IMPORTANT:

HERE IS YOUR REGISTRATION CODE TO ACCESS
YOUR PREMIUM McGRAW-HILL ONLINE RESOURCES.

For key premium online resources you need THIS CODE to gain access. Once the code is entered, you will be able to use the Web resources for the length of your course.

If your course is using **WebCT** or **Blackboard**, you'll be able to use this code to access the McGraw-Hill content within your instructor's online course.

Access is provided if you have purchased a new book. If the registration code is missing from this book, the registration screen on our Website, and within your WebCT or Blackboard course, will tell you how to obtain your new code.

Registering for McGraw-Hill Online Resources

TO gain access to your McGraw-Hill web resources simply follow the steps below:

(1) USE YOUR WEB BROWSER TO GO TO: **www.mhhe.com/unfinishedinteractive**

(2) CLICK ON **FIRST TIME USER**.

(3) ENTER THE REGISTRATION CODE* PRINTED ON THE TEAR-OFF BOOKMARK ON THE RIGHT.

(4) AFTER YOU HAVE ENTERED YOUR REGISTRATION CODE, CLICK **REGISTER**.

(5) FOLLOW THE INSTRUCTIONS TO SET-UP YOUR PERSONAL UserID AND PASSWORD.

(6) WRITE YOUR UserID AND PASSWORD DOWN FOR FUTURE REFERENCE.
KEEP IT IN A SAFE PLACE.

TO GAIN ACCESS to the McGraw-Hill content in your instructor's **WebCT** or **Blackboard** course simply log in to the course with the UserID and Password provided by your instructor. Enter the registration code exactly as it appears in the box to the right when prompted by the system. You will only need to use the code the first time you click on McGraw-Hill content.

Thank you, and welcome to your McGraw-Hill online Resources!

0-07-304428-8 BRINKLEY: THE UNFINISHED NATION: A BRIEF, INTERACTIVE HISTORY OF THE AMERICAN PEOPLE

MCGRAW-HILL
ONLINE RESOURCES

REGISTRATION CODE

W9-BFG-004

F329-CZ9S-AYUU-2Q8V-Y0WZ

THE UNFINISHED NATION

A BRIEF, INTERACTIVE HISTORY
OF THE AMERICAN PEOPLE
VOLUME II: FROM 1865

ALAN BRINKLEY

Columbia University

Boston   Burr Ridge, IL   Dubuque, IA   Madison, WI   New York   San Francisco   St. Louis
Bangkok   Bogotá   Caracas   Kuala Lumpur   Lisbon   London   Madrid   Mexico City
Milan   Montreal   New Delhi   Santiago   Seoul   Singapore   Sydney   Taipei   Toronto

Higher Education

THE UNFINISHED NATION: A BRIEF, INTERACTIVE HISTORY OF THE AMERICAN PEOPLE
VOLUME II: FROM 1865
Published by McGraw-Hill, a business unit of The McGraw-Hill Companies, Inc., 1221 Avenue of the Americas, New York, NY, 10020.
Copyright © 2005 by The McGraw-Hill Companies, Inc. All rights reserved. No part of this publication may be reproduced or distributed in any form or by any means, or stored in a database or retrieval system, without the prior written consent of The McGraw-Hill Companies, Inc., including, but not limited to, in any network or other electronic storage or transmission, or broadcast for distance learning.
Some ancillaries, including electronic and print components, may not be available to customers outside the United States.

This book is printed on acid-free paper.

1 2 3 4 5 6 7 8 9 0 DOW/DOW 0 9 8 7 6 5 4

ISBN   0-07-287911-4

Publisher: *Lyn Uhl*
Senior sponsoring editor: *Steve Drummond*
Developmental editors: *Jim Strandberg and Angela Kao*
Editorial coordinator: *Kimberly McGrath*
Marketing manager: *Katherine Bates*
Lead media producer: *Sean Crowley*
Lead project manager: *Susan Trentacosti*
Lead designer: *Gino Cieslik*
Senior production supervisor: *Carol A. Bielski*
Media project manager: *Kate Boylan*
Photo research coordinator: *Natalia C. Peschiera*
Photo researcher: *PhotoSearch, Inc.*
Art director: *Jeanne Schreiber*
Cover and interior design: *Maureen McCutcheon*
Cover images: *Martin Luther King: ©Corbis; Biotech scientist: ©Getty Images; Golden Gate Bridge: ©Corbis; Worker: ©Corbis; Scooter: ©Corbis.*
Typeface: *10.5/12 Janson*
Compositor: *GTS – Los Angeles, CA Campus*
Printer: *R.R. Donnelley and Sons, Inc.*

Library of Congress Control Number: 2004111909

www.mhhe.com

About the Author

ALAN BRINKLEY is the Allan Nevins Professor of History and Provost at Columbia University. He is the author of *Voices of Protest: Huey Long, Father Coughlin, and the Great Depression*, which won the 1983 National Book Award; *American History: A Survey; The End of Reform: New Deal Liberalism in Recession and War;* and *Liberalism and Its Discontents.* He was educated at Princeton and Harvard, and he has taught at Harvard, Princeton, the City University of New York Graduate School, and Oxford University, where he was the Harmsworth Professor of American History. He has been awarded the Joseph R. Levenson Memorial Teaching Prize at Harvard, and the Great Teacher Award at Columbia. He is a member of the American Academy of Arts and Sciences, a member of the boards of the New York Council for the Humanities and the National Humanities Center, and chairman of the board of the Century Foundation.

Brief Contents

Contents

CHAPTER 19

FROM STALEMATE TO CRISIS

CHAPTER 26
THE NEW DEAL

CHAPTER 27
THE GLOBAL CRISIS, 1921–1941

CHAPTER 28

AMERICA IN A WORLD AT WAR

CHAPTER 29

THE COLD WAR

CHAPTER 30
THE AFFLUENT SOCIETY

CHAPTER 33

FROM "THE AGE OF LIMITS" TO THE AGE OF REAGAN

THE AGE OF GLOBALIZATION

Preface

The story of the American past, which is the subject of this book, has undergone many transformations in recent decades. The past itself has not changed, of course, but the way Americans understand it has changed dramatically. And in the wake of those changes have come both new forms of presentation and new controversies.

The changes include both new ways of approaching historical scholarship and new approaches to teaching. Both inspired this book. Over the past decade there have been growing concerns among teachers of history over the rapidly growing amount of information that needs to be covered in an American history course. This has led instructors to reevaluate how they convey the story of America's past and what tools they employ in doing so. Many instructors have changed the type of texts they require for their students, choosing briefer volumes instead of more traditional and comprehensive books. Often, they choose a book that provides basic information, which they then supplement with other readings. *This* book is designed to provide students with the basic information they need and then allow instructors to fill in the rest of the story as they see fit.

The movement toward briefer texts also reflects a concern over the price that students have to pay for their books. This book is priced so that students can afford to purchase the text and so that instructors can supplement it with other materials. This affordable, briefer, more basic text answers the needs of both instructors and students and provides more flexibility for the teaching of American history.

The Unfinished Nation: A Brief, Interactive History of the American People also addresses another important issue that has become a considerable problem for instructors. Today's students have grown up in a visual world of computers, movies, television, and video games. How does an instructor relate the story of America's past to this generation of students? One answer is through increased use of visual material—photos, interactive maps, documentaries—that can both demonstrate an era's culture and inspire critical thinking about the past. We believe that the use of such visual material in conjunction with more traditional text-based materials actually enriches students' understanding of the past. Accompanying this text is our dynamic and versatile *Primary Source Investigator* CD-ROM which contains a wealth of images, original documents, interactive maps, and documentaries. This CD provides the visual images that will make history more vivid for students and will also give instructors new ways of employing these images in their teaching.

These changes in the tools of presentation reflect not just the market, but the changing character of historical understanding itself. The turbulence of our era has encouraged historians to ask new questions of the past—and thus to reinterpret it—in an effort to understand the tensions and contests that preoccupy us today. The popularity of history is growing even while the controversies surrounding it continue. Ours is an era of rapid and bewildering change which encourages people—particularly in the aftermath of the attacks of September 11, 2001, and the ensuing wars in Afghanistan and Iraq—to look to the past as way to deepen our understanding of the present. And as the population of the United States has become more diverse and as groups that once stood outside the view of scholarship have moved into its center, many historians have labored to reveal the immense complexity of their country's past. As America's economy and culture and power become more deeply involved in the life of the rest of the world, historians struggle to see the ways in which global forces have shaped the nation's development.

Historical narrative once recounted little beyond the experiences of great men and the unfolding of great public events. Today they attempt to tell a more complicated story, one that includes private as well as public lives, ordinary people as well as celebrated ones, differences as well as unity, international phenomena as well as national ones. This newer history seems fragmented at times, because it attempts to embrace so many more areas of human experience than the older narratives. It is often disturbing, because it reveals failures and injustices as well as triumphs. But it is also richer, fuller, and better suited to helping us understand our own diverse and contentious world.

I trust that this book will introduce readers to enough different aspects of American history to make them aware of its extraordinary richness and complexity. But I hope, too, that it will provide readers some sense of the shared experiences of Americans and of the forces that have sustained the United States as a nation.

My thanks to Kevin Murphy and Moshik Tenkin for their assistance on this book. I am, as always, grateful to the many people at McGraw-Hill who have helped with the editing and production of this book: Lyn Uhl, Steve Drummond, Kim McGrath, Jim Strandberg, Angela Kao, Katherine Bates, Susan Trentacosti, Gino Cieslik, Carol Bielski, and Natalia Peschiera.

I am also grateful to those readers of the original version of *The Unfinished Nation* who have offered me unsolicited comments, criticisms, and corrections. I hope they will continue to do so with this new venture. Suggestions can be sent to me at the Department of History, Columbia University, New York, NY 10027, or by e-mail at ab65@columbia.edu.

Alan Brinkley
Columbia University
New York, NY

Special Features and Useful Tools

This book and its companion *Primary Source Investigator* CD-ROM were created to portray both the diversity and the unity that have characterized the American experience, as well as to meet three particular needs often voiced by instructors and students:

1. American history survey texts continue to grow in size and frequently provide more information than can be covered in a single semester or quarter term. *The Unfinished Nation: A Brief, Interactive History of the American People* is approximately 200 pages shorter than other concise texts and is ideal for those who desire a more basic and accessible treatment of the American experience.

2. This text is priced to provide students and instructors with an affordable alternative. It also gives instructors the flexibility to assign supplementary works to accompany the book.

3. An outstanding technology package not only accompanies this text, but is integrated with the textbook. Features in the text direct the student to appropriate online and CD resources. At the heart of the technology package is McGraw-Hill's new *Primary Source Investigator (PSI)* CD-ROM, which accompanies each text and provides instant access to hundreds of documents, images, artifacts, audio recordings, and videos. *PSI* helps students practice the art of "doing history" on a real archive of historical sources. Students follow the three basic steps of *Ask, Research, Argue* to examine sources, take notes on them, and then save or print copies of the sources for other use (for example, inserting them into a paper or presentation). After researching a particular theme, individual, or time period, students can use *PSI*'s argument-outlining tool to walk them through the steps of writing an essay or building a presentation.

PEDAGOGICAL FEATURES

The telling of a good story is only part of the task facing those who teach American history. Instructors also have to engage students in the enterprise of learning and the more actively engaged they are, the more they learn. Pedagogical tools within a textbook have become an important complement to the narrative, aiding students in participating actively in the learning process. *The Unfinished Nation: A Brief, Interactive History of the American People* provides students with a clear, accessible, and useful pedagogical support.

Integration of *Primary Source Investigator* and Online Learning Center Material

Throughout the text, two icons lead readers to interactive learning tools in two locations. This icon appears whenever a relevant mini-documentary or primary source document is available on the *Primary Source Investigator* CD-ROM. Once students have worked with the documentary or document, they can continue their research by working with additional images, maps, interactive maps, time lines, and study aids.

The Online Learning Center icon appears in the text whenever interactive features such as "America in the World" and "Where Historians Disagree" essays are available on the book's website. Maps that have interactive version on the Online Learning Center display this icon in their captions. This icon also appears at the end of each chapter to remind readers of the study tools available on the Online Learning Center.

And finally, each chapter concludes with an Interactive Learning Guide that leads readers to chapter relevant key assets such as Mini-Documentaries, Interactive Maps, and Primary Sources on the *PSI* CD and the Online Learning Center. These assets are a sampling of what is available in our media package, and serve as entry points from which students can continue conducting their own historical research.

Chapter Introductions and Conclusions

Each chapter opens with a short introduction that sets the stage for understanding the materials. Chapters then end with conclusions that highlight key themes. These features preserve the engaging narrative style while satisfying the pedagogical dictum: "tell them what they'll learn, teach them, then tell them what they have learned."

Time Lines

One of the most commonly voiced frustrations for instructors is that students lack a sense of chronology. Each chapter of this book contains a time line focusing on significant events covered within the chapter narrative. These time lines have been placed at the beginning of each chapter.

Interactive Mapping Program

Because a sense of geography is essential to the study of history, the text includes a wealth of full-color maps with active-learning captions. These captions make specific reference to map content, to ideas within the narrative, and ask one or two questions of the student. Many of the maps have interactive versions on the book's Online Learning Center, indicated by the OLC icon.

Clear Headings and Marginal Notes

Each chapter features clear thematic titles and precise headings that guide students through the narrative. Marginal notes highlight key terms and concepts contained within the narrative.

For Further Reference Sections

The bibliographies that conclude each chapter provide students and instructors with suggestions of additional resources related to the material in the chapter.

DISTANCE LEARNING COURSE

Intelecom has developed a complete two-semester course, titled *The Unfinished Nation*, which combines fifty-two broadcast-quality videos with the material in *The Unfinished Nation* textbook to provide a rich, comprehensive treatment of American history. The videos include interviews with leading scholars, historical narratives, photographs and artifacts, dramatic recreations, and original maps and illustrations. The distance learning material may be offered as a traditional telecourse, as a telewebcourse (telecourse enhanced with online components), or as a complete online course. The videos and textbook are supported by a closely correlated telecourse study guide, which is available from McGraw-Hill. For more information on the distance learning course, visit Intelecom at www.intelecom.org, or contact your local McGraw-Hill representative.

SUPPLEMENTS

For the Instructor

Instructor's Resource CD-ROM

This CD-ROM gathers instructor's tools in one location. Instructors can illustrate classroom lectures and discussions with text-specific PowerPoint presentations, or incorporate the questions written for the Classroom Performance System (CPS). The Instructor's Manual and Test Bank are also included on this CD-ROM.

Instructor's Manual and Test Bank

Prepared by Roger Hall, Allan Hancock College, the comprehensive Instructor's Manual provides summaries, objectives, themes, points for discussion, map exercises, library exercises, essay questions, and bibliographies for each chapter. The Test Bank provides multiple levels and types of questions for each chapter of the text. Both the Instructor's Manual and Test Bank are available on the Instructor's Resource CD-ROM. The Instructor's Manual is also available on the text's Online Learning Center.

Computerized Test Bank

Available in Brownstone Diploma for Windows and Macintosh, this version of the Test Bank on CD-ROM allows instructors to customize each test to suit any course syllabus. The Computerized Test Bank is available on the Instructor's Resource CD-ROM.

Overhead Transparency Acetates

This comprehensive package of transparencies, most of them full-color, is designed to support the text's unique integrated art program.

U.S. History Video and CD-ROM Library

Contact your local sales representative for a complete listing of the many DVDs, videos, and CD-ROMs available from the Films for Humanities American History Catalog. Adoption requirements apply.

Lecture Launcher Clips

Available on either DVD or videotape, this two-volume set offers a total of twenty-one video clips to engage students in classroom lectures. Volume I begins with "America before the Americans" and ends with "Life in the West." Volume II begins with "Teddy Roosevelt and Yellow Journalism" and ends with "The Watergate Break-In."

Classroom Performance System (CPS)

CPS brings interactivity into the classroom or lecture hall. CPS is a wireless response system that gives instructors and students immediate feedback from the entire class. Each student uses a wireless response pad similar to a television remote to instantly respond to polling or quiz questions. CPS questions for each chapter of the book are available on the instructor's side of the Online Learning Center and on the Instructor's Resource CD-ROM.

Online Learning Center
www.mhhe.com/unfinishedinteractive

At the homepage of the text-specific website, instructors will find a series of online tools to meet a wide range of classroom needs. The Instructor's Manual and PowerPoint presentations can be downloaded by instructors, but are password-protected to prevent tampering. Instructors can create Web-based homework assignments or classroom activities by linking to the student's side of the Online Learning Center. Instructors can also create an interactive course syllabus using McGraw-Hill's PageOut (www.mhhe.com/pageout).

PageOut
www.mhhe.com/pageout

On the PageOut website, instructors can create their own course websites. PageOut requires no prior knowledge of HTML, no long hours of coding, and no design skills on the instructor's part. Simply plug the course information into a template and click on one of sixteen designs. The process takes no time at all and leaves instructors with a professionally designed website. Powerful features include an interactive course syllabus that lets instructors post content and links, an online gradebook, lecture notes, bookmarks, and even a discussion board where instructors and students can discuss course-related topics.

For the Student
Student Study Guide with Map Exercises

Prepared by Harvey H. Jackson and Bradley R. Rice, this study guide (available in two volumes) helps students process and master important concepts covered in the text. For each chapter of the text, the study guide offers valuable pedagogical tools such as chapter summaries and reviews, chapter outlines, objective questions, short answer and essay questions, and mapping exercises.

U.S. History Map Atlas

This is a valuable collection of more than fifty clear and colorful historical maps covering all major periods in American history. It is available for packaging with the textbook.

Online Learning Center
www.mhhe.com/unfinishedinteractive

At the homepage to the text-specific website, students can work with an interactive study guide, including online essay questions, time lines, mapping exercises, and a variety of objective questions to guide students through the text material. Also available are interactive "America in the World" boxes to contextualize American history within world history and "Where Historians Disagree" boxes to expose current controversies in the field. Additional links to related websites make the student side of the Online Learning Center a great place to begin Web-based research.

After the Fact Interactive CD-ROMs

Students can practice the art of historical detection on real historical controversies. Rich, visually appealing modules on the Salem witch trials, the freeing of the slaves, the passage of the Meat Inspection Act of 1906, and the changing roles of women after World War II introduce them to the three basic steps taken by practicing historians: ask, research, argue. Numerous original sources can be examined, including video, audio, maps, and still images. The CDs guide the students in constructing an argument based on their research.

PowerWeb: American History

This online supplement is a collection of readings delivered electronically, along with other tools for conducting research in history. In addition, student study tools, Web research tips and exercises, and free access to the Factiva search engine are included. A card with a password for accessing PowerWeb has been packaged free with the textbook.

Few periods in the history of the United States have produced as much bitterness as the era of Reconstruction—the years following the Civil War during which Americans attempted to reunite their shattered nation. To many white Southerners, Reconstruction was a vicious and destructive experience—a period when Northerners inflicted humiliation and revenge on the South. Northern defenders of Reconstruction, in contrast, argued that their policies were the only way to prevent Confederates from restoring Southern society to what it had been before the war.

To most African Americans at the time, and to many people of all races since, Reconstruction was notable for other reasons. Neither a vicious tyranny nor a thoroughgoing reform, it was, rather, a small but important first step in the effort to secure civil rights and economic power for the former slaves. Reconstruction did not provide African Americans with either the legal protections or the material resources to assure them anything like real equality. Most black men and women who continued to live in what came to be known as the New South had little power to resist their oppression.

And yet for all its shortcomings, Reconstruction did help African Americans create some new institutions and some important legal precedents that helped them survive and that ultimately, well into the twentieth century, became the basis of later efforts to win freedom and equality.

THE PROBLEMS OF PEACEMAKING

In 1865, when it became clear that the war was almost over, no one in Washington was certain about what to do. Abraham Lincoln could not negotiate a treaty with the defeated government; he continued to insist that the Confederate government had no legal right to exist. Yet neither could he simply readmit the Southern states into the Union.

The Aftermath of War and Emancipation

The Devastated South   The South after the Civil War was a desolate place. Towns had been gutted, plantations burned, fields neglected, bridges and railroads destroyed. Many white Southerners had almost no personal property. More than 258,000 Confederate soldiers had died in the war, and thousands more returned home wounded or sick. Some white Southerners faced starvation and homelessness.

If conditions were bad for Southern whites, they were far worse for Southern blacks. As soon as the war ended, hundreds of thousands of them left their plantations in search of a new life in freedom. But most had nowhere to go, and few had any possessions except the clothes they wore.

Competing Notions of Freedom

For blacks and whites alike, Reconstruction became a struggle to define the meaning of freedom. But the former slaves and the defeated whites had very different conceptions of what freedom meant.

Some blacks believed the only way to secure freedom was to have the government take land away from white people and give it to black people. Others asked only for legal equality, confident that they could advance successfully in American society once the formal obstacles to their advancement disappeared. But whatever their **Black Desire for Independence** particular demands, virtually all former slaves were united in their desire for independence from white control. Throughout the post–Civil War South, African Americans separated themselves from white institutions—pulling out of white-controlled churches and establishing their own, creating clubs and societies for their own people, and in some cases starting their own schools.

1863	1864	1865	1866	1867	1868	1869
Lincoln announces Reconstruction plan	Lincoln vetoes Wade-Davis bill	Lincoln assassinated; Johnson is president; Freedmen's Bureau; Joint Committee on Reconstruction	Republicans gain in congressional elections	Congressional Reconstruction begins	Grant elected president; Johnson impeached and acquitted; 14th Amendment ratified	Congress passes 15th Amendment

1872	1873	1875	1877	1883	1890s	1895	1896
Grant reelected	Panic and depression	"Whiskey ring" scandal	Hayes wins disputed election; Compromise of 1877 ends Reconstruction	Supreme Court upholds segregation	Jim Crow laws in South	Atlanta Compromise	*Plessy v. Ferguson*

For most white Southerners, freedom meant something very different. It meant the ability to control their own destinies without interference from the North or the federal government. And in the immediate aftermath of the war, they attempted to exercise this version of freedom by trying to restore their society to its antebellum form. When these white Southerners fought for what they considered freedom, they were fighting above all to preserve local and regional autonomy and white supremacy.

In the immediate aftermath of the war, the federal government's contribution to solving the question of the future of the South was modest. Federal troops remained in the South to preserve order and protect the freedmen. And in March 1865, Congress established the Freedmen's Bureau, an agency of the army directed by General Oliver O. Howard. The Freedmen's Bureau distributed food to millions of former slaves. It established schools, staffed by missionaries and teachers who had been sent to the South by Freedmen's Aid Societies and other private and church groups in the North. It made a modest effort to settle blacks on lands of their own. But the Freedmen's Bureau had authority to operate for only one year, and it was, in any case, far too small to deal effectively with the enormous problems facing Southern society. By the time the war ended, other proposals for reconstructing the South were emerging.

The Freedmen's Bureau

Plans for Reconstruction

Control of Reconstruction was in the hands of the Republicans, who were divided in their approach to the issue. Conservatives within the party insisted that the South accept the abolition of slavery, but they proposed few other conditions for the readmission of the seceded states. The Radicals, led by Representative Thaddeus Stevens of Pennsylvania and Senator Charles Sumner of Massachusetts, urged a much harsher course, including disenfranchising large numbers of Southern whites, protecting black civil rights, and confiscating the property of wealthy white Southerners and distributing the land among the freedmen. There was also a group of Republican Moderates, who rejected the most stringent demands of the Radicals but supported extracting at least some concessions on black rights.

Thaddeus Stevens and Charles Sumner

President Lincoln favored a lenient Reconstruction policy, and he believed that Southern Unionists could become the nucleus of new, loyal state governments. Lincoln announced his Reconstruction plan in December 1863, more than a year before the war ended. It offered a general amnesty to white Southerners—other than high officials of the Confederacy—who would pledge an oath of loyalty to the government. When 10 percent of a state's total number of voters in 1860 took the oath, those loyal voters could set up a state government. Lincoln also proposed extending suffrage to those African Americans who were educated, owned property, and had served in the Union army. Three Southern states—Louisiana, Arkansas, and Tennessee, all under Union occupation—reestablished loyal governments under the Lincoln formula in 1864.

The Radical Republicans were outraged at the mildness of Lincoln's program. In July 1864, they pushed their own plan through Congress in the form of the Wade-Davis Bill. It called for the president to appoint a provisional governor for each conquered state. When a majority of the white males of a state pledged their allegiance to the Union, the governor could summon a state constitutional convention, whose delegates were to be elected by voters who had never borne arms against the United States. The new state constitutions would be required to abolish slavery, disenfranchise Confederate civil and military leaders, and repudiate debts accumulated by the state governments during war. Only then would Congress readmit the states to the Union.

Wade-Davis Bill

Congress passed the bill a few days before it adjourned in 1864, and Lincoln disposed of it with a pocket veto. His action enraged the Radical leaders, and the pragmatic Lincoln realized he would have to accept at least some of the Radical demands.

The Death of Lincoln

What plan he might have produced no one can say. On the night of April 14, 1865, Lincoln and his wife attended a play at Ford's Theater in Washington. As they sat in the theater, John Wilkes Booth, an actor fervently committed to the Southern cause, entered the presidential box from the rear and shot Lincoln in the head. Early the next morning, the president died.

John Wilkes Booth

Lincoln's death produced something close to hysteria throughout the North, especially because it quickly became clear that Booth had been the leader of a conspiracy. One of his associates shot and

ABRAHAM LINCOLN This haunting photograph of Abraham Lincoln, showing clearly the weariness and aging that four years as a war president had created, was taken in Washington only four days before his assassination in 1865. *(The Library of Congress)*

wounded Secretary of State William Seward on the night of the assassination, and another abandoned at the last moment a scheme to murder Vice President Andrew Johnson. Booth himself escaped on horseback into the Maryland countryside, where, on April 26, he was cornered by Union troops and shot to death in a blazing barn. Eight other people were convicted by a military tribunal of participating in the conspiracy. Four were hanged.

To many Northerners, however, the murder of the president seemed evidence of an even greater conspiracy—one masterminded and directed by the unrepentant leaders of the defeated South. Militant Republicans exploited such suspicions relentlessly in the ensuing months.

Johnson and "Restoration"

Leadership of the Moderates and Conservatives fell to Lincoln's successor, Andrew Johnson of Tennessee. A Democrat until he had joined the

Union ticket with Lincoln in 1864, he became president at a time of growing partisan passions.

Johnson's Reconstruction Plan   Johnson revealed his plan for Reconstruction—or "Restoration," as he preferred to call it—soon after he took office, and he implemented it during the summer of 1865. Like Lincoln, he offered some form of amnesty to Southerners who would take an oath of allegiance. In most other respects, however, his plan resembled the Wade-Davis Bill. The president appointed a provisional governor in each state and charged him with inviting qualified voters to elect delegates to a constitutional convention. In order to win readmission to Congress, a state had to revoke its ordinance of secession, abolish slavery, and ratify the Thirteenth Amendment.

By the end of 1865, all the seceded states had formed new governments—some under Lincoln's plan, some under Johnson's—and awaited congressional approval of them. But Radicals in Congress vowed not to recognize the Johnson governments, **Hardening Northern Attitudes** for, by now, Northern opinion had become more hostile toward the South. Delegates to the Southern conventions had angered much of the North by their apparent reluctance to abolish slavery and by their refusal to grant suffrage to any blacks. Southern states had also seemed to defy the North by electing prominent Confederate leaders to represent them in Congress.

RADICAL RECONSTRUCTION

Reconstruction under Johnson's plan—often known as "presidential Reconstruction"—continued only until Congress reconvened in December 1865. At that point, Congress created a new Joint Committee on Reconstruction to frame a Reconstruction policy of its own. The period of "congressional" or "Radical" Reconstruction had begun.

The Black Codes

Meanwhile, events in the South were driving Northern opinion in even more radical directions. Throughout the South in 1865 and early 1866, state legislatures were enacting sets of laws known as the Black Codes, which authorized local officials to apprehend unemployed blacks, fine them for vagrancy, and hire them out to private employers to satisfy the fine. Some of the codes forbade blacks to own or lease farms or to take any jobs other than as plantation workers or domestic servants.

Congress first responded to the Black Codes by passing an act extending the life of the Freedmen's Bureau and widening its powers so that it could nullify work agreements forced on freedmen under the Black Codes. Then, in April 1866, Congress passed the first Civil Rights Act, which declared blacks to be citizens of the United States and gave the federal government power to intervene in state affairs to protect the rights of citizens. **Johnson's Vetoes** Johnson vetoed both bills, but Congress overrode him on each of them.

The Fourteenth Amendment

In April 1866, the Joint Committee on Reconstruction proposed a new amendment to the Constitution, which Congress approved in early summer and sent to the states for ratification. The Fourteenth Amendment offered the first constitutional definition of American citizenship. Everyone born in the United States, and everyone naturalized, was automatically a citizen and entitled to all the "privileges and immunities" guaranteed by the Constitution, including equal protection of the laws by both the state and national governments. **Citizenship for African Americans** The amendment also imposed penalties on states that denied suffrage to any adult male inhabitants. Finally, it prohibited former members of Congress or other former federal officials who had aided the Confederacy from holding any state or federal office unless two-thirds of Congress voted to pardon them.

Congressional Radicals offered to readmit to the Union any state whose legislature ratified the Fourteenth Amendment. Only Tennessee did so. All the other former Confederate states, along with Delaware and Kentucky, refused.

But by now, the Radicals were growing more confident and determined. Bloody race riots in New Orleans and other Southern cities were among the events that strengthened their hand. In the 1866 congressional elections, Johnson actively campaigned for Conservative candidates, but he did his own cause more harm than good with his intemperate speeches. The voters returned an overwhelming majority of Republicans, most of them Radicals, to Congress. Congressional Republicans were now strong enough to enact a plan of their own even over the president's objections.

The Congressional Plan

The Radicals passed three Reconstruction bills early in 1867 and overrode Johnson's vetoes of all of them. Under the congressional plan, Tennessee, which had ratified the Fourteenth Amendment, was promptly readmitted. But Congress rejected the Lincoln-Johnson governments of the other ten Confederate states and, instead, combined those states into five military districts. A military commander governed each district and had orders to register qualified voters (defined as all adult black males and those white males who had not participated in the rebellion). Once registered, voters would elect conventions to prepare new state constitutions, which had to include provisions for black suffrage. Once voters ratified the new constitutions, they could elect state governments. Congress had to approve a state's constitution, and the state legislature had to ratify the Fourteenth Amendment. Once that happened, and once enough states ratified the amendment to make it part of the Constitution, then the former Confederate states could be restored to the Union.

By 1868, seven of the ten former Confederate states (Arkansas, North Carolina, South Carolina, Louisiana, Alabama, Georgia, and Florida) had fulfilled these conditions (including ratification of the Fourteenth Amendment, which now became part of the Constitution) and were readmitted to the Union. Conservative whites held up the return of Virginia and Texas until 1869 and Mississippi until 1870. By then, Congress had added an additional requirement for readmission—ratification of another constitutional amendment, the Fifteenth, which forbade the states and the federal government to deny suffrage to any citizen on account of "race, color, or previous condition of servitude." Ratification by the states was completed in 1870.

To stop the president from interfering with their plans, the congressional Radicals passed two remarkable laws of dubious constitutionality in 1867. One, the Tenure of Office Act, forbade the president to remove civil officials, including members of his own cabinet, without the consent of the Senate. The principal purpose of the law was to protect the job of Secretary of War Edwin M. Stanton, who was cooperating with the Radicals. The other law, the Command of the Army Act, prohibited the president from issuing military orders except through

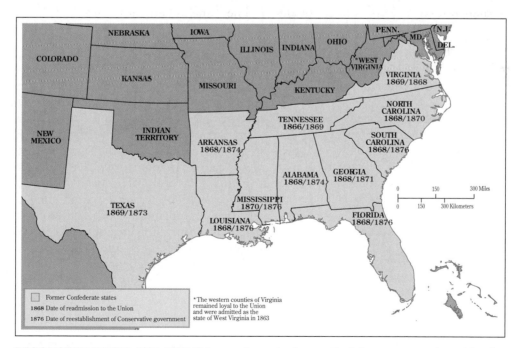

RECONSTRUCTION, 1866–1877 This map shows the former Confederate states and provides the dates when each was readmitted to the Union as well as a subsequent date when each state managed to return political power to traditional white, conservative elites—a process white southerners liked to call "redemption." ■ *What had to happen for a state to be readmitted to the Union? What had to happen before a state could experience "redemption"?*

the commanding general of the army (General Grant), who could not be relieved or assigned elsewhere without the consent of the Senate.

The congressional Radicals also took action to stop the Supreme Court from interfering with their plans. In 1866, the Court had declared in the case of *Ex parte Milligan* that military tribunals were unconstitutional in places where civil courts were functioning. Radicals in Congress immediately proposed several bills that would require two-thirds of the justices to support any decision overruling a law of Congress, would deny the Court jurisdiction in Reconstruction cases, would reduce its membership to three, and would even abolish it. The justices apparently took notice. Over the next two years, the Court refused to accept jurisdiction in any cases involving Reconstruction.

The Impeachment of the President

President Johnson had long since ceased to be a serious obstacle to the passage of Radical legislation, but he was still the official charged with administering the Reconstruction programs. As such, the Radicals believed, he remained a major impediment to their plans. Early in 1867, they began looking for a way to impeach him and remove him from office. A search for grounds for impeachment began. Republicans found them, they believed, when Johnson dismissed Secretary of War Stanton despite Congress's refusal to agree. Elated Radicals in the House quickly impeached the president and sent the case to the Senate for trial.

The trial before the Senate lasted throughout April and May 1868. The Radicals put heavy pressure on all the Republican senators, but the Moderates vacillated. On the first three charges to come to a vote, seven Republicans joined the Democrats and independents to support ac-

The President Acquitted

quittal. The vote was 35 to 19, one short of the constitutionally required two-thirds majority.

THE SOUTH IN RECONSTRUCTION

Reconstruction may not have accomplished what its framers intended, but it did have profound effects on the South.

The Reconstruction Governments

Critics labeled Southern white Republicans with the derogatory terms "scalawags"

"Scalawags" and "Carpetbaggers"

and "carpetbaggers." Many of the "scalawags" were former Whigs who had never felt comfortable in the Democratic Party or farmers who lived in remote areas where there had been little or no slavery. The "carpetbaggers" were white men from the North, most of them veterans of the Union army who looked on the South as a new frontier, more promising than the West.

The most numerous Republicans in the South were the black freedmen. In several states, African-

Freedmen

American voters held their own conventions to chart their future course. Freedmen had created their own churches after emancipation, and this religious independence also helped give them unity and self-confidence.

African Americans played a significant role in the politics of the Reconstruction South. They served as delegates to the constitutional conventions. They held public offices of practically every kind. Between 1869 and 1901, twenty blacks served in the United States House of Representatives, two in the Senate. They served, too, in state legislatures and in various other state offices. Southern whites complained loudly about "Negro rule," but the percentage of black officeholders was always far lower than the percentage of blacks in the population.

The record of the Reconstruction governments is mixed. Critics denounced them for corruption and financial extravagance, and there is some truth to both charges. But the corruption in the South was hardly unique to the Reconstruction governments. Corruption had been rife in some antebellum and Confederate governments, and it was at least as rampant in the Northern states. And the large state expenditures of the Reconstruction years were huge only in comparison with the meager budgets of the antebellum era. They represented an effort to provide services that antebellum governments had never offered.

Education

Perhaps the most important of the accomplishments of the Reconstruction governments was a dramatic improvement in Southern education. In the first years of Reconstruction, much of the impetus for educational reform in the South came from outside groups and from African Americans themselves. Over the opposition of many Southern whites, who feared that education would give blacks "false notions of equality," these reformers established a large network of schools for former slaves—4,000 schools by 1870, staffed by 9,000 teachers (half of them black), teaching 200,000 students. In the 1870s, Reconstruction governments began to build a comprehensive public school system in the South. By 1876, more than half of all white children and about 40 percent of all black children were attending schools in the South; all but a few were racially segregated. Several black "academies," offering more advanced education, also began operating. Gradually, these academies grew into a network of black colleges and universities.

Establishment of Black Schools

Landownership and Tenancy

The most ambitious goal of the Freedmen's Bureau, and of some Republican Radicals in Congress, was to reform landownership in the South. The effort failed. By June 1865, the bureau had settled nearly 10,000 black families on their own land—most of it drawn from abandoned plantations in areas occupied by the Union armies. By the end of that year, however, Southern plantation owners were returning and demanding the restoration of their property. President Johnson supported their demands, and the government eventually returned most of the confiscated lands to their original white owners.

Land Reform Thwarted

Even so, the distribution of landownership in the South changed considerably in the postwar years. Among whites, there was a striking decline in landownership. Some whites lost their land because of unpaid debt or increased taxes; some left the marginal lands they had owned to move to more fertile areas, where they rented. Among blacks, the proportion who owned land rose from virtually none to more than 20 percent.

Still, most blacks, and a growing minority of whites, did not own their own land during Reconstruction, and some who acquired land in the 1860s had lost it by the 1890s. Instead, they worked for others in one form or another. Many black agricultural laborers—perhaps 25 percent of the total—simply worked for wages. Most, however, became tenants of white landowners—that is, they worked their own plots of land and paid their landlords either a fixed rent or a share of their crop (hence the term "sharecropping"). As tenants and sharecroppers, blacks enjoyed at least the sense of working their own land, even if in most cases they could never hope to buy it. But tenantry also benefited landlords in some ways, relieving them of the cost of purchasing slaves and of responsibility for the physical well-being of their workers.

Rapid Growth of Sharecropping

Incomes and Credit

In some respects, the postwar years were a period of remarkable economic progress for African Americans in the South. The per capita income of blacks (when the material benefits of slavery are counted as income) rose 46 percent between 1857 and 1879, while the per capita income of whites declined 35 percent. African Americans were also able to work less than they had under slavery. Women and children were less likely to labor in the fields, and adult men tended to work shorter days. In all, the black labor force worked about one-third fewer hours during Reconstruction than it had been compelled to work under slavery—a reduction that brought the working schedule of blacks roughly into accord with that of white farm laborers.

But other developments were limiting these gains. While the black share of profits was increasing, the total profits of Southern agriculture were declining. Nor did the income redistribution of the postwar years lift many blacks out of poverty. Black per capita income rose from about one-quarter of white per capita income (which was itself low) to about one-half in the first few years after the war. After this initial increase, however, it rose hardly at all.

Persistent Black Poverty

Blacks and poor whites alike often found themselves virtually imprisoned by the crop-lien system. Few of the traditional institutions of credit in the South—the "factors" and banks—returned after the war. In their stead emerged a new system of credit, centered in large part on local country stores. Blacks and whites, landowners and tenants—all depended on these stores. And since

The "Crop-lien System"

farmers did not have the same steady cash flow as other workers, customers usually had to rely on credit from these merchants in order to purchase what they needed. Most local stores had no competition. As a result, they were able to set interest rates as high as 50 or 60 percent. Farmers had to give the merchants a lien (or claim) on their crops as collateral for the loans (thus the term "crop-lien system," generally used to describe Southern farming in this period). Farmers who suffered a few bad years in a row, as many did, could become trapped in a cycle of debt from which they could never escape.

One effect of this burdensome credit system was that Southern farmers became almost wholly dependent on cash crops—and most of all on cotton—because only such marketable commodities seemed to offer any possibility of escape from debt. The relentless planting of cotton contributed to an exhaustion of the soil. The crop-lien system, in other words, was not only helping to impoverish small farmers; it was also contributing to a general decline in the Southern agricultural economy.

The African-American Family in Freedom

A major reason for the rapid departure of so many blacks from plantations was the desire to find lost relatives. Thousands of African Americans wandered through the South looking for husbands, wives, children, or other relatives from whom they had been separated. Former slaves rushed to have their marriages sanctified by church and law.

Within the black family, the definition of male and female roles quickly came to resemble that within white families. Many women and children ceased working in the fields. Such work, they believed, was a badge of slavery. Instead, many women restricted themselves largely to domestic tasks. Still, economic necessity often compelled black women to engage in income-producing activities: working as domestic servants, taking in laundry, or helping their husbands in the fields. By the end of Reconstruction, half of all black women over the age of sixteen were working for wages. For a Where Historians Disagree essay on "The Origins of Segregation," visit the book's Online Learning Center for Chapter 15.

THE GRANT ADMINISTRATION

American voters in 1868 yearned for a strong, stable figure to guide them through the troubled years of Reconstruction. They turned trustingly to General Ulysses S. Grant.

The Soldier President

Grant could have had the nomination of either party in 1868. But believing that Republican Reconstruction policies were more popular in the North, he accepted the Republican nomination. The Democrats nominated former governor Horatio Seymour of New York. The campaign was a bitter one, and Grant's triumph was surprisingly narrow. Without the 500,000 new black Republican voters in the South, he would have had a minority of the popular vote.

> Grant Elected

Grant entered the White House with no political experience, and his performance was clumsy and ineffectual from the start. Except for Hamilton Fish, whom Grant appointed secretary of state, most members of the cabinet were ill-equipped for their tasks. Grant relied chiefly on established party leaders, and his administration used the spoils system even more blatantly than most of its predecessors. Grant also alienated the many Northerners who were growing disillusioned with the Radical Reconstruction policies. Some Republicans suspected, correctly, that there was also corruption in the Grant administration itself.

By the end of Grant's first term, therefore, members of a substantial faction of the party—who referred to themselves as Liberal Republicans—had come to oppose what they called "Grantism." In 1872 they bolted the party and nominated their own presidential candidate: Horace Greeley, publisher of the *New York Tribune*. The Democrats, somewhat reluctantly, named Greeley their candidate as well, hoping that the alliance with the Liberals would enable them to defeat Grant. But Grant won a substantial victory, polling 286 electoral votes to Greeley's 66.

> Liberal Republicans

The Grant Scandals

During the 1872 campaign, the first of a series of political scandals came to light. It involved the French-owned Crédit Mobilier construction company, which had helped build the Union Pacific Railroad. The heads of Crédit Mobilier had used their positions as Union Pacific stockholders to steer large fraudulent contracts to their construction company, thus bilking the Union Pacific of millions. To prevent investigations, the directors had given Crédit Mobilier stock to key members of Congress. But in 1872, Congress did conduct an investigation, which revealed that some highly placed Republicans—including Schuyler Colfax, now Grant's vice president—had accepted stock.

One dreary episode followed another in Grant's second term. Benjamin H. Bristow, Grant's third Treasury secretary, discovered that some of his officials and a group of distillers

The "Whiskey Ring"

operating as a "whiskey ring" were cheating the government out of taxes by filing false reports. Then a House investigation revealed that William W. Belknap, secretary of war, had accepted bribes to retain an Indian-post trader in office (the so-called Indian ring). Other, lesser scandals added to the growing impression that "Grantism" had brought rampant corruption to government.

The Greenback Question

Compounding Grant's, and the nation's, problems was a financial crisis, known as the Panic of 1873. It began with the failure of a leading investment banking firm, Jay Cooke and Company, which had invested too heavily in postwar railroad building. Debtors pressured the government to redeem federal war bonds with greenbacks, which would increase the amount of money in circulation. But Grant and most Republicans wanted a "sound" currency—based solidly on gold reserves—which would favor the interests of banks and other creditors. There was approximately $356 million in paper currency issued during the Civil War that was still in circulation. In 1873, the Treasury issued more in response to the panic. But in 1875, Republican leaders in Congress passed the Specie

Specie Resumption Act

Resumption Act. It provided that after January 1, 1879, the greenback dollars would be redeemed by the government and replaced with new certificates, firmly pegged to the price of gold. The law satisfied creditors, who had worried that debts would be repaid in paper currency of uncertain value. But

"resumption" made things more difficult for debtors, because the gold-based money supply could not easily expand.

In 1875, the "greenbackers" formed their own political organization: the National Greenback Party. It failed to gain widespread support, but it did keep the money issue alive. The question of the proper composition of the currency was to remain one of the most controversial and enduring issues in late-nineteenth-century American politics.

Republican Diplomacy

The Johnson and Grant administrations achieved their greatest successes in foreign affairs. The accomplishments were the work of two outstanding secretaries of state: William H. Seward and Hamilton Fish.

An ardent expansionist, Seward acted with as much daring as the demands of Reconstruction politics would permit. Seward accepted a Russian offer to sell Alaska for $7.2 million, despite criticism from

Purchase of Alaska

many who derided the purchase as "Seward's Folly." In 1867, Seward also engineered the American annexation of the tiny Midway Islands, west of Hawaii.

Hamilton Fish's first major challenge was resolving the longstanding controversy with England over the American claims that it had violated neutrality laws during the Civil War by permitting English shipyards to build ships (among them the *Alabama*) for the Confederacy. American demands that England pay for the damage these vessels had caused became known as the "*Alabama* claims." In 1871,

"Alabama Claims" Resolved

after a number of failed efforts, Fish forged an agreement, the Treaty of Washington, which provided for international arbitration.

THE ABANDONMENT OF RECONSTRUCTION

As the North grew increasingly preoccupied with its own political and economic problems, interest in Reconstruction began to wane. By the time Grant left office, Democrats had taken back seven of the governments of the former Confederate states. For three other states—South Carolina,

Louisiana, and Florida—the end of Reconstruction had to wait for the withdrawal of the last federal troops in 1877.

The Southern States "Redeemed"

In the states where whites constituted a majority—the states of the upper South—overthrowing Republican control was relatively simple. By 1872, all but a handful of Southern whites had regained suffrage. Now a clear majority, they needed only to organize and elect their candidates.

In other states, where blacks were a majority or where the populations of the two races were almost equal, whites used intimidation and violence to undermine the Reconstruction regimes. Secret societies—the Ku Klux Klan, the Knights of the White Camellia, and others—used terrorism to frighten or physically bar blacks from voting. Paramilitary organizations—the Red Shirts and White Leagues—armed themselves to "police" elections. Strongest of all, however, was the simple weapon of economic pressure. Some planters refused to rent land to Republican blacks; storekeepers refused to extend them credit; employers refused to give them work.

> Ku Klux Klan

The Republican Congress responded to this wave of repression with the Enforcement Acts of 1870 and 1871 (better known as the Ku Klux Klan Acts), which prohibited states from discriminating against voters on the basis of race. The laws also authorized the president to use federal troops to protect civil rights—a provision President Grant used in 1871 in nine counties of South Carolina. The Enforcement Acts discouraged Klan violence, which declined by 1872.

Waning Northern Commitment

But this Northern commitment to civil rights in the South did not last very long. After the adoption of the Fifteenth Amendment in 1870, some reformers convinced themselves that their long campaign on behalf of black people was now over. Former Radical leaders such as Charles Sumner and Horace Greeley now began calling themselves Liberals and denouncing what they viewed as black-and-carpetbag misgovernment. Within the South itself, many white Republicans now moved into the Democratic Party.

> Flagging Interest in Civil Rights

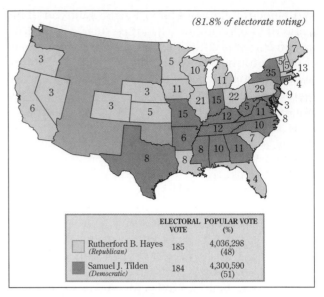

(81.8% of electorate voting)

	ELECTORAL VOTE	POPULAR VOTE (%)
Rutherford B. Hayes *(Republican)*	185	4,036,298 (48)
Samuel J. Tilden *(Democratic)*	184	4,300,590 (51)

THE ELECTION OF 1876 The election of 1876 was one of the most controversial in American history. As in the elections of 1824, 1888, and 2000, the winner of the popular vote—Samuel J. Tilden—was not the winner of the electoral college, which he lost by one vote. The final decision as to who would be president was not made until the day before the official Inauguration in March. ▪ *How did the Republicans turn this apparent defeat into a victory?*

For an interactive version of this map go to www.mhhe.com/unfinishedinteractive

The Panic of 1873 further undermined support for Reconstruction. In the congressional elections of 1874, the Democrats won control of the House of Representatives for the first time since 1861.

By the end of 1876, only three states were left in the hands of the Republicans—South Carolina, Louisiana, and Florida. In the state elections that year, Democrats (after using terrorist tactics) claimed victory in all three. But the Republicans claimed victory as well and were able to remain in office because of the presence of federal troops.

The Compromise of 1877

Grant had hoped to run for another term in 1876, but most Republican leaders—shaken by recent Democratic successes and the scandals with which Grant was associated—resisted. Instead, they settled on Rutherford B. Hayes, three-time governor of Ohio and a champion of civil service reform. The Democrats united behind Samuel J. Tilden, the reform governor of New York.

Although the campaign was a bitter one, there were few differences of principle between the candidates. The November election produced an apparent Democratic victory. Tilden carried the South and several large Northern states, and his popular margin over Hayes was nearly 300,000 votes. But disputed returns from Louisiana, South Carolina, Florida, and Oregon, whose electoral votes totaled 20, threw the election in doubt.

Disputed Election

The Constitution had established no method to determine the validity of disputed returns. The decision clearly lay with Congress, but it was not clear with which house or through what method. (The Senate was Republican, and the House was Democratic.) Members of each party naturally supported a solution that would yield them the victory. Finally, late in January 1877, Congress tried to break the deadlock by creating a special electoral commission composed of five senators, five representatives, and five justices of the Supreme Court. The congressional delegation would consist of five Republicans and five Democrats. The Court delegation would include two Republicans, two Democrats, and the only independent, Justice David Davis. But when the Illinois legislature elected Davis to the United States Senate, the justice resigned from the commission. His seat went instead to a Republican justice. The commission voted along straight party lines, 8 to 7, awarding every disputed vote to Hayes.

Special Electoral Commission

Behind the resolution of the deadlock, however, lay a series of elaborate compromises among leaders of both parties. When a Democratic filibuster threatened to derail the commission's report, Republican Senate leaders met secretly with Southern Democratic leaders to work out terms by which the Democrats would support Hayes. As the price of their cooperation, the Southern Democrats exacted several pledges: the appointment of at least one Southerner to the Hayes cabinet, control of federal patronage in their areas, generous internal improvements, federal aid for the Texas and Pacific Railroad, and withdrawal of the troops. Many powerful Southern Democrats believed that Republican programs of federal support for business and industry would help their region develop.

In his inaugural address, Hayes announced that the South's most pressing need was the restoration

AFRICAN-AMERICAN WORK AFTER SLAVERY Black men and women engaged in a wide range of economic activities in the aftermath of slavery. But discrimination by white Southerners and the former slaves' own lack of education limited most of them to relatively menial jobs. Many black women (including this former slave) earned money for their families by working as "washer women," doing laundry for white people. *(Historic New Orleans Collection (1981.324.1.242))*

of "wise, honest, and peaceful local self-government," and he soon withdrew the troops and let white Democrats take over the remaining southern state governments. That produced charges that he was paying off the South for acquiescing in his election. But the election had already created such bitterness that not even Hayes's promise to serve only one term could mollify his critics.

Federal Troops Withdrawn

The president and his party hoped to build up a "new Republican" organization in the South committed to modest support for black rights. But resentment of Reconstruction was so deep that supporting the party was politically impossible. The "solid" Democratic South, which would survive until the mid-twentieth century, was taking shape.

The Legacy of Reconstruction

Reconstruction made important contributions to the efforts of former slaves to achieve dignity and equality in American life. There was a significant redistribution of income. There was a more limited redistribution of landowner-

Lasting Contributions

ship. Perhaps most important, there was a largely successful effort by African Americans themselves to carve out a society and culture of their own.

Reconstruction was not as disastrous an experience for Southern white elites as most believed at the time. Within little more than a decade, the white South had regained control of its own institutions and, to a great extent, restored its traditional ruling class to power. The federal government imposed no drastic economic reforms on the region, and indeed few lasting political changes of any kind other than the abolition of slavery.

Reconstruction was notable, finally, for its limitations. For in those years the United States failed in its first serious effort to resolve its oldest and deepest social problem—the problem of race. What was

Limits of Reconstruction

more, the experience so disillusioned white Americans that it would be nearly a century before they would try again to combat racial injustice.

Given the odds confronting them, however, African Americans had reason for considerable pride in the gains they were able to make during Reconstruction. And future generations could be grateful for two great charters of freedom—the Fourteenth and Fifteenth Amendments to the Constitution—which, although widely ignored at the time, would one day serve as the basis for a "Second Reconstruction" that would renew the drive to bring freedom to all Americans.

THE NEW SOUTH

The agreement that helped settle the disputed election of 1876 was supposed to be the first step toward developing a stable, permanent Republican Party in the South. In that respect, at least, it failed. In the years following the end of Reconstruction, white southerners established the Democratic Party as the only viable political organization for the region's whites. Even so, the South did change in some of the ways the framers of the Compromise of 1877 had hoped.

The "Redeemers"

Many white southerners rejoiced at the restoration of

"Home Rule"

what they liked to call "home rule." But in reality, political power in the region was soon more restricted than at any time since the Civil War. Once again, most of the South fell under the control of a powerful, conservative oligarchy, whose members were known variously as the "Redeemers" or the "Bourbons."

In some places, this post-Reconstruction ruling class was much the same as the ruling class of the antebellum period. In other areas, however, the Redeemers constituted a genuinely new ruling class. They were merchants, industrialists, railroad developers, and financiers. Some of them were former planters, some of them northern immigrants, some of them ambitious, upwardly mobile white southerners from the region's lower social tiers. They combined a commitment to "home rule" and social conservatism with a commitment to economic development.

The various Bourbon governments of the New South behaved quite similarly. Virtually all the new Democratic regimes lowered taxes, reduced spending, and drastically diminished state services. One state after another eliminated or reduced its support for public school systems.

Industrialization and the "New South"

Many white southern leaders hoped to see their region become the home of a vigorous industrial economy, a "New South."

Henry Grady

Henry Grady, editor of the *Atlanta Constitution*, and other New South advocates seldom challenged white supremacy, but they did promote thrift, industry, and progress—qualities that prewar southerners had often denounced in northern society.

Southern industry did expand dramatically in the years after Reconstruction. Most visible was the growth in textile manufacturing. In the past, southern planters had usually shipped their cotton out of the region to manufacturers in the North or in Europe. Now textile factories appeared in the South itself—many of them drawn to the region by the abundance of water power, the ready supply of cheap labor, and the low taxes. The tobacco-processing industry, similarly, established an important foothold in the region. In the lower South, and particularly in Birmingham, Alabama, the iron industry grew rapidly.

Substantial Railroad Development Railroad development also increased substantially in the post-Reconstruction years. Between 1880 and 1890, trackage in the South more than doubled. And in 1886, the South changed the gauge (width) of its trackage to correspond with the standards of the North. No longer would it be necessary for cargoes heading into the South to be transferred from one train to another at the borders of the region.

Yet southern industry developed within strict limits, and its effects on the region were never even remotely comparable to the effects of industrialization on the North. The southern share of national manufacturing doubled in the last twenty years of the century, but it was still only 10 percent of the total. Even in those industries where development had been most rapid—textiles, iron, railroads—much of the capital had come from, and many of the profits thus flowed to, the North.

The growth of industry in the South required the region to recruit a substantial industrial work force for the first time. From the beginning, a high percentage of the factory workers were women. Heavy male casualties in the Civil War had helped create a large population of unmarried women who **Worker Exploitation** desperately needed employment. Hours were long and wages far below the northern equivalent; indeed, one of the greatest attractions of the South to industrialists was that employers were able to pay workers there as little as one-half what northern workers received. Life in most mill towns was rigidly controlled by the owners and managers of the factories. They rigorously suppressed attempts at protest or union organization. Company stores sold goods to workers at inflated prices and issued credit at exorbitant rates, and mill owners ensured

that no competing merchants were able to establish themselves in the community.

Some industries offered virtually no opportunities to African-American workers, but others did provide some employment for blacks. Some mill towns, therefore, were places where the black and white cultures came into close contact. This juxtaposition of cultures inhibited the growth of racial harmony and increased the determination of white leaders to take additional measures to protect white supremacy.

Tenants and Sharecroppers

The most important economic reality in the post-Reconstruction South was **Impoverished Agriculture** the impoverished state of agriculture. The 1870s and 1880s saw an acceleration of the process that had begun in the immediate postwar years: the imposition of systems of tenantry and debt peonage on much of the region; the reliance on a few cash crops rather than on a diversified agricultural system; and increasing absentee ownership of valuable farmlands.

Tenantry took several forms. Farmers who owned tools, equipment, and farm animals usually paid an annual cash rent for their land. But many farmers had no money or equipment at all. Landlords would supply them with land, a crude house, a few tools, seed, and sometimes a mule. In return, the farmers would promise the landlord a large share of the annual crop. After paying their landlords and their local furnishing merchants, these "sharecroppers" seldom had anything left to sell on their own.

African Americans and the New South

The "New South creed" was not the property of whites alone. Many African Americans were attracted to the vision of progress and self-improvement as well. Some blacks succeeded in elevating themselves into a distinct middle class. These were former slaves who managed to acquire property, establish small businesses, or enter professions. They believed strongly that education was vital to the future of their people, and they expanded the network of black colleges and institutes into an important educational system.

Booker T. Washington   The chief spokesman for this commitment to education was Booker T. Washington, founder and president of the Tuskegee Institute in Alabama. Born into slavery, Washington had worked his way out of poverty after acquiring an education (at Virginia's Hampton Institute). He urged other blacks to follow the same road to self-improvement.

Washington's message was both cautious and hopeful. African Americans should attend school, learn skills, and establish a solid footing in agriculture and the trades. Blacks should, moreover, refine their speech, improve their dress, and adopt habits of thrift and personal cleanliness; they should, in short, adopt the standards of the white middle class. Only thus, he claimed, could they win the respect of the white population.

In a famous speech in Georgia in 1895, Washington outlined a controversial philosophy of race relations that became widely known **Atlanta Compromise** as the Atlanta Compromise. Blacks, he said, should forgo agitating for political rights and concentrate on self-improvement. Washington offered a powerful challenge to those whites who wanted to discourage African Americans from acquiring an education or winning any economic gains. But his message was also intended to assure whites that blacks would not challenge the system of segregation, which southern governments were in the process of creating.

The Birth of Jim Crow

Few white southerners had ever accepted the idea of racial equality. That the former slaves acquired any legal and political rights at all after emancipation was in large part the result of their own efforts and critical federal support. That outside support all but vanished after 1877, when federal troops withdrew and the Supreme Court stripped the Fourteenth and Fifteenth Amendments of much of their significance. In the so-called civil rights cases of 1883, the Court ruled that the Fourteenth Amendment prohibited state governments from discriminating against people because of race but did not restrict private organizations or individuals from doing so.

Eventually, the Court also validated state legislation that institutionalized the separation of the races. In *Plessy* v. *Ferguson* (1896), a case involving a Louisiana **Plessy v. Ferguson**

TUSKEGEE INSTITUTE, 1881
From these modest beginnings, Booker T. Washington's Tuskegee Institute in Alabama became the preeminent academy offering technical and industrial training to black men. It deliberately de-emphasized the traditional liberal arts curricula of most colleges. Washington considered such training less important than developing practical skills. *(Bettmann/Corbis)*

law that required separate seating arrangements for the races on railroads, the Court held that separate accommodations did not deprive blacks of equal rights if the accommodations were equal. In *Cumming* v. *County Board of Education* (1899), the Court ruled that communities could establish schools for whites only, even if there were no comparable schools for blacks.

Even before these decisions, white southerners were working to separate the races to the greatest extent possible. They were particularly determined to strip African Americans of the right to vote. In some states, disenfranchisement had begun almost as soon as Reconstruction ended. But in other areas, black voting continued for some time after Reconstruction—largely because conservative whites believed they could control the black electorate.

In the 1890s, however, franchise restrictions became much more rigid. During those years, some small white farmers began to demand complete black disenfranchisement—

Black Disenfranchisement

because they objected to the black vote being used against them by the Bourbons. At the same time, many members of the conservative elite began to fear that poor whites might unite politically with poor blacks to challenge them.

In devising laws to disenfranchise black males, the southern states had to find ways to evade the Fifteenth Amendment. Two devices emerged before 1900 to accomplish this goal. One was the poll tax or some form of property qualification; few blacks were prosperous enough to meet such requirements. Another was the "literacy" or "understanding" test, which required voters to demonstrate an ability to read and to interpret the Constitution. Even those African Americans who could read had a hard time passing the difficult test white officials gave them.

Laws restricting the franchise and segregating schools were only part of a network of state and local statutes—known as the

Jim Crow Laws

Jim Crow laws—that by the first years of the twentieth century had institutionalized an elaborate system of segregation. Blacks and whites could not ride together in the same railroad cars, sit in the same waiting rooms, use the same washrooms, eat in the same restaurants, or sit in the same theaters. Blacks had no access to many public parks, beaches, or picnic areas; they could not be patients in many hospitals. Much of the new legal structure did no more than confirm what had already been widespread social practice in the South. But the Jim Crow laws also stripped blacks of many of the modest social, economic, and political gains they had made in the late nineteenth century.

More than legal efforts were involved in this process. The 1890s witnessed a dramatic increase in white violence against blacks. The worst such violence—lynching of blacks by white mobs—reached appalling levels. In the nation as a whole in the 1890s, there was an average of 187 lynchings each year, more than 80 percent of them in the South. The vast majority of victims were black. Those who participated in lynchings often saw their actions as a legitimate form of law enforcement, and some victims of lynchings had in fact committed crimes. But lynchings were also a means by which whites controlled the black population through terror and intimidation.

The rise of lynchings shocked the conscience of many white Americans in a way that other forms of racial injustice did not. In 1892 Ida B. Wells, a commit-

Ida B. Wells

ted black journalist, launched an anti-lynching movement with a series of impassioned articles after the lynching of three of her friends. The movement gradually gathered strength, attracting substantial support from whites in both the North and South. Its goal was a federal anti-lynching law, which would allow the national government to do what state and local governments in the South were generally unwilling to do: punish those responsible for lynchings.

But the substantial southern white opposition to lynchings stood as an exception to the general white support for suppression of African Americans. Indeed, just as in the antebellum period, the shared commitment to white supremacy helped dilute class animosities between poorer whites and the Bourbon oligarchies. Economic issues tended to play a secondary role to race in southern politics. For a Where Historians Disagree essay on "The Origins of Segregation," visit Chapter 15 of the book's Online Learning Center.

CONCLUSION

Reconstruction was a profoundly important moment in American history. Despite the bitter political battles in Washington and throughout the South, the most important result of the effort to reunite the nation after its long and bloody war was a reshaping of the lives of ordinary people in all regions of the nation.

In the North, Reconstruction solidified the power of the Republican Party. The expansion of the northern economy accelerated, drawing more and more of its residents into a burgeoning commercial world.

In the South, Reconstruction fundamentally rearranged the relationship between the region's white and black citizens. Only for a while did Reconstruction permit African Americans to participate actively and effectively in southern politics. After a few years, the forces of white supremacy forced most African Americans to the margins of the southern political world, where they would mostly remain until the 1960s.

In other ways, the lives of southern blacks changed dramatically and permanently. Overwhelmingly, they left the plantations. Some sought work in towns and cities. Some left the region altogether. But the great majority began farming as tenants and sharecroppers on land owned by whites. The result was a form of economic bondage, driven by debt, only scarcely less oppressive than the legal bondage of slavery. Within this system, however, African Americans managed to carve out a much larger sphere of social and cultural activity than they had ever been able to create under slavery. Black churches proliferated, African-American schools emerged in some communities, and black colleges began to operate in the region. Some former slaves owned businesses and flourished.

Strenuous efforts by "New South" advocates to advance industry and commerce produced significant results in a few areas. But the South on the whole remained an overwhelmingly rural society with a sharply defined class structure. It was also a region with a deep commitment among its white citizens to the subordination of African Americans—a commitment solidified when white southerners erected an elaborate legal system of segregation (the "Jim Crow" laws). The promise of the great Reconstruction amendments to the Constitution—the Fourteenth and Fifteenth—remained largely unfulfilled in the South as the century drew to its close.

INTERACTIVE LEARNING

On the *Primary Source Investigator CD-ROM*, check out a number of valuable tools for further exploration of the content of this chapter.

Interactive Maps
- U.S. Elections (Map M7)
- Barrow Plantation (Map M18)
- African-Americans and Crop Lien (Map M19)

Primary Sources
Documents, images, and maps related to the Reconstruction era following the Civil War. Some highlights include:

- Examples of Black Codes passed by Southern states and communities early in the aftermath of the Civil War
- A political cartoon about Reconstruction by Thomas Nast
- Several firsthand accounts from former slaves

*Online Learning Center
(www.mhhe.com/unfinishedinteractive)*
Explore this rich website, providing additional exploration of the material covered in this chapter, online versions of the interactive maps included on the Primary Source Investigator CD-ROM, as well as several study aids, including a multiple-choice quiz, essay questions, a glossary, and other valuable tools. In the Online Learning Center for this chapter look for two *Interactive Feature Essays* on:

- **Where Historians Disagree: The Origins of Segregation**

FOR FURTHER REFERENCE

Eric Foner, *Reconstruction: America's Unfinished Revolution, 1863–1877* (1988), the most important modern synthesis of Reconstruction scholarship, emphasizes the radicalism of Reconstruction and the agency of freed people in the process of political and economic renovation. David W. Blight, *Race and Reunion: The Civil War in American Memory* (2001) is an excellent study of the ways in which Americans reinterpreted the Civil War in the late nineteenth century. Amy Dru Stanley, *From Bondage to Contract: Wage Labor, Marriage, and the Market in the Age of Slave Emancipation* (1998) and Jeffrey R. Kerr-Ritchie, *Freedpeople in the Tobacco South: Virginia, 1860–1900* (1999) are important examinations of African-American labor during and after Emancipation. Thomas Holt, *Black over White: Negro Political Leadership in South Carolina During Reconstruction* (1977) examines Reconstruction in the state where black political power reached its apex. C. Vann Woodward, *Origins of the New South* (1951), a classic work on the history of the South after Reconstruction, argues that a rising middle class defined the economic and political transformation of the New South. Edward Ayers, *The Promise of the New South* (1992) offers a rich portrait of social and cultural life in the New South. Jacqueline Jones, *Labor of Love, Labor of Sorrow* (1985) examines the lives of African-American women after Emancipation. Mia Bay, *The White Image in the Black Mind: African-American Ideas about White People, 1830–1925* (2000) is a valuable study of African-American attitudes toward white society. Leon Litwack, *Been in the Storm So Long: The Aftermath of Slavery* (1979) is a major study of the experiences of freed slaves. C. Vann Woodward, *The Strange Career of Jim Crow* (rev. 1974) claims that segregation emerged only gradually across the South after Reconstruction. The "Woodward Thesis" has been challenged by, among others, Joel Williamson, *After Slavery: The Negro in South Carolina During Reconstruction* (1965); John W. Cell, *The Highest Stage of White Supremacy: The Origins of Segregation in South Africa and the American South* (1982); and Howard N. Rabinowitz, *Race Relations in the Urban South, 1865–1890* (1978).

16

The Conquest of the Far West

(National Archives and Records Administration)

MINI-DOCUMENTARY
The Curtis Legacy

By the mid-1840s migrants from the eastern regions of the nation had settled in the West in substantial numbers. By the end of the Civil War, the West had become legendary in the eastern states. No longer the Great American Desert, it was now the "frontier": an empty land awaiting settlement and civilization; a place of wealth, adventure, opportunity, and untrammeled individualism.

In fact, the real West of the mid-nineteenth century bore little resemblance to its popular image. It was a diverse land, with many different regions, climates, and resources. And the English-speaking migrants of the late nineteenth century did not find an empty, desolate land. They found Indians, Mexicans, French and British Canadians, Asians, and others, some of whose families had been living in the West for generations.

THE SOCIETIES OF THE FAR WEST

The Far West was in fact many lands. It contained some of the most arid land in the United States, and some of the wettest. It contained the flattest plains and the highest mountains. And it contained many peoples.

The Western Tribes

The largest and most important western population group before the great white migration from the East was the Indian tribes. Some were members of eastern tribes who had been forcibly resettled west of the Mississippi. But most were members of tribes indigenous to the West.

The western tribes had developed a number of patterns of civilization. More than 300,000 Indians (among them the Serrano, Chumash, Pomo, Maidu, Yurok, and Chinook) had lived on the Pacific coast before the arrival of Spanish settlers, supporting themselves through fishing, foraging, and simple agriculture. The Pueblos of the Southwest had long lived largely as farmers and had established permanent settlements there.

The most widespread Indian groups in the West were the Plains Indians. They were, in fact, made up of many different tribal and language groups. Some lived more or less sedentary lives as farmers. But many of the Plains tribes subsisted largely through hunting buffalo. Riding small but powerful horses, the tribes

Plains Indians

moved through the grasslands following the herds. When a band halted, it constructed tepees as temporary dwellings. The buffalo, or bison, provided the economic basis for the Plains Indians' way of life. The flesh of the large animal was their principal source of food, and its skin supplied materials for clothing, shoes, tepees, blankets, robes, and utensils. "Buffalo chips"—dried manure—provided fuel; buffalo bones became knives and arrow tips; buffalo tendons formed the strings of bows.

The Plains warriors proved to be the most formidable foes white settlers had encountered. But the various tribes were usually unable to unite against white aggression. At times, tribal warriors faced white forces who were being assisted by guides and even fighters from other, usually rival, tribes. Some tribes, however, were able to overcome their divisions and unite effectively. By the mid-nineteenth century, for example, the Sioux, Arapaho, and Cheyenne had forged a powerful alliance that dominated the northern plains. That proved no protection, however, against the greatest danger to the tribes: ecological and economic decline. Indians were highly vulnerable to eastern infectious diseases. And the tribes were, of course, at a considerable disadvantage in any long-term battle with an economically and industrially advanced people.

Indian Disadvantages

Hispanic New Mexico

For centuries, much of the Far West had been part of, first, the Spanish Empire and, later, the Mexican

	1862	1865–1867	1866	1869	1873	1874	1876
T I M E L I N E	Homestead Act	Sioux Wars	Western cattle bonanza begins	Transcontinental railroad completed	Barbed wire invented	Black Hills gold rush	Battle of Little Bighorn
	1877	**1882**	**1885**	**1887**	**1889**	**1890**	**1893**
	Desert Land Act	Chinese Exclusion Act	Twain's *Huckleberry Finn*	Dawes Act	Oklahoma opened to white settlement	Battle of Wounded Knee	Turner's "Frontier Thesis"

Republic. When the United States acquired its new lands there in the 1840s, it acquired many Mexican residents at the same time.

In New Mexico, the centers of Spanish-speaking society were the farming and trading communities the Spanish had established in the seventeenth century. When the United States acquired title to New Mexico in the aftermath of the Mexican War, General Stephen Kearny—who had commanded the American troops in the region during the conflict—tried to establish a territorial government out of the approximately 1,000 Anglo-Americans in the region, ignoring the over 50,000 Hispanics. There were widespread fears among the Hispanics and Indians that the new American rulers of the region would confiscate their lands. In 1847, before the new government had established itself, Taos Indians rebelled; they killed the new governor and other Anglo-American officials before being subdued by United States Army forces. New Mexico remained under military rule until the United States finally organized a territorial government there in 1850. The United States Army finally broke the power of the Navajo, Apache, and other tribes in the region. The defeat of the tribes led to substantial Hispanic migration into other areas of the Southwest.

Taos Indian Rebellion

The Anglo-American presence in the Southwest grew rapidly once the railroads established lines into the region in the 1880s and early 1890s. With the railroads came extensive new ranching, farming, and mining. The expansion of economic activity in the region attracted a new wave of Mexican immigrants, who moved across the border in search of work. The English-speaking proprietors of the new enterprises restricted most Mexicans to the lowest-paying and least stable jobs.

Hispanic California and Texas

In California, Spanish settlement began in the eighteenth century with a string of Christian missions along the Pacific coast. The missionaries and the soldiers who accompanied them gathered most of the coastal Indians into their communities. In the 1830s, after the new Mexican government began reducing the power of the church, the mission society largely collapsed. In its place emerged a secular Mexican aristocracy, which controlled a chain of large estates in the fertile lands west of the Sierra mountains. For them, the acquisition of California by the United States was disastrous. So vast were the numbers of English-speaking immigrants that the *californios* (as the Hispanic

Anglo-American Onslaught

residents of the region were known) had little power to resist the onslaught. English-speaking prospectors organized to exclude them from the mines during the gold rush. Many *californios* also lost their lands—either through corrupt business deals or through outright seizure.

Increasingly, Mexicans and Mexican Americans became part of the lower end of the state's working class, clustered in *barrios* in Los Angeles or elsewhere or laboring as migrant farmworkers. Even small Hispanic landowners who managed to hang on to their farms found themselves unable to raise livestock, as once-communal grazing lands fell under the control of powerful Anglo ranchers.

Hispanics Oppressed A similar pattern occurred in Texas after it joined the United States. Many Mexican landowners lost their land—some as a result of fraud and coercion, some because they could not compete with the enormous Anglo-American ranching kingdoms that were emerging. In 1859, angry Mexicans, led by the rancher Juan Cortina, raided the jail in Brownsville and freed all the Mexican prisoners inside. But such resistance had little long-term effect. As in California, Mexicans in southern Texas became an increasingly impoverished working class relegated largely to unskilled farm or industrial labor.

The Chinese Migration

At the same time that Europeans were crossing the Atlantic in search of opportunities in the New World, many Chinese were crossing the Pacific in hopes of better lives. Not all came to the United States. Many Chinese moved to Hawaii, Australia, Latin America, South Africa, and even the Caribbean—some as "coolies" (indentured servants).

Increasing Chinese Immigration A few Chinese traveled to the American West even before the gold rush, but after 1848 the flow increased dramatically. By 1880, more than 200,000 Chinese had settled in the United States. Almost all came as free laborers. For a time, white Americans welcomed the Chinese. Very quickly, however, white opinion turned hostile—in part because the Chinese were so industrious and successful that some white Americans began considering them rivals.

In the early 1850s, large numbers of Chinese immigrants joined the hunt for gold. Many of them

A CHINESE FAMILY IN SAN FRANCISCO Like many other Americans, Chinese families liked to pose for photographic portraits in the late nineteenth century. And like many other immigrants, they often sent them back to relatives in China. This portrait of Chun Duck Chin and his seven-year-old son Chun Jan Yut was taken in a studio in San Francisco in the 1870s. *(The National Archives and Records Administration)*

were well-organized, hardworking prospectors, and for a time some of them enjoyed considerable success. But opportunities for Chinese to prosper in the mines were fleeting. In 1852, the California legislature began trying to exclude the Chinese from gold mining by enacting a "foreign miners" tax. Gradually, the effect of the discriminatory laws, the hostility of white miners, and the declining profitability of the surface mines drove most Chinese out of prospecting.

As mining declined as a source of wealth and jobs for the Chinese, railroad employment grew. Beginning in 1865, over 12,000 Chinese found work building the transcontinental railroad. In fact, Chinese workers formed 90 percent of the labor force of the Central Pacific. The company preferred them to white laborers because they worked hard, made few demands, and accepted relatively low wages.

Work on the Central Pacific was arduous and often dangerous. In the winter, many Chinese tunneled into snow banks at night to create warm sleeping areas for themselves, even though such tunnels frequently collapsed, suffocating those inside. In the spring of 1866, 5,000 Chinese railroad workers rebelled against the terrible conditions of their work and went on strike demanding higher wages and a shorter workday. The company isolated them, surrounded them with strikebreakers, and starved them into submission.

In 1869 the transcontinental railroad was completed, and thousands of Chinese lost their jobs. Some moved into agricultural work, usually in menial positions. Increasingly, however, the Chinese flocked to cities. By far the largest single Chinese community was in San Francisco. Much of community life there, and in other "Chinatowns" throughout the West, revolved around organizations that functioned as something like benevolent societies and filled many of the roles that political machines often served in immigrant communities in eastern cities. They were often led by prominent merchants. These organizations became, in effect, employment brokers, unions, arbitrators of disputes, defenders of the community against outside persecution, and dispensers of social services. They also organized the elaborate festivals and celebrations that were such a conspicuous and important part of life in Chinatowns.

Other Chinese organizations were secret societies, known as "tongs." And some of the tongs were violent criminal organizations, involved in the opium trade and prostitution. Few people outside the Chinese communities were aware of their existence, except when rival tongs engaged in violent conflict (or "tong wars").

In San Francisco and other western cities, the Chinese usually occupied the lower rungs of the employment ladder. Many worked as common laborers, servants, and unskilled factory hands. Some established their own small businesses, especially laundries. They moved into this business because laundries could be started with very little capital and required only limited command of English. By the 1890s, Chinese constituted over two-thirds of all the laundry workers in California.

During the earliest Chinese migrations to California, virtually all the women who made the journey did so because they had been sold into prostitution in China. As late as 1880, nearly half the Chinese women in California were prostitutes. Gradually, however, the number of Chinese women increased, and Chinese men in America became more likely to form families.

Anti-Chinese Sentiments

As Chinese communities grew larger and more conspicuous, anti-Chinese sentiment among white residents became increasingly strong. Anti-Chinese activities, some of them violent, reflected the resentment of many white workers toward Chinese laborers for accepting low wages and thus undercutting union members. As the political value of attacking the Chinese grew in California, the Democratic Party took up the call. So did the Workingmen's Party of California—created in 1878 by Denis Kearney, an Irish immigrant—which gained significant political power in the state in large part on the basis of its hostility to the Chinese.

In 1882, Congress responded to the political pressure and the growing violence by passing the Chinese Exclusion Act, which banned Chinese immigration into the United States for ten years and barred Chinese already in the country from becoming naturalized citizens. Congress renewed the law for another ten years in 1892 and made it permanent in 1902. It had a dramatic effect on the Chinese population, which declined by more than 40 percent in the forty years after the act's passage.

Migration from the East

The scale of the post–Civil War migration to the American West dwarfed everything that had preceded it. In previous decades, the settlers had come in thousands. Now they came in millions. Most of the new settlers were from the established Anglo-American societies of the eastern United States, but substantial numbers were foreign-born immigrants from Europe: Scandinavians, Germans, Irish, Russians, Czechs, and others.

They came to the West for many reasons. Settlers were attracted by gold and silver deposits, by the shortgrass pasture for cattle and sheep, and ultimately by the sod of the plains and the meadowlands of the mountains. The completion of the great transcontinental railroad line in 1869 encouraged settlement. So did the land policies of the federal government. The Homestead Act of 1862 permitted settlers to buy plots of 160 acres for a small fee if they occupied the land they purchased for five years and improved it.

Homestead Act of 1862

Supporters of the Homestead Act believed it would create new markets and new outposts of commercial agriculture for the nation's growing economy. But a unit of 160 acres, while ample in much of the East, was too small for the grazing and grain farming of the Great Plains. Eventually, the federal government provided some relief. The Timber Culture Act (1873) permitted homesteaders to receive grants of 160 additional acres if they planted 40 acres of trees on them. The Desert Land Act (1877) provided that claimants could buy 640 acres at $1.25 an acre provided they irrigated part of their holdings within three years. These and other laws ultimately made it possible for individuals to acquire as much as 1,280 acres of land at little cost.

Political organization followed on the heels of settlement. By the mid-1860s, territorial governments were in operation in Nevada, Colorado, Dakota, Arizona, Idaho, Montana, and Wyoming. Statehood rapidly followed for Nevada, Nebraska, and Colorado. In 1889, North and South Dakota, Montana, and Washington won admission; Wyoming and Idaho entered the next year. Congress denied Utah statehood until its Mormon leaders convinced the government in 1896 that polygamy (the practice of men taking several wives) had been abandoned. At the turn of the century, only Arizona, New Mexico, and Oklahoma remained outside the Union.

New Western States

THE CHANGING WESTERN ECONOMY

Among many other things, the great wave of Anglo-American and European settlement transformed the economy of the Far West. The new American settlers tied the West firmly to the growing industrial economy of the East.

Labor in the West

As commercial activity increased, many farmers, ranchers, and miners found it necessary to recruit a paid labor force. The labor shortage of the region led to higher wages for some workers than were typical in most areas of the East. But working conditions were often arduous, and job security was almost nonexistent. Once a railroad was built or a mine played out, thousands of workers could find themselves suddenly unemployed. Competition from Chinese immigrants also forced some Anglo-Americans and Europeans out of work.

Even more than in many parts of the East, the western working class was highly multiracial. English-speaking whites worked alongside African Americans and immigrants from southern and eastern Europe, as they did in the East. Even more, they worked with Chinese, Filipinos, Mexicans, and Indians. But the work force was highly stratified along racial lines. In almost every area of the western economy, white workers (whatever their ethnicity) occupied the upper tiers of employment, while the lower tiers consisted overwhelmingly of nonwhites.

Multiracial Working Class

The western economy was, however, no more a single entity than the economy of the East. In the late nineteenth century, the region produced three major industries: mining, ranching, and commercial farming.

The Arrival of the Miners

The first economic boom in the Far West came in mining. It began around 1860 and flourished until the 1890s. Then it abruptly declined.

News of a gold or silver strike in an area would start a stampede, followed by several stages of settlement. Individual prospectors would exploit the first shallow deposits of ore largely by hand, with pan and placer mining. After these surface deposits dwindled, corporations moved in to engage in lode or quartz mining, which dug deeper beneath the surface. Then, as those deposits dwindled, commercial mining either disappeared or continued on a restricted basis, and ranchers and farmers established a more permanent economy.

Mining Booms

The first great mineral strikes (other than the California gold rush) occurred just before the Civil War. In 1858, gold was discovered in the Pike's Peak district of what would soon be the territory of Colorado; the following year, 50,000 prospectors stormed in. Denver and other mining camps blossomed into "cities" overnight. Almost as rapidly as it had developed, the boom ended. Later, the discovery of silver near Leadville supplied a new source of mineral wealth.

While the Colorado rush of 1859 was still in progress, news of another strike drew miners to Nevada. Gold had been found in the Washoe district. But even more plentiful and more valuable was the silver found in the great Comstock Lode and other Washoe veins. The first

Comstock Lode Discovered

prospectors to reach the Washoe fields came from California, and from the beginning, Californians dominated the settlement and development of Nevada. In a remote desert without railroad transportation, the territory produced no supplies of its own, and everything had to be shipped from California to Virginia City, Carson City, and other roaring camp towns. When the first placer (or surface) deposits ran out, Californian and eastern capitalists bought the claims of the pioneer prospectors and began to use the more difficult process of quartz mining, which enabled them to retrieve silver from deeper veins. For a few years these outside owners reaped tremendous profits: from 1860 to 1880 the Nevada lodes yielded bullion worth $306 million. After that, the mines quickly played out.

The next important mineral discoveries came in 1874, when gold was found in the Black Hills of southwestern Dakota Territory. Prospectors swarmed into the remote area. Like the others, the boom flared for a time, until surface resources faded and corporations took over from the miners. One enormous company, the Homestake, came to dominate the fields.

Although the gold and silver discoveries generated the most popular excitement, in the long run other, less glamorous natural resources proved more important to the development of the West. The great Anaconda copper mine launched by William Clark in 1881 marked the beginning of an industry that would remain important to Montana for many decades. In other areas, mining operations had significant success with lead, tin, quartz, and zinc.

Men greatly outnumbered women in the mining towns, and younger men in particular had difficulty finding female companions of comparable age. Those

Gender Disparity

women who did gravitate to the new communities often came with their husbands. Single women, or women whose husbands were earning no money, did work for wages at times, as cooks, laundresses, and tavern keepers. And in the sexually imbalanced mining communities, there was always a ready market for prostitutes.

The thousands of people who flocked to the mining towns in search of quick wealth and failed to find it often remained as wage laborers in corporate mines, working in almost uniformly terrible conditions. In the 1870s, one worker in every thirty was disabled in the mines, and one in every eighty was killed.

The Cattle Kingdom

A second important element of the changing economy of the Far West was cattle ranching. The open range provided a huge area where cattle raisers could graze their herds.

The western cattle industry was Mexican and Texan

Mexican Roots

by ancestry. Long before citizens of the United States entered the Southwest, Mexican ranchers had developed the techniques and equipment that the cattlemen and cowboys of the Great Plains later employed. Americans in Texas adopted these methods and carried them to the northernmost ranges of the cattle kingdom. Texas also had the largest herds of cattle in the country. From Texas, too, came the small, muscular horses (broncos and mustangs) that enabled cowboys to control the herds.

At the end of the Civil War, an estimated 5 million cattle roamed the Texas ranges. Eastern markets were offering good prices for steers in any condition, and the challenge facing the cattle industry was getting the animals from the range to the railroad centers. Early in 1866, some Texas cattle ranchers began driving their combined herds, some 260,000 head, north to Sedalia, Missouri, on the Missouri Pacific Railroad. The caravan suffered heavy losses. But the drive proved that cattle could be driven to distant markets and pastured along the

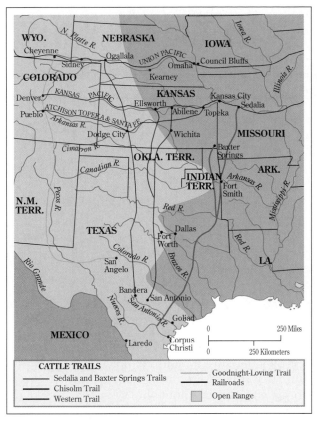

THE CATTLE KINGDOM, c. 1866–1887 Cattle ranching and cattle drives are among the most romanticized features of the nineteenth-century West. This map shows two important characteristics of the "cattle kingdom" in the 1860s and 1870s. One is the vast expanse of "open range." ▮ *Why was that necessary for the great cattle drives, and what eventually ended it?* The other is the dense network of trails and railroads that together made possible the commerce in cattle.

For an interactive version of this map go to www.mhhe.com/unfinishedinteractive

trail. This earliest of the "long drives" established the first, tentative link between the isolated cattle breeders of west Texas and the booming urban markets of the East.

With the precedent of the long drive established, the next step was to find an easier route through more accessible country. Market facilities grew up at Abilene, Kansas, on the Kansas Pacific Railroad, and for years the town reigned as the railhead of the cattle kingdom. But by the mid-1870s, agricultural development in western Kansas was eating away at the open-range land. Cattlemen had to develop other trails and other market outlets. As the railroads began to reach farther west, Dodge City and Wichita in Kansas, Ogallala and Sidney in Nebraska, Cheyenne and Laramie in Wyoming, and Miles City and Glendive in Montana all began to rival Abilene as major centers of stock herding.

There had always been an element of risk and speculation in the open-range cattle business. Rustlers and Indians frequently seized large numbers of animals. But as settlement of the plains increased, new forms of competition arose. Sheep breeders from California and Oregon brought their flocks onto the range to compete for grass. Farmers ("nesters") from the East threw fences around their claims, blocking trails and breaking up the open range. A series of "range wars" erupted out of the tensions between these competing groups.

"Range Wars"

Accounts of the lofty profits to be made in the cattle business tempted eastern, English, and Scottish capital to the plains. Increasingly, the structure of the cattle economy became corporate; in one year, twenty corporations with a combined capital of $12 million were chartered in Wyoming. The result of this frenzied, speculative expansion was that the ranges became overstocked. There was not enough grass to support the crowding herds or sustain the long drives. Two severe winters, in 1885–1886 and 1886–1887, with a searing summer between them, stung and scorched the plains. Hundreds of thousands of cattle died; streams and grass dried up; princely ranches and costly investments disappeared in a season.

The open-range industry never recovered, and railroads displaced the trail as the route to market for livestock. But established cattle ranches survived, grew, and prospered, eventually producing more beef than ever.

THE ROMANCE OF THE WEST

The West occupied a special place in the Anglo-American imagination in the nineteenth century. Many white Americans continued to consider it a romantic place, a wilderness where individuals could experience true freedom.

PROMOTING THE WEST
Buffalo Bill's Wild West show was popular all over the United States, and indeed through much of the world. He was so familiar a figure that many of his posters contained only his picture with the words "He is Coming." This more conventional poster announces a visit of the show to Brooklyn.
(Culver Pictures, Inc.)

The Western Landscape and the Cowboy

Part of the reason was the spectacular natural landscape of the West. Painters of the new "Rocky Mountain School"—of whom the best known were Albert Bierstadt and Thomas Moran—celebrated the new West in grandiose canvases, some of which were taken on tours around the eastern and midwestern states and attracted enormous crowds, eager for a vision of the Great West.

> "Rocky Mountain School"

Gradually, the interest in paintings of the West inspired a growing wave of tourism. In the 1880s and 1890s, resort hotels began to spring up near some of the most spectacular landscapes in the region.

Even more appealing than the landscape was the rugged, free-spirited lifestyle that many Americans associated with the West. Many nineteenth-century Americans came to romanticize, especially, the figure of the cowboy. Western novels such as Owen Wister's *The Virginian* (1902) romanticized the cowboy's supposed freedom from traditional social constraints, his affinity with nature, even his supposed propensity for violence. Wister's character was a semi-educated man whose natural decency, courage, and compassion made him a powerful symbol of the

> Cowboys Mythologized

supposed virtues of the "frontier." But *The Virginian* was only the most famous example of a type of literature that soon swept throughout the United States: novels and stories about the West, and about the lives of cowboys in particular, that appeared in boys' magazines, pulp novels, theater, and even serious literature.

One reason for the widespread admiration of the cowboy was the remarkable popularity of the Wild West shows that traveled throughout the United States and Europe. The most successful were the shows of Buffalo Bill Cody, a former Pony Express rider and Indian fighter. Cody's Wild West show exploited his own fame. But it was mainly popular for its romanticization of the West and of the life of the cowboy. It included re-enactments of Indian battles and displays of horsemanship and riflery (many of them by the famous sharpshooter Annie Oakley). Buffalo Bill and his imitators confirmed the popular image of the West as a place of romance and glamour and helped keep that image alive for later generations.

The Idea of the Frontier

Yet it was not simply the particular character of the new West that made it so important to the nation's imagination. Since the earliest moments of European settlement in America, the image of the open frontier to the west had always inspired those who dreamed of starting life anew.

Romantic Vision of the Frontier Mark Twain gave voice to this romantic vision of the frontier in a series of novels and memoirs. In *The Adventures of Tom Sawyer* (1876) and *The Adventures of Huckleberry Finn* (1885), he produced characters who repudiated the constraints of organized society and attempted to escape into a more natural world. For Huck Finn, the vehicle of escape was a small raft on the Mississippi, but the yearning for freedom reflected a larger vision of the West as the last refuge from the constraints of civilization.

The painter and sculptor Frederic Remington also captured the romance of the West. He portrayed the cowboy as a natural aristocrat, much like Wister's *Virginian*, living in a natural world in which all the normal supporting structures of "civilization" were missing. Remington became one of the most successful artists of the nineteenth century.

Theodore Roosevelt also contributed to the romanticizing of the West. He traveled to the Dakota badlands in the mid-1880s to help himself recover from the sudden death of his young wife. In the 1890s, he published a four-volume history, *The Winning of the West*, with a heroic account of the spread of white civilization into the frontier.

Frederick Jackson Turner The clearest and most influential statement of the romantic vision of the frontier came from the historian Frederick Jackson Turner, in a memorable paper he delivered to a meeting of the American Historical Association in Chicago in 1893 entitled "The Significance of the Frontier in American History." In it he boldly claimed that the experience of expansion into the frontier had stimulated individualism, nationalism, and democracy. It had kept opportunities for advancement alive. "Now," Turner concluded, "the frontier has gone and with its going has closed the first period of American history."

"Passing of the Frontier" In accepting the idea of the "passing of the frontier," many Americans were acknowledging the end of one of their most cherished myths. As long as it had been possible for them to consider the West an empty, open land, it was possible to believe that there were constantly revitalizing opportunities in American life. Now there was a vague and ominous sense of opportunities foreclosed. For a Where Historians Disagree essay on "The Frontier and the West," visit Chapter 16 of the book's Online Learning Center website.

THE DISPERSAL OF THE TRIBES

Having imagined the West as a "virgin land" awaiting civilization by white people, many Americans tried to force the region to match their image of it. That meant, above all, ensuring that the Indian tribes would not remain obstacles to the spread of white society.

White Tribal Policies

The traditional policy of the federal government was to regard the tribes simultaneously as independent nations (with which the United States could negotiate treaties) and as wards of the president (who would exercise paternalistic authority over the Indians). The concept of Indian sovereignty had supported the government's attempt to erect a permanent frontier between whites and Indians. But the belief in tribal sovereignty was not strong enough to withstand the pressure of white settlers eager for access to Indian lands.

"Concentration" Policy By the early 1850s, the idea of establishing one great enclave in which many tribes could live gave way to a new reservations policy known as "concentration." In 1851, the government assigned all the tribes their own defined reservations, confirmed by individual treaties—often negotiated with unauthorized "representatives" chosen by whites, people known sarcastically as "treaty chiefs." The new arrangement divided the tribes from one another and made them easier to control. It allowed the government to force tribes into scattered locations and to take over the most desirable lands for white settlement. But it did not survive for long.

In 1867, Congress established the Indian Peace Commission to recommend a new Indian policy. The commission recommended that the government move all the Plains tribes into two large reservations—one in Indian Territory (Oklahoma), the other in the Dakotas. At a series of meetings with the tribes, government agents cajoled, bribed, and tricked their representatives into agreeing to treaties establishing the new reservations.

But this "solution" worked little better than previous ones. Part of the problem was the abysmal way in which the Bureau of Indian Affairs administered the reservations. But the problem was also a result

Buffalo Herds Decimated

of the relentless slaughtering by whites of the buffalo herds. After the Civil War, hunters swarmed over the plains, killing the huge animals. Some Indian tribes (notably the Blackfeet) also began killing large numbers of buffalo to sell in the booming new market. In 1865, there had been at least 15 million buffalo; a decade later, fewer than a thousand of the great beasts survived. By destroying the buffalo herds, whites were destroying the Indians' source of food and supplies.

The Indian Wars

There was almost incessant fighting between whites and Indians from the 1850s to

Growing Indian Resistance

the 1880s. Indian warriors attacked wagon trains, stagecoaches, and isolated ranches, often in retaliation for earlier attacks on them by whites. As the United States Army became more deeply involved in the fighting, the tribes began to focus more of their attacks on white soldiers.

At times, this small-scale fighting escalated. During the Civil War, the eastern Sioux in Minnesota, cramped on a small reservation and exploited by corrupt white agents, suddenly rebelled. Led by Little Crow, they killed more than 700 whites before being subdued by a force of regulars and militiamen. Thirty-eight of the Indians were hanged, and the tribe was exiled to the Dakotas.

At the same time, fighting flared up in eastern Colorado, where the Arapaho and Cheyenne were coming into conflict with white miners. Bands of Indians attacked stagecoach lines and settlements in an effort to regain territory they had lost. In response to these incidents, whites called up a large territorial militia. The governor urged all friendly Indians to congregate at army posts for protection before the army began its campaign. One Arapaho and Cheyenne band under Black Kettle camped near Fort Lyon on Sand Creek in November 1864. Some members of the party were warriors, but Black Kettle believed he was under official protec-

tion and exhibited no hostile intention. Nevertheless, Colonel J. M. Chivington led a volunteer militia force to the unsuspecting camp and massacred 133 people, 105 of them women and children. Black Kettle himself escaped the Sand Creek massacre. But

Sand Creek Massacre

four years later, in 1868, he and his Cheyennes, some of whom were now at war with the whites, were caught on the Washita River, near the Texas border, by Colonel George A. Custer. White troops killed the chief and his people.

At the end of the Civil War, white troops stepped up their wars against the western Indians on several fronts. The most serious and sustained conflict was in Montana, where the army was attempting to build a road, the Bozeman Trail, to connect Fort Laramie, Wyoming, to the new mining centers. The western Sioux resented this intrusion into the heart of their buffalo range. Led by one of their great chiefs, Red Cloud, they so harried the soldiers and the construction party that the road could not be used.

But it was not only the United States military that harassed the tribes. It was also unofficial violence by white vigilantes who engaged in what became known as "Indian hunting."

"Indian Hunting"

Sometimes the killing was in response to Indian raids on white communities. But considerable numbers of whites were committed to the goal of literal "elimination" of the tribes whatever their behavior. In California, civilians killed close to 5,000 Indians between 1850 and 1880—one of many factors (disease and poverty being the more important) that reduced the Indian population of the state from 150,000 before the Civil War to 30,000 in 1870.

The treaties negotiated in 1867 brought a temporary lull to many of the conflicts. But new forces soon shattered the peace again. In the early 1870s, more waves of white settlers, mostly miners, began to penetrate some of the lands in Dakota Territory supposedly guaranteed to the tribes in 1867. Indian resistance flared anew. In the northern plains, the Sioux rose up in 1875 and left their reservation. When white officials ordered them to return, bands of warriors gathered in Montana and united under two great leaders: Crazy Horse and Sitting Bull. Three army columns set out to round them up and force them back onto the reservation. With the

Custer Defeated

expedition, as colonel of the famous Seventh Cavalry, was the colorful and controversial George A. Custer. At the Battle of the Little Bighorn in southern Montana in 1876, an unprecedentedly large army, perhaps 2,500 tribal warriors, surprised Custer and part of his regiment, surrounded them, and killed every man.

But the Indians did not have the political organization or the supplies to keep their troops united. Soon the warriors drifted off in bands to elude pursuit or search for food, and the army ran them down singly and returned them to Dakota. The power of the Sioux quickly collapsed.

One of the most dramatic episodes in Indian history occurred in Idaho in 1877. The Nez Percé were a small tribe, some of whose members had managed to live in Oregon into the 1870s without ever signing a treaty with the United States. But under pressure from white settlers, the government forced them to move onto a reservation. With no realistic prospect of resisting, the Indians began the journey to the reservation; but on the way, several younger Indians killed four white settlers.

MINI-DOCUMENTARY: The Curtis Legacy

The leader of the band, Chief Joseph, persuaded his followers to flee from the expected retribution.

Chief Joseph

American troops pursued and attacked them, only to be driven off in a battle at White Bird Canyon. After that, the Nez Percé scattered and became part of a remarkable chase. Joseph moved with 200 warriors and 350 women, children, and old people in an effort to reach Canada. Pursued by four columns of American soldiers, the Indians covered 1,321 miles in seventy-five days, repelling or evading the army time and again. They were finally caught just short of the Canadian boundary. Some escaped and slipped across the border; but Joseph and most of his followers finally gave up. "Hear me, my chiefs," Joseph said after meeting with the American general Nelson Miles. "I am tired. My heart is sick and sad. From where the sun now stands, I will fight no more forever."

The last Indians to maintain organized resistance against the whites were the Chiricahua Apaches. The two ablest chiefs of this fierce tribe were Mangas Colorados and Cochise. Mangas was murdered during the Civil War by white soldiers who tricked him into surrendering, and in 1872 Cochise agreed to peace in exchange for a reservation that included some of the tribe's traditional land. But Cochise died in 1874, and his successor, Geronimo, fought

THE SURRENDER OF GERONIMO The great Apache warrior Geronimo (front row, third from right) sits with members of his diminished band after surrendering to United States troops in 1886. The two men at front row, left, are Geronimo's half brothers. The young boy in the front row, right, is his son. *(Smithsonian Institution, National Anthropological Archives, Bureau of American Ethnology Collection)*

on for more than a decade longer, leading warriors in intermittent raids against white outposts. With each raid, however, the number of warring Apaches dwindled, as some warriors died and others drifted away to the reservation. By 1886, Geronimo's band consisted of only about 30 people, including women and children, while his white pursuers numbered perhaps 10,000. Geronimo recognized the odds and surrendered.

The Apache wars were the most violent of all the Indian conflicts, and they produced brutality on both sides. But it was the whites who committed the most flagrant atrocities. That did not end with the conclusion of the Apache wars. Another tragic encounter occurred in 1890 as a result of a religious revival among the Sioux. As other tribes had done in trying times in the past, many of these Indians turned to a prophet who led them in a religious revival.

This time the prophet was Wovoka, a Paiute who inspired a fervent spiritual awakening that began in Nevada and spread quickly to the plains. The new revival emphasized the coming of a messiah, but its most conspicuous feature was a mass, emotional "Ghost Dance," which inspired ecstatic, mystical visions among many participants. One of these visions was an image of a retreat of white people from the plains and a restoration of the great buffalo herds. White agents on the Sioux reservation watched the dances in bewilderment and fear; some believed they might be the preliminary to hostilities.

"Ghost Dance"

On December 29, 1890, the Seventh Cavalry tried to round up a group of about 350 cold and starving Sioux at Wounded Knee, South Dakota. Fighting broke out in which about 40 white soldiers and up to 200 of the Indians died. An Indian may have fired the first shot, but the battle soon turned into a one-sided massacre, as the white soldiers turned their new machine guns on the Indians and mowed them down in the snow.

Wounded Knee Massacre

The Dawes Act

Even before the Ghost Dance and Wounded Knee tragedies, the federal government had moved to destroy the tribal structure that had always been the cornerstone of Indian culture. Reversing its policy of nearly fifty years, Congress abolished the practice by which tribes owned reservation lands communally. The action was designed to force Indians to become landowners and farmers, to abandon their collective society and culture and become part of white civilization.

The Dawes Severalty Act of 1887 provided for the gradual elimination of most tribal ownership of land and the allotment of tracts to individual owners: 160 acres to the head of a family, 80 acres to a single adult or orphan, 40 acres to each dependent child. Adult owners were given United States citizenship, but unlike other citizens, they could not gain full title to their property for twenty-five years (supposedly to prevent them from selling the land to speculators).

In applying the Dawes Act, the Bureau of Indian Affairs relentlessly promoted the idea of assimilation. Not only did agents of the bureau try to move Indian families onto their own plots of land; they also took many Indian children away from their families and sent them to boarding schools. They moved as well to stop Indian religious rituals and encouraged the spread of Christianity and the creation of Christian churches on the reservations.

Assimilation Promoted

Few Indians were prepared for this wrenching change. In any case, administration of the Dawes Act was so corrupt and inept that ultimately the government abandoned most efforts to enforce it. Much of the reservation land, therefore, was never distributed to individual owners.

THE RISE AND DECLINE OF THE WESTERN FARMER

The arrival of the miners, the empire building of the cattle ranchers, the dispersal of the Indian tribes—all served as a prelude to the decisive phase of white settlement of the Far West. Even before the Civil War, farmers had begun moving into the plains region. By the 1870s, what was once a trickle had become a deluge. Farmers poured into the plains and beyond, enclosed land that had once been hunting territory for Indians and open range for cattle, and established a new agricultural region.

For a time in the late 1870s and early 1880s, the new western farmers flourished, enjoying the fruits of an agricultural economic boom. Beginning in the mid-1880s, however, the boom turned to bust, and the western agricultural economy began a long, steady decline.

Farming on the Plains

Many factors combined to produce the surge of western agricultural settlement, but the most important was the railroads. Before the Civil War, the Great Plains had been accessible only through a difficult journey by wagon. But beginning in the 1860s, a great new network of railroad lines developed. It made huge areas of settlement accessible for the first time.

The building of the transcontinental line—completed in 1869 when the two lines met at Promontory Point, Utah—was a dramatic achievement. But the construction of subsidiary lines in the following years proved of greater importance. State governments subsidized railroad development by offering direct financial aid, favorable loans, and more than 50 million acres of land (on top of the 130 million acres the federal government had provided). Although built and operated by private corporations, the railroads were in many respects public projects.

The railroads spurred agricultural settlement by making access to the Great Plains easier. But the railroad companies also actively promoted settlement. The companies set rates so low for settlers that almost anyone could afford the trip west. And they sold much of their land at very low prices and with liberal credit.

Cheap Rail Rates

Contributing further to the great surge of white agricultural expansion was a pronounced but temporary change in the climate of the Great Plains. For several years in succession, beginning in the 1870s, rainfall in the Plains states was well above average. White Americans now rejected the old idea that the region was the Great American Desert.

Even under the most favorable conditions, farming on the plains presented special problems. First was the problem of fencing. Farmers had to enclose their land, but materials for traditional wood or stone fences were unavailable. In the mid-1870s, however, two Illinois farmers, Joseph H. Glidden and I. L. Ellwood, solved this problem by developing and marketing barbed wire, which became standard equipment on the plains.

The second problem was water. Water was scarce even when rainfall was above average. After 1887, a series of dry seasons began, and lands that had been fertile now returned to semidesert. Some farmers dealt with the problem by using deep wells pumped by steel windmills, by turning to what was called dry-land farming (a system of tillage designed to conserve moisture in the soil by covering it with a dust blanket), or by planting drought-resistant crops. In many areas of the plains, however, only large-scale irrigation could save the endangered farms. But irrigation projects of the necessary magnitude required government assistance, and neither the federal nor the state governments were prepared to fund the projects.

Scarce Water

Most of the people who moved into the region had previously been farmers in the Middle West, the East, or Europe. In the booming years of the early 1880s, with land values rising, the new farmers had no problem obtaining extensive and easy credit. But the arid years of the late 1880s changed the farmers' prospects. Tens of thousands of farmers could not pay their debts and were forced to abandon their farms. There was, in effect, a reverse migration: white settlers moving back east. Those who remained continued to suffer from falling prices and persistent indebtedness.

Reverse Migration

Commercial Agriculture

By the late nineteenth century the sturdy, independent farmer of popular myth was being replaced by the commercial farmer—attempting to do in the agricultural economy what industrialists were doing in the manufacturing economy. Commercial farmers specialized in cash crops that were sold in national or world markets. They did not often make their own household supplies or grow their own food but bought them from merchants. This kind of farming, when it was successful, raised farmers' living standards. But it also made them dependent on bankers and interest rates, railroads and freight rates, national and European markets, world supply and demand. And unlike the capitalists of the industrial order, they could not regulate their production or influence the prices of what they sold.

Between 1865 and 1900, farm output increased dramatically, not only in the United States but in

Brazil, Argentina, Canada, Australia, New Zealand, Russia, and elsewhere. At the same time, modern forms of communication and transportation—the telephone, the telegraph, steam navigation, railroads—were creating new markets around the world for agricultural goods. Beginning in the 1880s,

Overproduction

worldwide overproduction led to a drop in prices for most agricultural goods and hence to great economic distress for many of the more than 6 million American farm families. Commercial farming made some people fabulously wealthy. But the farm economy as a whole was suffering a significant decline relative to the rest of the nation.

The Farmers' Grievances

American farmers were painfully aware that something was wrong. But few yet understood the implications of national and world overproduction. Instead, they concentrated their attention and anger on more immediate, more comprehensible—and no less real—problems: inequitable freight rates, high interest charges, and an inadequate currency.

Grievances against Railroads

The farmers' first and most burning grievance was against the railroads. In many cases, the railroads charged higher rates for farm goods than for other goods, and higher rates in the South and West than in the Northeast. Railroads also controlled elevator and warehouse facilities in buying centers and charged arbitrary storage rates.

Farmers also resented the institutions controlling credit—banks, loan companies, insurance corporations. Since sources of credit in the West and South were few, farmers had to take loans on whatever terms they could get, often at interest rates of from 10 to 25 percent. Many farmers had to pay these loans back in years when prices were dropping and currency was becoming scarce. As a result, expansion of the currency became an increasingly important issue to farmers.

Belief in Conspiracy

A third grievance concerned prices. A farmer could plant a large crop at a moment when its price was high and find that by the time of the harvest the price had declined. Farmers' fortunes rose and fell in response to unpredictable forces. But many farmers became convinced that "middlemen"—speculators, bankers, agents—were conspiring to fix prices. Many farmers also came to believe that manufacturers in the East were colluding to keep the prices of farm goods low and the prices of industrial goods high. Although farmers sold their crops in a competitive world market, they bought manufactured goods in a domestic market protected by tariffs and dominated by trusts and corporations.

The Agrarian Malaise

These economic difficulties helped produce a series of social and cultural resentments. In part, this was a result of the isolation of farm life. Farm families in some parts of the country were virtually cut off from the outside world. During the winter months and spells of bad weather, the loneliness and boredom could become nearly unbearable. Many farmers lacked access to adequate education for their children, to proper medical facilities, to recreational or cultural activities, to virtually anything that might give them a sense of being members of a community. Older farmers felt the sting of watching their children leave the farm for the city. They felt the humiliation of being ridiculed as "hayseeds" by the new urban culture that was coming to dominate American life.

The result of this sense of isolation and obsolescence was a growing malaise among

Isolation and Obsolescence

farmers, a discontent that would help create a national political movement in the 1890s. It found reflection, too, in the literature that emerged from rural America. Writers usually romanticized the rugged life of the cowboy and the western miner. For the farmer, however, the image was usually different. Hamlin Garland, for example, reflected the growing disillusionment in a series of novels and short stories. In the past, Garland wrote in the introduction to his novel *Jason Edwards* (1891), the agrarian frontier had seemed to be "the Golden West, the land of wealth and freedom and happiness." Now, however, the bright promise had faded. "So this is the reality of the dream!" a character in *Jason Edwards* exclaims. "A shanty on a barren plain, hot and lone as a desert. My God!" Once, sturdy yeoman farmers had viewed themselves as the backbone of American life. Now they were becoming painfully aware that their position was declining in relation to the rising urban-industrial society to the east.

To many Americans in the late nineteenth century, the West seemed an untamed "frontier" in which hardy pioneers were creating a new society. The reality of the West in these years, however, was very different. White Americans were moving into the vast regions west of the Mississippi at a remarkable rate, and many of them were indeed settling in lands far from any civilization they had ever known. But the West was not an empty place. It contained a large population of Indians, with whom the white settlers sometimes lived uneasily and sometimes battled, but almost always in the end pushed aside and relocated onto lands whites did not want. There were significant numbers of Mexicans in some areas, small populations of Asians in others, and African Americans moving in from the South in search of land and freedom. The West was not a barren frontier, but a place of many cultures.

The West was also tied to the emerging capitalist-industrial economy of the East. The miners who flooded into California, Colorado, Nevada, the Dakotas, and elsewhere were responding to the demand in the East for gold and silver, but even more for iron ore, copper, lead, zinc, and quartz. Cattle and sheep ranchers produced meat, wool, and leather for eastern consumers and manufacturers. Farmers grew crops for sale in national and international commodities markets. The West certainly looked different from the East. But the growth of the West was very much a part of the growth of the rest of the nation. And the culture of the West, despite the romantic images embraced by easterners and westerners alike, was at its heart as much a culture of economic growth and capitalist ambition as was the culture of the rest of the nation.

INTERACTIVE LEARNING

On the *Primary Source Investigator CD-ROM*, check out a number of valuable tools for further exploration of the content of this chapter.

Mini-Documentary Movie

- **The Curtis Legacy** A serious look at a well-known photographer who documented native peoples for years and some of the historical problems with his work (Doc D11)

Interactive Maps

- Indian Expulsion (Map M8)
- Mining Towns (Map M14)

Primary Sources

Documents, images, and maps related to the settlement of the American West following the Civil War, and the dispersal of the native peoples in the process. Some highlights include:

- A photograph of the Carlisle Indian School

- Documents pertaining to the Workingmen's Party and their anti-Chinese rhetoric
- The text of the Dawes Act of 1887, the federal policy which broke up Indian tribal lands

 Online Learning Center (www.mhhe.com/unfinishedinteractive)

Explore this rich website, providing additional exploration of the material covered in this chapter, online versions of the interactive maps included on the Primary Source Investigator CD-ROM, as well as several study aids, including a multiple-choice quiz, essay questions, a glossary, and other valuable tools. Also in the Online Learning Center for this chapter look for this *Interactive Feature Essay:*

- **Where Historians Disagree: The Frontier and the West**

FOR FURTHER REFERENCE

Frederick Jackson Turner's *The Frontier in American History* (1920) is a classic argument on the centrality of the frontier experience to American democracy, an argument that frames much recent history of the West, which rejects the Turner thesis. Patricia Nelson Limerick's *The Legacy of Conquest: The Unbroken Past of the American West* (1987) argues that the West was not a frontier but rather an inhabited place conquered by Anglo-Americans. Richard White, *"It's Your Misfortune and None of My Own": A History of the American West* (1991), is an outstanding general history of the region that revises many myths about the West. Ronald Takaki, *Strangers from a Different Shore: A History of Asian Americans* (1989), surveys the Asian-American experience as immigrants to America's western shore. John Mack Faragher, *Women and Men on the Overland Trail* (1979) examines the social experience of westering migrants and Peggy Pascoe, *Relations of Rescue: The Search for Female Authority in the American West, 1874–1939* (1990) describes the female communities of the West. William Cronon, *Nature's Metropolis and the Great West* (1991) describes the relationships among economies and environments in the West. Jon Gjerde, *The Minds of the West: Ethnocultural Evolution in the Rural Middle West, 1830–1914* (1997) examines the impact of the ethnicity on the shaping of the agrarian West. Robert Wooster, *The Military and United States Indian Policy, 1865–1902* (1988) examines the military campaigns against the Indians in the late nineteenth century. Frederick E. Hoxie, *A Final Promise: The Campaign to Assimilate the Indians, 1880–1920* (1984) examines U.S. policies toward Native Americans in the years after the end of the Indian Wars, and Mark David Spence, *Dispossessing the Wilderness: Indian Removal and the Making of the National Parks* (1999) revises a familiar story. John Mack Faragher, *Daniel Boone* (1992) is a study of one of the West's most fabled figures, and Joy S. Kasson, *Buffalo Bill's Wild West: Celebrity, Memory, and Popular History* (2000) describes one of the regon's most accomplished mythmakers. Richard Slotkin, *The Fatal Environment: The Myth of the Frontier in the Age of Industrialization* (1985) and *Gunfighter Nation* (1992) are provocative cultural studies of the idea of the West. Henry Nash Smith, *Virgin Land* (1950) is a classic study of the West in American culture. *The West* (1996), a documentary film by Stephen Ives and Ken Burns, offers a broad history of the region, along with a companion book of the same title by Geoffrey C. Ward.

17

Industrial Supremacy

(Bettmann/CORBIS)

"Twenty-five years after the death of Lincoln, America had become, in the quantity and value of her products, the first manufacturing nation of the world. What England had accomplished in a hundred years, the United States had achieved in half the time." So wrote the historians Charles and Mary Beard in the 1920s, expressing the amazement many Americans felt when they considered the remarkable expansion of their industrial economy in the late nineteenth century.

In fact, America's rise to industrial supremacy was not as sudden as such observers suggested. The nation had been building a manufacturing economy since early in the nineteenth century. But Americans were clearly correct in observing that the accomplishments of the last three decades of the nineteenth century overshadowed all the earlier progress.

The remarkable growth did much to increase the wealth and improve the lives of many Americans. But such benefits were very unequally shared. While industrial titans and a growing middle class were enjoying a prosperity without precedent in the nation's history, workers, farmers, and others were experiencing an often painful ordeal that slowly edged the United States toward a great economic and political crisis.

SOURCES OF INDUSTRIAL GROWTH

Many factors contributed to the growth of American industry: abundant raw materials; a large and growing labor supply; a surge in technological innovation; the emergence of a talented and often ruthless group of entrepreneurs; a federal government eager to assist the growth of business; and an expanding domestic market for the products of manufacturing.

Industrial Technologies

The rapid emergence of new technologies was one of the principal sources of late-nineteenth-century industrial growth. Some of the most important innovations were in communications. In 1866, Cyrus W. Field laid a transatlantic telegraph cable to Europe. During the next **Alexander Graham Bell** decade, Alexander Graham Bell developed the first telephone with commercial capacity. In the 1890s, the Italian inventor Guglielmo Marconi was taking the first steps toward the development of radio; the technology he developed quickly found its way to the United States. Other inventions that speeded the pace of business organization were the typewriter (by Christopher L. Sholes in 1868), the

cash register (by James Ritty in 1879), and the calculating or adding machine (by William S. Burroughs in 1891).

Among the most revolutionary innovations was the introduction in the 1870s of electricity as a source of light and power. Among the pioneers of electric lighting were Charles F. Brush, who devised the arc **Impact of Electric Power** lamp for street illumination, and Thomas A. Edison, who invented the incandescent lamp (or lightbulb). Edison and others designed improved generators and built large power plants to furnish electricity to whole cities. By the turn of the century, electric power was becoming commonplace in street railway systems, in factories, and increasingly in offices and homes.

Particularly important to trade and industry was the development of new, high-efficiency steam engines capable of powering larger ships at faster speeds than ever imagined in the past. The new high-speed freighters, for example, made it cheaper for Britain to buy wheat grown in Canada and the United States than to grow it at home. The introduction of refrigerated ships in the 1870s made it possible to transport meat from North America and even Australia and Asia to Europe.

1859	1866	1870	1873	1876	1877	1879	1881
First oil well drilled	National Labor Union founded First transatlantic cable	Rockefeller founds Standard Oil	Carnegie Steel founded Economic panic	Bell invents telephone	Nationwide railroad strike	Edison invents electric light bulb	American Federation of Labor founded

1886	1888	1892	1893	1894	1901	1903	1914
Haymarket bombing	Bellamy's *Looking Backward*	Homestead steel strike	Depression begins	Pullman strike	Morgan creates U. S. Steel	Wright brothers' airplane flight	Ford introduces factory assembly lines

TIME LINE

The Technology of Iron and Steel Production

Perhaps the most important technological development in a nation whose economy rested so heavily on railroads and urban construction was the revolutionizing of iron and steel production. Iron production had developed slowly in the United States through most of the nineteenth century; steel production had developed hardly at all by the end of the Civil War. In the 1870s and 1880s, however, iron production soared as railroads added 40,000 new miles of track, and steel production made great strides toward what would soon be its dominance in the metals industry.

The rise of steel was itself the product of technological discovery. An Englishman, Henry Bessemer, and an American, William Kelly, had developed, almost simultaneously, a process for converting iron into the much more durable and versatile steel.

Bessemer Process (The process, which took Bessemer's name, consisted of blowing air through molten iron to burn out the impurities and create a much stronger metal.) The Bessemer process also relied on the discovery by the British metallurgist Robert Mushet that ingredients could be added to the iron during conversion to

transform it into steel, to give it additional strength. In 1868, the New Jersey ironmaster Abram S. Hewitt introduced from Europe another method of making steel—the open-hearth process. These techniques made possible the production of steel in great quantities and large dimensions.

The steel industry emerged first in western Pennsylvania and eastern Ohio. That was partly because iron ore could be found there in abundance. It was also because the new forms of steel production created a demand for new kinds of fuel—and particularly for the anthracite (or hard) coal that was plentiful in Pennsylvania. Later, new techniques made it possible to use soft bituminous coal, also easily mined in western Pennsylvania. As a result, Pittsburgh quickly became the center of the steel world. But the industry was growing so fast that new sources of ore were soon necessary. The upper peninsula of Michigan, the Mesabi Range in Minnesota, and the area around Birmingham, Alabama, became important ore-producing centers, and new centers of steel production grew up near them.

Until the Civil War, iron and steel furnaces were mostly made of stone and usually built against the side of a **New Blast Furnaces** hill. In the 1870s and after, however, furnaces were redesigned as cylindrical iron shells lined with brick. These furnaces were 75 feet tall and higher and could produce over 500 tons a week.

As the steel industry spread, new transportation systems emerged to serve it. The steel production in the Great Lakes region was possible only because of the availability of steam freighters that could carry ore on the lakes. The demand for vessels capable of transporting oil and the development of the new and more powerful steam engine encouraged, in turn, the design of larger and heavier freighters. Shippers used new steam engines to speed the unloading of ore, a task that previously had been performed, slowly and laboriously, by men and horses.

| New Transportation Systems |

There was even a closer relationship between the emerging steel companies and the railroads. Steel manufacturers provided rails and parts for cars to the railroads; railroads were both markets for and transporters of manufactured steel. But the relationship soon became more intimate than that. The Pennsylvania Railroad, for example, literally created the Pennsylvania Steel Company.

The steel industry's need for lubrication for its machines helped create another important new industry in the late nineteenth century—oil. The existence of petroleum reserves in western Pennsylvania had been common knowledge for some time. Not until the 1850s, however, after Pennsylvania businessman George Bissell showed that the substance could be burned in lamps and that it could also yield such products as paraffin, naphtha, and lubricating oil, was there any sense of its commercial value. Bissell raised money to begin drilling; and in 1859, Edwin L. Drake, one of Bissell's employees, established the first oil well near Titusville, Pennsylvania. Demand for petroleum grew quickly, and promoters soon developed other fields in Pennsylvania, Ohio, and West Virginia.

| Rise of the Petroleum Industry |

The Airplane and the Automobile

Among the technological innovations that were to have the farthest-reaching impact on the United States was the automobile. Two technologies were critical to its development. One was the creation of gasoline, which was the result of an extraction process developed in the late nineteenth century by which lubricating oil and fuel oil were removed separately from crude oil. As early as the 1870s, designers in France, Germany, and Austria had begun to develop an "internal combustion engine," which used the expanding power of burning gas to drive pistons. A German, Nicolaus August Otto, created a gas-powered "four-stroke" engine in the mid-1860s, but he did not develop a way to untether it from gas lines. One of Otto's former employees, Gottfried Daimler, later perfected an engine that could be used in automobiles.

The American automobile industry developed rapidly in the aftermath of these breakthroughs. Charles and Frank Duryea built the first gasoline-driven motor vehicle in America in 1903. Three years later, Henry Ford produced the first of the famous cars that would bear his name. In 1895, there were only four automobiles on the American highways. By 1917, there were nearly 5 million.

| Henry Ford |

The search for a means of human flight was as old as civilization, and had been almost entirely futile until the late nineteenth century when engineers, scientists, and tinkerers began to experiment with aeronautic devices. Balloonists began to consider ways to make dirigibles useful vehicles of transportation. Others experimented with kites and gliders. Two brothers in Ohio, Wilbur and Orville Wright, owned a bicycle shop in which they began to construct a glider that could be propelled through the air by an internal-combustion engine. Four years after they began their experiments, Orville made a celebrated test flight near Kitty Hawk, North Carolina, in which an airplane took off by itself and traveled 120 feet in 12 seconds. By the fall of 1904, they had improved the plane to the point where they were able to fly over 23 miles.

| The Wright Brothers |

Although the first working airplane was built in the United States, aviation technology was slow to gain a foothold in America. Most of the early progress in airplane design occurred in France, where there was substantial government funding for research and development. The U.S. government created the National Advisory Committee on Aeronautics in 1915, twelve years after the Wright brothers' flight, and American airplanes became a significant presence in Europe during World War I.

But the prospects for commercial flight seemed dim until the 1920s, when Charles Lindbergh's famous solo flight from New York to Paris electrified the nation and the world.

Research and Development

The rapid development of new industrial technologies persuaded many business leaders to sponsor their own research. General Electric created one of the first corporate laboratories in 1900. The emergence of corporate research and development laboratories coincided with a decline in government support for research. That helped corporations to attract skilled researchers. It also decentralized the sources of research funding and ensured that inquiry would move in many different directions, and not just along paths determined by the government.

Corporate Research and Development

A rift began to emerge between scientists and engineers. Engineers became increasingly tied up with the research and development agendas of corporations. Many scientists continued to scorn this "commercialization" of knowledge and preferred to stick to basic research. Even so, American scientists were more closely connected to practical challenges than were their European counterparts, and some joined engineers in corporate research and development laboratories, which over time began to sponsor not just practical but also basic research.

The Science of Production

Central to the growth of the automobile and other industries were changes in the techniques of production. By the turn of the century, many industrialists were embracing the new principles of "scientific management," often known as "Taylorism" after its leading theoretician, Frederick Winslow Taylor. Taylor urged employers to reorganize the production process by subdividing tasks. This would speed up production; it would also make workers more interchangeable and thus diminish a manager's dependence on any particular employee. If properly managed by trained experts, he claimed, workers using modern machines could perform simple tasks at much greater speed, greatly increasing productive efficiency.

"Taylorism"

The most important change in production technology in the industrial era was the emergence of

THE ASSEMBLY LINE Workers in the Ford Motor Company's plant in Highland Park, Michigan, guide auto bodies down a ramp onto chassis that have moved into position from below. This was the final stage of the assembly line, which Henry Ford pioneered and which by 1914 (when this photograph was taken) had become common in other industries as well. *(Henry Ford Museum and Greenfield Village)*

mass production and, along with it, the moving assembly line, which Henry Ford introduced in his auto-

Assembly Line

mobile plants in 1914. The assembly line was both a particular place—a factory through which automobiles moved as they were being assembled by workers who specialized on particular tasks—and a concept. The concept stressed the complete interchangeability of parts. General Motors adopted the same philosophy, and even proceeded to demonstrate it at a motor works in England in 1906—when three Cadillacs were dismantled, their engines disassembled, the pieces mixed up with one another, and then completely reassembled by several mechanics, who then turned on the engines and drove them onto a track. Automobile production relied on other technologies, too, in particular the intensive use of electricity. The revolutionary assembly-line technique enabled Ford to raise the wages and reduce the hours of his workers while cutting the base price of his Model T from $950 in 1914 to $290 in 1929. It became a standard for many other industries.

Railroad Expansion and the Corporation

But the principal agent of industrial development in the late nineteenth century was the expansion of the railroads. Railroads gave industrialists access to distant markets and sources of raw materials. They were the nation's largest businesses and created new forms of corporate organization. And they were America's biggest investors, stimulating economic growth through their own expenditures on construction and equipment.

Total railroad trackage increased from 30,000 miles in 1860 to 193,000 in

Importance of Government Subsidies

1900. Subsidies from federal, state, and local governments were vital to this expansion. Equally important was the emergence of great railroad combinations, many of them dominated by one or two individuals. The achievements (and excesses) of these tycoons—Cornelius Vanderbilt, James J. Hill, Collis R. Huntington, and others—became symbols of concentrated economic power. But railroad development was less significant for the individual barons it created than for its contribution to the growth of a new institution: the modern corporation.

There had been various forms of corporations in America since colonial times, but the modern corporation emerged as a major force only after the Civil War. By then, railroad magnates and other industrialists realized that their great ventures could not be financed by any single person.

Under the laws of incorporation passed in many states in the 1830s and 1840s, business organizations could raise money by selling stock to members of the public; after the Civil War, one industry after another began doing so. What made the stocks more appealing than they had been in the past was that investors now had only "limited liability"—that is,

"Limited Liability"

they risked only the amount of their investments; they were not liable for any debts the corporation might accumulate beyond that point. The ability to sell stock to a broad public made it possible for entrepreneurs to gather vast sums of capital and undertake great projects.

The Pennsylvania and other railroads were among the first to adopt the new corporate form of organization. But incorporation quickly spread beyond the railroad industry. In steel, the central figure was Andrew Carnegie, a Scottish immigrant who had worked his way up from modest beginnings and in 1873 opened his own steelworks in Pittsburgh. Soon he dominated the industry. With his associate Henry Clay Frick, he bought up coal mines, operated a fleet of ore ships, and acquired railroads. He financed his vast undertakings not only out of his own profits but out of the sale of stock. Then, in 1901, he sold out for $450 million to the banker J. Pierpont Morgan, who merged the Carnegie interests with others to create the giant United States Steel Corporation—a $14 billion enterprise that controlled almost two-thirds of the nation's steel production.

There were similar developments in other industries. Gustavus Swift developed a small meatpacking company into a national corporation. Isaac Singer patented a sewing machine in 1851 and created I. M. Singer and Company—one of the first modern manufacturing corporations.

Large, national business enterprises needed more systematic administrative structures. As a result, corporate leaders introduced a set of managerial techniques that relied on systematic division of responsibilities, a carefully designed hierarchy of

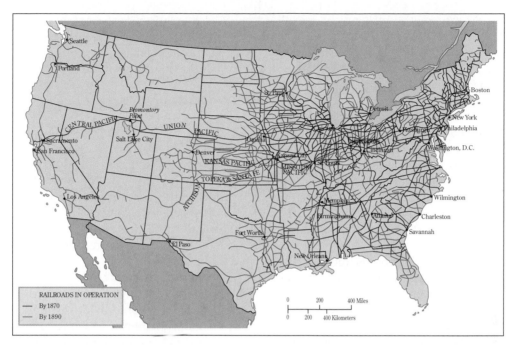

RAILROADS, 1870–1890 This map illustrates the rapid expansion of railroads in the late nineteenth century. In 1870, there was already a dense network of rail lines in the Northeast and Middle West, illustrated here by the red lines. The green lines show the further expansion of rail coverage between 1870 and 1890, much of it in the South and the areas west of the Mississippi River. ▌ *Why were railroads so essential to the nation's economic growth in these years?*

OLC **For an interactive version of this map go to www.mhhe.com/unfinishedinteractive**

control, careful cost-accounting procedures, and perhaps above all a new breed of business executive: the "middle manager," who formed a layer of command between workers and owners. Efficient administrative capabilities helped make possible another major feature of the modern corporation: consolidation.

Businessmen created large, consolidated organizations primarily through two methods. One was "horizontal integration"—the combining of a number of firms engaged in the same enterprise into a single corporation. The consolidation of many different railroad lines into one company was an example. Another method, which became popular in the 1890s, was "vertical integration"—the taking over of all the different businesses on which a company relied for its primary function. Carnegie Steel, which came to control not only steel mills but mines, railroads, and other enterprises, was an example of vertical integration.

 "Horizontal Integration" and "Vertical Integration"

The most celebrated corporate empire of the late nineteenth century was John D. Rockefeller's Standard Oil. Shortly after the Civil War, Rockefeller launched a refining company in Cleveland and immediately began trying to eliminate his competition. Allying himself with other wealthy capitalists, he proceeded methodically to buy out competing refineries. In 1870, he formed the Standard Oil Company of Ohio, which in a few years had acquired twenty of the twenty-five refineries in Cleveland, as well as plants in Pittsburgh, Philadelphia, New York, and Baltimore.

So far, Rockefeller had expanded only horizontally. But soon he began expanding vertically as well. He built his own barrel factories, terminal warehouses, and pipelines. Standard Oil owned its own freight cars and **Standard Oil** developed its own marketing organization. By the 1880s, Rockefeller had established such dominance within the petroleum industry that to much of the nation he served as a leading symbol of monopoly.

Rockefeller and other industrialists saw consolidation as a way to cope with what they believed was the greatest curse of the modern economy: "cutthroat competition." Most businessmen claimed to believe in free enterprise and a competitive marketplace, but in fact they feared that substantial competition could spell instability and ruin for all.

As the movement toward combination accelerated, new vehicles emerged to facilitate it. The railroads began with so-called pool arrangements—informal agreements among various companies to stabilize rates and divide markets. But if even a few firms in an industry were unwilling to cooperate (as was almost always the case), the pool arrangements collapsed.

The failure of the pools led to new techniques of consolidation. At first, the most successful such technique was the creation of the "trust"—pioneered by Standard Oil in the early 1880s and perfected by the banker J. P. Morgan. Under a trust agreement, stockholders in individual corporations transferred their stocks to a small group of trustees in exchange for shares in the trust itself. Owners of trust certificates often had no direct control over the decisions of the trustees; they simply received a share of the profits. The trustees themselves, on the other hand, might own only a few companies but could exercise effective control over many.

In 1889, New Jersey changed its laws of incorporation to permit companies to buy up other companies. Other states soon followed. That made the trust unnecessary and permitted actual corporate mergers. Rockefeller, for example, quickly relocated Standard Oil to New Jersey and created there what became known as a "holding **"Holding Company"** company"—a central corporate body that would buy up the stock of various members of the Standard Oil trust and establish direct, formal ownership of the corporations in the trust.

By the end of the nineteenth century, 1 percent of the corporations in America were able to control more than 33 percent of the manufacturing. A system of economic organization was emerging that lodged enormous power in the hands of very few men—the great bankers of New York such as J. P. Morgan, industrial titans such as Rockefeller, and others.

The industrial giants of the era were clearly responsible for substantial economic growth. They were also creating the basis for one of the greatest public controversies of their era: a raging debate over concentrated economic and political power that continued well into the twentieth century.

CAPITALISM AND ITS CRITICS

The rise of big business was not without its critics. Farmers and workers saw a threat to their ability to control their own destinies. Middle-class critics pointed to the corruption that the new industrial titans seemed to produce. The growing criticisms challenged the captains of industry to create a defense of the new corporate economy.

Survival of the Fittest

The new rationale for capitalism rested squarely on an older ideology of individualism. The new industrial economy, its defenders argued, was not shrinking opportunities for individual advancement. It was providing every individual with a chance to succeed and attain great wealth.

There was an element of truth in such claims, but only a small element. Before the Civil War there had been few millionaires in America; by 1892 there were more than 4,000. Some of them—Carnegie, Rockefeller, and a few others—were in fact "self-made men." But most of the new business tycoons had begun their careers from positions of privilege and wealth. Nor was their rise to power and prominence always a result simply of hard work and ingenuity, as they liked to claim. It was also a result of ruthlessness and, at times, rampant corruption.

Nevertheless, most tycoons continued to claim that they had attained their wealth and power through hard work and thrift. Those who succeeded, they argued, deserved their success, and those who failed had earned their failure through their own laziness, stupidity, or carelessness. Such assumptions became the basis of a popular social theory of the late nineteenth century: Social Darwinism, **Social Darwinism** the application of Charles Darwin's laws of evolution and natural selection among species to human society. Just as only the fittest survived in the process of evolution, so in human society only the fittest individuals survived in the marketplace.

The English philosopher Herbert Spencer was the first and most important proponent of this theory. Society, he argued, benefited from the elimination of the unfit and the survival of the strong and talented. Spencer's teachings found prominent supporters among American intellectuals, most notably William Graham Sumner of Yale, who promoted similar ideas in lectures, articles, and a famous 1906 book, *Folkways*.

Social Darwinism appealed to corporate leaders because it seemed to legitimize their success. It did not, however, have very much to do with the realities of the corporate economy.

Corporate Wealth Legitimated

At the same time that businessmen were celebrating the virtues of competition and the free market, they were making active efforts to protect themselves from competition and to replace the natural workings of the marketplace with control by great combinations. Vicious competitive battle was in fact the very thing that American businessmen most feared.

The Gospel of Wealth

Some businessmen attempted to temper the harsh philosophy of Social Darwinism with a gentler idea: the "gospel of wealth." People of great wealth, they argued, had not only great power but great responsibilities. It was their duty to use their riches to advance social progress. Andrew Carnegie elaborated on the creed in his 1901 book,

Gospel of Wealth

The Gospel of Wealth, in which he wrote that people of wealth should consider all revenues in excess of their own needs "trust funds" to be used for the good of the community. Carnegie was only one of many industrialists who devoted large parts of their fortunes to philanthropy.

The notion of private wealth as a public blessing existed alongside another popular concept: the notion of great wealth as something available to all. Russell H. Conwell, a Baptist minister, became the most prominent spokesman for the idea by delivering one lecture, "Acres of Diamonds," more than 6,000 times between 1880 and 1900. Conwell told a series of stories, which he claimed were true, of individuals who had found opportunities for extraordinary wealth in their own backyards. (One such story involved a modest farmer who discovered a vast diamond mine in his own fields in the course of working his land.) Most of the millionaires in the country, Conwell claimed (inaccurately), had begun on the lowest rung of the economic ladder and had worked their way to success.

Horatio Alger was the most famous promoter of the success story.

Horatio Alger

Alger was originally a minister in a small town in Massachusetts but was driven from his pulpit as a result of a scandal connected to his active, but usually hidden, homosexuality. He moved to New York, where he wrote his celebrated novels: *Ragged Dick*, *Tom the Bootblack*, *Sink or Swim*, and many others, more than 100 in all. The basic story was almost always the same: A young boy, perhaps an orphan, makes his perilous way through life on the rough streets of the city by selling newspapers or peddling matches. One day, his energy and determination catches the eye of a wealthy man, who gives him a chance to improve himself. Through honesty, charm, hard work, and aggressiveness, the boy rises in the world to become a successful man.

The purpose of writing, Alger claimed, was twofold. He wanted to "exert a salutary influence upon the class of whom [I] was writing, by setting before them inspiring examples of what energy, ambition, and an honest purpose may achieve." He also wanted to show his largely middle-class readers "the life and experiences of the friendless and vagrant children to be found in all our cities."

But Alger's intentions probably had little to do with the success of his books. Most Americans of the late nineteenth and early twentieth centuries were attracted to Alger because his stories helped them to believe that it is possible for individuals to rise in the world with willpower and hard work. Alger's admirers came to ignore his own misgivings about industrialism and to portray his books purely as a celebration of (and justification for) laissez-faire capitalism and the accumulation of wealth.

Alternative Visions

Alongside the celebrations of competition and the justifications for great wealth stood a group of alternative philosophies, challenging the corporate ethos and at times capitalism itself.

One such philosophy emerged in the work of the sociologist Lester Frank Ward. In *Dynamic Sociology* (1883) and other books, he argued that civilization was not governed by natural selection but by human intelligence. In contrast to Sumner, who believed that state intervention to remodel the environment was futile, Ward thought that an active government engaged in positive planning was society's best hope.

Other Americans adopted more radical approaches to reform. Some dissenters found a home in the Socialist Labor Party,

Socialist Labor Party

founded in the 1870s and led for many years by Daniel De Leon, an immigrant from the West Indies. Although De Leon attracted a modest following in the industrial cities, the party never became a major political force. A dissident faction of De Leon's party, eager to forge stronger ties with organized labor, broke away and in 1901 formed the more enduring American Socialist Party.

Other radicals gained a wider following. Among them was the California writer and activist Henry George.

Henry George's "Single Tax"

His *Progress and Poverty*, published in 1879, became one of the best-selling non-fiction works in American publishing history. George blamed social problems on the ability of a few monopolists to grow wealthy as a result of rising land values. An increase in the value of land, he claimed, was not a result of any effort by the owner. It was an "unearned increment," produced by the growth of society around the land. Such profits were rightfully the property of the community. He proposed a "single tax" on land, to replace all other taxes, which would return the increment to the people. The tax, he argued, would destroy monopolies, distribute wealth more equally, and eliminate poverty.

Rivaling George in popularity was Edward Bellamy, whose utopian novel *Looking Backward*, published in 1888, sold more than 1 million copies. It described the experiences of a young Bostonian who went into a hypnotic sleep in 1887 and awoke in the year 2000 to find a new social order in which want, politics, and vice were unknown. The new society had emerged through a peaceful, evolutionary process: the large trusts of the late nineteenth century had continued to grow in size and to combine with one another until ultimately they formed a single, great trust, controlled by the government, which distributed the abundance of the industrial economy equally among all the people. "Fraternal cooperation" had replaced competition. Class divisions had

"MODERN COLOSSUS OF (RAIL) ROADS" Cornelius Vanderbilt, known as the "Commodore," accumulated one of America's great fortunes by consolidating several large railroad companies under his control in the 1860s. His name became a synonym not only for enormous wealth, but also (in the eyes of many Americans) for excessive corporate power—as suggested in this cartoon, showing him standing astride his empire and manipulating its parts. *(Culver Pictures, Inc.)*

disappeared. Bellamy labeled the philosophy behind this vision "nationalism."

The Problems of Monopoly

Relatively few Americans questioned capitalism itself. But by the end of the century, a wide range of groups had begun to assail monopoly and economic concentration. They blamed monopoly for creating artificially

Economic Concentration Challenged

high prices. In the absence of competition, they argued, monopolistic industries could charge whatever prices they wished; railroads, in particular, charged very high rates along some routes because their customers had no choice but to pay them. Artificially high prices, moreover, contributed to the economy's instability. Beginning in 1873, the economy fluctuated erratically, producing severe recessions every five or six years, each worse than the last.

THE ORDEAL OF THE WORKER

Most workers in the late nineteenth century experienced a real rise in their standard of living. But they did so at the cost of arduous and often dangerous working conditions, diminishing control over their own work, and a growing sense of powerlessness.

The Immigrant Work Force

The industrial work force expanded dramatically in the late nineteenth century. The source of that expansion was a massive migration into industrial cities—immigration of two sorts. The first was the continuing flow of rural Americans into factory towns and cities. The second was the great wave of immigration from abroad (primarily from Europe, but also from Asia, Canada, Mexico, and other areas) in the decades following the Civil War. The 25 million immigrants who arrived in the United States between 1865 and 1915 were more than four times the number who had arrived in the previous fifty years.

Rapidly Expanding Working Class

In the 1870s and 1880s, most of the immigrants came from England, Ireland, and northern Europe. By the end of the century, however, the major sources of immigrants had shifted, with large numbers of southern and eastern Europeans (Italians, Poles, Russians, Greeks, Slavs, and others) moving into the country and into the industrial work force.

The new immigrants were coming to America in part to escape poverty and oppression in their homelands. But they were also lured by expectations of new opportunities. Railroads tried to lure immigrants into their western landholdings by distributing misleading advertisements overseas. Industrial employers actively recruited immigrant workers under the Labor Contract Law, which—until its repeal in 1885—permitted them to pay for the passage of

Labor Contract Law

workers in advance and deduct the amount later from their wages. Even after the repeal of the law, employers continued to encourage the immigration of unskilled laborers.

The arrival of these new groups introduced heightened ethnic tensions into the dynamics of the working class. Low-paid Poles, Greeks, and French Canadians began to displace higher-paid British and Irish workers in the textile factories of New England. Italians, Slavs, and Poles emerged as a major source of labor for the mining industry. Chinese and Mexicans competed with Anglo-Americans and African Americans in mining, farmwork, and factory labor in California, Colorado, and Texas.

Growing Ethnic Tensions

Wages and Working Conditions

At the turn of the century, the average income of the American worker was $400 to $500 a year—below the $600 figure that many believed was the minimum required to maintain a reasonable level of comfort. Nor did workers have much job security. All were vulnerable to the boom-and-bust cycle of the industrial economy, and some lost their jobs because of technological advances. Even those who kept their jobs could find their wages suddenly and substantially cut in hard times.

American laborers faced a wide array of other hardships as well. For first-generation workers accustomed to the patterns of agrarian life, there was a difficult adjustment to the nature of modern industrial labor: the performance of routine, repetitive tasks on a strict and monotonous schedule. To skilled artisans whose once-valued tasks were now performed by machines, the new system was impersonal and demeaning. Most factory laborers worked ten-hour days, six days a week. Industrial accidents were frequent.

Harsh Work Conditions

The decreasing need for skilled work in factories induced many employers to increase the use of women and children, whom they could hire for lower wages than adult males. By 1900, 20 percent of all manufacturing workers were women. Most women worked in a few industries where unskilled and semi-skilled machine labor (as opposed to heavy manual labor) prevailed. The textile industry remained the largest single industrial employer of women. (Domestic service remained the most common female

SPINDLE BOYS Young boys, some of them barefoot, clamber along the great textile machines in a Georgia cotton mill adjusting spindles. Many of them were the children of women who worked in the plants. The photograph is by Lewis Hine. *(Bettmann/Corbis)*

occupation overall.) Women worked for wages well below the minimum necessary for survival.

At least 1.7 million children under sixteen years of age were employed in facto-ries and fields; 10 percent of all girls aged ten to fifteen, and 20 percent of all boys, held jobs. Under public pressure, thirty-eight states passed child labor laws in the late nineteenth century. But 60 percent of child workers were em-ployed in agriculture, which was typically exempt from the laws. And even for children employed in factories, the laws merely set a minimum age of twelve years and a maximum workday of ten hours.

Child Labor

Emerging Unionization

Laborers attempted to fight back against such con-ditions by creating national unions. But at first their efforts met with little success.

There had been craft unions in America since well before the Civil War. Alone, however, individ-ual unions could not hope to exert significant power. And during the turbulent recession years of the 1870s, unions faced widespread public hostil-ity. When labor disputes turned bitter and violent, as they occasionally did, much of the public in-stinctively blamed the workers for the trouble, rarely the employers. Particularly alarming to middle-class Americans was the emergence of the

"Molly Maguires" in the an-thracite coal region of west-ern Pennsylvania. This militant labor organization sometimes used violence and even murder in its battle with coal operators. Much of the violence, however, was deliberately instigated by informers and agents employed by the mine owners, who wanted a pretext for ruthless measures to suppress unionization.

"Molly Maguires"

Excitement over the Molly Maguires paled beside the near hysteria that gripped the country during the railroad strike of 1877, which began when the eastern rail-roads announced a 10 percent wage cut. The strike soon expanded into something approaching a class war. Strikers disrupted rail service from Baltimore to St. Louis, destroyed equipment, and rioted in the streets of Pittsburgh and other cities. State militias were called out, and in July President Hayes ordered federal troops to suppress the disorders in West Virginia. In Baltimore, eleven demonstrators died and forty were wounded in a conflict between work-ers and militiamen. In Philadelphia, the state militia killed twenty people when the troops opened fire on thousands of workers and their families who were attempting to block the railroad crossings. In all, over 100 people died before the strike finally col-lapsed several weeks after it had begun.

Railroad Strike of 1877

The Knights of Labor

The first major effort to create a genuinely national labor organization was the founding in 1869 of the Noble Order of the Knights of Labor, under the leadership of Uriah S. Stephens. Membership was open to all who "toiled," a definition that included all workers, most business and professional people, and virtually all women. The only excluded groups were lawyers, bankers, liquor dealers, and professional gamblers. The Knights of Labor championed an eight-hour workday and the abolition of child labor, but they were more interested in long-range reform of the economy. The Knights hoped to replace the "wage system" with a new "cooperative system," in which workers would themselves control a large part of the economy.

For several years, the Knights remained a secret fraternal organization. But in the late 1870s, under the leadership of Terence V. Powderly, the order moved **Terence V. Powderly** into the open and entered a period of spectacular expansion. By 1886, it claimed a total membership of over 700,000. Local unions or assemblies associated with the Knights launched a series of railroad and other strikes in the 1880s in defiance of Powderly's wishes. Their failure helped discredit the organization. By 1890, the membership of the Knights had shrunk to 100,000. A few years later, the organization disappeared altogether.

The AFL

Even before the Knights began to decline, a rival association appeared. In 1881, representatives of a number of craft unions formed the Federation of Organized Trade and Labor Unions of the United States and Canada. Five years later, this body took the name it has borne ever since, the American Federation of Labor (AFL).

Rejecting the Knights' idea of one big union for everybody, the Federation was an association of craft unions. Samuel Gompers, the **Samuel Gompers** powerful leader of the AFL, concentrated on labor's immediate objectives: wages, hours, and working conditions. As one of its first objectives, the AFL demanded a national eight-hour workday and called for a general strike if the goal was not achieved by May 1, 1886. On that day, strikes and demonstrations for a shorter workday took place all over the country.

In Chicago, a strike was already in progress at the McCormick Harvester Company. City police had been harassing the strikers, and labor and radical leaders called a protest meeting at Haymarket Square on **Haymarket Bombing** May 1. When the police ordered the crowd to disperse, someone threw a bomb that killed seven policemen and injured sixty-seven others. The police, who had killed four strikers the day before, fired into the crowd and killed four more people. Conservative, property-conscious Americans demanded retribution. Chicago officials finally rounded up eight anarchists and charged them with murder, on the grounds that their statements had incited whoever had hurled the bomb. All eight scapegoats were found guilty after a remarkably injudicious trial. Seven were sentenced to death. One of them committed suicide, four were executed, and two had their sentences commuted to life imprisonment.

To most middle-class Americans, the Haymarket bombing was an alarming symbol of social chaos and radicalism. "Anarchism" now became in the public mind a code word for terrorism and violence, even though most anarchists were relatively peaceful. For the next thirty years, the specter of anarchism remained one of the most frightening concepts in the American imagination. It was a constant obstacle to the goals of the **Labor Discredited** AFL and other labor organizations, and it did particular damage to the Knights of Labor. However much they tried to distance themselves from radicals, labor leaders were always vulnerable to accusations of anarchism.

The Homestead Strike

The Amalgamated Association of Iron and Steel Workers was the most powerful trade union in the country. Its members were skilled workers, in great demand by employers, and thus had long been able to exercise significant power in the workplace. In the mid-1880s, however, demand for skilled workers was in decline. In the Carnegie system, which was coming to dominate the steel industry, the union was able to maintain a foothold in only one of the corporation's three major factories—the Homestead plant near Pittsburgh.

By 1890, Carnegie and his chief lieutenant, Henry Clay Frick, had decided that the Amalgamated **Henry Clay Frick** "had to go." Over the next two years, they repeatedly cut wages at Homestead. At first, the union acquiesced, aware that it was not strong enough to wage a successful strike. But in 1892, when the company stopped even discussing its decisions with the union and gave it two days to accept another wage cut, the Amalgamated called for a strike.

Frick abruptly shut down the plant and called in 300 guards from the Pinkerton Detective Agency to enable the company to hire nonunion workers. The Pinkertons approached the plant by river, on barges, on July 6, 1892. The strikers poured gasoline on the water, set it on fire, and then met the Pinkertons at the docks with guns and dynamite. A pitched battle broke out. After several hours of fighting, which killed three guards and ten strikers and injured many others, the Pinkertons surrendered.

But the workers' victory was temporary. The governor of Pennsylvania sent the state's entire National Guard contingent, some 8,000 men, to Homestead. Production resumed, with strikebreakers now protected by troops. And public opinion turned against the strikers when a radical made an attempt to assassinate Frick. Slowly, workers drifted

Government Intervention

back to their jobs, and finally—four months after the strike began—the Amalgamated surrendered. By 1900, every major steel plant in the Northeast had broken with the Amalgamated. Its membership shrank from a high of 24,000 in 1891 to fewer than 7,000 a decade later.

The Pullman Strike

A dispute of greater magnitude, if less violence, was the Pullman strike in 1894. The Pullman Palace Car Company manufactured railroad sleeping and parlor cars, which it built and repaired at a plant near Chicago. There the company constructed a 600-acre town, Pullman, and rented its trim, orderly houses to the employees. George M. Pullman, owner of the company, saw the town as a model—a solution to the problems of industrial workers. But many residents chafed at the regimentation (and the high rents). In the winter of 1893–1894, the Pullman Company slashed wages by about 25 percent, citing its own declining revenues in the depression, without reducing the rent it charged its employees. Workers went on strike and persuaded the militant American Railway Union, led by Eugene V. Debs, to support them by refusing to handle Pullman cars and equipment.

BREAKING THE PULLMAN STRIKE Company C of the 15th United States Infantry, called into service by President Grover Cleveland to break a widespread railroad strike in 1894, poses here before a special patrol train near Rock Island, Illinois. The strike began when workers at the Pullman Palace Car Company outside Chicago walked off the job to protest wage cuts and rent increases. Their walkout generated broad support from other railroad workers and even from the governor of Illinois, John Peter Altgeld, who refused to call out the state militia to keep the trains running. Cleveland, however, had little sympathy for striking workers and he used his authority as president to protect the delivery of the mails to call out federal troops to break the strike. *(Bettmann/Corbis)*

American Railway Union Within a few days thousands of railroad workers were on strike, and transportation from Chicago to the Pacific coast was paralyzed.

Unlike most elected politicians, the governor of Illinois, John Peter Altgeld, was a man with demonstrated sympathies for workers. He refused to call out the militia to protect employers. Bypassing Altgeld, railroad operators asked the federal government to send regular army troops to Illinois, using the pretext that the strike was preventing the movement of mail on the trains. In July 1894, President Grover Cleveland ordered 2,000 troops to the Chicago area. A federal court issued an injunction forbidding the union to continue the strike. When Debs and his associates defied it, they were arrested and imprisoned, and the strike quickly collapsed.

Sources of Labor Weakness

The last decades of the nineteenth century were years in which labor, despite militant organizing efforts, made few real gains. Industrial **Few Gains for Labor** wages rose hardly at all. Labor leaders won a few legislative victories—the abolition of the Contract Labor Law, the establishment of an eight-hour day for government employees, compensation for some workers injured on the job, and others. But many such laws were not enforced. There were widespread strikes and protests, but few real gains. The end of the century found most workers with less political power and less control of the workplace than they had had forty years before.

Workers failed to make greater gains for many reasons. The principal labor organizations represented only a small percentage of the industrial work force; the AFL, the most important, excluded unskilled workers, and along with them most women, blacks, and recent immigrants. Divisions within the work force contributed further to union weakness. Tensions among different ethnic and racial groups kept laborers divided.

Another source of labor weakness was the shifting nature of the work force. Many **The Nature of the Workforce** immigrant workers came to America intending to earn some money and then return home. Other workers were in constant motion, moving from one job to another, one town to another, seldom in a single place long enough to establish any institutional ties or exert any real power. Above all, workers faced corporate organizations of vast wealth and power, which were generally determined to crush any efforts by workers to challenge their prerogatives. And as the Homestead and Pullman strikes suggest, the corporations usually had the support of local, state, and federal authorities, who were willing to send in troops to crush labor uprisings.

Despite the creation of new labor unions, despite a wave of strikes and protests, workers in the late nineteenth century failed on the whole to create successful organizations or to protect their interests. In the battle for power within the emerging industrial economy, almost all the advantages seemed to lie with capital. **Capital's Strength**

In the four decades following the end of the Civil War, the United States propelled itself into the forefront of the industrializing nations of the world. Large areas of the nation remained overwhelmingly rural, to be sure. But even so, America's economy, and along with it the nation's society and culture, was being profoundly transformed.

New technologies, new forms of corporate management, and new supplies of labor helped make possible the rapid growth of the nation's industries and the construction of its railroads. The factory system contributed to the growth of the nation's cities. Immigration provided a steady supply of new workers for the growing industrial economy. The result was a steady increase in national wealth, rising living standards for much of the population, and the creation of great new fortunes.

But industrialization did not spread its fruits evenly. Large areas of the country, most notably the South, and large groups in the population, most notably minorities, women, and recent immigrants, profited relatively little from economic growth. Industrial workers experienced arduous conditions of labor. Small merchants and manufacturers found themselves overmatched by great new combinations.

CONCLUSION

Industrialists strove to create a rationale for their power and to persuade the public that everyone had something to gain from it. But many Americans remained skeptical of modern capitalism, and some—workers struggling to form unions, reformers denouncing trusts, socialists envisioning a new world, and many others—created broad and powerful critiques of the new economic order. Industrialization brought both progress and pain to late-nineteenth-century America. Controversies over its effects defined the era and would continue to define the first decades of the twentieth century.

INTERACTIVE LEARNING

 On the *Primary Source Investigator CD-ROM*, check out a number of valuable tools for further exploration of the content of this chapter.

Interactive Map
- Transportation Revolution (Map M12)

Primary Sources
Documents, images, and maps related to industrialization, economic growth, and labor strife in the late nineteenth century. Some highlights include:

- Thomas Edison's patent for the lightbulb
- An excerpt from a Haymarket bombing suspect's autobiography

- Original railroad maps showing the expansion of transportation networks
- Panoramic photographs of the era's giant industrial plants

 Online Learning Center
(www.mhhe.com/unfinishedinteractive)
Explore this rich website, providing additional exploration of the material covered in this chapter, online versions of the interactive maps included on the Primary Source Investigator CD-ROM, as well as several study aids, including a multiple-choice quiz, essay questions, a glossary, and other valuable tools.

FOR FURTHER REFERENCE

Robert Wiebe's *The Search for Order, 1877–1920* (1968) is a classic analysis of America's evolution from a society of island communities to a national urban society. Alfred D. Chandler, Jr., describes the new business practices that made industrialization possible in *The Visible Hand: The Managerial Revolution in American Business* (1977) and *Scale and Scope: The Dynamics of Industrial Capitalism* (1990). Olivier Zunz offers a provocative analysis of the social underpinnings of the new corporate order in *Making America Corporate, 1870–1920* (1990) and *Why the American Century?* (1998). David F. Noble, *America by Design: Science, Technology, and the Rise of Corporate Capitalism* (1977) and David Hounshell, *From the American System to Mass Production, 1800–1932* (1984) discuss the explosion of science and technology in the era of rapid industrialization. Daniel Rodgers, *The Work Ethic in Industrial America, 1850–1920* (1978) is an important intel-lectual history of the way Americans viewed industrial workers. David Montgomery, *The Fall of the House of Labor: The Workplace, the State, and American Labor Activism, 1865–1925* (1987) analyzes the way industrialization shaped (and was shaped by) the workers, their expertise, and the strong cultural traditions of the shop floor. Kevin Kenny, *Making Sense of the Molly Maguires* (1998) examines labor radicalism and Elliott J. Gorn, *Mother Jones: The Most Dangerous Woman in America* (2001) explores the career of a celebrated labor firebrand. Alice Kessler-Harris documents the tremendous movement of women into the work force in this period in *Out to Work: A History of Wage-Earning Women in the United States* (1982). John L. Thomas, *Alternative America: Henry George, Edward Bellamy, Henry Demarest Lloyd, and the Adversary Tradition* (1983) examines some important critics of corporate capitalism.

18 The Age of the City

(Christopher Cardozo, Inc.)

MINI-DOCUMENTARY Age of Immigration

T he face of American society changed in countless ways in response to the growth of industry and commerce. No change was more profound, however, than the growing size and influence of cities.

THE NEW URBAN GROWTH

The movement of people from the countryside to the city was not unique to the United States. But Americans found urbanization particularly jarring. The urban population increased sevenfold in the half-century after the Civil War. And in 1920, the census revealed that for the first time, a majority of the American people lived in "urban" areas—defined as communities of 2,500 people or more.

Natural increase accounted for only a small part of the urban growth. Urban families experienced a high rate of infant mortality, a declining fertility rate, and a high death rate from disease. Without immigration, cities would have grown relatively slowly.

The Migrations
The late nineteenth century was an age of unprecedented geographical mobility, as Americans left the declining agricultural regions of the East at a dramatic rate. Some of those who left were moving to the newly developing farmlands of the West. But almost as many were moving to the cities of the East and the Midwest.

Among those leaving rural America were blacks escaping the poverty and oppression they faced in the rural South. They were also seeking new opportunities in cities. Factory jobs for blacks were rare and professional opportunities almost nonexistent. Urban blacks tended to work as cooks, janitors, and domestic servants, as well as in other service occupations. Because many such jobs were considered women's work, black women often outnumbered black men in the cities.

The most important source of urban population growth in the late nineteenth century, however, was the arrival of great numbers of new immigrants from abroad. Some came from Canada, Latin America, and—particularly on the West Coast—China and Japan. But the greatest number

Southern and Eastern European Immigrants

came from Europe. After 1880, the flow of new arrivals began to include large numbers of people from southern and eastern Europe.

In earlier years, most new immigrants from Europe (particularly Germans and Scandinavians) had arrived with at least some money and education. Most of them arrived at one of the major port cities on the Atlantic coast (the greatest number in New York, through the famous immigrant depot on Ellis Island) and then headed west. But the new immigrants generally lacked the capital to buy farmland and lacked the education to establish themselves in professions. So, like similarly poor Irish immigrants before the Civil War, they settled overwhelmingly in industrial cities, where they worked largely in unskilled jobs.

MINI-DOCUMENTARY: Age of Immigration

The Ethnic City
By 1890, most of the population of the major urban areas consisted of immigrants: 87 percent of the population in Chicago, 80 percent in New York, 84 percent in Milwaukee and Detroit.

Diverse Immigrant Populations

Equally striking was the diversity of the new immigrant populations. In other countries experiencing heavy immigration in this period, most of the new arrivals were coming from one or two sources. But in the United States, no single national group dominated.

Most of the new immigrants were rural people, and for many the adjustment to city life was painful. To help ease the transition, some national groups formed close-knit ethnic communities within the cities, neighborhoods often called "immigrant ghettoes." There they could find newspapers and theaters in their native languages, stores selling their native foods, and organizations that provided links with their national pasts. Many immigrants also maintained close ties with their native countries. They stayed in touch with relatives who had remained behind. Some returned to their homelands after a relatively short time; others helped bring the rest of their families to America.

1869	1870	1871	1872	1876	1882	1884	1890
First inter-collegiate football game	NYC opens first elevated railroads	Boston and Chicago fires	Boss Tweed convicted	Baseball's National League founded	Congress restricts Chinese immigration	First "skyscraper" in Chicago	Riis's *How the Other Half Lives*

1891	1894	1895	1897	1901	1903	1906	1910
Basketball invented	Immigration Restriction League formed	Crane's *The Red Badge of Courage*	Boston opens first subway in America	Baseball's American League founded	First World Series	San Francisco earthquake and fire Sinclair's *The Jungle*	NCAA founded

TIME LINE

TOTAL IMMIGRATION, 1860–1900 Over 10 million immigrants from abroad entered the United States in the last forty years of the nineteenth century, with particularly high numbers arriving in the 1880s and 1890s. This chart shows the pattern of immigration in five-year intervals. ■ *What external events might help explain some of the rises and falls in the rates of immigration in these years?*

The cultural cohesiveness of the ethnic communities clearly eased the pain of separation from the immigrants' native lands. What role it played in helping immigrants become absorbed into the economic life of America is a more difficult question to answer. Some ethnic groups advanced economically more rapidly than others. One explanation is that, by huddling together in ethnic neighborhoods, immigrant groups tended to reinforce the cultural values of their previous societies. When those values were particularly well suited to economic advancement, as was—for example, the high value Jews placed on education— ethnic identification may have helped members of a group to improve their lots. When other values predominated—maintaining community solidarity, strengthening family ties—progress could be less rapid.

Importance of Ethnic Ties

But other factors were at least as important in determining how well immigrants fared. Immigrants who aroused strong racial prejudice among native-born whites found it very difficult to advance, whatever their talents. Those white immigrants who arrived with a valuable skill or with some capital did better than those who did not. And over time, those

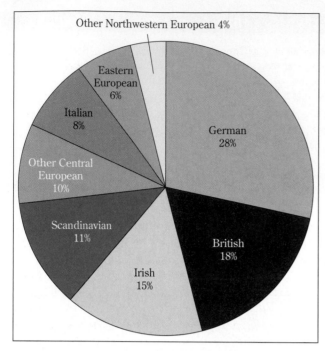

Other Northwestern European 4%

Eastern European 6%

Italian 8%

Other Central European 10%

Scandinavian 11%

Irish 15%

British 18%

German 28%

SOURCES OF IMMIGRATION FROM EUROPE,
1860–1900 This pie chart shows the sources of European immigration in the late nineteenth century. The largest number of immigrants continued to come from traditional sources (Britain, Ireland, Germany, Scandinavia), but the beginnings of what in the early twentieth century would become a major influx of immigrants from new sources—southern and eastern Europe in particular—are already visible here. Immigration from other sources—Mexico, South and Central America, and Asia—was also significant during this period. ▮ *Why would these newer sources of European and other kinds of immigration create controversy among older-stock Americans?*

who lived in cities where people of their own nationality came to predominate—for example, the Irish in New York and Boston, or the Germans in Milwaukee—gained an advantage as they learned to exert their political power.

Assimilation and Exclusion

Despite the many differences among the various immigrant communities, virtually all groups had certain things in common. Most immigrants shared the experience of living in cities. Most were young. And in most communities of the foreign-born, the strength of ethnic ties had to compete against another powerful force: the desire for assimilation.

Many of the new arrivals had come to America with romantic visions of the New World. And how-

ever disillusioning they might find their first contact with the United States, they usually retained the dream of becoming true "Americans." Second-generation immigrants were particularly likely to attempt to break with the old ways. Young women, in particular, sometimes rebelled against parents who tried to arrange (or prevent) marriages or who opposed women entering the workplace.

Native-born Americans encouraged immigrants to assimilate in countless ways. **Assimilation Encouraged** Public schools taught children in English, and employers often insisted that workers speak English on the job. Most non-ethnic stores sold mainly American products, forcing immigrants to adapt their diets, clothing, and lifestyles to American norms. Church leaders encouraged their parishioners to adopt American ways. Some even embraced reforms to make their religion more compatible with the norms of the new country. Reform Judaism, imported from Germany in the late nineteenth century, was an effort by American Jewish leaders to make their faith less "foreign" to the dominant culture.

The arrival of these vast numbers of new immigrants provoked fear and resentment among some native-born Americans in much the same way earlier arrivals had done. The rising nativism provoked political responses. In 1887, Henry Bowers, a self-educated lawyer, founded the American Protective Association, a group committed to stopping immigration. By 1894, membership in the organization reportedly reached 500,000, with chapters throughout the Northeast and Midwest. That same year, five Harvard alumni founded a more genteel organization—the Immigration Restriction League— in Boston. They proposed **Immigration Restriction League** screening immigrants through literacy tests and other standards, to separate the "desirable" from the "undesirable."

The government responded to popular concern about immigration even earlier. In 1882 Congress excluded the Chinese, denied entry to "undesirables"— convicts, paupers, the mentally incompetent—and placed a tax of 50 cents on each person admitted. Later legislation of the 1890s enlarged the list of those barred from immigrating.

But these laws kept out only a small number of aliens, and more ambitious restriction proposals made little progress in Congress. That was because immigration was providing a cheap and plentiful labor supply to the rapidly growing economy, and many argued that America's industrial development would be impossible without it. For an America in the World feature essay on "Global Migrations," visit Chapter 18 of the book's Online Learning Center.

THE URBAN LANDSCAPE

The city was a place of remarkable contrasts. It had homes of almost unimaginable size and grandeur and hovels of indescribable squalor. It had conveniences unknown to earlier generations and problems that seemed beyond the capacity of society to solve.

The Creation of Public Space

In the eighteenth and early nineteenth centuries, cities had grown up haphazardly. By the mid-nineteenth century, however, reformers, planners, and others began to call for a more ordered vision of the city.

Among the most important innovations of the mid-nineteenth century were city parks, which reflected the desire of a growing number of urban leaders to provide an antidote to the congestion of the city. Parks, they argued, would allow city residents a healthy escape from the strains of urban life by reacquainting them with the natural world. The most successful promoters of this notion were the landscape designers Frederick Law Olmsted and Calvert Vaux, who together in the late 1850s designed New York's Central Park. Instead of the ordered, formal spaces common in some European cities, they created instead a space that seemed to be entirely natural. Central Park was from the start one of the most popular and admired public spaces in the world.

Central Park

At the same time that cities were creating great parks, they were also creating great public buildings: libraries, museums, theaters, concert and opera halls. New York's Metropolitan Museum of Art was only the largest and best known of many great museums taking shape in the late nineteenth century. In one city after another, new public libraries appeared as if to confirm the city's role as a center of learning and knowledge.

Wealthy residents of cities were the principal force behind the creation of the art museums, concert halls, opera houses, and at times even parks. As their own material and social aspirations grew, they wanted the public life of the city to provide them with amenities to match their expectations.

As both the size and the aspirations of cities increased, urban leaders launched monumental projects to remake the way their cities looked. Some cities began to clear away older neighborhoods and streets and create grand avenues lined with impressive buildings. A particularly important event in inspiring this effort to remake the city was the 1893 Columbian Exposition in Chicago, a world's fair constructed to honor the 400th anniversary of Columbus's first voyage to America. At the center of the wildly popular exposition was a cluster of neoclassical buildings—the "Great White City"—arranged symmetrically around a formal lagoon. It became the inspiration for what became known as the "city beautiful" movement, led by the architect of the Great White City, Daniel Burnham. The movement strove to impose a similar order and symmetry on the disordered life of cities around the country. Only rarely, however, were planners able to overcome the obstacles of private landowners and complicated urban politics.

Daniel Burnham

The effort to remake the city did not focus only on redesigning the existing landscapes. It occasionally led to the creation of entirely new ones. In Boston in the late 1850s, a large area of marshy tidal land was gradually filled in to create the neighborhood known as "Back Bay." The landfill project was one of the largest public works projects ever undertaken in America to that point. But Boston was not alone. Chicago reclaimed large areas from Lake Michigan as it expanded and at one point raised the street level for the entire city to help avoid the problems the marshy land created. In New York and other cities, the response to limited space was not so much creating new land as annexing adjacent territory. A great wave of annexations expanded the boundaries of many American cities in the 1890s and beyond.

"Back Bay"

The Search for Housing

One of the greatest urban problems was providing housing for the new residents pouring into the cities. For the prosperous, housing was seldom a worry. The availability of cheap labor reduced the cost of building and permitted anyone with even a moderate income to afford a house. Some of the richest urban residents lived in mansions located in exclusive neighborhoods in the heart of the city—Fifth Avenue in New York, Back Bay and Beacon Hill in Boston, Society Hill in Philadelphia, Lake Shore Drive in Chicago, Nob Hill in San Francisco, and many others.

Many of the moderately well-to-do took advantage of less expensive land on the edges of the city and settled in new suburbs, linked to the downtowns by trains or streetcars. Chicago in the 1870s, for example, connected nearly 100 residential suburbs to the downtown by railroad. Real estate developers worked to create suburban **Railroad Suburbs** communities that would appeal to the nostalgia for the countryside that many city dwellers felt. Affluent suburbs were notable for lawns, trees, and houses designed to look manorial.

Most urban residents, however, could not afford either to own a house in the city or to move to the suburbs. Instead, they stayed in the city centers and rented. Landlords tried to squeeze as many rent-paying residents as possible into the smallest available space. In Manhattan, for example, the average population density in 1894 was 143 people per acre. In the cities of the South, poor blacks lived in crumbling former slave quarters. In Boston, immigrants moved into cheap three-story wooden houses ("triple deckers"). In Baltimore and Philadelphia, the new arrivals crowded into narrow brick row houses. And in New York and many other cities, they lived in tenements.

The word "tenement" had originally referred simply to a multiple-family rental building, but by the late nineteenth century it had become a term for slum dwellings only. The first tenements, built in 1850, had been hailed as a great improvement in housing for the poor. But most were, in fact, miserable places, with many windowless rooms and little or no plumbing or heating. Jacob Riis, a Danish immigrant and New York newspaper reporter and photographer, shocked many **Jacob Riis** middle-class Americans with his descriptions and pictures of tenement life in his 1890 book, *How the Other Half Lives*. But the solution reformers often adopted was simply to raze slum dwellings without building any new housing to replace them.

A TENEMENT LAUNDRY
Immigrant families living in tenements, in New York and in many other cities, earned their livelihoods as they could. This woman, shown here with her children, was typical of many working-class mothers who found income-producing activities they could pursue in the home (in this case laundry). The room, dominated by large vats and piles of other people's laundry, is also the family's home, as the crib and religious pictures make clear. *(Bettmann/Corbis)*

Urban Technologies: Transportation and Construction

Urban growth posed monumental transportation challenges. Streetcars drawn on tracks by horses had been introduced into some cities even before the Civil War. But the horsecars were not fast enough, so many communities developed new forms of mass transit. In 1870, New York opened its first elevated railway, whose noisy, steam-powered trains moved rapidly above the city streets on massive iron structures. New York, Chicago, San Francisco, and other cities also experimented with cable cars, towed by continuously moving underground cables. Richmond, Virginia, introduced the first electric trolley line in 1888, and in 1897 Boston opened the first American subway. At the same time, cities were developing new techniques of road and bridge building. One of the great technological marvels of the 1880s was the completion of the Brooklyn Bridge in New York—a dramatic steel-cable suspension span designed by John A. Roebling.

Cities were growing upward as well as outward. In Chicago, the construction in 1884 of the first modern "skyscraper"—

Skyscrapers

by later standards a relatively modest building, ten stories high—launched a new era in urban architecture. Critical to the creation of the skyscraper was a new technology of construction, which emerged as a result of several related developments. One was the creation of new kinds of steel girders, capable of supporting much greater tension than the metals of the past. Still another was the invention and development of the passenger elevator. And another was the search for ways to protect cities from the ravages of great fires. Steel-frame construction was, among other things, a way to make cities more fireproof. Once the technology existed to permit the construction of tall buildings, there were few obstacles to building taller and taller structures. The early Chicago skyscrapers paved the way for some of the great construction marvels later in the twentieth century.

STRAINS OF URBAN LIFE

The increasing congestion of the city and the absence of adequate public services produced serious hazards. Crime, fire, disease, and indigence all placed strains on the capacities of metropolitan institutions, and both governments and private agencies were for a time poorly equipped to respond.

Fire and Disease

One serious problem was fire. In one major city after another, fires destroyed large downtown areas. Chicago and Boston suffered "great fires" in 1871. Other cities experienced similar disasters. The great fires were terrible experiences, but they were also important events in the development of the cities involved. They encouraged the construction of fireproof buildings and the development of professional fire departments. They also forced cities to rebuild at a time when new technological and architectural innovations were available.

An even greater hazard than fire was disease, especially in poor neighborhoods with inadequate sanitation facilities. Few municipal officials recognized the relationship of improper sewage disposal and

Inadequate Sanitation

water contamination to such epidemic diseases as typhoid fever and cholera; many cities lacked adequate systems for disposing of human waste until well into the twentieth century. Flush toilets and sewer systems began to appear in the 1870s, but they could not solve the problem as long as sewage continued to flow into open ditches or streams, polluting cities' water supplies.

Environmental Degradation

Modern notions of environmental science were unknown to most Americans in the late nineteenth and early twentieth centuries. But the environmental degradation of many American cities was a visible and disturbing fact of life in those years. The frequency of fires, the dangers of disease and plague, the crowding of working-class neighborhoods were all examples of the environmental costs of industrialization and urbanization.

Improper disposal of human and industrial waste was a common feature of almost all large cities in these years. That contributed to the pollution of rivers and lakes, and also in many cases to the compromising of the city's drinking water. The presence of domestic animals—especially horses, the principal means of transportation until the late nineteenth century—contributed as well to the environmental problems.

Air quality in many cities was poor as well. Air

Air Pollution

pollution from factories and from stoves and furnaces in offices, homes, and other buildings was constant and at times severe. The incidence of respiratory infection and related diseases was much higher in cities than it was in rural areas, and it accelerated rapidly in the late nineteenth century.

By the early twentieth century, reformers were actively crusading to improve the environmental conditions of cities. New sewage and drainage systems were created to protect drinking water from sewage disposal. By 1910, most large American cities had constructed sewage disposal systems to protect the drinking water of their inhabitants and to prevent the great bacterial plagues that impure water had helped create in the past—such as the yellow fever epidemic in Memphis that killed 5,000 people.

In 1912, the federal government created the Public Health Service, which was charged with preventing such occupational diseases as tuberculosis

Public Health Service

and anemia and carbon dioxide poisoning, which were common in the garment industry and other trades. It attempted to create common health standards for all factories; but since the agency had few powers of enforcement, it had limited impact. The creation of the Occupational Health and Safety Administration in 1970, which gave government the authority to require employers to create safe and healthy workplaces, was a legacy of the Public Health Service's early work.

Urban Poverty, Crime, and Violence

Above all, perhaps, the expansion of the city spawned widespread poverty. Public agencies and private philanthropic organizations offered some relief. But they were generally poorly funded and dominated by middle-class people who believed that too much assistance would breed dependency. Most tried to restrict aid to the "deserving poor"—those who truly could not help themselves. Charitable organizations conducted "investigations" to separate the "deserving" from the "undeserving." Other charitable societies, such as the Salvation Army, concentrated more on religious revivalism than on the relief of the homeless and hungry.

Middle-class people grew particularly alarmed over the rising number of poor children in the cities, some of them orphans or runaways. These "street arabs," as they were often called, attracted more attention from reformers than any other group.

Poverty and crowding bred crime and violence. The murder rate rose rapidly in the late nineteenth century, from 25 murders for every million people in 1880 to over 100 by the end of the century. That reflected

Growing Crime Rate

in part a very high level of violence in some nonurban areas: the South, where lynching and homicide were particularly high; and the West, where the instability of new communities created much violence. But the cities contributed their share to the increase in crime as well. Native-born Americans liked to believe that crime was a result of the violent proclivities of immigrant groups, and they cited the rise of gangs and criminal organizations in various ethnic communities. But native-born Americans in the cities were as likely to commit crimes as immigrants. The rising crime rates encouraged many cities to develop more professional police forces. But police forces themselves could spawn corruption and brutality, particularly since jobs on them were often filled through political patronage.

Some members of the middle class, fearful of urban insurrections, felt the need for even more substantial forms of protection. Urban national guard groups built imposing armories on the outskirts of affluent neighborhoods and stored large supplies of weapons and ammunition in preparation for uprisings that, in fact, virtually never occurred.

The city was a place of strong allure and great excitement. Yet it was also a place of alienating impersonality and, to some, exploitation. Theodore Dreiser's novel *Sister Carrie* (1900) exposed one troubling aspect of urban life: the plight of single women (like Dreiser's heroine, Carrie) who moved from the countryside into the city and found themselves without any means of support. Carrie first took an ill-paying job in a Chicago shoe factory; then she drifted into a life of "sin," exploited by predatory men.

The Machine and the Boss

Newly arrived immigrants were much in need of institutions to help them adjust to American urban life. For many residents of the inner cities, the principal source of assistance was the political "machine."

The urban machine owed its existence to the power vacuum that the chaotic growth of cities had created. It was also a product of the potential voting power of large immigrant communities. Out of that combination emerged the urban "bosses." The principal function of the political boss was simple: to win votes for his organization. That meant winning the loyalty of his constituents. To do so, a boss might provide them with occasional relief—a basket of groceries or a bag of coal. He might step in to save those arrested for petty crimes from jail. When he could, he found work for the unemployed. Above all, he rewarded many of his followers with patronage: with jobs in city government or agencies such as the police; with jobs building or operating the new transit systems; and with opportunities to rise in the political organization itself.

Function of the Urban "Boss"

Machines were also vehicles for making money. Politicians enriched themselves and their allies through various forms of graft and corruption. A politician might discover where a new road or streetcar line was to be built, buy land near it, and sell it at a profit when property values rose as a result of the construction. There was also covert graft. Officials received kickbacks from contractors in exchange for contracts to build public projects, and they sold franchises for the operation of public utilities. The most famously corrupt city boss was William M. Tweed, boss of New York City's Tammany Hall in the 1860s and 1870s, whose extravagant use of public funds on projects that paid kickbacks to the organization landed him in jail in 1872.

William M. Tweed

The urban machine was not without competition. Reform groups frequently mobilized public outrage at the corruption of the bosses and often succeeded in driving machine politicians from office. But the reform organizations typically lacked the permanence of the machine.

THE RISE OF MASS CONSUMPTION

In the last decades of the nineteenth century a distinctive middle-class culture began to exert a powerful influence over the whole of American life.

Other groups in society advanced less rapidly, or not at all, but almost no one was unaffected by the rise of the new urban, consumer culture.

Patterns of Income and Consumption

Incomes were rising for almost everyone in the industrial era, although at highly uneven rates. The most conspicuous result of the new economy was the creation of vast fortunes, but perhaps the most important result for society as a whole was the growth and increasing prosperity of the middle class. The salaries of clerks, accountants, middle managers, and other "white-collar" workers rose by an average of a third between 1890 and 1910. Working-class incomes rose in those years as well, although from a much lower base and often more slowly. The iron and steel industries saw workers' hourly wages increase by a third between 1890 and 1910; but industries with large female work forces saw more modest increases, as did almost all industries in the South. Wages for African Americans, Mexicans, and Asians also rose more slowly than those for other workers.

Rising Income

Rising incomes created new markets for consumer goods. Affordable products and new merchandising techniques soon made many consumer goods available to this mass market for the first time. A good example of such changes was the emergence of ready-made clothing. In the early nineteenth century, most Americans had made their own clothing. The invention of the sewing machine and the spur that the Civil War (and its demand for uniforms) gave to the manufacture of clothing helped create an enormous industry devoted to producing ready-made garments. By the end of the century, almost all Americans bought their clothing from stores. Partly as a result, much larger numbers of people became concerned with personal style. Interest in women's fashion, for example, had once been a luxury reserved for the relatively affluent. Now middle-class and even working-class women could strive to develop a distinctive style of dress.

Ready-made Clothing

Buying and preparing food also became a critical part of the new consumerism. The development and mass production of tin cans in the 1880s created a large new industry devoted to packaging and selling canned food and condensed milk. Refrigerated

THE MONTGOMERY WARD DEPARTMENT STORE This advertising poster for the Montgomery Ward department store in downtown Chicago dates from about 1880. The designer has stripped away the outside walls to reveal the vast array of goods inside what the poster calls "the enormous establishment." *(Chicago Historical Society (ICHi-01622))*

railroad cars made it possible for perishable foods to be transported over long distances without spoiling. Artificially frozen ice enabled many households to afford iceboxes. The changes brought improved diets and better health.

Chain Stores, Mail-Order Houses, and Department Stores

Changes in marketing also altered the way Americans bought goods. New "chain stores" could usually offer a wider array of goods at lower prices than the small local stores with which they competed. The Atlantic and Pacific Tea Company (the A & P) began a national network of grocery stores in the 1870s. F. W. Woolworth built a chain of dry goods stores. Sears and Roebuck established a large market for its mail-order merchandise by distributing an enormous catalog each year.

In larger cities, the emergence of great department stores helped transform buying habits. Marshall Field in Chicago created one of the first American department stores—a place deliberately designed to produce a sense of wonder and excitement. Similar stores emerged in New York, Brooklyn, Boston, Philadelphia, and other cities.

Marshall Field

Women as Consumers

The rise of mass consumption had particularly dramatic effects on women. Women's clothing styles changed much more rapidly and dramatically than men's, which encouraged more frequent purchases. The availability of new food products changed the way women shopped and cooked. Canning and refrigeration meant greater variety in the diet. It also meant that food did not always have to be eaten on the day it was purchased.

The consumer economy produced new employment opportunities for women as salesclerks and waitresses. And it spawned the creation of a new movement in which women were to play a vital role: the consumer protection movement. The National Consumers League, formed in the 1890s under the leadership of Florence Kelley, attempted to mobilize the power of women as consumers to force retailers and manufacturers to improve wages and working conditions.

National Consumers League

LEISURE IN THE CONSUMER SOCIETY

Closely related to the growth of consumption was a growing interest in leisure time. Members of the urban middle and professional classes had large blocks of time during which they were not at work—evenings, weekends, even paid vacations. Working hours in many factories declined, from an average of nearly seventy hours a week in 1860 to under sixty in 1900. The lives of many Americans were becoming more compartmentalized, with clear distinctions between work and leisure. The change produced a search for new forms of recreation and entertainment.

Redefining Leisure
It also produced a redefinition of the idea of "leisure." In earlier eras, relatively few Americans had considered leisure a valuable thing. On the contrary, many equated it with laziness or sloth. In the late nineteenth century, however, the beginnings of a redefinition of leisure appeared. The economist Simon Patten was one of the first intellectuals to articulate this new view of leisure. In *The Theory of Prosperity* (1902), *The New Basis of Civilization* (1910), and other works, he challenged the assumption that the normal condition of civilization was a scarcity of

Simon Patten

goods. In earlier times, Patten argued, fear of scarcity had caused people to place a high value on thrift, self-denial, and restraint. But industrial economies could create enough wealth to satisfy not just the needs, but also the desires, of all.

As Americans became more accustomed to leisure as a normal part of their lives, they began to look for new experiences with which to entertain themselves. In cities, in particular, the demand for popular entertainment produced a rich mix of spectacles, recreations, and other activities.

Mass entertainment occasionally bridged differences of class, race, or gender. But it could also be sharply divided. Saloons and some sporting events tended to be male preserves. Shopping and going to tea rooms and luncheonettes was more characteristic of female leisure. Theaters, pubs, and clubs were often specific to particular ethnic communities or work groups. When the classes did meet in public spaces, there was often considerable conflict over what constituted appropriate public behavior. Elites in New York City, for example, tried to prohibit anything but quiet, "genteel" activities in Central Park, while working-class people wanted to use the public spaces for sports and entertainments.

Spectator Sports
Among the most important responses to the search for entertainment was the rise of organized spectator sports, and especially baseball. A game much like baseball—known as "rounders" and derived from cricket—had enjoyed limited popularity in Great Britain in the early nineteenth century. Versions of the game began to appear in America in the early 1830s. By the end of the Civil War, interest in the game had grown rapidly. More than 200 amateur or semiprofessional teams and clubs existed, many of which joined a national association and proclaimed a set of standard rules. The first salaried team, the Cincinnati Red Stockings, was formed in 1869. Other cities fielded professional teams, and in 1876 the teams banded together in the National League. A rival league, the American Association, soon appeared. It eventually collapsed, but in 1901 the American League emerged to replace it. And in 1903, the first modern World Series was played, in which the American League Boston Red Sox beat the National League Pittsburgh Pirates. By then,

Baseball

baseball had become an important business and a great national preoccupation.

Baseball had great appeal to working-class males. The second most popular game, football, appealed at first to a more elite segment of the male population, in part because it originated in colleges and universities. The first intercollegiate football game in America occurred between Princeton and Rutgers in 1869. Early intercollegiate football bore only an indirect relation to the modern game; it was more similar to what is now known as rugby. By the late 1870s, however, the game was becoming standardized and was taking on the outlines of its modern form.

| Basketball Invented |

Basketball was invented in 1891 at Springfield, Massachusetts, by Dr. James A. Naismith, a Canadian working as athletic director for a local college. Boxing, which had long been concentrated primarily among the lower classes, became by the 1880s a more popular and, in some places, more reputable sport.

Participation in the major sports of the era was almost exclusively the province of men, but several sports emerged in which women became important participants. Golf and tennis experienced a rapid increase in participation among relatively wealthy men and women. Bicycling and croquet also enjoyed widespread popularity among women as well as men. Women's colleges introduced their students to more strenuous sports as well—track, crew, swimming, and (beginning in the late 1890s) basketball.

Music, Theater, and Movies

Other forms of popular entertainment developed in the cities in response to the large potential markets there. Many ethnic communities maintained their own theaters. Urban theaters also introduced new and distinctively American entertainment forms: the musical comedy, which evolved gradually from the comic operettas of Europe;

| Vaudeville |

and vaudeville, a form of theater adapted from French models, which consisted of a variety of acts (musicians, comedians, magicians, jugglers, and others) and was, at least in the beginning, inexpensive to produce. As the economic potential of vaudeville grew, some promoters—most prominently Florenz Ziegfeld of New York—staged much more elaborate spectacles.

Vaudeville was also one of the few entertainment media open to black performers. They brought to it elements of the minstrel shows they had earlier developed for black audiences. Some minstrel singers (including the most famous, Al Jolson) were whites wearing heavy makeup (or "blackface"), but most were black. They performed music based on the gospel and folk tunes of the plantation and on the jazz and ragtime of black urban communities. They also tailored their acts to white prejudices, ridiculing blacks by acting out demeaning stereotypes.

The most important form of mass entertainment was the movies. Thomas Edison and others had created the technology of the motion picture in the 1880s. Soon after that, short films became available to individual viewers watching peepshows in pool halls, penny arcades, and amusement parks. Soon, larger projectors made it possible to project the images onto big screens, which permitted substantial audiences to see films in theaters. By 1900, Americans were becoming attracted in large numbers to these early movies—usually plotless films of trains or waterfalls or other spectacles. D. W. Griffith carried

| D. W. Griffith |

the motion picture into a new era with his silent epics—*The Birth of a Nation* (1915), *Intolerance* (1916), and others—which introduced serious (if racist) plots and elaborate productions to filmmaking. Motion pictures were the first truly mass entertainment medium.

Patterns of Public and Private Leisure

Many Americans spent their leisure time in places where they would find not only entertainment but also other people. Thousands of working-class New Yorkers spent evenings in dance halls, vaudeville houses, and concert halls. More affluent New Yorkers enjoyed afternoons in Central Park, where a principal attraction was seeing other people (and being seen by them). Moviegoers were attracted not just by the movies themselves but by the energy of the audiences at lavish new "movie palaces," just as sports fans were drawn by the crowds as well as by the games.

Perhaps the most striking example of popular, public entertainment was Coney Island, the famous amusement

| Coney Island |

park and resort on a beach in Brooklyn. The greatest of the Coney Island attractions, Luna Park, opened

POSTCARD FROM LUNA PARK
Visitors to Coney Island sent postcards to friends and relatives by the millions, and those cards were among the most effective promotional devices for the amusement parks. This one shows the brightly lit entrance to Luna Park, Coney Island's most popular attraction for many years. *(Bettmann/Corbis)*

in 1903. It provided rides and stunts, and also lavish reproductions of exotic places and spectacular adventures: Japanese gardens, Venetian canals with gondoliers, a Chinese theater, a simulated trip to the moon, and re-enactments of such disasters as burning buildings and earthquakes. A year later, a competing company opened Dreamland, which featured a 375-foot tower, a three-ring circus, chariot races, and a Lilliputian village from *Gulliver's Travels.* The popularity of Coney Island in these years was phenomenal. Thousands of people flocked to the large resort hotels that lined the beaches. Many thousands more made day trips by train and (after 1920) subway. In 1904, the average daily attendance at Luna Park alone was 90,000 people.

Most people who found Coney Island appealing did so in part because it provided them with an escape from the genteel standards of behavior that governed so much of American life at the time. In the amusement parks of Coney Island, decorum was often forgotten, and people delighted in finding themselves in situations that in any other setting would have seemed embarrassing or improper: women's skirts blown above their heads with hot air; people pummeled with water and rubber paddles by clowns; hints of sexual freedom as strangers were forced to come into physical contact with one another on rides and amusements.

Not all popular entertainment, however, involved public events. So-called dime novels, cheaply bound and widely circulated, became popular after the Civil War,

Dime Novels

with detective stories, tales of the "Wild West," sagas of scientific adventure, and novels of "moral uplift." Publishers also distributed sentimental novels of romance, which developed a large audience among women, as did books about animals and about young children growing up. Louisa May Alcott's *Little Women* sold more than 2 million copies.

The Technologies of Mass Communication

American publishing and journalism experienced an important change in the decades following the Civil War. Between 1870 and 1910, the circulation of daily newspapers increased nearly ninefold, a rate three times as great as the rate of population increase. And while standards varied widely from one paper to another, American journalism was developing a professional identity. Salaries of reporters increased; many newspapers began separating the reporting of news from the expression of opinion; and newspapers themselves became important businesses.

The transformation of publishing and journalism was to a large degree a result of new technologies of communication. The emergence of national press services, for example, was a product of the telegraph, which made it possible to supply news and features from around the nation and the world. By the turn of the century newspaper chains had emerged as well, linked together by their own internal wire services. The most powerful was owned by

| William Randolph Hearst |

William Randolph Hearst, who by 1914 controlled nine newspapers and two magazines. New printing technologies were making possible more elaborate layouts, the publication of color pictures, and, by the end of the century, the printing of photographs. These advances helped publishers not only to make their stories more vivid but also to attract more advertisers.

The Telephone

The most important new technology of communication was the telephone, which Alexander Graham Bell had first demonstrated in 1876 (p. 270). In its first years, the telephone was a relatively impractical tool. Those who subscribed to telephone service had to have direct wire links to everyone else they wished to call. In 1878, the first "switchboard" opened in New Haven, Connecticut, opening the way for more practical uses of the telephone. Once there was a switchboard, a telephone subscriber needed only a line to the central telephone office from which connections could be made to any other subscriber. A new occupation—the "telephone operator"—was born. The

| The Bell System |

Bell System, which controlled all American telephone service, hired young white women to work as operators, hoping that a pleasant female voice would make the experience of using the telephone more appealing, or less irritating, to customers. Telephone signals were very weak at first, and callers could seldom reach anyone more than a few miles away. In an effort to increase the range of telephones, engineers created the "repeater," which periodically strengthened the signal as it moved over distances. By 1914, however, the repeaters had improved to the point that it was now practical to envision a transcontinental line.

In its early years, the telephone was an almost entirely commercial instrument. Of the nearly 7,400 telephone customers in the New York-New Jersey area in 1891, 6,000 were businesses and organizations. Even the residential telephones tended to belong to doctors or business managers.

The growing reach of the telephone made the Bell System (formally named American Telephone and Telegraph, or AT&T) one of the most powerful corporations in America. Central to its success was an early decision by executives that the company would exclusively build and own all telephone instruments and then lease them to subscribers. That made it possible for AT&T to control both the equipment and the telephone service itself, and to exclude any competitors in either field. It also gave AT&T effective control over the local telephone companies allied with it.

HIGH CULTURE IN THE URBAN AGE

In addition to the important changes in popular culture that accompanied the rise of cities and industry, there were profound changes in the realm of "high culture." The distinction between "highbrow" and "lowbrow" culture was largely new to the industrial era. In the early nineteenth century, most cultural activities had targeted people of all classes. By the late nineteenth century, however, elites were developing a cultural and intellectual life quite separate from the popular amusements of the urban masses.

Literature and Art in Urban America

One of the strongest impulses in American literature was the effort to re-create urban social reality. This trend toward realism found an early voice in

| Literary Realism |

Stephen Crane, who—although perhaps best known for his novel of the Civil War, *The Red Badge of Courage* (1895)—created a sensation in 1893 when he published *Maggie: A Girl of the Streets*, a grim picture of urban poverty and slum life. Theodore Dreiser, Frank Norris, and Upton Sinclair were similarly drawn to social issues as themes. Kate Chopin, a southern writer, encountered widespread public abuse after publication of her shocking novel, *The Awakening*, in 1899. It described a young wife and mother who abandoned her family in search of personal fulfillment. William Dean Howells, in *The Rise of Silas Lapham* and other works, described what he considered the shallowness and corruption in ordinary American lifestyles.

American art through most of the nineteenth century had been overshadowed by the art of Europe. By 1900, however, a number of American artists broke from the Old World traditions. Winslow Homer was vigorously American in his paintings of New England maritime life and other native subjects. James McNeil Whistler was one of the first Western artists to introduce Oriental themes into American and European art.

By the first years of the new century, some American artists were turning away from the traditional academic style (a style perhaps most identified in America by the portraitist John Singer Sargent). Members of the so-called

Ashcan School

Ashcan School produced work startling in its naturalism and stark in its portrayal of the social realities of the era. John Sloan portrayed the dreariness of American urban slums; George Bellows caught the vigor and violence of his time in paintings and drawings of prizefights; Edward Hopper explored the loneliness of the modern city. The Ashcan artists were also among the first Americans to appreciate expressionism and abstraction; and they showed their interest in new forms in 1913 when they helped stage the famous "Armory Show" in New York City, which displayed works of the French postimpressionists and of some American moderns.

The Impact of Darwinism

Perhaps the most profound intellectual development in the late nineteenth century was the widespread acceptance of the theory of evolution, associated most prominently with the English naturalist Charles Darwin. Darwin argued that the human species had evolved from earlier forms of life through a process of "natural selection." History, Darwin suggested, was not the working out of a divine plan. It was a random process dominated by the fiercest or luckiest competitors.

The theory of evolution met widespread resistance at first from educators, theologians, and even many scientists. By the end of the century, however, the evolutionists had converted most

Resistance to Evolution

members of the urban professional and educated classes. Even many middle-class Protestant religious leaders had accepted the doctrine, making significant alterations in theology to accommodate it. Unseen by most urban Americans at the time, however, the rise of Darwinism was contributing to a deep schism between the new, cosmopolitan culture of the city—which was receptive to new ideas such as evolution—and the more tradi-

tional, provincial culture of some rural areas—which remained more wedded to fundamentalist religious beliefs and older values. Thus the late nineteenth century saw not only the rise of a liberal Protestantism in tune with new scientific discoveries but also the beginning of an organized Protestant fundamentalism.

Darwinism helped spawn other new intellectual currents. There was the Social Darwinism of William Graham Sumner and others, which industrialists used so enthusiastically to justify their favored position in American life. But there were also more sophisticated philosophies, among them a doctrine that became known as "prag-matism." William James, a

"Pragmatism"

Harvard psychologist (and brother of the novelist Henry James), was the most prominent publicist of the new theory. According to the pragmatists, modern society should rely for guidance not on inherited ideals and moral principles but on the test of scientific inquiry. No idea or institution (not even religious faith) was valid, they claimed, unless it worked, unless it stood the test of experience.

A similar concern for scientific inquiry was influencing the social sciences. Sociologists such as Edward A. Ross and Lester Frank Ward urged applying the scientific method to the solution of social and political problems. Historians such as Frederick Jackson Turner and Charles Beard argued that economic factors more than spiritual ideals had been the governing force in historical development. John Dewey proposed a new approach to education that placed less emphasis on the rote learning of traditional knowledge and more on flexible, democratic schooling.

The implications of Darwinism also promoted the growth of anthropology and encouraged some scholars to begin examining other cultures in new ways. Some white Americans began to look at Indian society, for example, as a coherent culture with its own norms and values that were worthy of respect and preservation.

Toward Universal Schooling

The growing demand for specialized skills and knowledge naturally created a growing demand for education. The late nineteenth century, therefore, was a time of rapid expansion of schools and universities.

One example was the spread of free public primary and secondary education. By

Spread of Free Public Schooling

1900, compulsory school attendance laws were in effect in thirty-one states and territories. Education was still far from universal, however. Rural areas lagged far behind urban-industrial ones in funding public education. In the South, many blacks had access to no schools at all.

Educational reformers tried to extend educational opportunities to the Indian tribes as well. In the 1870s, reformers recruited small groups of Indians to attend Hampton Institute (a primarily black college). In 1879 they organized the Carlisle Indian Industrial School in Pennsylvania. Like many black colleges, Carlisle emphasized practical "industrial" education. Ultimately, however, these reform efforts failed.

Universities and the Growth of Science and Technology

Colleges and universities were also proliferating rapidly in the late nineteenth century. They benefited particularly from the Morrill Land Grant Act of 1862, by which the federal government had donated public land to states for the establishment of colleges. Sixty-nine "land-grant" institutions were established in the last decades of the century—among them the state university systems of California, Illinois, Minnesota, and Wisconsin. Other universities benefited from millions of dollars contributed by business and financial titans. Rockefeller, Carnegie, and others gave generously to such schools as Columbia, Chicago, Harvard, Northwestern, Princeton, Syracuse, and Yale. Other philanthropists founded new universities or reorganized older ones and perpetuated their family names—Vanderbilt, Johns Hopkins, Cornell, Duke, Tulane, and Stanford.

| Economic Impact of Higher Education |

These and other universities played a vital role in the economic development of the United States in the late nineteenth century and beyond. The land-grant institutions were specifically mandated to advance knowledge in "agriculture and mechanics." From the beginning, therefore, they were committed not just to abstract knowledge, but to making discoveries that would be of practical use to farmers and manufacturers. Private universities emerged that served many of the same purposes: the Massachusetts Institute of Technology, founded in 1865, which soon became the nation's premier engineering school; Johns Hopkins University in Baltimore, founded in 1876, which did much to advance medical scholarship; the Rockefeller Institute for Medical Research in New York (later

Rockefeller University); the Carnegie Institution. By the early twentieth century, even much older and more traditional universities were beginning to form relationships with the private sector and the government, doing research that did not just advance knowledge for its own sake but that was directly applicable to practical problems of the time.

Medical Science

Both the culture of and the scientific basis for medical care was changing rapidly in the early twentieth century. Most doctors were beginning to accept the new medical assumption that there were underlying causes to particular symptoms—that a symptom was not itself a disease. They were also beginning to make use of new or improved technologies such as the X-ray that made it possible to distinguish among different diseases. Laboratory tests could now identify infections such as typhoid and dysentery, a critical first step toward finding effective treatments. At about the same time, pharmaceutical research was beginning to produce some important new medicines. Aspirin was first synthesized in 1899. Other researchers were beginning to experiment with chemicals that might destroy diseases in the blood, an effort that eventually led to various forms of chemotherapy. In 1906, an American surgeon, G. W. Crile, became the first physician to use blood transfusion in treatment. In the past, patients often lost so much blood during operations that extensive surgery could be fatal for that reason alone. With transfusions, it became possible to conduct much more elaborate operations.

The widespread acceptance of the germ theory of disease **Germ Theory Accepted** had important implications. Physicians quickly discovered that exposure to germs did not by itself necessarily cause disease, and they began looking for the other factors that determined who got sick and who did not. Among the factors they eventually discovered were general health, previous medical history, diet and nutrition, and eventually genetic predisposition. The awareness of the importance of infection in spreading disease also encouraged doctors to sterilize their instruments and use surgical gloves.

By the early twentieth century, American physicians and surgeons were generally recognized as among the best in the world, and American medical education was beginning to attract students from many **Declining Mortality** other countries. These improvements in medical knowledge and training, along with improvements in sanitation and public health, did much to reduce infection and mortality in most American communities.

Education for Women

The post–Civil War era saw an important expansion of educational opportunities for women, although such opportunities continued to lag far behind those available to men and were denied to black women.

Most public high schools accepted women readily, but opportunities for higher education were fewer. At the end of the Civil War, only three American colleges were coeducational. In the years after the war, many of the land-grant colleges and universities in the Midwest and such private universities as Cornell and Wesleyan began to admit women along with men. But coeducation was less crucial to women's education in this period than was the creation of a network of women's colleges.

Women's Colleges

Mount Holyoke in central Massachusetts had begun its life in 1836 as a "seminary" for women; it became a full-fledged college in the 1880s, at about the same time that entirely new female institutions were emerging: Vassar, Wellesley, Smith, Bryn Mawr, Wells, and Goucher. A few of the larger private universities created separate colleges for women on their campuses (Barnard at Columbia and Radcliffe at Harvard, for example).

The female college was part of an important phenomenon in the history of modern American women: the emergence of distinctive women's communities outside the family.

Emergence of Women's Communities

The life of the college produced a spirit of sorority and commitment among educated women that had important effects in later years. Most female college graduates ultimately married, but they married at a more advanced age than their noncollege counterparts. A significant minority, perhaps over 25 percent, did not marry at all, but devoted themselves to careers. The growth of female higher education clearly became for some women a liberating experience, persuading them that they had roles to perform other than those of wives and mothers.

The extraordinary growth of American cities in the last decades of the nineteenth century led to both great achievements and enormous problems. Cities became centers of learning, art, and commerce. They produced great advances in technology, transportation, architecture, and communications. They provided their residents—and their many visitors—with varied and dazzling experiences, so much so that people increasingly left the countryside to move to the city.

But cities were also places of congestion, filth, disease, and corruption. With populations expanding too rapidly for services to keep up, most American cities in this era struggled with makeshift techniques to solve the basic problems of providing water, disposing of sewage, building roads, running public transportation, fighting fire, stopping crime, and preventing or curing disease. City governments, many of them dominated by political machines and ruled by party bosses, were often models of inefficiency and corruption—although in their informal way they also provided substantial services to the working-class and immigrant constituencies who needed them most. Yet they also managed to oversee great public projects: the building of parks, museums, opera houses, and theaters, usually in partnership with private developers.

The city brought together races, ethnic groups, and classes of extraordinary variety—from the families of great wealth that the new industrial age was creating to the vast working class that crowded into densely packed neighborhoods sharply divided by nationality. The city also spawned new forms of popular culture. It created temples of consumerism: shops, boutiques, and above all department stores. And it created forums for public recreation and entertainment: parks, theaters, athletic fields, amusement parks, and later movie palaces.

Urban life created anxiety among those who lived within the cities and among those who observed them from afar. But in fact, American cities adapted reasonably successfully to the demands their growth made of them and learned to govern themselves if not entirely honestly and efficiently, at least adequately to allow them to survive and grow.

CONCLUSION

INTERACTIVE LEARNING

 On the *Primary Source Investigator CD-ROM* check out a number of valuable tools for further exploration of the content of this chapter.

Mini-Documentary Movie

- **Age of Immigration.** A study of the flood of immigration into the United States in the late nineteenth and early twentieth centuries (Doc D14)

Interactive Map

- Streetcar Suburbs (Map M17)

Primary Sources

Documents, images, and maps related to urbanization, immigration, and the rise of mass consumption in the late nineteenth century. Some highlights include:

- The text of the Chinese Exclusion Act of 1882

- Images from the new urban world: a tenement dwelling, Bohemian cigarmakers at work in their living quarters, and young children asleep in the street

Online Learning Center
(www.mhhe.com/unfinishedinteractive)
Explore this rich website, providing additional exploration of the material covered in this chapter, online versions of the interactive maps included on the Primary Source Investigator CD-ROM, as well as several study aids, including a multiple-choice quiz, essay questions, a glossary, and other valuable tools. Also in the Online Learning Center for this chapter look for an *Interactive Feature Essay:*

- **America in the World: Global Migrations**

FOR FURTHER REFERENCE

Lewis Mumford, author of *The City in History* (1961), was America's foremost critic and chronicler of urbanization through the mid-twentieth century. John Bodnar provides a synthetic history of immigration in *The Transplanted: a History of Immigrants in America* (1985), which challenges an earlier classic study by Oscar Handlin, *The Uprooted: The Epic Story of the Great Migrations that Made the American People,* 2nd ed. (1973). Henry Yu, *Thinking Orientals: Migration, Contact, and Exoticism in Modern America* (2001) is a provocative examination of aspects of Asian immigration. Desmond King, *Making Americans: Immigration, Race, and the Origins of Diverse Democracy* (2000) examines responses to immigration. The new urban mass culture of America's cities is the subject of William Leach, *Land of Desire: Merchants, Power, and the Rise of a New American Culture* (1993) and Kathy Peiss, *Cheap Amusements: Working Women and Leisure in Turn-of-the-Century New York* (1986). Sven Beckert, *The Moneyed Metropolis: New York City and the Consolidation of the American Bourgeoisie, 1850–1896* (2001) and Stuart Blumin, *The Emergence of the Middle Class: Social Experience in the American City, 1760–1900* (1989) examine the rise of the urban middle class. Sarah Deutsch, *Women and the City: Gender, Space, and Power in Boston, 1870–1940* (2000), reveals the world of women in the emergence of the modern city. T. J. Jackson Lears, *No Place of Grace: Antimodernism and the Transformation of American Culture, 1880–1920* (1981) chronicles patterns of resistance to the new culture. Roy Rosenzweig and Elizabeth Blackmar, *The Park and the People: A History of Central Park* (1992) studies the creation of America's most famous public park. Edwin G. Burroughs and Mike Wallace, *Gotham: A History of New York City to 1898* (1998) is a thorough history of New York's remarkable growth. Christine Stansell, *American Moderns: Bohemian New York and the Creation of a New Century* (2001) examines the rise of a modern urban sensibility. John F. Kasson, *Amusing the Million: Coney Island at the Turn of the Century* (1978) is an illustrated history and interpretation of the amusement park's place in American culture. *Coney Island* (1991), a film by Ric Burns, presents a colorful history of America's favorite seaside resort. The documentary film *Baseball* (1994) by Ken Burns—and the companion book by the same name, by Geoffrey C. Ward—provide sweeping narratives of the national pastime, its origins in the age of the city, and its wider social context of race relations, immigration, and popular culture. *New York* (1999–2001), a film by Ric Burns, is a sweeping documentary history of the city, accompanied by a companion book, Ric Burns et al., *New York: an Illustrated History* (1999).

19

From Stalemate to Crisis

The enormous changes America was experiencing in the late nineteenth century strained not only the nation's traditional social arrangements but its political institutions as well. Industrialization and urbanization had produced considerable progress, but they had also created disorder and despair. Gradually, Americans began to look to government for leadership in their search for stability and social justice. Yet American government during much of this period responded with apparent passivity and confusion. Its leaders, for the most part, seemed political mediocrities. The issue with which it was concerned were often irrelevant to the nation's most serious problems. Rather than taking active leadership of the nation's dramatic transformation, the American political system for nearly two decades after the end of Reconstruction was locked in a rigid stalemate— watching the remarkable changes that were occurring in the nation and doing little to affect them. The result was a set of problems and grievances that festered and grew without any natural outlet. Thus it was not surprising that in the 1890s the United States entered a period of national crisis.

THE POLITICS OF EQUILIBRIUM

To modern eyes, the nature of the American political system in the late nineteenth century appears paradoxical. The two political parties enjoyed a strength and stability that neither was ever to know again. And yet the federal government was doing little of importance. In fact, most Americans engaged in political activity not because of an interest in particular issues but because of broad regional, ethnic, or religious sentiments.

The Party System

The most striking feature of the late-nineteenth-century party system was its remarkable stability. From the end of Reconstruction until the late 1890s, the electorate was divided evenly between the Republicans and the Democrats. Sixteen states were solidly and consistently Republican, and fourteen states (most of them in the South) were solidly and consistently Democratic. Only five states were usually in doubt, and their voters generally decided the results of national elections. The Republican Party captured the presidency in all but two of the elections of the era, but the party was not really as dominant as those victories suggest. In the five presidential elections beginning in 1876, the average popular-vote margin separating the Democratic and Republican candidates was 1.5 percent. The congressional

Stability and Stalemate

balance was similarly stable, with the Republicans generally controlling the Senate and the Democrats generally controlling the House.

As striking as the balance between the parties was the intensity of public loyalty to them. Voter turnout in presidential elections between 1860 and 1900 averaged over 78 percent of all eligible voters (as compared with only about 50 percent in recent decades). Large groups of potential voters were disfranchised: women in most states; almost all blacks and many poor whites in the South. But for adult white males outside the South, there were few franchise restrictions. The remarkable turnout represented a genuinely mass-based politics.

High Turnout

What explains this extraordinary loyalty to the two political parties? It was not, certainly, that the parties took distinct positions on important public issues. They did so rarely. Party loyalties reflected other factors. Region was perhaps the most important. To white southerners, loyalty to the Democratic Party was a matter of unquestioned faith. It was the vehicle by which they had triumphed over Reconstruction, the vehicle by which they preserved white supremacy. To many northerners, Republican loyalties were equally intense. To them, the party of Lincoln remained a bulwark against slavery and treason.

Religious and ethnic differences also shaped party loyalties. The Democratic Party

Cultural Basis of Party Loyalty

1867	1880	1881	1883	1884	1887	1888
National Grange founded	Garfield elected president	Garfield assassinated Arthur becomes president	Pendleton Act	Cleveland elected president	Interstate Commerce Act	Benjamin Harrison elected president

1890	1892	1893	1894	1896	1990
Sherman Antitrust Act Sherman Silver Purchase Act McKinley Tariff	Cleveland elected president People's Party formed	Economic depression begins Sherman Silver Purchase Act repealed	Coxey's Army	McKinley elected president	Gold Standard Act

TIME LINE

attracted most of the Catholic voters, most of the recent immigrants, and most of the poorer workers. The Republican Party appealed to northern Protestants, citizens of old stock, and much of the middle class. Among the few substantive issues on which the parties took clearly different stands were matters connected with immigrants. Republicans tended to support measures restricting immigration and to favor temperance legislation, which many believed would help discipline immigrant communities. Catholics and immigrants viewed such proposals as assaults on them and their cultures; the Democratic Party followed their lead.

Party identification, then, was usually more a reflection of cultural inclinations than a calculation of economic interest. Individuals might affiliate with a party because their parents had done so, or because it was the party of their region, their church, or their ethnic group.

The National Government

One reason the two parties managed to avoid substantive issues was that the federal government did relatively little. The government in Washington was responsible for delivering the

Weak Federal Government

mails, for maintaining a national military, for conducting foreign policy, and for collecting tariffs and taxes. It had few other responsibilities and few institutions with which it could have undertaken additional responsibilities even if it had chosen to do so.

There was one significant exception. From the end of the Civil War to the early twentieth century, the federal government administered a system of annual pensions for Union Civil War veterans who had retired from work and for their widows. Some reformers hoped to make the system permanent and universal, but their efforts failed, in part because the Civil War pension system was awash in party patronage and corruption. Other reformers—believers in "good government"—saw elimination of the pension system as a way to fight graft, corruption, and party rule. When the Civil War generation died out, the pension system died with it.

In most other respects, the United States in the late nineteenth century was a society without a modern, national government. The most powerful national political institutions were the two political parties. The national leaders of both parties were primarily concerned not with policy but with office—with winning elections and controlling patronage.

Presidents and Patronage

The power of party bosses had an important effect on the power of the presidency. The office had great symbolic importance, but its occupants were unable to do very much except distribute government appointments. A new president and his tiny staff had to make almost 100,000 appointments; and even in that function, presidents had limited latitude, since they had to avoid offending the various factions within their own parties.

Sometimes that proved impossible, as the presidency of Rutherford B. Hayes (1877–1881) demonstrated. By the end of his term, two groups—the Stalwarts, led by Roscoe Conkling of New York, and the Half-Breeds, captained by James G. Blaine of Maine—were competing for control of the Republican Party. Rhetorically, the Stalwarts favored traditional, professional machine politics, while the Half-Breeds favored reform. In fact, both groups were mainly interested in a larger share of the patronage pie.

Stalwarts and Half-Breeds

The battle over patronage overshadowed all else during Hayes's presidency. His one important initiative—an effort to create a civil service system—attracted no support from either party. And his early announcement that he would not seek reelection only weakened him further.

The Republicans managed to retain the presidency in 1880 in part because they agreed on a ticket that included a Stalwart and a Half-Breed. After a long convention deadlock, they nominated James A. Garfield, an Ohio congressman Half-Breed, for president and Chester A. Arthur of New York, a Stalwart, for vice president. The Democrats nominated General Winfield Scott Hancock, a minor Civil War commander with no national following. Benefiting from the end of the recession of 1879, Garfield won a decisive electoral victory, although his popular-vote margin was very thin.

Garfield began his presidency by trying to defy the Stalwarts in his appointments. He soon found himself embroiled in an ugly public quarrel with both Conkling and other Stalwarts. It was never resolved. On July 2, 1881, only four months after his inauguration, Garfield was shot twice while standing in the Washington railroad station by an apparently deranged gunman (and unsuccessful office seeker) who shouted, "I am a Stalwart and Arthur is president now!" Garfield lingered for nearly three months but finally died.

Garfield Assassinated

Chester A. Arthur, who succeeded Garfield, had spent a political lifetime as a close ally of Roscoe Conkling. But on becoming president, he tried—like Hayes and Garfield before him—to follow an independent course. To the dismay of the Stalwarts, Arthur kept most of Garfield's appointees in office and supported civil service reform. In 1883, Congress passed the first national civil service measure, the

REVOLT AMONG REPUBLICANS Many Republican reformers, believers in "good government," were aghast when their party nominated James G. Blaine for president in 1884. Blaine, a former Speaker of the House, U. S. senator, and secretary of state, was controversial after a long career of wily political maneuvering and because of the scandals that continually attached themselves to his name. This cartoon by Joseph Keppler in the political magazine *Puck* shows Republican leaders responding with horror to "the writing on the wall," and to the dire consequences they believed would follow the nomination of Blaine. *(New York Public Library)*

| Pendleton Act | Pendleton Act, which required that some federal jobs be filled by competitive written examinations rather than by patronage. Relatively few offices fell under civil service at first, but by the mid-twentieth century most federal employees were civil servants.

Cleveland, Harrison, and the Tariff

In the election of 1884, the Republican candidate was Senator James G. Blaine of Maine—known to some as "the Plumed Knight" but to others as a symbol of seamy party politics. A group of "liberal Republicans," known by their critics as "mugwumps," announced they would bolt the party and support an honest Democrat. Rising to the bait, the Democrats nominated Grover Cleveland, the "reform" governor of New York.

In a campaign filled with personal invective, what may have decided the election was the last-minute introduction of a religious controversy. Shortly before the election, a delegation of Protestant ministers called on Blaine in New York City; their spokesman, Dr. Samuel Burchard, referred to the Democrats as the party of "rum, Romanism, and rebellion." Blaine was slow to repudiate Burchard's indiscretion, and Democrats quickly spread the news that Blaine had tolerated a slander on the Catholic Church. Cleveland's

| Cleveland Elected | narrow victory was probably a result of an unusually heavy Catholic vote for the Democrats in New York.

Grover Cleveland was respected for his opposition to politicians, grafters, pressure groups, and Tammany Hall. He was the embodiment of an era in which few Americans believed the federal government could, or should, do very much. Cleveland had always doubted the wisdom of protective tariffs (taxes on imported goods designed to protect domestic producers). The existing high rates, he believed, were responsible for the annual surplus in federal revenues, which was tempting Congress to pass "reckless" and "extravagant" legislation, which he frequently vetoed. In December 1887, therefore, he asked Congress to reduce the tariff rates. Democrats in the House approved a tariff reduction, but Senate Republicans defiantly passed a bill of their own actually raising the rates. The resulting deadlock made the tariff an issue in the election of 1888.

The Democrats renominated Cleveland and supported tariff reductions. The Republicans settled on former senator Benjamin Harrison of Indiana, who was obscure but respectable; and they endorsed protection. | Election of 1888 | The campaign was the first since the Civil War to involve a clear question of economic difference between the parties. Harrison won an electoral majority of 233 to 168, but Cleveland's popular vote exceeded Harrison's by 100,000.

New Public Issues

Benjamin Harrison had few visible convictions, and he made no effort to influence Congress. And yet during Harrison's passive administration, public opinion was beginning to force the government to confront some of the pressing social and economic issues of the day. Most notably, perhaps, sentiment was rising in favor of legislation to curb the power of trusts.

By the mid-1880s, fifteen western and southern states had adopted laws prohibiting combinations that restrained competition. But corporations found it easy to escape limitations by incorporating in states such as New Jersey and Delaware that offered them special privileges. If antitrust legislation was to be effective, its supporters believed, it would have to come from the national government. Responding to growing popular demands, both houses of Congress passed the Sherman Antitrust Act in July 1890, al- | Sherman Antitrust Act | most without dissent. But for over a decade after its passage, the Sherman Act—indifferently enforced and steadily weakened by the courts—had virtually no impact. As of 1901, the Justice Department had instituted many antitrust suits against unions, but only fourteen against business combinations; there had been few convictions.

The Republicans were more interested in the tariff. | Tariff Rates Raised | Representative William McKinley of Ohio and Senator Nelson W. Aldrich of Rhode Island drafted the highest protective measure ever proposed to Congress. Known as the McKinley Tariff, it became law in October 1890. But Republican leaders apparently misinterpreted public sentiment, for the party suffered a stunning reversal in the 1890 congressional election. The Republicans' substantial Senate majority was slashed to 8; in the House, the party retained only 88 of the 323 seats. Nor were the Republicans able to recover in the course of the next two years. In the presidential election of 1892, Benjamin Harrison once again supported protection; Grover Cleveland, renominated by the Democrats, once again opposed it. A new third party, the People's Party, with James B. Weaver as its candidate, advocated more substantial economic reform. Cleveland won 277 electoral votes to Harrison's 145 and had a popular margin of 380,000. Weaver showed some significant strength, but still ran far behind. For the first time since 1878, the Democrats won a majority of both houses of Congress.

The policies of Cleveland's second term were much like those of his first—hostile to active efforts to deal with social or economic problems. Again, he supported a tariff reduction, which the House approved but the Senate weakened. Cleveland denounced the result but allowed it to become law as the Wilson-Gorman Tariff.

But public pressure was growing in the 1880s for other reforms, among them regulation of the railroads. Farm organizations in the Midwest (most notably the Grangers) had persuaded several state legislatures to pass regulatory legislation in the early 1870s. But in 1886, the Supreme Court ruled one of the Granger Laws in Illinois unconstitutional. According to the Court, the law was an attempt to control interstate commerce and thus infringed on the exclusive power of Congress. Later, the courts limited the powers of the states to regulate commerce even within their own boundaries.

Effective railroad regulation, it was now clear, could come only from the federal government. Congress grudgingly responded to public pressure in 1887 with the Interstate Commerce Act, which banned discrimination in rates between long and short hauls, required that railroads publish their rate schedules and file them with the government, and declared that all interstate rail rates must be "reasonable and just." A five-person agency, the Interstate Commerce Commission (ICC), was to administer the act. But it had to rely on the courts to enforce its rulings. For almost twenty years after its passage, the Interstate Commerce Act—which was, like the Sherman Act, haphazardly enforced and narrowly interpreted by the courts—was without much practical effect.

Interstate Commerce Act

THE AGRARIAN REVOLT

No group watched the performance of the federal government in the 1880s with more dismay than American farmers. The serious problems that afflicted them helped produce one of the most powerful movements of political protest in American history: what became known as Populism.

The Grangers

The first major farm organization was the National Grange of the Patrons of Husbandry, founded in 1867. From it emerged a network of local organizations that tried to teach new scientific agricultural techniques to members. But when the depression of 1873 caused a sharp decline in farm prices, membership rapidly increased and the direction of the organization changed. Granges in the Midwest began to organize marketing cooperatives, and they promoted political action to curb the monopolistic practices of the railroads and warehouses. At their peak, Grange supporters controlled the legislatures in most of the midwestern states. The result was the Granger Laws of the early 1870s, by which many states imposed strict regulations on railroad rates and practices. But the destruction of the new regulations by the courts, combined with the political inexperience of many Grange leaders and the return of prosperity in the late 1870s, produced a dramatic decline in the power of the association by the end of the decade.

National Grange of the Patrons of Husbandry

The Alliances

The successor to the Granges began to emerge even before the Granger movement had faded. As early as 1875, farmers in parts of the South were banding together in so-called Farmers' Alliances. By 1880, the Southern Alliance had more than 4 million members; and a comparable Northwestern Alliance was taking root in the plains states and the Midwest.

Like the Granges, the Alliances established stores, banks, processing plants, and other facilities for their members—to free them from dependence on the hated "furnishing merchants" who kept so many farmers in debt. Some Alliance leaders, however, saw the movement in larger terms: as an effort to build a new kind of society in

Social Goals of the Farmers' Alliances

which economic competition might give way to co-operation. Alliance lecturers traveled throughout rural areas lambasting the concentrated power of the great corporations and financial institutions.

Although the Alliances quickly became far more widespread than the Granges had ever been, their cooperatives did not always work well, partly because the market forces operating against them were sometimes too strong to be overcome and partly because the cooperatives themselves were often mismanaged. These economic frustrations helped push the movement into a new phase: the creation of a national political organization.

In 1889, the Southern and Northwestern Alliances agreed to a loose merger. The next year the Alliances held a national convention at Ocala, Florida, and produced a statement of their goals known as the Ocala Demands. In the 1890 off-year elections, candidates supported by the Alliances won partial or complete control of the legislatures in twelve states. They also won six governorships, three seats in the Senate, and approximately fifty in the House of Representatives. Dissident farmers drew enough encouragement from the results to contemplate further political action.

Alliance leaders discussed plans for a third party at meetings in Cincinnati in May 1891 and St. Louis in February 1892. Then, in July 1892, 1,300 delegates poured into Omaha, Nebraska, to proclaim the creation of the new party, approve an official set of principles, and nominate candidates for the presidency and vice presidency. The new organization's official name was the People's Party, but it was commonly referred to as Populism.

People's Party Established

The election of 1892 demonstrated the potential power of the new movement. The Populist presidential candidate—James B. Weaver of Iowa—polled more than 1 million votes. Nearly 1,500 Populist candidates won election to state legislatures and local offices. The party elected three governors, five senators, and ten congressmen. It could also claim the support of many Republicans and Democrats in Congress who had been elected by appealing to Populist sentiment.

The Populist Constituency

Populism's Limited Appeal

Already, however, there were signs of the limits of Populist strength. Populism had great appeal to farmers, particularly small farmers. But Populism failed to move much beyond that group. Its leaders made energetic efforts to include labor within the coalition. In addition to courting the Knights of Labor, the new party added a labor plank to its platform—calling for shorter hours for workers and restrictions on immigration, and denouncing the use of private detective agencies as strikebreakers. But Populism never attracted any substantial labor support, in part because the economic interests of labor and the interests of farmers were often at odds.

In the South in particular, white Populists struggled with the question of accepting African Americans in the party. Indeed there was an important black component to the movement—a network of "Colored Alliances" that by 1890 numbered over 1.25 million members. But most white Populists were willing to accept the assistance of blacks only as long as it was clear that whites would remain indisputably in control. When southern conservatives began to attack the Populists for undermining white supremacy, the interracial character of the movement quickly faded.

Populist Ideas

The Populists spelled out their program of reform first in the Ocala Demands of 1890 and then, even more clearly, in the Omaha platform of 1892. They proposed a system of "subtreasuries," a network of government-owned ware-houses, where farmers could deposit their crops. Using those crops as collateral, growers could then borrow money from the government at low rates of interest and wait for the price of their goods to go up before selling them. In addition, the Populists called for the abolition of national banks; the end of absentee ownership of land; the direct election of United States senators (which would weaken the power of conservative state legislatures); and other devices to improve the ability of the people to influence the political process. They called as well for regulation or government ownership of railroads, telephones, and telegraphs. And they demanded a system of government-operated postal savings banks, a graduated income tax, the inflation of the currency, and, later, the remonetization of silver.

The Populists' Reform Program

Some Populists were openly anti-Semitic. Others were anti-intellectual, antieastern, and antiurban.

But bigotry was not the dominant force behind Populism. The movement was a serious effort to find solutions to real problems. Populism was less a critique of capitalism than a challenge to what the Populists considered the brutal and chaotic way in which the economy was developing. Progress and growth should continue, they urged, but should be strictly defined by the needs of individuals and com-munities. Visit Chapter 19 of the book's Online Learning Center for a Where Historians Disagree essay on "Populism."

THE CRISIS OF THE 1890s

The rising agrarian protest was only one of many indications of the national political crisis emerging in the 1890s. There was a severe depression, which began in 1893. There was widespread labor unrest. There was the failure of either major party to respond to the growing distress. And there was the rigid conservatism of Grover Cleveland, who took office for the second time just when the economy collapsed.

The Panic of 1893
The Panic of 1893 precipitated the most severe depression the nation had ever experienced. It began in March 1893, when the Philadelphia and Reading Railroads declared bankruptcy, unable to meet demands for payment by British banks from which they had borrowed large sums. Two months later, the National Cordage Company failed as well. Together, the two corporate failures triggered a collapse of the stock market. And since many of the major New York banks were heavy investors in the market, a wave of bank failures soon began. That caused a contraction of credit, which meant that many businesses went bankrupt.

| America's Interconnected Economy |

The depression reflected, among other things, the degree to which all parts of the American economy were now interconnected. And the depression showed how dependent the economy was on the health of the railroads. When the railroads suffered, everything suffered.

Once the panic began, its effects spread with startling speed. Within six months, more than 8,000 businesses, 156 railroads, and 400 banks failed. Already low agricultural prices tumbled further. Up to 1 million workers lost their jobs. The depression was unprecedented not only in its severity but also in its persistence. Although there was slight improvement beginning in 1895, prosperity did not fully return until after 1898.

In 1894, Jacob S. Coxey, an Ohio businessman and Populist, began advocating an inflation of the currency and a massive public works program to create jobs for the unemployed. When it became clear that his proposals were making no progress in Congress, Coxey organized a march of the unemployed (known as "Coxey's Army") to Washington to present his demands to the government. Congress took no action on the demands.

There were major labor upheavals as well during the decade—of which the Homestead and Pullman strikes were only the most

| Homestead and Pullman Strikes |

prominent examples. To many middle-class Americans, the worker unrest was a sign of dangerous social instability, even perhaps a revolution. Labor radicalism was seldom far from the public mind.

The Silver Question
Populists, and many others, blamed the depression on an inadequate supply of money. Conservatives blamed it on a lack of commitment to a "sound currency." The "money question," therefore, became one of the burning issues of the era.

The heart of the debate was over what would form the basis of the dollar, what would lie behind it and give it value. Most people assumed that currency was worthless if there was not something concrete behind it—precious metal (specie), which holders of paper money could collect if they presented their currency to a bank or to the Treasury.

During most of its existence as a nation, the United States had recognized two metals—gold and silver—as a basis for the dollar, a formula known as "bimetallism." In the 1870s, however, that had

| "Bimetallism" |

changed. The official ratio of the value of silver to the value of gold for purposes of creating currency (the "mint ratio") was 16 to 1: sixteen ounces of silver equaled one ounce of gold. But the actual commercial value of silver was much higher than that. Owners of silver could get more by selling it for

COXEY'S ARMY Jacob S. Coxey's "army" of the unemployed marches toward Washington in 1894 to demand relief from the federal government. Although several thousand people started out from various parts of the country to join the army, only about 400 actually reached the Capital. The protest disbanded after Coxey and several others were arrested for "trespassing" on the grounds of the United States Capitol. *(Culver Pictures, Inc.)*

manufacture into jewelry and other objects than they could by taking it to the mint for conversion to coins. So they stopped taking it to the mint, and the mint stopped coining silver.

In 1873, Congress passed a law officially discontinuing silver coinage. Few objected at the time. But later in the 1870s, the market value of silver fell well below the official mint ratio. Silver was suddenly available for coinage again, and it soon became clear that Congress had foreclosed a potential method of expanding the currency. Before long, many Americans concluded that a conspiracy of bankers had been responsible for the "demonetization" of silver, and they referred to the law as the "Crime of '73."

Two groups of Americans were especially determined to undo the "Crime of '73." One consisted of silver-mine owners and their allies, now eager to have the government take their surplus silver and pay them much more than the market price. The other group consisted of farmers, who wanted an increase in the quantity of money—an inflation of the currency—as a means of raising the prices of farm products and easing payment of debts. The inflationists demanded that the government return at once to "free silver"—that is,

"Free Silver"

to the "free and unlimited coinage of silver" at the old ratio of 16 to 1. Congress responded with the Sherman Silver Purchase Act of 1890, which required the government to purchase (but not coin) silver and pay for it in gold.

At the same time, the nation's gold reserves were steadily dropping. And the Panic of 1893 intensified the demands on those reserves. President Cleveland believed that the chief cause of the weakening gold reserves was the Sherman Silver Purchase Act. Early in his second administration,

Sherman Silver Purchase Act Repealed

therefore, Congress responded to his request and repealed the act—although only after a bitter and divisive battle.

"A Cross of Gold"

Republicans, watching the failure of Cleveland and the Democrats to deal effectively with the depression, were confident of success in 1896. Party leaders settled on former congressman William McKinley,

McKinley Nominated

author of the 1890 tariff act and now governor of Ohio, as the party's presidential candidate. The tariff, they believed, should be the principal issue in the campaign. But their platform also opposed the free coinage of silver. Thirty-four delegates from the mountain and plains states walked out in protest and joined the Democratic Party.

The Democratic convention of 1896 was unusually tumultuous. Southern and western delegates, eager for a way to compete with the Populists, were determined to seize control of the party from conservative easterners and incorporate some Populist demands—among them free silver—into the Democratic platform. They wanted as well to nominate a pro-silver candidate. The divided platform committee presented two reports to the convention. The majority report, the work of westerners and southerners, called for tariff reduction, an income tax, "stricter control" of trusts and railroads, and free silver. The minority report, the product of the party's eastern wing, opposed the free coinage of silver.

Defenders of the gold standard seemed to prevail in the debate, until the final speech. Then William Jennings Bryan, a handsome, thirty-six-year-old congressman from Nebraska, delivered a defense of free silver that became one of the most famous political speeches in American history. The closing passage sent his audience into a frenzy: "If they dare to come out in the open and defend the gold standard as a good thing, we will fight them to the uttermost. Having behind us the producing masses of this nation and the world, supported by the commercial interests, the laboring interests and the toilers everywhere, we will answer their demand for a gold standard by saying to them: 'You shall not press down upon

"Cross of Gold" Speech

the brow of labor this crown of thorns; you shall not crucify mankind upon a cross of gold.'" It became known as the "Cross of Gold" speech.

In the glow of Bryan's speech, the convention voted to adopt the pro-silver platform. Perhaps more important, the agrarians embraced Bryan as their leader. The following day, Bryan was nominated for president.

The Populists had expected both major parties to adopt conservative programs and nominate conservative candidates, leaving the Populists to represent the growing forces of protest. But now the Democrats had stolen much of their thunder. The Populists faced the choice of naming their own candidate and splitting the protest vote or endorsing Bryan and losing their identity as a party. Many Populists argued that "fusion"

"Fusion"

with the Democrats would destroy their party. But the majority concluded that there was no viable alternative. Amid considerable acrimony, the convention voted to support Bryan.

The Conservative Victory

The business and financial community contributed lavishly to the Republican campaign in 1896. From his home at Canton, Ohio, McKinley conducted a dignified "front-porch" campaign before pilgrimages

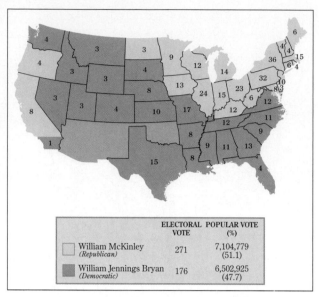

	ELECTORAL VOTE	POPULAR VOTE (%)
☐ William McKinley *(Republican)*	271	7,104,779 (51.1)
■ William Jennings Bryan *(Democratic)*	176	6,502,925 (47.7)

ELECTION OF 1896 The results of the presidential election of 1896 are, as this map shows, striking for the regional differentiation they reveal. William McKinley won the election by a comfortable but not enormous margin, but his victory was not broad-based. He carried all the states of the Northeast and the industrial Midwest, along with California and Oregon, but virtually nothing else. Bryan carried the entire South and almost all of the agrarian West. ▌ *What campaign issues in 1896 help account for the regional character of the results?*

For an interactive version of this map go to www.mhhe.com/unfinishedinteractive

of the Republican faithful, customary behavior in an age when many Americans considered it undignified for anyone to campaign too openly for the presidency.

Bryan showed no such restraint. He became the first presidential candidate in

Emergence of Modern Campaigning

American history to stump the country systematically. He traveled 18,000 miles (mostly in the West and South) and addressed an estimated 5 million people. His revivalistic, camp-meeting style pleased old-stock Protestants, but it alienated many of the immigrant Catholics and other ethnics who normally voted Democratic. Employers, meanwhile, warned workers that a Bryan victory would cost them their jobs.

On election day, McKinley polled 271 electoral votes to Bryan's 176 and received 51.1 percent of the popular vote to Bryan's 47.7. Bryan carried only those areas of the South and West where miners or struggling staple farmers predominated. For the

| Demise of the Populist Party |

Populists and their allies, the election results were a disaster. They had gambled everything on their "fusion" with the Democratic Party and lost. Within months of the election, the People's Party began to dissolve.

McKinley and Prosperity

The administration of William McKinley saw a return to relative calm. McKinley and his allies worked actively on only one issue: the need for higher tariff rates. Within weeks of McKinley's inauguration, the administration won approval of the Dingley Tariff, raising duties to the highest point in American history. The administration dealt more gingerly with the explosive silver question. McKinley sent a commission to Europe to

| Gold Standard Act |

explore the possibility of an agreement with Great Britain and France on free coinage of silver. As he and everyone else anticipated, the effort produced no agreement. The Republicans then enacted the Currency, or Gold Standard, Act of 1900, which confirmed the nation's commitment to the gold standard.

And so the "battle of the standards" ended in victory for the forces of conservatism. Economic developments at the time seemed to vindicate them. Prosperity returned beginning in 1898. Foreign crop failures sent United States farm prices surging upward, and American business entered another cycle of booming expansion. Prosperity and the gold standard, it seemed, were closely allied.

But while the free-silver movement had failed, it had raised an important question for the American economy. In the quarter-century before 1900, the nations of the Western world had experienced a spectacular growth in productive facilities and population. Yet the supply of money had not kept pace with economic progress. Had it not been for a dramatic increase in the gold supply in the late 1890s, Populist predictions of financial disaster might in fact have proved correct. In 1898, two and a half times as much gold was produced as in 1890, and the currency supply was soon inflated far beyond anything Bryan and the free-silver forces had proposed.

By then, however, Bryan—like many other Americans—was becoming engaged with another major issue: the nation's growing involvement in world affairs and its increasing flirtation with imperialism.

For nearly three decades after the battles over Reconstruction, the electorate was relatively evenly divided between the two major parties, which differed with one another on only a few issues. The national government, never fully dominated by either party, remained small and inconsequential. Except for Indian tribes, people engaged in international trade (who were thus subject to tariffs), and the many northern Civil War veterans who received federal pensions, few Americans had any direct contact with the government in Washington except to receive mail from the federal post office.

Beneath the placid surface of national politics, however, great social issues were creating deep divisions in American life. Battles between employers and workers intensified. American farmers became increasingly resentful of their declining fortunes. Men and women throughout the country grew angry about corruption in government and excessive power in the hands of a few corporate leaders. When a great depression began in 1893, these social tensions exploded to the surface.

The most visible sign of the challenge to politics was the Populist movement. The Populists created their own political party, showed impressive strength in several elections, and then—in 1896— joined with the Democrats to nominate William Jennings Bryan for president. But the forces for insurgency were no match for the forces of established institutions. After a campaign notable for its hysterical attacks on Bryan and "free silver" (making silver a basis for issuing currency in addition to

CONCLUSION

gold), Bryan lost the election to William McKinley. Perhaps more important, the election became the occasion for an electoral realignment that left the Republicans the clear majority party for the next three decades.

The Republican victory did not, however, end the battle over power and corruption in American life. It simply redirected it into other channels. The challenges to the old politics soon made themselves felt as more conventional reform movements that became known, collectively, as progressivism.

INTERACTIVE LEARNING

On the ***Primary Source Investigator CD-ROM,*** check out a number of valuable tools for further exploration of the content of this chapter.

Interactive Map
- U.S. Elections (Map M7)

Primary Sources
Documents, images, and maps related to the political and economic turmoil of the 1890s. Some highlights include:

- Excerpts from the Interstate Commerce Act

- The Sherman Antitrust Act

*Online Learning Center
(www.mhhe.com/unfinishedinteractive)*
Explore this rich website, providing additional exploration of the material covered in this chapter, online versions of the interactive maps included on the Primary Source Investigator CD-ROM, as well as several study aids, including a multiple-choice quiz, essay questions, a glossary, and other valuable tools. Also in the Online Learning Center for this chapter, look for an *Interactive Feature Essay:*

- **Where Historians Disagree: Populism**

FOR FURTHER REFERENCE

Morton Keller, *Affairs of State: Public Life in Late Nineteenth-Century America* (1977) is an important study of politics and government after Reconstruction. Nell Irvin Painter, *Standing at Armageddon: The United States, 1877–1919* (1987) explores the multicultural dimensions of industrialization, emphasizing the particularly cataclysmic effect of industrialization on minority populations and on race relations. Martin J. Sklar, *The Corporate Reconstruction of American Capitalism, 1890–1916* (1988), offers an interpretation of the evolution of American business practice and, by extension, American politics and society. Two significant books charting the growing capacities of the American state during this period are Theda Skocpol, *Protecting Soldiers and Mothers: The Political*

Origins of Social Policy in the United States (1992) and Stephen Skowronek, *Building a New American State: The Expansion of National Administrative Capacities, 1877–1920* (1982). Richard Hofstadter's *The Age of Reform: From Bryan to FDR* (1955) and Lawrence Goodwyn's *The Populist Moment* (1978) offer sharply contrasting characterizations of the Populist and progressive reform movements of this time. Other important studies of Populism include John D. Hicks, *The Populist Revolt* (1931), a classic account, and Steven Hahn, *The Roots of Southern Populism: Yeoman Farmers and the Transformation of the Georgia Upcountry* (1983). Michael Kazin, *The Populist Persuasion: An American History* (1995) places Populist ideas in a broad historical context.

20

The Imperial Republic

(CORBIS)

Throughout the first half of the nineteenth century, the government, through purchase or conquest, had continually acquired new lands: the trans-Appalachian West, the Louisiana Territory, Florida, Texas, Oregon, California, New Mexico, Alaska. It was the nation's "Manifest Destiny," many Americans believed, to expand into new realms.

In the last years of the nineteenth century, with little room left for territorial growth on the North American continent, those who favored expansion set their eyes beyond the nation's shore. The United States began to consider joining England, France, Germany, and others in the great imperial drive that was bringing much of the nonindustrial world under the control of the industrial powers of the West.

STIRRINGS OF IMPERIALISM

For over two decades after the Civil War, the United States expanded geographically hardly at all. By the 1890s, however, some Americans were ready—indeed, eager—to resume the course of Manifest Destiny that had inspired their ancestors to wrest an empire from Mexico.

The New Manifest Destiny

Several developments helped shift American attention to lands across the seas. The experience of sub-

Sources of Imperialism

jugating the Indian tribes had established a precedent for exerting colonial control over dependent peoples. The supposed "closing of the frontier" produced fears that natural resources would soon dwindle. The depression that began in 1893 encouraged some businessmen to look for new markets abroad. Americans were, moreover, well aware of the imperialist fever that was raging through Europe. It was leading the major powers to partition most of Africa among themselves and to turn covetous eyes on the Far East and the feeble Chinese Empire. Some Americans feared that their nation would be left out.

Scholars and others found a philosophic justification for expansionism in Charles Darwin's theories. They contended that nations or "races," like biological species, struggled constantly for existence and that only the fittest could survive. For strong nations to dominate weak ones was, therefore, in accordance with the laws of nature.

Alfred Thayer Mahan

The ablest and most effective advocate of imperialism

was Alfred Thayer Mahan, a captain and later admiral in the navy. Mahan's thesis—presented in *The Influence of Sea Power upon History* (1890) and other works—was simple: Countries with sea power were the great nations of history. Mahan believed America should, at the least, acquire defensive bases in the Caribbean and the Pacific and take possession of Hawaii and other Pacific islands. He feared that the United States did not have a large enough navy to play the great role he envisioned. But during the 1870s and 1880s, the government launched a shipbuilding program that by 1898 had moved the United States to fifth place among the world's naval powers, and by 1900 to third.

Hemispheric Hegemony

James G. Blaine, who served as secretary of state in the Republican administrations of the 1880s, led the early efforts to expand American influence into Latin America. In October 1889, he helped organize the first Pan-American Congress, which attracted delegates from nineteen nations. They agreed to create the Pan-American Union, an organization that served as a clearinghouse for distributing information to the member nations. But they rejected Blaine's more substantive proposals: an inter-American customs union and arbitration procedures for hemispheric disputes.

The second Cleveland administration also took a lively interest in Latin America. In 1895, it supported

Venezuelan Dispute

Venezuela in a dispute with Great Britain over the boundary between Venezuela and British Guiana. When the British ignored American demands that

1875	1878	1887	1889	1890	1893	1895
Reciprocity treaty with Hawaii	U.S. gains base at Pago Pago	U.S. gains base at Pearl Harbor	First Pan-American Congress	Mahan's *The Influence of Sea Power upon History*	Revolution in Hawaii	Venezuelan boundary dispute

1898	1898–1902	1899	1990	1901	1946
Battleship *Maine* sunk

War with Spain

Treaty of Paris

U.S. annexes Hawaii, Philippines, Puerto Rico | Philippines revolt | Open Door notes | Boxer Rebellion

McKinley reelected | Platt Amendment | U.S. grants Philippines independence |

TIME LINE

the matter be submitted to arbitration, the Cleveland administration began threatening England with war. The British government finally realized that it had stumbled into a genuine diplomatic crisis and agreed to arbitration.

Hawaii and Samoa

Hawaii Coveted The islands of Hawaii in the mid-Pacific had been an important way station for American ships in the China trade since the early nineteenth century. By the 1880s, the navy was looking covetously at Pearl Harbor on the island of Oahu as a possible base for American ships. Pressure for an increased American presence in Hawaii was emerging from another source as well: the growing number of Americans living on the islands.

Settled by Polynesian people beginning in about 1500 B.C., Hawaii had developed an agricultural and fishing society in which different islands lived more or less self-sufficiently. When the first Americans arrived in Hawaii in the 1790s on merchant ships from New England, there were perhaps a half-million people living there.

Battles among rival communities were frequent, as ambitious chieftains tried to consolidate power over their neighbors. In 1810, after a series of such battles, King Kamehameha I established his dominance over the other chieftains on Hawaii. He welcomed American traders and helped them develop a thriving trade between Hawaii and China. But Americans soon wanted more than trade. Missionaries began settling there in the early nineteenth century, and in the 1830s, William Hooper, a Boston trader, became the first of many Americans to buy land and establish a sugar plantation on the islands.

The arrival of these merchants, missionaries, and planters was devastating to **Growing American Dominance** native Hawaiian society. The newcomers inadvertently brought infectious diseases to which the Hawaiians were tragically vulnerable. By the mid-nineteenth century, more than half the native population had died. But the Americans brought other incursions as well. Missionaries worked to replace native religion with Christianity. Other white settlers introduced liquor, firearms, and a commercial economy, all of which eroded the traditional character of Hawaiian society. By the 1840s, American planters had spread throughout the islands; and an American settler, G. P. Judd, had become prime minister of

Hawaii under King Kamehameha III, who had agreed to establish a constitutional monarchy.

In 1887, the United States negotiated a treaty with Hawaii that permitted it to open a naval base at Pearl Harbor. By then, growing sugar for export to America had become the basis of the Hawaiian economy—as a result of an 1875 agreement allowing Hawaiian sugar to enter the United States duty-free. The American-dominated sugar plantation system displaced native Hawaiians from their lands and relied heavily for workers on Asian immigrants.

Native Hawaiians did not accept these changes
Queen Liliuokalani
without protest. In 1891, they elevated a powerful nationalist to the throne: Queen Liliuokalani. But her brief reign coincided with newly militant efforts by the Americans to seize power. In 1890, Congress had eliminated the 1875 exemption from tariffs for Hawaiian sugar planters. The result was devastating to the economy of the islands. American planters concluded that the only way to recover was to become part of the United States (and hence exempt from its tariffs). In 1893 they staged a revolution and called on the United States for protection. After the American minister ordered marines from a warship in Honolulu harbor to go ashore to aid the rebels, the queen yielded her authority.

A provisional government, dominated by Americans, immediately sent a dele-
Hawaii Annexed
gation to Washington to negotiate a treaty of annexation. Debate over the treaty continued until 1898, when Congress finally approved the agreement.

Three thousand miles south of Hawaii, the Samoan islands had also long served as a port for American ships in the Pacific trade. As American commerce with Asia increased, the American navy began eyeing the Samoan harbor at Pago Pago. In 1878, the Hayes administration extracted a treaty from Samoan leaders for an American naval station there. It bound the United States to arbitrate any differences between Samoa and other nations.

But Great Britain and Germany were also interested in the islands, and they too secured treaty rights from the native princes. For the next ten years the three powers jockeyed for dominance in Samoa. Finally, they agreed to create a tripartite protectorate, with the native chiefs exercising only nominal authority. The arrangement failed to halt the rivalries of its members, and in 1899, the United States and Germany divided the islands between them, compensating Britain with territories elsewhere in the Pacific. The United States retained the harbor at Pago Pago. For an America in the World feature essay on "Imperialism," visit Chapter 20 of the book's Online Learning Center.

WAR WITH SPAIN

Imperial ambitions had thus begun to stir within the United States well before the late 1890s. But a war with Spain in 1898 turned those stirrings into overt expansionism.

Controversy over Cuba

The Spanish-American War emerged out of events in Cuba. Cubans had been resisting Spanish rule intermittently since at least 1868, when they began a long but unsuccessful fight for independence. Many Americans had sympathized with the Cubans during that first ten-year struggle, but the United States did not intervene.

In 1895, the Cubans rose up again. This rebellion pro-
Cuban Revolt
duced a ferocity on both sides that horrified Americans. The Cubans deliberately devastated the island to force the Spaniards to leave. The Spanish, commanded by General Valeriano Weyler (known in the American press as "Butcher" Weyler), confined civilians in certain areas to hastily prepared concentration camps, where they died by the thousands, victims of disease and malnutrition. The Spanish had used equally savage methods during the earlier struggle in Cuba without shocking American sensibilities. But the revolt of 1895 attracted unprecedented attention in the United States. That was partly because a growing population of Cuban émigrés in the United States gave extensive support to the Cuban Revolutionary Party (whose headquarters was in New York). They helped publicize its leader, José Martí, who was killed in Cuba in 1895. Later, Cuban Americans formed other clubs and associations to support the cause of *Cuba Libre* (Free Cuba).

But it was also because the events in Cuba were reported more fully and flamboyantly by American

THE YELLOW PRESS AND THE WRECK OF THE *MAINE* No evidence was ever found tying the Spanish to the explosion in Havana harbor that destroyed the American battleship *Maine* in February 1898. Indeed, most evidence indicated that the blast came from inside the ship, a fact that suggests an accident rather than sabotage. Nevertheless, newspapers ran sensational stories about the incident that were designed to arouse public sentiment in support of a war against the Spanish. This front-page from Pulitzer's New York *World* is an example of the lurid coverage the event received. *(The Granger Collection, New York)*

"Yellow Press" newspapers, and particularly by the new "yellow press" of William Randolph Hearst and Joseph Pulitzer. Pulitzer's *World*, which began publishing in New York in 1883, launched the age of yellow journalism—a term probably derived originally from the *World*'s lavish use of color, especially yellow. But before long, the term came to be used to describe a sensationalist style of reporting and writing, and a self-conscious effort to reach a mass market. The success of the *World*, whose circulation reached 250,000 by 1886, spawned imitators. Most prominent among them was Hearst's *New York Journal*, which cut its price to one cent after Hearst bought it in 1895, copied many of the *World*'s techniques, and within a year raised its circulation to 400,000. The competition between these two great "yellow" journals soon drove both to new levels of sensationalism. Their success inspired newspapers in other cities around the nation to copy their techniques.

The civil war in Cuba gave both papers their best opportunities yet for combining sensational reporting with shameless appeals to patriotism and moral outrage. They avidly published exaggerated reports of Spanish atrocities against the Cuban rebels. When the American battleship *Maine* mysteriously exploded in Havana harbor in 1898, both papers immediately blamed Spanish authorities (without any evidence). The *Journal* offered a $50,000 reward for information leading to the conviction of those responsible for the explosion. In the three days following the *Maine* explosion, the *Journal* sold over 3 million copies, a new world's record for newspaper circulation. The *World* exploited the destruction of the *Maine* less successfully, but it soon made up for it in its highly sensationalized coverage of the war itself. Hearst boasted at times that the conflict in Cuba was "the *Journal*'s war" and even sent a cable to one of his reporters in Cuba saying: "You furnish the pictures, and I'll furnish the war."

Despite the mounting storm of indignation against Spain, President Cleveland refused to intervene in the conflict. But when McKinley became president in 1897, he formally protested Spain's "uncivilized and inhuman" conduct, causing the Spanish government (fearful of American intervention) to recall Weyler, modify the concentration policy, and grant the island a qualified autonomy.

But whatever chances there were for a peaceful settlement vanished as a result of two dramatic incidents in February 1898. The first occurred when a Cuban agent stole a private letter written by Dupuy de Lôme, the Spanish minister in Washington, and turned

de Lôme Letter

it over to the American press. It described McKinley as a weak man and "a bidder for the admiration of the crowd." This was no more than what many Americans, including some Republicans, were saying about their president. But coming from a foreigner, it created intense popular anger. Dupuy de Lôme promptly resigned.

The *Maine*

While excitement over the de Lôme letter was still high, the American battleship *Maine* blew up in Havana harbor with a loss of more than 260 people. Many Americans assumed that the Spanish had sunk the ship, particularly when a naval court of inquiry reported that an external explosion by a submarine mine had caused the disaster. (Later evidence suggested that the disaster was actually the result of an accidental explosion inside one of the engine rooms.) War hysteria swept the country, and Congress unanimously appropriated $50 million for military preparations.

McKinley still hoped to avoid a conflict. But others in his administration (including Theodore Roosevelt) were clamoring for war. In March 1898, at McKinley's request, Spain agreed to stop the fighting and eliminate its concentration camps; but it refused to negotiate with the rebels and reserved the right to resume hostilities at its discretion. That satisfied neither public opinion nor Congress. A few days later, McKinley asked for and, on April 25, received a congressional declaration of war.

"A Splendid Little War"

Secretary of State John Hay called the Spanish-American conflict "a splendid little war." Declared in April, it was over in August. That was in part because Cuban rebels had already greatly weakened

the Spanish resistance, which made the American intervention in many respects little more than a "mopping up" exercise. Only 460 Americans were killed in battle or died of wounds, although some 5,200 perished of disease. Casualties among Cuban insurgents, who continued to bear the brunt of the struggle, were much higher.

Yet the American war effort was not without difficulties. United States soldiers faced serious supply problems: a shortage of modern rifles and ammunition, **Logistical Difficulties** uniforms too heavy for the warm Caribbean weather, inadequate medical services, and skimpy, almost indigestible food. The regular army numbered only 28,000 troops and officers, most of whom had experience in quelling Indian outbreaks but none in larger-scale warfare. That meant that the United States had to rely heavily on National Guard units, commanded for the most part by leaders without military experience.

A significant proportion of the American invasion force consisted of black soldiers. Among them were members of the four black regiments in the regular army, who had been stationed on the frontier to defend white settlements against Indians and were now transferred east to fight in Cuba. As the black soldiers traveled through the South toward the training camps, some resisted the rigid segregation to which they were subjected. Black soldiers in Georgia deliberately made use of a "whites only" park; in Florida, they beat a soda-fountain operator for refusing to serve them; in Tampa, white provocations and black retaliation led to a night-long riot that left thirty wounded.

Racial tensions continued in Cuba itself, where African Americans played crucial **Racial Tensions in the Military** roles in important battles and won many medals. Nearly half the Cuban insurgents fighting with the Americans were black, but unlike their American counterparts they were fully integrated into the rebel army. The sight of black Cuban soldiers fighting alongside whites as equals gave African Americans a stronger sense of the injustice of their own position.

Seizing the Philippines

Assistant Secretary of the Navy Theodore Roosevelt was an ardent imperialist and an active proponent of war. As the tension with Spain rose, Roosevelt unilaterally strengthened the navy's Pacific squadron

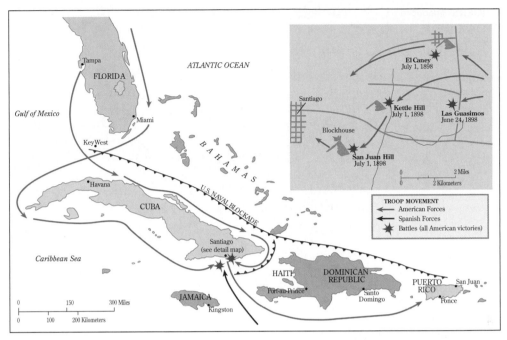

THE SPANISH-AMERICAN WAR IN CUBA, 1898 The military conflict between the United States and Spain in Cuba was a brief affair. The Cuban rebels and an American naval blockade had already brought the Spanish to the brink of defeat. The arrival of American troops was simply the final blow. In the space of about a week, U.S. troops won four decisive battles in the area around Santiago in southeast Cuba. ▌ *What were the implications of the war in Cuba for Puerto Rico?*

 For an interactive version of this map go to www.mhhe.com/unfinishedinteractive

and instructed its commander, Commodore George Dewey, to attack Spanish naval forces in the Philippines, a colony of Spain, in the event of war.

Immediately after war was declared, Dewey sailed for the Philippines. On May 1, 1898, he steamed into Manila Bay and completely destroyed the aging Spanish fleet there. Several months later, after the arrival of an American expeditionary force, the Spanish surrendered the city of Manila itself.

| Dewey Victorious |

The Battle for Cuba

Cuba, however, remained the principal focus of American military efforts. At first, the American commanders planned a long period of training before actually sending troops into combat. But when a Spanish fleet under Admiral Pascual Cervera slipped past the American navy into Santiago harbor, on the southern coast of Cuba, plans changed quickly. The American Atlantic fleet quickly bottled

Cervera up in the harbor. And the army's commanding general, Nelson A. Miles, hastily altered his strategy and ordered a force of 17,000 to leave Tampa in June to attack Santiago.

General William R. Shafter, the American commander in Cuba, moved toward Santiago. On the way he met and defeated Spanish forces at Las Guasimos and, a week later, El Caney and San Juan Hill. At the center of the fighting during all these engagements was a cavalry unit known as the Rough Riders. Nominally commanded by General Leonard Wood, its real leader was Colonel Theodore Roosevelt. Roosevelt rapidly emerged as a hero of the conflict. His fame rested in large part on his role in leading a bold, if perhaps reckless, charge up Kettle Hill (a charge that was a minor part of the larger battle for the adjacent San Juan Hill) directly into the face of Spanish guns. Roosevelt himself emerged unscathed, but nearly a hundred of his soldiers were killed or

| Theodore Roosevelt's Rough Riders |

THE ROUGH RIDERS Theodore Roosevelt, center, poses with some of the Rough Riders after their famous charge in the Battle of San Juan Hill. The brigade had an unofficial anthem: "Rough, rough, we're the stuff. We want to fight, and we can't get enough." (*Theodore Roosevelt Association*)

wounded. He remembered the battle as "the great day of my life."

Although Shafter was now in position to assault Santiago, his army was so weakened by sickness that disaster seemed imminent. But unknown to the Americans, the Spanish government had by now decided that Santiago was lost. On July 3, Cervera tried to escape the harbor. The waiting American squadron destroyed his entire fleet. On July 16, the commander of the Spanish ground forces in Santiago surrendered. At about the same time, an American army landed in Puerto Rico and occupied it. On August 12, Spain signed an armistice recognizing Cuban independence, ceding Puerto Rico to the United States, and accepting American occupation of Manila until the two nations reached a final agreement on the Philippines.

Puerto Rico Occupied

Puerto Rico and the United States

The island of Puerto Rico had been a part of the Spanish Empire since 1508. The native people of the island, the Arawaks, disappeared almost entirely as a result of infectious diseases, Spanish brutality, and poverty. Puerto Rican society developed, therefore, with a Spanish ruling class and a large African workforce for the coffee and sugar plantations.

Puerto Rican resistance to Spanish rule began to emerge in the nineteenth century. Uprisings occurred intermittently beginning in the 1820s; the most important of them—the so-called Lares Rebellion—was, like the others, effectively crushed by the Spanish in 1868. But the growing resistance did prompt some reforms: the abolition of slavery in 1873, representation in the Spanish parliament, and other changes. Demands for independence continued to grow, and in 1898 Spain granted the island a degree of independence. But before the changes had any chance to take effect, control of Puerto Rico shifted to the United States.

American military forces occupied the island during the war. They remained in control until 1900, when the Foraker Act ended military rule and established a formal colonial government. In 1917, Congress passed the Jones Act, which declared Puerto Rico to be United States territory and made all Puerto Ricans American citizens.

Foraker Act

The Puerto Rican sugar industry flourished as it took advantage of the American market that was now open to it without tariffs. The growing emphasis on sugar as a cash crop and the transformation of many Puerto Rican farmers into paid laborers led to a reduction in the growing of food for the island and a higher reliance on imported goods. When international sugar prices were high, Puerto Rico did well. When they dropped, the island's economy sagged, pushing the many plantation workers—already desperately poor—into destitution.

The Debate over the Philippines

If the annexation of Puerto Rico produced relatively

■ Annexation Debated

little controversy, the annexation of the Philippines occasioned a long and impassioned debate. Controlling a nearby Caribbean island fit reasonably comfortably into America's sense of itself as the dominant power in the Western Hemisphere. Controlling a large territory thousands of miles away seemed different and more ominous.

McKinley claimed to be reluctant to support annexation. But, according to his own accounts, he emerged from an "agonizing night of prayer" convinced that there were no acceptable alternatives. Returning the Philippines to Spain would be "cowardly and dishonorable," he claimed. Turning the islands over to another imperialist power would be "bad business and discreditable." Granting them independence would be irresponsible; the Filipinos were "unfit for self government." The only solution was "to take them all and to educate the Filipinos, and uplift and Christianize them." Growing popular support for annexation and the pressure of the imperialist leaders of his party undoubtedly helped him reach this decision.

The Treaty of Paris, signed in December 1898, brought a formal end to the Spanish-American War. It confirmed the terms of the armistice concerning Cuba, Puerto Rico, and Guam. American negotiators had startled the Spanish by demanding that they also cede the Philippines to the United States, but an offer of $20 million for the islands softened Spain's resistance. The Spanish negotiators accepted all the American terms.

In the United States Senate, however, resistance was fierce. During debate over ratification of the treaty, a powerful anti-imperialist movement arose. Among the anti-imperialists were some of the nation's wealthiest and most influential figures. Some believed simply that imperialism was immoral. Some feared "polluting" the American population by introducing "inferior" Asian races into it. Industrial workers feared being undercut by a flood of cheap laborers from the new colonies. Conservatives feared that the large standing army and entangling foreign alliances they thought imperialism would require would threaten American liberties. Sugar growers and others feared unwelcome competition

■ Anti-Imperialist League

from the new territories. The Anti-Imperialist League, established by upper-class Bostonians, New Yorkers, and others late in 1898, waged a vigorous campaign against ratification of the Paris treaty.

Favoring ratification was an equally varied group. Some businessmen believed

Supporters of Annexation ■

annexation would position the United States to dominate the Asian trade. And most Republicans saw partisan advantages in acquiring valuable new territories through a war fought and won by a Republican administration. Perhaps the strongest argument in favor of annexation, however, was the apparent ease with which it could be accomplished. The United States, after all, already possessed the islands.

When anti-imperialists warned of the danger of acquiring heavily populated territories whose people might have to become citizens, the imperialists had a ready answer: The nation's long-standing policies toward Indians—treating them as dependents rather than as citizens—had created a precedent for annexing land without absorbing people.

The fate of the treaty remained in doubt for weeks, until it received the unexpected support of William Jennings Bryan. Bryan was a fervent anti-imperialist who hoped to move the issue out of the Senate and make annexation the subject of a national referendum in 1900, when he expected to be the Democratic presidential candidate again. Bryan persuaded a number of anti-imperialist Democrats to support the treaty so as to set up the 1900 debate. The Senate ratified it finally on February 6, 1899.

But Bryan miscalculated. If the campaign of 1900 was in

Election of 1900 ■

fact a debate on the Philippines, as Bryan tried to make it, the election proved beyond doubt that the nation had decided in favor of imperialism. Once again, Bryan ran against McKinley, and once again, McKinley won. It was not only the issue of the colonies, however, that ensured McKinley's victory. The Republicans were the beneficiaries of growing national prosperity—and also of the colorful personality of their vice presidential candidate, Theodore Roosevelt.

THE REPUBLIC AS EMPIRE

The new American empire was a small one by the standards of the imperial powers of Europe. But it embroiled the United States in the politics of both

Europe and the Far East in ways it had tried to avoid in the past. It also drew Americans into a brutal war in the Philippines.

Governing the Colonies

Three of the new American dependencies—Hawaii, Alaska, and Puerto Rico—presented relatively few problems. They received territorial status (and their residents American citizenship) relatively quickly: Hawaii in 1900, Alaska in 1912, and Puerto Rico (in stages) by 1917. The navy took control of Guam and Tutuila.

Cuba was a thornier problem. American military forces, commanded by General Leonard Wood, remained there until 1902 to prepare the island for independence. They built roads, schools, and hospitals; reorganized the legal, financial, and administrative systems; and introduced medical and sanitation reforms. But when Cuba drew up a constitution that made no reference to the United States, Congress responded by passing the Platt Amendment in 1901 and pressuring Cuba into incorporating the amendment's terms into its constitution. The Platt Amendment barred Cuba from making treaties with other nations; it gave the United States the right to intervene in Cuba to preserve independence, life, and property; and it required Cuba to permit American naval stations on its territory. The amendment left Cuba with only nominal political independence. And American investors poured into Cuba, buying up plantations, factories, railroads, and refineries. Resistance to "Yankee imperialism" produced intermittent revolts against the Cuban government. American troops occupied the island from 1906 to 1909 after one such rebellion; they returned again in 1912, to suppress a revolt by black plantation workers. As in Puerto Rico and Hawaii, sugar production increasingly dominated the island's economic life and subjected it to the same cycle of booms and busts that so plagued other sugar-producing appendages of the United States economy.

Platt Amendment

The Philippine War

Americans did not like to think of themselves as imperial rulers in the European mold. Yet like other imperial powers, the United States soon discovered that subjugating another people required strength and at times brutality. That, at least, was the lesson of the American experience in the Philippines.

The conflict in the Philippines is the least remembered of all American wars. It was also one of the longest (it lasted from 1898 to 1902) and one of the most vicious. It involved 200,000 American troops and resulted in 4,300 American deaths. The number of Filipinos killed in the conflict is still in dispute, but it seems likely that at least 50,000 natives (and perhaps many more) died. The American occupiers faced guerrilla tactics in the Philippines very similar to those the Spanish occupiers had faced prior to 1898 in Cuba. And they soon found themselves drawn into the same pattern of brutality that had outraged so many Americans when Weyler had used them in the Caribbean.

The Filipinos had been rebelling against Spanish rule even before 1898. And as soon as they realized the Americans had come to stay, they rebelled against them as well. Ably led by Emilio Aguinaldo, Filipinos harried the American army of occupation from island to island for more than three years. At first, American commanders believed the rebels had only a small popular following. But by early 1900, General Arthur MacArthur, an American commander in the islands, was writing: "I have been reluctantly compelled to believe that the Filipino masses are loyal to Aguinaldo and the government which he heads."

Emilio Aguinaldo

To MacArthur and others, that was not a reason to moderate American tactics or conciliate the rebels. It was a reason to adopt more severe measures. Gradually, the American military effort became more systematically vicious and brutal. Captured Filipino guerrillas were summarily executed. On some islands, entire communities were evacuated—the residents forced into concentration camps while American troops destroyed their villages. A spirit of savagery grew among American soldiers, who came to view the Filipinos as almost subhuman and at times seemed to take pleasure in killing almost arbitrarily.

The Philippines Brutally Subjugated

By 1902, reports of the brutality and of the American casualties had soured the American public on the war. But by then, the occupiers had established control over most of the islands. The key to their victory was the March 1901 capture of

FILIPINO PRISONERS American troops guard captured Filipino guerrillas in Manila. The suppression of the Filipino insurrection was a much longer and costlier military undertaking than the Spanish-American War, by which the United States first gained possession of the islands. *(The Library of Congress)*

Aguinaldo. Fighting continued intermittently until as late as 1906; but American possession of the Philippines was now secure.

In the summer of 1901, the military transferred authority over the islands to William Howard Taft, who became the first civilian governor. Taft gave the Filipinos broad local autonomy. The Americans also built roads, schools, bridges, and sewers; instituted major administrative and financial reforms; and established a public health system. Filipino self-rule slowly increased. But not until July 4, 1946, did the islands finally gain their independence.

> Gradual Shift to Self-rule

The Open Door

The acquisition of the Philippines greatly increased the already strong American interest in Asia. Americans were particularly concerned about the future of China. By 1900, England, France, Germany, Russia, and Japan were beginning to carve up China among themselves, pressuring the Chinese government for "concessions" that gave them effective economic control over various regions. In some cases, they simply seized Chinese territories and claimed them as their own "spheres of influence." Many Americans feared the process would soon cut them out of the China trade altogether.

Eager for a way to protect American interests in China without risking war, McKinley issued a statement in September 1898 saying the United States wanted access to China but no special advantages there: "Asking only the open door for ourselves, we are ready to accord the open door to others." Later, Secretary of State John Hay translated the president's words into policy when he addressed identical messages—which became known as the "Open Door notes"—to England, Germany, Russia, France, Japan, and Italy. He asked them to approve three principles: Each nation with a "sphere of influence" in China was to allow other nations to trade freely and equally in its sphere. The principles he outlined would allow the United States to trade with the Chinese without fear of interference.

> Hay's "Open Door Notes"

But the Open Door proposals were coolly received in Europe and Japan. Russia openly rejected

THE AMERICAN SOUTH PACIFIC EMPIRE, 1900 Except for Puerto Rico, all of the colonial acquisitions of the United States in the wake of the Spanish-American War occurred in the Pacific. The new attraction of imperialism persuaded the United States to annex Hawaii in 1898. The war itself gave America control of the Philippines, Guam, and other, smaller Spanish possessions in the Pacific. ▮ *What was the reaction in the United States to the acquisition of this new empire?*

them; the other powers claimed to accept them in principle but to be unable to act unless all the powers agreed. Hay, unperturbed, simply announced that all the powers had accepted the principles of the Open Door and that the United States expected them to observe those principles. But unless the United States was willing to resort to war, it could not prevent any nation that wanted to violate the Open Door from doing so.

No sooner had the diplomatic maneuvering over the Open Door ended than the Boxers, a secret Chinese martial-arts society, launched a revolt against foreigners in China.

The Boxer Rebellion

The climax of the Boxer Rebellion was a siege of the entire foreign diplomatic corps in the British embassy in Beijing (Peking). The imperial powers (including the United States) sent an international expeditionary force into China to rescue the diplomats. In August 1900, it fought its way into Beijing and broke the siege.

McKinley and Hay had agreed to American participation so as to secure a voice in the settlement of the uprising and to prevent the partition of China. Hay now won support for his Open Door approach from England and Germany and then induced the other participating powers to accept compensation from the Chinese for the damages the Boxer Rebellion had caused. Chinese territorial integrity survived at least in name, and the United States retained access to its lucrative trade.

A Modern Military System

The war with Spain had revealed glaring deficiencies in the American military system. Had the United States been fighting a more powerful nation, disaster might have resulted. After the war, McKinley appointed Elihu Root, an able New York corporate lawyer, as secretary of war to supervise a major overhaul of the armed forces.

Root's reforms enlarged the maximum size of the regular army from 25,000 to 100,000. They established federal army standards for the National Guard, ensuring that never again would the nation fight a war with volunteer regiments. They sparked

Creation of the Modern Military

the creation of a system of officer training schools, including the Army Staff College at Fort Leavenworth, Kansas, and the Army War College in Washington, D.C. And in 1903, they established a general staff (named the Joint Chiefs of Staff) to act as military advisers to the secretary of war. As a result of the new reforms, the United States entered the twentieth century with something resembling a modern military system.

CONCLUSION

After more than a century of continual expansion on the North American continent, in the 1890s the United States acquired a substantial empire far from its own shores. But the rise of American imperialism was a halting and contested process.

In the beginning, America's new internationalism took the form of a supposedly humanitarian intervention in a civil war in Spanish Cuba. The American public, inflamed by lurid journalistic accounts of Spanish atrocities inflicted on innocent Cubans, helped push the United States into a short, victorious war with Spain. Through the efforts of some committed internationalists in the McKinley administration, the Spanish-American War was soon transformed from a fight to free Cuba into a fight to wrest important colonies from Spain. At its end, the United States found itself in possession of substantial new territories in the Caribbean (including Puerto Rico) and an important territory in the Pacific—the Philippines. A vigorous domestic anti-imperialist movement failed to stop the annexationist drive, and by 1899 the United States found itself in possession of colonies.

Taking the colonies proved easier than holding them. In the Philippines, American forces became bogged down in a four-year war with Filipino rebels. The new colonial rulers soon pacified the Philippines, but not before souring much of the American public on the effort. In part as a result, the territories the United States acquired in the aftermath of the Spanish-American War marked not only the beginning but the end of American territorial imperialism.

INTERACTIVE LEARNING

On the ***Primary Source Investigator CD-ROM,*** check out a number of valuable tools for further exploration of the content of this chapter.

Interactive Map
- The Spanish-American War, 1898 (Map M20)

Primary Sources
Documents, images, and maps related to the Spanish-American War of 1898 and the rise of American imperialism in this era. Some highlights include:

- Text of the Joint Resolution of Congress annexing Hawaii

- A video clip of Theodore Roosevelt and the Rough Riders

 Online Learning Center *(www.mhhe.com/unfinishedinteractive)*
Explore this rich website, providing additional exploration of the material covered in this chapter, online versions of the interactive maps included on the Primary Source Investigator CD-ROM, as well as several study aids, including a multiple-choice quiz, essay questions, a glossary, and other valuable tools. Also in the Online Learning Center for this chapter look for an *Interactive Feature Essay* on:

- **America in the World: Imperialism**

FOR FURTHER REFERENCE

Walter LaFeber, *The New Empire: An Interpretation of American Expansion, 1860–1898* (1963) and Ernest May, *Imperial Democracy* (1961) are important introductions to the subject. David F. Healy, *U.S. Expansionism: Imperialist Urge in the 1890s* (1970) is a contrasting view. Walter LaFeber, *The Cambridge History of American Foreign Policy, Vol. 2: The Search for Opportunity, 1865–1913* (1993) is an important overview. William Appleman Williams, *The Tragedy of American Diplomacy*, rev. ed. (1972) is a classic revisionist work on the origins and tragic consequences of American imperialism, supplemented by his *Empire as a Way of Life: An Essay on the Causes and Character of America's Present Predicament* (1982). David M. Pletcher, *The Diplomacy of Trade and Investment: American Economic Expansion in the Hemisphere, 1865–1900* (1998) examines the economic roots of American intervention in Latin America. Anders Stephanson, *Manifest Destiny: American Expansionism and the Empire of Right* (1995) is a short and provocative history of Americans' ideology of expansionism. Robert L. Beisner's *Twelve Against Empire* (1968) chronicles the careers of the leading opponents of imperial expansion. Emily S. Rosenberg, *Spreading the American Dream: American Economic and Cultural Expansion, 1890–1945* (1982) is a provocative cultural interpretation. Gerald F. Linderman, *The Mirror of War: American Society and the Spanish-American War* (1974) examines the social meaning of the war within the United States. Stuart Creighton Miller, *"Benevolent Assimilation": The American Conquest of the Philippines, 1899–1903* (1982) describes the American war in the Philippines. Michael Hunt, *The Making of a Special Relationship: The United States and China to 1914* (1983) is a good introduction to the subject. Matthew Frye Jacobson, *Barbarian Virtues: The United States Encounters Foreign Peoples at Home and Abroad, 1876–1917* (2000) is a broad overview of the interplay between imperialism and immigration.

21

The Rise of Progressivism

MINI-DOCUMENTARY Votes for Women

(Schlesinger Library, Radcliffe College, Harvard University)

Well before the turn of the century, many Americans had become convinced that the rapid industrialization and urbanization of their society had created intolerable problems—that the nation's most pressing need was to impose order on the growing chaos and to curb industrial society's most glaring injustices. In the early years of the new century, that outlook acquired a name: progressivism.

Not even those who called themselves progressives could always agree on what the word "progressive" really meant, for it was a phenomenon of great scope and diversity. But it was also one that rested on an identifiable set of central assumptions. It was, first, an optimistic vision. Progressives believed, as their name implies, in the idea of progress. They believed that continued growth and advancement were the nation's destiny. But progressives believed, too, that growth and progress could not continue to occur recklessly, as they had in the late nineteenth century. The "natural laws" of the marketplace were not sufficient to create the order and stability that the growing society required. Purposeful human intervention was necessary to solve the nation's problems. Progressives did not always agree on the form that intervention should take, but most believed that government should play an important role in the process.

THE PROGRESSIVE IMPULSE

Beyond these central premises, progressivism flowed outward in a number of different directions. One powerful impulse was the spirit of "antimonopoly," the fear of concentrated power and the urge to limit and disperse authority and wealth. A second progressive impulse was a belief in the importance of social cohesion: the belief that the welfare of any single person is dependent on the welfare of society as a whole. And a third progressive impulse was the belief that social order was a result of intelligent social organization and rational procedures for guiding social and economic life. Many progressives made use of all these ideas at times, and others as well, as they tried to restore order and stability to their turbulent society.

The Muckrakers and the Social Gospel

Among the first to articulate the new spirit of reform was a group of journalists who were committed to exposing scandal, corruption, and injustice. They became known as the "muckrakers" after Theodore Roosevelt accused one of them of raking up muck through his writings.

At first, their major targets were the trusts and particularly the railroads. Exposés of the great corporate organizations began to appear as early as the 1860s, when Charles Francis Adams, Jr., and others uncovered corruption among the railroad barons. Decades later, Ida Tarbell produced a scorching study of the Standard Oil trust. By the turn of the century, however, many muckrakers were turning their attention to government. Among the most influential was Lincoln Steffens, a reporter for *McClure's Magazine*. His portraits of "machine government" and "boss rule" in cities had a tone of studied moral outrage that was reflected in the title of his series and of the book that emerged from it, *The Shame of the Cities*. The muckrakers reached the peak of their influence in the first decade of the twentieth century. They investigated governments, labor unions, and corporations. They explored the problems of child labor, immigrant ghettoes, prostitution, and family disorganization. They denounced the waste and destruction of natural resources, the subjugation of women, even occasionally the oppression of blacks.

Many reformers became committed to the idea of what was known as "social justice." A clear

Lincoln Steffens

1873	1889	1893	1895	1899	1900
Women's Christian Temperance Union founded	Jane Addams opens Hull House	Anti-Saloon League founded	National Association of Manufacturers founded	Veblen's *A Theory of the Leisure Class*	Galveston, Texas, creates commission government Robert La Follette elected Wisconsin governor

1902	1909	1911	1912	1919	1920
Ida Tarbell's exposé of Standard Oil	Croly's *The Promise of American Life* NAACP formed	Triangle Shirtwaist fire	U.S. Chamber of Commerce founded	18th Amendment (prohibition)	19th Amendment (woman suffrage)

TIME LINE

expression of that concern was the rise within American Protestantism of the "Social Gospel," the effort to make faith into a tool of social reform. The Salvation Army, which began in England but soon spread to the United States, was a Christian social welfare organization with a vaguely military structure. By 1900, it had recruited 3,000 "officers" and 20,000 "privates" and was offering both material aid and spiritual service to the urban poor. In addition, many ministers, priests, and rabbis left traditional parish work to serve in the troubled cities. Charles Sheldon's *In His Steps* (1898), the story of a young minister who abandoned a comfortable post to work among the needy, sold more than 15 million copies. The engagement of religion with reform helped bring a powerful moral impulse to progressivism.

The Settlement House Movement
One of the strongest elements of progressive thought was the belief that the environment shaped individual development. Ignorance, poverty, even criminality, progressives argued, were not the result of inherent moral or genetic failings or of the workings of providence. They were, rather, the effects of an unhealthy environment. To elevate the distressed, therefore, required an improvement of the conditions in which the distressed lived.

Nothing produced more distress, many reformers believed, than the crowded immigrant neighborhoods of American cities. One response to the problems of such communities, borrowed from England, was the settlement house. Staffed by members of the educated middle class, settlement houses sought to help immigrant families adapt to the language and customs of their new country. The most famous was Hull House, which opened in

Hull House

1889 in Chicago as a result of the efforts of Jane Addams.

Central to the settlement houses were the efforts of educated women. Indeed, the movement became a training ground for many important female leaders of the twentieth century, among them Eleanor Roosevelt. The settlement houses also helped spawn the profession of social work—a profession in which women were to play an important role. The professional social worker combined a compassion for the poor with a commitment to scientific study and efficient organization.

The Allure of Expertise

Progressives involved in humanitarian efforts often placed high value on knowledge and expertise. That belief found expression through the writings of a group of scholars and intellectuals who envisioned a new civilization in which the expertise of scientists and engineers would be put into the service of the economy and society. Among the most influential of these theorists was the social scientist Thorstein Veblen. Harshly critical of the industrial tycoons—the "leisure class," as he satirically described them in his first major work, *A Theory of the Leisure Class* (1899)—Veblen proposed instead a new economic system in which power would reside in the hands of highly trained engineers. Only they, he argued, could fully understand the "machine process" by which modern society must be governed.

> Knowledge and Expertise Valued

In practical terms, the impulse toward expertise and organization helped produce the idea of scientific management, or "Taylorism" (see p. 273). It encouraged the development of modern mass-production techniques and, above all, the assembly line. It inspired a revolution in American education and the creation of a new area of inquiry—social science, the use of scientific techniques in the study of society and its institutions. It also helped create a movement toward organization among the expanding new group of middle-class professionals.

The Professions

The late nineteenth century saw a dramatic expansion in the number of Americans engaged in administrative and professional tasks. Industries needed managers, technicians, and accountants as well as workers. Cities required commercial, medical, legal, and educational services. New technologies required scientists and engineers. By the turn of the century, the people performing these services had come to constitute a new middle class.

> The New Middle Class

This new middle class created the modern, organized professions. The idea of professionalism had been a frail one in America even as late as 1880. But as the demand for professional services increased, so did the pressures for reform.

Among the first to respond was the medical profession. Throughout the 1890s, doctors began forming local associations and societies. In 1901, they reorganized the American Medical Association (AMA) into a national professional society. The AMA quickly called for strict, scientific standards for admission to the practice of medicine. State and local governments responded by creating medical schools in their universities and by passing new laws that required the licensing of all physicians and that restricted licenses to those practitioners approved by the profession.

> American Medical Association

THE INFANT WELFARE SOCIETY, CHICAGO The Infant Welfare Society was one of many "helping" organizations in Chicago and other large cities—many of them closely tied to the settlement houses—that strove to help immigrants adapt to American life and create safe and healthy living conditions. Here, a volunteer helps an immigrant mother learn to bathe her baby sometime around 1910. *(Chicago Historical Society, ICHi-20216)*

There was similar movement in other professions. By 1916, lawyers in all forty-eight states had established professional bar associations. Increasingly, aspiring lawyers found it necessary to enroll in graduate programs, and the nation's law schools accordingly expanded greatly. Businessmen supported the creation of schools of business administration and established their own national organizations: the National Association of Manufacturers in 1895 and the United States Chamber of Commerce in 1912. Farmers responded to the new order by forming, through the National Farm Bureau Federation, a network of agricultural organizations.

Limiting Entry into the Professions Among the chief purposes of the new professionalism was guarding entry into the professions. This was only partly an effort to defend the professions from the untrained and incompetent. The admission requirements also protected those already in the professions from excessive competition. Some professions used their entrance requirements to exclude blacks, women, immigrants, and other "undesirables" from their ranks. Others used them simply to keep the numbers down, to ensure that demand for the services of existing members would remain high.

Women and the Professions

American women found themselves excluded from most of the emerging professions. But a substantial number of middle-class women—particularly those emerging from the new women's colleges and from the coeducational state universities—nevertheless entered professional careers.

A few women managed to establish themselves as physicians, lawyers, engineers, scientists, and corporate managers. Most, however, turned by necessity to those professions that society considered suitable for women. The most important of these was teaching. Indeed, in the late nineteenth century, more than two-thirds of all grammar-school teachers were women. For educated black women, in particular, teaching was often the only professional opportunity they could hope to find.

Women also dominated other professional activities. Nursing had become primarily a women's field around the time of the Civil War, when it was still considered a menial occupation, akin to domestic service. But by the early twentieth century, it too

was adopting professional standards. Women also found opportunities as librarians. And many women entered academia—often studying at predominantly male institutions that permitted women to earn advanced degrees, among them the University of Chicago, MIT, and Columbia, and then finding professional opportunities in the new and expanding women's colleges.

"Helping" Professions The "women's professions" had much in common with other professions. But they also had distinctive qualities. Careers such as teaching, nursing, and library work were "helping" professions. Women's workplaces—schools, hospitals, and libraries—had a vaguely "domestic" or "feminine" image, which enabled men to reconcile the idea of female professional work with prevailing ideas about the proper role of women in society.

WOMEN AND REFORM

The prominent role of women in reform movements is one of the most striking features of progressivism. Women became important reformers even though they could not vote in most states, seldom held office, and had footholds in only a few professions. But their relative insulation from political and professional life in some ways enhanced their ability to wield influence, for it enabled them to tie their causes to the idea of a nonpartisan, nurturing culture uncontaminated by economic or political interests.

The "New Woman"

The phenomenon of the "new woman" was a product of the social and economic changes of the era. By the end of the nineteenth century, almost all income-producing activity had moved out of the home and into the factory or the office. At the same time, many women were having fewer children. For wives and mothers who did not work for wages, home and family were less all-consuming. Hence more and more women began looking for activities outside the home.

There were also more women who lived outside traditional families altogether. Approximately 10 percent of all American women in the last decades of the nineteenth century never married, and single women were among the most prominent female re-formers of the time. Some of these women lived alone. Others lived with other women, often in long-term relationships known as "Boston mar-riages." The divorce rate also rose rapidly, from one divorce for every twenty-one marriages in 1880 to one in nine by 1916.

"Boston Marriages"

Higher levels of education also contributed to the prominence of women in reform activities. The proliferation of women's colleges and of coeduca-tional public universities in the late nineteenth cen-tury produced the first generation of women in which significant numbers had educations above the high-school level (p. 301). The new colleges also helped create female communities, within which women could find support for their ambitions and companionship for their activities.

The Clubwomen

In the vanguard of many progressive social reforms was a large network of women's clubs. The clubs began largely as cultural organizations to provide middle- and upper-class women with an outlet for their intellectual energies. In 1892, when women formed the General Federa-tion of Women's Clubs to co-ordinate the activities of local organizations, there were more than 100,000 mem-bers in nearly 500 clubs. By 1917, there were over 1 million members.

Importance of Women's Clubs

By the early twentieth century, the clubs were be-coming more concerned with making a contribu-tion to social reform. Much of what they did was uncontroversial: planting trees; supporting schools, libraries, and settlement houses; building hospitals and parks. But many women's clubs also supported such controversial measures as child labor laws, worker compensation, pure food and drug legisla-tion, occupational safety, reforms in Indian policy, and—beginning in 1914—woman suffrage.

Black women occasionally joined clubs domi-nated by whites. But African Americans also formed clubs of their own, some of which affiliated with the General Federation, but more of which became part of the independ-ent National Association of Colored Women. Some black clubs crusaded against lynching and called for con-

National Association of Colored Women

gressional legislation to make lynching a federal crime. Others protested aspects of segregation.

The women's club movement raised few overt challenges to prevailing assumptions about the proper role of women in society. But it did represent an important effort by women to define a space for themselves in the public world without openly chal-lenging the existing, male-dominated order.

The importance of the club movement did not, however, lie simply in what it did for middle-class women. It lay also in what those women did for the working-class people they at-tempted to help. The women's club movement was an important force in winning passage of state (and ultimately federal) laws that regulated the condi-tions of woman and child labor, that established government inspection of workplaces, that regu-lated the food and drug industries, and that applied new standards to urban housing.

Importance of the Club Movement

Woman Suffrage

The largest single reform movement of the pro-gressive era was the fight for woman suffrage. It was the culmination of many decades of struggle by women to obtain basic political rights. But it was also the product of forces peculiar to the early twentieth century.

MINI-DOCUMENTARY: Votes for Women

It is sometimes difficult for today's Americans to understand why the suffrage (or right-to-vote) issue could have become the source of such enormous controversy in the early twentieth century. But at the time, suffrage seemed to many of its critics a very rad-ical demand—in part be-cause of the way some of its supporters promoted it. Throughout the late nineteenth century, many suf-frage advocates presented their views in terms of "natural rights," arguing that women deserved the same rights as men—including, first and foremost, the right to vote. Elizabeth Cady Stanton, for exam-ple, wrote in 1892 of woman as "the arbiter of her own destiny . . . if we are to consider her as a citizen, as a member of a great nation, she must have the same rights as all other members." A woman's role as "mother, wife, sister, daughter" was "incidental" to her larger role as a part of society.

Radical Implications of Suffrage

This was an argument that boldly challenged the views of many men (and even many women) who believed that society required a distinctive female "sphere" in which women would serve first and foremost as wives and mothers. And so a powerful antisuffrage movement emerged. There were antisuffrage organizations, newspapers, and political crusades. Antisuffragists associated suffrage with divorce, promiscuity, and neglect of children.

The suffrage movement began to overcome this opposition in the first years of the twentieth century. That was in part because suffragists were becoming better organized and more politically sophisticated than their opponents. Under the leadership of Anna Howard Shaw, a Boston social worker, and Carrie Chapman Catt, a journalist from Iowa, the National American Woman Suffrage Association **NAWSA** grew from a membership of about 13,000 in 1893 to over 2 million in 1917.

But the movement also gained strength because many of its leaders began to justify suffrage in less threatening ways. Suffrage, some supporters began to argue, would allow women to bring their special and distinct virtues more widely to bear on society's problems. It was, they claimed, precisely because women occupied a distinct sphere—because as mothers and wives and homemakers they had special sensitivities to bring to public life—that woman suffrage could make such an important contribution to politics. In particular, many suffragists argued that enfranchising women would help the temperance movement by giving its largest group of supporters a political voice. Some suffrage advocates claimed that once women had the vote, war would become a thing of the past, since women would—through their maternal instincts and their calming, peaceful influence—help curb the natural belligerence of men.

The triumphs of the suffrage movement began in 1910. That year, Washington became the first state in fourteen years to extend suffrage to women. California joined it a year later, and in 1912 four **Nineteenth Amendment Ratified** other western states did the same. In 1913, Illinois became the first state east of the Mississippi to embrace woman suffrage. And in 1917 and 1918, New York and Michigan did so. By 1919, thirty-nine states had granted women the right to vote in at least some elections; fifteen had allowed them full participation. In 1920, finally, suffragists won ratification of the Nineteenth Amendment, which guaranteed political rights to women throughout the nation.

To some feminists, however, the victory seemed incomplete. Alice Paul, the head of the militant National **Alice Paul** Woman's Party (founded in 1916), argued that the Nineteenth Amendment alone would not be sufficient to protect women's rights. Women needed more: a constitutional amendment that would provide clear, legal protection for their rights and would prohibit all discrimination on the basis of sex. But for many years Alice Paul's argument found limited support even among suffragists.

THE ASSAULT ON THE PARTIES

Sooner or later, most progressive goals required the involvement of government. Only government could effectively counter the powerful private interests that threatened the nation. But American government was, progressives believed, poorly adapted to meet their demands. Before they could reform society effectively, they would first have to reform government. In the beginning, at least, many progressives believed that such reform should start with an assault on the political parties.

Early Attacks

Attacks on party dominance had been frequent in the late nineteenth century. Greenbackism and Populism had been efforts to break the hammerlock with which the Republicans and Democrats controlled public life. The Independent Republicans (or mugwumps) had attempted to challenge the grip of partisanship, and former mugwumps became important supporters of progressive political reform activity.

The early assaults enjoyed some success. In the 1880s and 1890s, for example, most states adopted the secret ballot. Prior to that, the political parties **Secret Ballot** themselves had printed ballots (or "tickets") with only the party's candidates listed, which they distributed to their supporters, who then simply went to the polls to deposit the tickets in the ballot box. The old system had made it possible for bosses to monitor the voting behavior of their constituents.

The new ballot—printed by the government and distributed at the polls, where it was filled out and deposited in secret—helped chip away at the power of the parties over the voters.

By the late 1890s, critics of the parties were expanding their goals. Party rule could be broken, they believed, in two ways. It could be broken by increasing the power of the people, by permitting them to express their will directly at the polls. And it could be broken by placing more power in the hands of nonpartisan, nonelective officials.

Municipal Reform

Many progressives believed the impact of party rule was most damaging in the cities. Municipal government, therefore, became their first target. Muckraking journalists were especially successful in arousing public outrage at corruption and incompetence in city politics.

The muckrakers struck a responsive chord among a powerful group of urban middle-class progressives, who set out to destroy the power of machines. They faced formidable opposition. In addition to challenging the powerful city bosses and their entrenched political organizations, they attacked a large group of special interests: saloon owners, brothel keepers, businessmen who had established lucrative relationships with the urban machines. Finally, there was the great constituency of urban working people, many of them recent immigrants, for whom the machines were a source of needed jobs and services. Gradually, however, the reformers gained in political strength and began to score some important victories.

Urban Machines Challenged

An early and influential success came in Galveston, Texas, where the old city government proved completely unable to deal with the effects of a destructive tidal wave in 1900. Capitalizing on public dismay, reformers won approval of a new city charter that replaced the mayor and council with an elected, nonpartisan commission. In 1907, Des Moines, Iowa, adopted its own version of the commission plan, and other cities followed.

City-Manager Plan

Another approach was the city-manager plan, by which elected officials hired an outside expert—often a professionally trained business manager or engineer—to take charge of the government. The city manager would presumably remain untainted by the corrupting influence of politics. By the end of the progressive era, almost 400 mostly smaller cities were operating under commissions, and another 45 employed city managers.

In other cities, reformers organized to challenge the municipal electoral process. Some cities made the election of mayors nonpartisan or moved them to years when no presidential or congressional races were in progress. Reformers tried to make city-council members run at large so as to limit the influence of ward leaders and district bosses. They tried to strengthen the power of the mayor at the expense of the city council, on the assumption that reformers were more likely to get a sympathetic mayor elected than to win control of the entire council.

Statehouse Progressivism

Other progressives turned to state government as an agent for reform. They looked with particular scorn on state legislatures, whose members were, they believed, generally incompetent, often corrupt, and almost always controlled by party bosses. Many reformers began looking for ways to circumvent the legislatures by increasing the power of the electorate.

Two of the most important changes were innovations first proposed by Populists in the 1890s: the initiative and the referendum. The

Initiative and Referendum

initiative allowed reformers to submit new legislation directly to the voters in general elections. The referendum provided a method by which actions of the legislature could be returned to the electorate for approval. By 1918, more than twenty states had enacted one or both of these reforms.

The direct primary and the recall were, similarly, efforts to limit the power of parties and improve the quality of elected officials. The primary election was an attempt to take the selection of candidates away from the bosses and give it to the people. (In the South, it was also a device for excluding African Americans from voting.) The recall gave voters the right to remove a public official from office through a special election, which could be called after a sufficient number of citizens had signed a petition. By 1915 every state in the nation had instituted primary elections for at least some offices. The recall

ROBERT LA FOLLETTE CAMPAIGNING IN WISCONSIN After three terms as governor of Wisconsin, La Follette began a long career in the United States Senate in 1906, during which he worked uncompromisingly for advanced progressive reforms. *(Wisconsin Historical Society)*

encountered more strenuous opposition, but some states adopted it as well.

Robert M. La Follette

The most celebrated state-level reformer was Robert M. La Follette of Wisconsin. Elected governor in 1900, he helped turn his state into a "laboratory of progressivism." The Wisconsin progressives won approval of direct primaries, initiatives, and referendums. They regulated railroads and utilities. They passed laws to regulate the workplace and provide compensation for laborers injured on the job. They taxed inherited fortunes and nearly doubled state levies on railroads and other corporate interests.

Parties and Interest Groups

The reformers did not, of course, eliminate parties from American political life. But they did diminish the parties' centrality. Evidence of that came from, among other things, the decline in voter turnout. In the late nineteenth century, up to 81 percent of eligible voters routinely turned out for national elections. In the early twentieth century, the figure declined markedly. In the presidential election of 1900, 73 percent of the electorate voted. By 1912, the figure had dropped to about 59 percent.

At the same time that parties were declining, other power centers were emerging to compete with them:

what have become known as "interest groups": professional organizations, trade associations representing particular businesses and industries, labor organizations, farm lobbies, and many others. Social workers, the settlement house movement, women's clubs, and others learned to operate as interest groups. A new pattern of politics, in which many individual interests organized to influence government directly rather than operating through party structures, was taking shape.

Emergence of "Interest Groups"

SOURCES OF PROGRESSIVE REFORM

Middle-class reformers, most of them from the East, dominated the public image and much of the substance of progressivism. But they were not alone in seeking to improve social conditions. Working-class Americans, African Americans, westerners, even party bosses also played crucial roles.

Labor, the Machine, and Reform

Although the American Federation of Labor remained largely aloof from many of the reform efforts, some unions nevertheless played important roles in reform battles. In San Francisco, for example, workers in the Building Trades Council spearheaded the formation of the new Union Labor Party, committed to a program of reform almost indistinguishable from that of middle-class and elite progressives in the city. Between 1911 and 1913, in significant part because of the new party's efforts, California passed a child labor law, a workmen's compensation law, and a limitation on working hours for women. Union pressures contributed to the passage of similar laws in many other states as well.

One result of the assault on the parties was a change in the party organizations themselves. Party bosses sometimes turned their machines into vehicles of social reform. One example was New York's Tammany Hall, the nation's oldest and most notorious city machine. Its astute leader, Charles Francis Murphy, began in the early years of the century to fuse the techniques of boss rule with some of the concerns of social reformers. Tammany used its political power to improve working conditions and eliminate the worst abuses of the industrial economy.

In 1911, a terrible fire swept through the factory of the Triangle Shirtwaist Company in New York's

Triangle Shirtwaist Fire

Washington Square; 146 workers, most of them women, died. Many of them had been trapped inside the burning building because management had locked the emergency exits. For the next three years, a state commission studied not only the background of the fire but the general condition of the industrial workplace. By 1914, the commission had issued a series of reports calling for major reforms in the conditions of labor. When its recommendations reached the New York legislature, its most effective supporters were not middle-class progressives but two Tammany Democrats from working-class backgrounds: Senator Robert F. Wagner and Assemblyman Alfred E. Smith. With the support of Murphy and the backing of other Tammany legislators, they steered through a series of laws that imposed strict regulations on factory owners and established effective mechanisms for enforcement.

Western Progressives

The American West produced some of the most notable progressive leaders of the time: Hiram Johnson of California, George Norris of Nebraska, William Borah of Idaho, and others—almost all of whom spent at least some of their political careers in the United States Senate. That was because for western states, the most important target of reform energies was the federal government, which exercised a kind of authority in the West that it had never possessed in the East.

Reforming the Federal Government

Many of the most important issues to the future of the West required action above the state level. Disputes over water, for example, almost always involved rivers and streams that crossed state lines. More significant, perhaps, the federal government exercised enormous power over the lands and resources of the western states and provided substantial subsidies to the region in the form of land grants and support for railroad and water projects. Huge areas of the West remained (and still remain) public lands, controlled by Washington; and much of the growth of the West was (and continues to be) a result of federally funded dams and water projects.

Because so much authority in the region rested in federal bureaucracies that state and local governments could not control, political parties in most of the West were relatively weak. That was one reason why western states could move so quickly and decisively to embrace reforms that parties did not like. It is also why aspiring politicians were much quicker to look to Washington as a place from which they could influence their region.

African Americans and Reform

The question of race received serious attention from relatively few white progressives, except among those white southerners who believed that the construction of legalized segregation was a progressive reform. But among African Americans themselves, the progressive era produced some significant challenges to existing racial norms.

African Americans faced greater obstacles than any other group in challenging their own oppressed status and seeking reform. That was one reason why so many had embraced the message of Booker T. Washington in the late nineteenth century, to work for immediate self-improvement rather than

W. E. B. DU BOIS AT HIS DESK
Although W. E. B. Du Bois never developed a large popular following, he was the acknowledged leader of the black elite in the early twentieth century. He was the first African American to earn a doctorate at Harvard University, and he published a number of distinguished works of history and sociology. He also served as editor of *The Crisis,* the newspaper of the NAACP (which he had helped to found). *(Schomburg Center/Art Resource, NY)*

long-range social change. By the turn of the century, however, a powerful new approach was emerging. The chief spokesman for this approach was W. E. B. Du Bois, a Harvard-trained sociologist and historian.

W. E. B. Du Bois

In *The Souls of Black Folk* (1903), Du Bois launched an open attack on Washington's "Atlanta Compromise," first presented in a speech in Atlanta, which had urged blacks to postpone efforts to achieve political equality and concentrate on self-improvement. Rather than content themselves with education at the trade and agricultural schools, Du Bois advocated, talented blacks should accept nothing less than a full university education. They should aspire to the professions. They should, above all, fight for immediate progress on civil rights. In 1905, Du Bois and a group of his supporters met at Niagara Falls—on the Canadian side of the border because no hotel on the American side of the Falls would have them—and launched what became known as the Niagara Movement. Four years later, they joined with white progressives sympathetic to their cause to form the National Association for the Advancement of Colored People (NAACP). In the years that followed, the new organization led the drive for equal rights, using as one of its principal weapons lawsuits in the federal courts. Visit Chapter 21 of

NAACP Founded

 the book's Online Learning Center for a Where Historians Disagree essay on "Progressive Reform."

CRUSADES FOR ORDER AND REFORM

Reformers directed many of their energies at the political process. But they also crusaded on behalf of what they considered moral issues. There were campaigns to eliminate alcohol from national life, to curb prostitution, to regulate divorce. There were efforts to restrict immigration and to curb the power of monopoly. There were crusades to resolve what many considered long-standing injustices, of which the most prominent was the campaign for woman suffrage.

The Temperance Crusade
Many progressives considered the elimination of alcohol from American life a necessary step in restoring order to society. Workers in settlement houses and social agencies abhorred the effects of drinking on working-class families: Scarce wages vanished as workers spent hours in saloons; drunkenness spawned violence, and occasionally murder. Women, in particular, saw alcohol as a source of some of the greatest problems of working-class wives and mothers. Employers complained

that workers often missed time on the job because of drunkenness or, worse, came to the factory intoxicated and performed their tasks sloppily and dangerously. And political reformers, who looked on the saloon (correctly) as one of the central institutions of the machine, saw an attack on drinking as part of an attack on the bosses. Out of such varied sentiments emerged the temperance movement.

Temperance had been a major reform movement before the Civil War, mobilizing large numbers of people in a crusade with strong religious overtones. Beginning in the 1870s, it experienced a major resurgence. In 1873, temperance advocates formed the

| WCTU |

Women's Christian Temperance Union (WCTU), led after 1879 by Frances Willard. By 1911, it had 245,000 members. In 1893, the Anti-Saloon League joined the temperance movement and, along with the WCTU, began to press for the legal abolition of saloons. Gradually, that demand grew to include the complete prohibition of the sale and manufacture of alcoholic beverages.

Pressure for prohibition grew steadily through the first decades of the new century. By 1916, nineteen states had passed prohibition laws. American entry into World War I, and the moral fervor it unleashed, provided the last push to the advocates of prohibition. In 1917, advocates of prohibition steered through Congress a constitutional amendment embodying their demands. Two years later, after ratification by every state in the nation except Connecticut and Rhode Island (with large populations of Catholic

| Eighteenth Amendment Ratified |

immigrants opposed to prohibition), the Eighteenth Amendment became law.

Immigration Restriction

Virtually all reformers agreed that the growing immigrant population had created social problems, but there was wide disagreement on how best to respond. Some progressives believed that helping the new residents adapt to American society was the proper approach. Others argued that the only solution was to limit the flow of new arrivals.

| Growing Nativism |

In the first decades of the century, the arguments of this second group gradually gained strength. New scholarly theories argued that the introduction of immigrants into American society was diluting the purity of the nation's racial stock. The "science" of eugenics spread the belief that human inequalities were hereditary and that immigration was contributing to the multiplication of the unfit. A special federal commission of supposed experts, chaired by Senator William P. Dillingham of Vermont, issued a report filled with statistics and scholarly testimony. It argued that the newer immigrant groups—largely southern and eastern Europeans—had proved themselves less assimilable than earlier immigrants. Immigration, the report implied, should be restricted by nationality. Even many people who rejected racial arguments supported limiting immigration as a way to solve such problems as overcrowding, unemployment, and social unrest.

The combination of these concerns gradually won for the nativists the support of some of the nation's leading public figures. Powerful opponents—employers who saw immigration as a source of cheap labor, immigrants themselves, and the immigrants' political representatives—managed to block the restriction movement for a time. But by the beginning of World War I the nativist tide was clearly rising.

The Dream of Socialism

At no time in the history of the United States to that point, and in few times after it, did radical critiques of the capitalist system attract more support than in the period between 1900 and 1914.

| Socialist Party of America |

The Socialist Party of America grew during the progressive era into a force of considerable strength. In 1912, its durable leader and perennial presidential candidate, Eugene V. Debs, received nearly 1 million ballots. Strongest in urban immigrant communities (particularly among Germans and Jews), it attracted the loyalties, too, of a substantial number of Protestant farmers in the South and Midwest.

Virtually all socialists agreed on the need for basic structural changes in the economy, but they differed on the extent of those changes and the tactics necessary to achieve them. Some endorsed the radical goals of European Marxists (a complete end to capitalism and private property); others envisioned a more moderate reform that would allow small-scale private enterprise to survive. Militant groups within the party favored direct action. Most conspicuous was the radical labor union the Industrial Workers of the World (IWW), whose members were

| IWW |

known to their opponents as "Wobblies." Under

the leadership of William ("Big Bill") Haywood, the IWW advocated a single union for all workers. The Wobblies were widely believed to have been responsible for the dynamiting of railroad lines and power stations and other acts of terror, although their use of violence was greatly exaggerated by their opponents.

More moderate socialists dominated the party. They emphasized gradual education of the public to the need for change. But by the end of World War I, because the party had refused to support the war effort and because of a growing wave of antiradicalism, socialism was in decline as a significant political force.

Decentralization and Regulation

Many reformers agreed with the socialists that the greatest threat to the nation's economy was excessive centralization of power and concentration of wealth. They argued that the federal government should ensure the survival of genuine economic competition. This viewpoint came to be identified particularly closely with Louis D. Brandeis, a brilliant lawyer and later a justice of the Supreme Court, who spoke and wrote widely (most notably in his 1913 book, *Other People's Money*) about the "curse of bigness."

Other progressives were less enthusiastic about the virtues of competition. More important to them was efficiency, which they believed economic concentration encouraged. Government, they argued, should not fight "bigness," but should guard against abuses of power by large institutions. It should distinguish between "good trusts" and "bad trusts." Since economic consolidation was destined to remain a permanent feature of American society, continuing oversight by a strong, modernized government was essential. One of the most important spokesmen for this emerging "nationalist" position was Herbert Croly, whose 1909 book, *The Promise of American Life*, became an influential progressive document. One of those who came to endorse that position was Theodore Roosevelt, who became for a time the most powerful symbol of the reform impulse at the national level.

Herbert Croly

CONCLUSION

A powerful surge of reform efforts emerged in the last years of the nineteenth century and the first years of the twentieth—reforms intended to deal with the vexing problems that the rise of the modern industrial economy had caused. American reformers at the time thought of themselves as "progressives."

The reforms were of a bewildering variety—efforts to improve the moral fabric of families and communities; efforts to make politics more efficient and less corrupt; efforts to tame or discipline the great industrial combinations of the time; efforts to empower some groups and restrict or control others. The ideas that lay behind these reforms were similarly various. "Progressivism" was a remarkably heterogeneous movement, united—if it was united at all—by the common belief among reformers that progress was indeed possible and that purposeful human intervention in the life of society and its economy was necessary. The reform crusades gained strength steadily from the 1880s onward. By the early years of the twentieth century, reform was beginning to transform the character of society and the nature of American politics.

INTERACTIVE LEARNING

On the *Primary Source Investigator CD-ROM,* check out a number of valuable tools for further exploration of the content of this chapter.

Mini-Documentary Movie

- **Votes for Women**. The story of the fight by women for the right to vote in the United States, culminating with the ratification of the Nineteenth Amendment. (Doc D15)

Interactive Map

• Woman Suffrage (Map M16)

Primary Sources

Documents, images, and maps related to the rise of Progressivism. Some highlights include:

• The Nineteenth Amendment to the U.S. Constitution, which gave women the right to vote

• Images of women hanging pro-suffrage posters and a video clip of women suffragists meeting with President Roosevelt

Online Learning Center
(www.mhhe.com/unfinishedinteractive)
Explore this rich website, providing additional exploration of the material covered in this chapter, online versions of the interactive maps included on the Primary Source Investigator CD-ROM, as well as several study aids, including a multiple-choice quiz, essay questions, a glossary, and other valuable tools. Also in the Online Learning Center for this chapter look for an *Interactive Feature Essay* on:

• **Where Historians Disagree: Progressive Reform**

FOR FURTHER REFERENCE

Richard Hofstadter, *The Age of Reform: From Bryan to FDR* (1955) is a classic, and now controversial, analysis of the partly psychological origins of the Populist and progressive movements. Robert Wiebe, *The Search for Order, 1877–1920* (1967) is an important organizational interpretation of the era. Gabriel Kolko makes a distinctly revisionist argument that business conservatism was at the heart of the progressive movement in *The Triumph of Conservatism* (1963). Alan Dawley, *Struggles for Justice: Social Responsibility and the Liberal State* (1991) is a sophisticated synthetic account of progressive movements and their ideas. John Milton Cooper, *The Pivotal Decades: The United States, 1900–1920* (1990) is a good narrative history of the period. Arthur S. Link and Richard L. McCormick, *Progressivism* (1983) is a brief interpretation. Daniel T. Rodgers, *Atlantic Crossings: Social Politics in a Progressive Age* (1998) is an important study of the passage of progressive ideas back and forth across the Atlantic. For powerful insights into pragmatism, an important philosophical underpinning to much reform, see Robert Westbrook, *John Dewey and American Democracy* (1991) and Louis Menand, *The Metaphysical Club: A Story of Ideas* (2001). Thomas L. Haskell, *The Emergence of Professional Social Science* (1977) is an important study of the social sciences and professionalism. Paul Starr, *The Social Transformation of American Medicine* (1982) is a pathbreaking study of the emergence of modern systems of health care. Morton J. Horwirtz, *The Transformation of American Law, 1870–1960: The Challenge to Legal Orthodoxy* (1992) is an important, controversial study of the way the legal world responded to economic and social change. Nancy Cott, *The Grounding of American Feminism* (1987) studies the shifting roles and beliefs of women. Kathryn Kish Sklar, *Florence Kelley and the Nation's Work: The Rise of Women's Political Culture, 1830–1900* (1995) examines the impact of female reformers on the progressive movement and the nation's political culture as a whole. Linda Gordon, *The Great Arizona Orphan Abduction* (1999) is the story of an early twentieth-century event that reveals the power of race, religion, and gender in dealing with immigrants. Paula Giddings, *When and Where I Enter: The Impact of Black Women on Race and Sex in America* (1984) is a good introduction to the intersection of gender and race. Glenda Gilmore, *Gender and Jim Crow: Women and the Politics of White Supremacy in North Carolina, 1896–1920* (1996) examines the role of gender in the construction of segregation. Louis Harlan, *Booker T. Washington: The Making of a Black Leader* (1956) and *Booker T. Washington: The Wizard of Tuskegee* (1983) are parts of an outstanding multivolume biography, as are David Levering Lewis, *W. E. B. Du Bois: Biography of a Race* (1993) and *W. E. B. Du Bois: The Fight for Equality and the American Century* (2000).

22 The Battle for National Reform

(Theodore Roosevelt, *John Singer Sargent. White House Historical Association (White House Collection) (56)*)

Efforts to reform the industrial economy encountered repeated frustrations at the state and local levels, so beginning early in the twentieth century, reformers began to look to the federal government. As at the state and local levels, however, the national government—mired in partisan politics—seemed poorly suited to serve as an agent of reform. Progressives attempted to make it more responsive to their demands. Some reformers, for example, urged an end to the system by which state legislatures elected the members of the United States Senate; they proposed instead a direct popular election, which they believed would force the Senate to react more directly to public demands. The Seventeenth Amendment, passed by Congress in 1912 and ratified by the states in 1913, provided for that change.

But even a reformed Congress, progressives believed, could not be expected to provide the kind of coherent leadership their agenda required. Congress was too clumsy, too divided, too tied to local, parochial interests. If the federal government was truly to fulfill its mission, most reformers agreed, it would require leadership from the presidency.

THEODORE ROOSEVELT AND THE PROGRESSIVE PRESIDENCY

To a generation of progressive reformers, Theodore Roosevelt was an idol. Yet Roosevelt was in many respects decidedly conservative. He earned his extraordinary popularity less because of the extent of his reforms than because of his ebullient public personality and because he invested the presidency with something of its modern status as the center of national political life.

The Accidental President

When President William McKinley suddenly died in September 1901, an assassination victim, Roosevelt (who had been elected vice president less than a year before) was only forty-two years old, the youngest man ever to assume the presidency. Already, however, he had achieved a reputation as something of a wild man. Party boss Mark Hanna exclaimed, "Now look, that damned cowboy is president of the United States!" But Roosevelt as president became a champion of cautious, moderate change.

Roosevelt's Vision of Federal Power
Roosevelt envisioned the federal government not as the agent of any particular interest but as a mediator of the public good. This attitude found expression in his policy toward industrial combinations. At the heart of that was his desire to win for government the power to investigate the activities of corporations and publicize the results. The pressure of educated public opinion, he believed, would eliminate most corporate abuses.

Roosevelt engaged in a few highly publicized efforts to break up combinations, among them a 1902 suit against a great new railroad combination in the Northwest, the Northern Securities Company. But he was not a trustbuster at heart, and his use of antitrust law did not mark any serious effort to reverse the trend toward economic concentration.

A similar commitment to establishing the government as an impartial regulatory mechanism shaped Roosevelt's policy toward labor. In the past, federal intervention in industrial disputes had almost always meant action on behalf of employers. Roosevelt was willing to consider labor's position as well. When a 1902 strike by the United Mine Workers dragged on long enough to endanger coal supplies for the coming winter, Roosevelt asked both the operators and the miners to accept federal arbitration; and he threatened to dispatch federal troops to seize the mines when the owners refused. They soon relented. Arbitrators awarded the strikers a 10 percent wage increase and a nine-hour day.

Reform was not Roosevelt's main priority during his first years as president. He was too concerned

1901	1902	1903	1904	1906	1908
McKinley assassinated Theodore Roosevelt becomes president	Northern Securities antitrust case	Panamanian independence	Roosevelt Corollary Roosevelt elected president	Hepburn Railroad Regulation Act Meat Inspection Act	Taft elected president

1909	1912	1913	1914	1915	1916
Payne-Aldrich Tariff U.S. troops in Nicaragua	Wilson elected president	16th Amendment (income tax) 17th Amendment (direct election of U.S. senators) Federal Reserve Act	Federal Trade Commission Act Panama Canal opened	U.S. troops in Haiti	U.S. troops in Mexico

TIME LINE

with winning an election in his own right, which meant not antagonizing the Republican Old Guard. By early 1904, Roosevelt had all but neutralized his opposition within the party. He won its presidential nomination with ease. And in the general election, where he faced a pallid conservative Democrat, Alton B. Parker, he captured over 57 percent of the popular vote.

The Square Deal

During the 1904 campaign, Roosevelt boasted that he had worked in the anthracite coal strike to provide everyone with a "square deal." In his second term, he set out to extend this square deal further. One of his first targets was the powerful railroad industry. The Interstate Commerce Act of 1887, establishing the Interstate Commerce Commission (ICC), had been an early effort to regulate the industry, but over the years the courts had sharply limited its influence. The Hepburn Railroad Regulation Act of 1906 sought to restore some regulatory authority to the government by giving the ICC authority to inspect the books of railroad companies.

Hepburn Railroad Regulation Act

Roosevelt also pressured Congress to enact the Pure Food and Drug Act, which restricted the sale of dangerous or ineffective medicines. When Upton Sinclair's powerful novel *The Jungle* appeared in 1906, featuring appalling descriptions of conditions in the meatpacking industry, Roosevelt insisted on passage of the Meat Inspection Act, which ultimately helped eliminate many diseases once transmitted in impure meat. Starting in 1907, he proposed even more stringent measures: an eight-hour day for workers, broader compensation for victims of industrial accidents, inheritance and income taxes, regulation of the stock market, and others. But conservative opposition blocked much of this agenda and was responsible for a widening gulf between the president and the conservative wing of his party.

Roosevelt and the Environment

Roosevelt's aggressive policies on behalf of conservation contributed to that gulf. Using executive powers, he restricted private development on millions of acres of undeveloped government land by adding them to the national forest system. When conservatives in Congress restricted his authority over public lands in 1907, Roosevelt and his chief forester, Gifford Pinchot, worked to seize all the forests and many of the water power sites still in the public domain before the bill became law.

BOYS IN THE MINES These young boys, covered in grime and no more than twelve years old, pose at the entrance to the coal mine in Pennsylvania where they worked. The rugged conditions in the mines were one cause of the great strike of 1902, in which Theodore Roosevelt intervened. *(Lewis Hine/Corbis)*

Roosevelt was the first president to take an active interest in the new conservation movement, and his policies had a lasting effect on environmental policies. Many people who considered themselves "conservationists" promoted policies to protect land for carefully managed development. That was in part a result of the influence of Pinchot, the first director of the National Forest Service, who supported rational and efficient use of the wilderness. As a result, the most important legacy of Roosevelt's conservation policy was to establish the government's role as manager of the continuing development of the wilderness.

The Old Guard may have opposed Roosevelt's efforts to extend government control over vast new lands. But they eagerly supported another important aspect of Roosevelt's natural resource policy: public reclamation and irrigation projects. In 1902, the president backed the National Reclamation Act, which provided federal funds for the construction of dams, reservoirs, and canals in the West—projects that would open new lands for cultivation and, years later, provide cheap electric power.

Despite his sympathy with Pinchot's vision of conservation, Roosevelt also shared some of the concerns of the naturalists—those within the conservation movement committed to protecting the natural beauty of the land and the health of its wildlife from human intrusion. Roosevelt even spent four days camping in the Sierras with John Muir, the nation's leading preservationist and the founder of the Sierra Club. And he added significantly to the National Park System, whose purpose was to protect public land from any exploitation or development at all.

The contending views of the early conservation movement came to a head beginning in 1906 in a sensational controversy over the Hetch Hetchy Valley in Yosemite National Park—a spectacular, high-walled valley highly popular with naturalists. But many residents of San Francisco, worried about finding enough water to serve their growing population, saw Hetch Hetchy as an ideal place for a reservoir.

For over a decade, a battle raged between naturalists and the advocates of the dam, a **Preservation versus "Rational Use"** battle that consumed the energies of John Muir for the rest of his life. To Pinchot, the issue was the practical one of whether "leaving this valley in a state of nature is greater than using it for the benefit of the city of San Francisco." Muir helped place a referendum question on the ballot in 1908, certain that the residents of the city would oppose the project "as soon as light is cast upon it." Instead, San Franciscans approved the dam by a huge margin. Construction of the dam finally began after World War I.

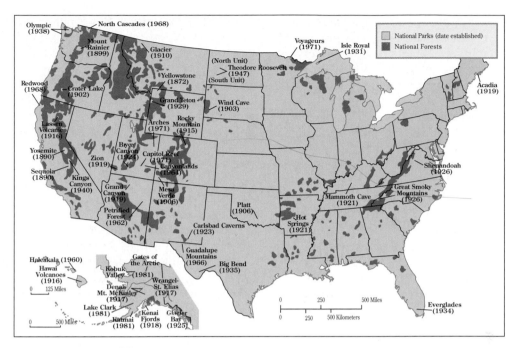

ESTABLISHMENT OF NATIONAL PARKS AND FORESTS This map illustrates the steady growth throughout the late nineteenth and twentieth centuries of the systems of national parks and national forests in the United States. ▌ *What is the difference between national parks and national forests?*

This setback for the naturalists was not, however, a total defeat. The fight against Hetch Hetchy helped mobilize a new coalition of people committed to preservation, not "rational use," of wilderness and made clear that the casual exploitation of natural wonders would no longer be unopposed.

Panic and Retirement

Despite the flurry of reforms Roosevelt was able to enact, the government still had relatively little control over the industrial economy. That became clear in 1907, when a serious recession began. Conservatives blamed Roosevelt's "mad" economic policies for the disaster. And while the president naturally (and correctly) disagreed, he nevertheless acted quickly to reassure business leaders that he would not interfere with their private recovery efforts.

J. P. Morgan

The financier J. P. Morgan helped construct a pool of the assets of several New York banks to prop up shaky financial institutions. The key to the arrangement, he told the president, was the purchase by U.S. Steel of the shares of the Tennessee Coal and Iron Company, currently held by a threatened New York bank. He would need assurances that the purchase would not prompt antitrust action. Roosevelt agreed, and the plan proceeded.

Roosevelt loved being president, and many people assumed he would run for the office again in 1908 despite the long-standing tradition of presidents serving no more than two terms. But the Panic of 1907 and Roosevelt's reform efforts had so alienated conservatives in his own party that he might have had difficulty winning the Republican nomination for another term. In 1904, moreover, he had made a public promise to step down four years later. And so, after nearly eight energetic years in the White House, Theodore Roosevelt, fifty years old, retired from public life—briefly.

THE TROUBLED SUCCESSION

William Howard Taft, who assumed the presidency in

William Howard Taft

1909, had been Theodore Roosevelt's hand-picked successor; progressive reformers believed him to be one of their own. But Taft had also been a restrained and moderate jurist; conservatives expected him to abandon Roosevelt's aggressive use of presidential powers. By seeming acceptable to almost everyone, Taft easily won election to the White House in 1908. He received his party's nomination virtually uncontested. His victory in the general election in November—over William Jennings Bryan, running for the Democrats for the third time—was a foregone conclusion.

Four years later, however, Taft would leave office the most decisively defeated president of the twentieth century. Taft's failure was a result in part of his failure to match Roosevelt's personal dynamism. More significant, however, was that having come into office as the darling of progressives and conservatives alike, he soon found that he could not please both groups. Gradually he found himself pleasing the conservatives and alienating the progressives.

Taft and the Progressives

Taft's first problem arose in the opening months of the new administration, when he called Congress into special session to lower protective tariff rates. But the president made no effort to overcome the opposition of the congressional Old Guard, arguing that it would violate the constitutional doctrine of separation of powers if he were to intervene in legislative matters. The result was the feeble Payne-Aldrich Tariff, which reduced tariff rates scarcely at all.

| Payne-Aldrich Tariff |

A sensational controversy broke out late in 1909 that helped destroy Taft's popularity with reformers for good. Many progressives had been unhappy when Taft replaced Roosevelt's secretary of the interior, James R. Garfield, an aggressive conservationist, with Richard A. Ballinger, a more conservative corporate lawyer. Suspicion of Ballinger grew when he attempted to invalidate Roosevelt's removal of nearly 1 million acres of forests and mineral reserves from the public lands available for private development.

In the midst of this mounting concern, Louis Glavis, an Interior Department investigator, charged the new secretary with having once connived to turn over valuable public coal lands in Alaska to a private syndicate for personal profit. Glavis took the evidence to Gifford Pinchot, still head of the Forest Service. Pinchot took the charges to the president. Taft investigated them and decided they were groundless. But Pinchot leaked the story to the press and asked Congress to investigate the scandal. The president discharged him for insubordination, and the congressional committee appointed to study the controversy, dominated by Old Guard Republicans, exonerated Ballinger. But progressives supported Pinchot. The controversy aroused as much public passion as any dispute of its time; and when it was over, Taft had alienated the supporters of Roosevelt completely and, it seemed, irrevocably.

| Pinchot-Ballinger Controversy |

The Return of Roosevelt

During most of these controversies, Roosevelt was away on a safari in Africa and a tour of Europe. To the American public, however, he remained a formidable presence. His return to New York in the spring of 1910 was a major public event. Roosevelt insisted that he had no plans to reenter politics, but within a month he announced that he would embark on a national speaking tour. Furious with Taft, he was becoming convinced that he alone was capable of reuniting the Republican Party.

The real signal of Roosevelt's decision to assume leadership of Republican reformers came in a speech he gave on September 1, 1910, in Osawatomie, Kansas. In it he outlined a set of principles, which he labeled the "New Nationalism," that made clear he had moved a considerable way from the cautious reform conservatism of the first years of his presidency. He argued that social justice was possible only through the efforts of a strong federal government whose executive acted as the "steward of the public welfare." He supported graduated income and inheritance taxes, workers' compensation for industrial accidents, regulation of the labor of women and children, tariff revision, and firmer regulation of corporations.

| Roosevelt's "New Nationalism" |

Spreading Insurgency

The congressional elections of 1910 provided further evidence of how far the progressive revolt had spread. In primary elections, conservative Republicans suffered defeat after defeat. In the general election, the Democrats won control of the House of Representatives and gained strength in the Senate. But Roosevelt still denied any presidential

ROOSEVELT AT OSAWATOMIE
Roosevelt's famous speech at Osawatomie, Kansas, in 1910 was the most radical of his career and openly marked his break with the Taft administration and the Republican leadership. *(Brown Brothers)*

ambitions. Two events, however, changed his mind. The first, on October 27, 1911, was the announcement by the administration of a suit against U.S. Steel, which charged, among other things, that the 1907 acquisition of the Tennessee Coal and Iron Company had been illegal. Roosevelt had approved that acquisition in the midst of the 1907 panic, and he was enraged by the implication that he had acted improperly.

Roosevelt was still reluctant to become a candidate for president, because Senator Robert La Follette, the great Wisconsin progressive, had been working since 1911 to secure the presidential nomination for himself. But La Follette's candidacy stumbled in February 1912 when, exhausted, and distraught over the illness of a daughter, he appeared to suffer a nervous breakdown during a speech in Philadelphia. Roosevelt announced his candidacy on February 22.

T. R. versus Taft

For all practical purposes, the campaign for the Republican nomination had now become a battle between Roosevelt, the champion of the progressives, and Taft, the candidate of the conservatives. Roosevelt scored overwhelming victories in all thirteen presidential primaries. Taft, however, remained the choice of most party leaders.

The battle for the nomination at the Chicago convention revolved around an unusually large number of contested delegates: 254 in all. Roosevelt needed fewer than half the disputed seats to clinch the nomination. But the Republican National Committee, controlled by the Old Guard, awarded all but 19 of them to Taft. At a rally the night before the convention opened, Roosevelt addressed 5,000 cheering supporters and announced that if the party refused to seat his delegates, he would continue his own candidacy outside the party. The next day, he led his supporters out of the convention, and out of the party. The convention then nominated Taft on the first ballot.

Roosevelt summoned his supporters back to Chicago in August for another convention, this one to launch the new Progressive Party and nominate himself as its presidential candidate. Roosevelt approached the battle feeling, as he put it, "fit as a bull moose" (thus giving his new party an enduring nickname). But by then, he was aware that his cause was virtually hopeless. That was partly because many of the insurgents who had supported him during the primaries refused to follow him out of the Republican Party. It was also because of the man the Democrats had nominated for president.

The "Bull Moose" Party

WOODROW WILSON AND THE NEW FREEDOM

The 1912 presidential contest was not simply one between conservatives and reformers. It was also one between two brands of progressivism. And it was one that matched the two most important national leaders of the early twentieth century in unequal contest.

Woodrow Wilson

At the 1912 Democratic Convention in Baltimore in June, Champ Clark, the conservative Speaker of the House, was unable to assemble the two-thirds majority necessary for nomination because of progressive opposition. Finally, on the forty-sixth ballot, Woodrow Wilson, the governor of New Jersey and the only genuinely progressive candidate in the race, emerged as the party's nominee.

Wilson had been a professor of political science at Princeton until 1902, when he was named president of the university. Elected governor of New Jersey in 1910, he demonstrated a commitment to reform. During his two years in the statehouse, he earned a national reputation for winning passage of progressive legislation. As a presidential candidate in 1912, Wilson presented a progressive program that came to be called the "New Freedom." Wilson's **"New Freedom"** New Freedom differed from Roosevelt's New Nationalism most clearly in its approach to economic policy and the trusts. Roosevelt believed in accepting economic concentration and using government to regulate and control it. Wilson seemed to side with those who believed that the proper response to monopoly was not to regulate it but to destroy it.

The 1912 presidential campaign was something of an anticlimax. William Howard Taft barely campaigned at all. Roosevelt campaigned energetically (until a gunshot wound from a would-be assassin forced him to the sidelines), but he failed to draw many Democratic progressives away from Wilson. In November, Roosevelt and Taft split the Republican vote; Wilson held onto most Democrats and won. He polled only a plurality of the popular vote: 42 percent, compared with 27 percent for Roosevelt, 23 percent for Taft, and 6 percent for the

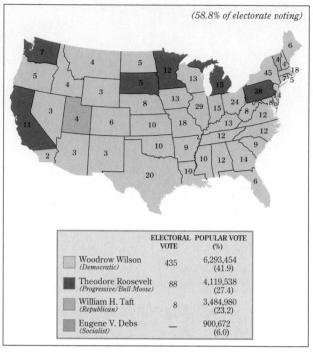

(58.8% of electorate voting)

	ELECTORAL VOTE	POPULAR VOTE (%)
Woodrow Wilson *(Democratic)*	435	6,293,454 (41.9)
Theodore Roosevelt *(Progressive/Bull Moose)*	88	4,119,538 (27.4)
William H. Taft *(Republican)*	8	3,484,980 (23.2)
Eugene V. Debs *(Socialist)*	—	900,672 (6.0)

ELECTION OF 1912 The election of 1912 was one of the most unusual in American history because of the dramatic schism within the Republican party. Two Republican presidents—William Howard Taft, the incumbent, and Theodore Roosevelt, his predecessor—ran against each other in 1912, opening the way for a victory by the Democratic candidate Woodrow Wilson, who won with only about 42 percent of the popular vote. A fourth candidate, the socialist Eugene V. Debs, received a significant 6 percent of the vote. ▮ *What events caused the schism between Taft and Roosevelt?*

For an interactive version of this map go to www.mhhe.com/unfinishedinteractive

socialist Eugene Debs. But in the electoral college, Wilson won 435 of the 531 votes.

The Scholar as President

More than Taft, more even than Roosevelt, Wilson concentrated the powers of the executive branch in his own hands. He exerted firm control over his cabinet, and he delegated real authority only to those whose loyalty to him was beyond question. Perhaps the clearest indication of his style of leadership was the identity of his most powerful adviser: Colonel Edward M. House, an intelligent and ambitious Texan whose only claim to authority was his personal intimacy with the president.

In legislative matters, Wilson skillfully used his position as party leader to weld together a coalition that would support his program. Democratic majorities in both houses of Congress made his task easier. Wilson's first triumph as president was a substantial lowering of the protective tariff. The Underwood-Simmons Tariff provided cuts substantial enough, progressives believed, to introduce real competition into American markets and thus to help break the power of trusts. To make up for the loss of revenue under the new tariff, Congress approved a graduated income tax. This first

Income Tax Adopted

modern income tax imposed a 1 percent tax on individuals and corporations earning over $4,000, with rates ranging up to 6 percent on incomes over $500,000.

Wilson held Congress in session through the summer to work on a major reform of the American banking system: the Federal Reserve Act, which Congress passed and which the president signed on December 23, 1913. It created twelve regional banks, each to be owned and controlled by the individual banks of its district. The regional Federal Reserve banks would hold a certain percentage of the assets of their member banks in reserve; they would use those reserves to support loans to private banks at an interest (or "discount") rate that the Federal Reserve system would set; they would issue a new type of paper currency—Federal Reserve notes—that would become the nation's basic medium of trade and would be backed by the government. Most important, perhaps, they would be able to shift funds quickly to troubled areas—to meet increased demands for credit or to protect imperiled banks. Supervising and regulating the entire system was a national Federal Reserve Board, whose members were appointed by the president.

In 1914, Wilson proposed two measures to deal with the problem of monopoly. There was a proposal to create a federal agency through which the government would help business police itself. There were also proposals to strengthen the government's ability actually to break up trusts. The two measures

Federal Trade Commission Act

took shape as the Federal Trade Commission Act and the Clayton Antitrust Act.

The Federal Trade Commission Act created a regulatory agency that would help businesses determine in advance whether their actions would be acceptable to the government. The agency would also have authority to launch prosecutions against "unfair trade practices," which the law did not define, and it would have wide power to investigate corporate behavior. The act, in short, increased the government's regulatory authority significantly. Wilson signed it happily. But he seemed to lose interest in the Clayton Antitrust Bill and did little to protect it from conservative assaults, which greatly weakened it.

Retreat and Advance

By the fall of 1914, Wilson believed that the program of the New Freedom was essentially complete. He refused to support the movement for woman suffrage. Deferring to southern Democrats, he condoned the reimposition of segregation in the agencies of the federal government. When progressives attempted to enlist his support for new reform legislation, he dismissed their proposals as unconstitutional or unnecessary.

The elections of 1914, however, shattered the president's complacency. Democrats suffered major losses in the House of Representatives, and voters who in 1912 had supported the Progressive Party began returning to the Republicans. Wilson would not be able to rely on a divided opposition when he ran for reelection. By the end of 1915, therefore, Wilson had begun to support a second flurry of reforms. In January 1916, he appointed Louis Brandeis to the Supreme Court, making him not only the first Jew but the most advanced progressive to serve there. Later, he supported a measure to make it easier for farmers to receive credit and one creating a system of workers' compensation for federal employees.

In 1916, Wilson supported the Keating-Owen Act. The measure prohibited the shipment across state lines of goods produced by underage children, thus giving an expanded importance to the constitutional clause assigning Congress the task of regulating interstate commerce. (It would be some years before the Supreme Court would uphold this interpretation of the clause; the Court invalidated the Keating-Owen Act in 1918.) The president similarly supported measures that used federal taxing authority as a vehicle for legislating social change. After the Court struck down Keating-Owen, a new law attempted to achieve the same goal by imposing a heavy tax on the products of child labor. (The Court later struck it down, too.) And the Smith-Lever Act of 1914 demonstrated another way in which the federal government could influence local behavior; it offered matching federal grants to states that agreed to support agricultural extension education.

| Limiting Child Labor |

THE "BIG STICK": AMERICA AND THE WORLD, 1901–1917

American foreign policy during the progressive years reflected many of the same impulses that were motivating domestic reform. But more than that, it reflected the nation's new sense of itself as a world power.

Roosevelt and "Civilization"

Theodore Roosevelt believed in the value and importance of using American power in the world (a conviction he once described by citing the proverb, "Speak softly, but carry a big stick"). But he also believed that an important distinction existed between the "civilized" and "uncivilized" nations of the world. "Civilized" nations, as he defined them, were predominantly white and Anglo-Saxon or Teutonic; "uncivilized" nations were generally nonwhite, Latin, or Slavic. Equally important was economic development. Civilized nations were, by Roosevelt's definition, producers of industrial goods; uncivilized nations were suppliers of raw materials and markets. There was, he believed, an economic relationship between the two parts that was vital to both of them. A civilized society, therefore, had the right and duty to intervene in the affairs of a "backward" nation to preserve order and stability. That belief was one important reason for Roosevelt's early support of the development of American sea power. By 1906, the American navy had attained a size and strength surpassed only by that of Great Britain.

| Justifying Intervention |

Protecting the "Open Door" in Asia

In 1904 the Japanese staged a surprise attack on the Russian fleet at Port Arthur in southern Manchuria, a province of China that both Russia and Japan hoped to control. Roosevelt agreed to a Japanese request to mediate an end to the conflict. Russia, faring badly in the war, had no choice but to agree. At a peace conference in Portsmouth, New Hampshire, in 1905, Roosevelt extracted from the embattled Russians a recognition of Japan's territorial gains and from the Japanese an agreement to cease the fighting and expand no further. At the same time, he negotiated a secret agreement with the Japanese to ensure that the United States could continue to trade freely in the region. But in the years that followed, relations between the United States and Japan deteriorated. Having destroyed the Russian fleet at Port Arthur, Japan now emerged as the preeminent naval power in the Pacific and soon began to exclude American trade from many of the territories it controlled. Roosevelt took no direct action against Japan, but he sent sixteen battleships of the new American navy (known as the "Great White Fleet" because the ships were painted white for the voyage) on an unprecedented journey around the world that included a call on Japan.

| "Great White Fleet" |

The Iron-Fisted Neighbor

Roosevelt took a particular interest in events in Latin America, embarking on a series of ventures in the Caribbean and South America. He established a pattern of American intervention in the region that would long survive his presidency.

Crucial to Roosevelt's thinking was an incident early in his administration. In 1902, the government of Venezuela began to renege on debts to European bankers. Naval forces of Britain, Italy, and Germany blockaded the Venezuelan coast in response. Then German ships began to bombard a Venezuelan port. Roosevelt used the threat of American naval power to pressure the German navy to withdraw.

The incident helped persuade Roosevelt that European intrusions into Latin America could result not only from aggression but from instability or irresponsibility (such as defaulting on debts) within the Latin American nations themselves. As a result,

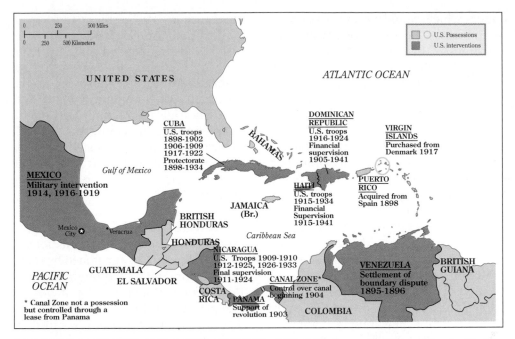

THE UNITED STATES AND LATIN AMERICA, 1895–1941 Except for Puerto Rico, the Virgin Islands, and the Canal Zone, the United States had no formal possessions in Latin America and the Caribbean in the late nineteenth century and the first half of the twentieth. But as this map reveals, the U.S. exercised considerable influence in these regions throughout this period—political and economic influence, augmented at times by military intervention. ▌ *What were some of the most frequent reasons for American intervention in Latin America?*

 For an interactive version of this map go to www.mhhe.com/unfinishedinteractive

 "Roosevelt Corollary" Announced

in 1904 he announced what came to be known as the "Roosevelt Corollary" to the Monroe Doctrine. The United States, he claimed, had the right not only to oppose European intervention in the Western Hemisphere but also to intervene itself in the domestic affairs of its neighbors if those neighbors proved unable to maintain order and national sovereignty on their own.

The immediate motivation for the Roosevelt Corollary was a crisis in the Dominican Republic. A revolution had toppled its corrupt and bankrupt government in 1903, but the new regime proved no better able than the old to make good on the country's $22 million in debts to European nations. Roosevelt established, in effect, an American receivership, assuming control of Dominican customs and distributing 45 percent of the revenues to the Dominicans and the rest to foreign creditors. This

arrangement lasted, in one form or another, for more than three decades.

In 1902, the United States granted political independence to Cuba, but only after the new government had agreed to the so-called Platt Amendment (named after Senator Thomas Platt of Pennsylvania) to its constitution. The amendment gave the United States the right to prevent any foreign power from intruding into the new nation. In 1906, when domestic uprisings threatened the island's stability, American troops landed in Cuba, quelled the fighting, and remained there for three years.

The Panama Canal

The most celebrated accomplishment of Roosevelt's presidency was the construction of the Panama Canal, which linked the Atlantic and the Pacific. At first, Roosevelt and many others favored a route across Nicaragua, which would permit a sea-level canal requiring no locks. But they soon turned instead to the Isthmus of Panama in Colombia, the site of an earlier, failed effort by a French company to construct a channel. Although the Panama route was not at sea level, it was shorter than the one in Nicaragua, and construction was already about 40 percent complete.

Roosevelt dispatched John Hay, his secretary of state, to negotiate an agreement with Colombian diplomats that would allow construction to begin without delay. Under heavy American pressure, the Colombian chargé d'affaires, Tomas Herrán, signed an agreement giving the United States perpetual rights to a six-mile-wide "canal zone" across Colombia; in return, the United States would pay Colombia $10 million and an annual rental of $250,000. The treaty produced outrage in the Colombian senate, which refused to ratify it. Colombia then sent a new representative to Washington with instructions to demand at least $20 million from the Americans plus a share of the payment to the French.

Roosevelt was furious and began to look for ways to circumvent the Colombian government. Philippe Bunau-Varilla, chief engineer of the French canal project, was a ready ally. In November 1903, he helped organize a revolution in Panama with the support of the United States. Roosevelt landed troops in Panama to "maintain order." Their presence prevented Colombian forces from suppressing the rebellion, and three days later Roosevelt recognized Panama as an independent nation. The new Panamanian government quickly agreed to the terms the Colombian senate had rejected. Work on the canal proceeded rapidly, and it opened in 1914.

Panamanian Revolt

Taft and "Dollar Diplomacy"

Like his predecessor, William Howard Taft worked to advance the nation's economic interests overseas. But he showed little interest in Roosevelt's larger vision of world stability. Taft's secretary of state, Philander C. Knox, worked aggressively to extend American investments into less-developed regions. Critics called his policies "Dollar Diplomacy."

It was particularly visible in American policy in the Caribbean. When a revolution broke out in

Nicaragua in 1909, the administration quickly sided with the insurgents and sent American troops into the country to seize the customs houses. As soon as peace was restored, Knox encouraged American bankers to offer substantial loans to the new government, thus increasing Washington's financial leverage over the country. When the new pro-American government faced an insurrection less than two years later, Taft again landed American troops in Nicaragua, this time to protect the existing regime.

Nicaragua Occupied

Diplomacy and Morality

Woodrow Wilson faced international challenges of a scope and gravity unmatched by those of any president before him. Although the greatest test of Wilsonian diplomacy did not occur until World War I, many of the qualities that he would bring to that ordeal were evident in his foreign policy from his first moments in office.

Having already seized control of the finances of the Dominican Republic in 1905, the United States established a military government there in 1916 when the Dominicans refused to accept a treaty that would have made the country a virtual American protectorate. The military occupation lasted eight years. In Haiti, Wilson landed the marines in 1915 to quell a revolution. American military forces remained in the country until 1934, and American officers drafted the new Haitian constitution adopted in 1918. When Wilson began to fear that the Danish West Indies might be about to fall into the hands of Germany, he bought the colony from Denmark and renamed it the Virgin Islands. Concerned about the possibility of European influence in Nicaragua, he signed a treaty with that country's government winning for the United States the right to intervene in Nicaragua's internal affairs to protect American interests. In all of these actions, Wilson was displaying an approach to Latin America very similar to the approaches of Roosevelt and Taft.

Intervention in Haiti and the Dominican Republic

But Wilson's view of America's role in the Western Hemisphere (and the world) was not entirely similar to the views of his predecessors. That became clear in his dealings with Mexico. For many years, under the friendly auspices of the dictator

Porfirio Díaz, American businessmen had been establishing an enormous economic presence in Mexico. In 1910, however, Díaz had been overthrown by the popular leader Francisco Madero, who seemed hostile to American businesses in Mexico. The United States encouraged a reactionary general, Victoriano Huerta, to depose Madero early in 1913, and the Taft administration prepared to recognize the new Huerta regime. Before it could do so,

Recognition Withheld

however, the new government murdered Madero, and Woodrow Wilson took office in Washington. The new president announced that he would never recognize Huerta's "government of butchers."

The conflict dragged on for years. At first, Wilson hoped that simply by refusing to recognize Huerta he could help topple the regime and bring to power the opposing Constitutionalists, led by Venustiano Carranza. But when Huerta established a full military dictatorship in October 1913, the president became more assertive. In April 1914, an officer in Huerta's army briefly arrested several American sailors from the U.S.S. *Dolphin* who had gone ashore in Tampico. The men were immediately released, but the American admiral demanded that the Huerta forces fire a twenty-one-gun salute to the American flag as a public display of penance. The Mexicans refused. Wilson used the trivial incident as a pretext for seizing the Mexican port of Veracruz.

Wilson had envisioned a bloodless action, but in a clash

Veracruz Incident

with Mexican troops in Veracruz, the Americans killed 126 of the defenders and suffered 19 casualties of their own. Now at the brink of war, Wilson began to look for a way out. His show of force, however, had helped strengthen the position of the Carranza faction, which captured Mexico City in August and forced Huerta to flee the country. At last, it seemed, the crisis might be over.

But Wilson was not yet satisfied. He reacted angrily when Carranza refused to accept American guidelines for the creation of a new government, and he briefly considered throwing his support to still another aspirant to leadership: Carranza's erstwhile lieutenant Pancho Villa. When Villa's military position deteriorated, however, Wilson abandoned him and finally, in October 1915, granted preliminary recognition to the Carranza government. Villa retaliated in January 1916 by taking sixteen American mining engineers from a train in northern Mexico and shooting them. Two months later, he led his soldiers across the border into Columbus, New Mexico, where they killed seventeen more Americans.

With the permission of the Carranza government, Wilson ordered General John J. Pershing to lead an expedi-

Pershing Expedition

tionary force across the Mexican border in pursuit

PANCHO VILLA AND HIS TROOPS Pancho Villa (fourth from left) poses with some of the leaders of his army, whose members Americans came to consider bandits once they began staging raids across the U.S. border. He was a national hero in Mexico. *(Brown Brothers)*

of Villa. The American troops never found Villa, but they did engage in two ugly skirmishes with Carranza's army. Again, the United States and Mexico stood at the brink of war. But at the last minute, Wilson drew back. He withdrew American troops from Mexico, and in March 1917, he at last granted formal recognition to the Carranza regime. By now, however, Wilson's attention was turning elsewhere—to the far greater international crisis engulfing the European continent.

CONCLUSION

Driven by the great surge of reform energies emerging throughout the United States, American national politics in the early twentieth century itself became an important battleground for progressives. The rise of national reform was a result of many things, but two in particular.

First, many reformers discovered that success required the engagement of the federal government in their efforts. Second, two national leaders helped transform the federal government into a visible and muscular vehicle of reform. Theodore Roosevelt's eight years as president changed popular expectations of the office and launched a significant reform agenda. Woodrow Wilson, who defeated not only Roosevelt's ill-fated successor William Howard Taft in 1912, but also Roosevelt himself, running as a third-party challenger, became the most successful legislative president of the early twentieth century by winning passage of a broad and ambitious reform agenda of his own.

Roosevelt, Taft, and Wilson also contributed to a continuation, and indeed an expansion, of America's active role in international affairs, in part as an effort to abet the growth of American capitalism and in part as an attempt to impose American standards of morality and democracy on other parts of the world. Similar mixtures of ideals and self-interest would soon guide the United States into a great world war.

INTERACTIVE LEARNING

On the *Primary Source Investigator CD-ROM,* check out a number of valuable tools for further exploration of the content of this chapter.

Interactive Maps
- U.S. Elections (Map M7)
- The United States and Latin America, 1895–1941 (Map M21)

Primary Sources
Documents, images, and maps related to progressivism on the national stage, highlighted by the presidencies of Theodore Roosevelt and Woodrow Wilson. Some highlights include:

- Text of the congressional act establishing Yellowstone National Park

- Photographs taken of the stockyards
- Correspondence between President Roosevelt and author Upton Sinclair
- The text of the 1906 Meat Inspection Act, and an image of a promotional poster for an early movie version of *The Jungle*

*Online Learning Center
(www.mhhe.com/unfinishedinteractive)*

Explore this rich website, providing additional exploration of the material covered in this chapter, online versions of the interactive maps included on the Primary Source Investigator CD-ROM, as well as several study aids, including a multiple-choice quiz, essay questions, a glossary, and other valuable tools.

FOR FURTHER REFERENCE

John Milton Cooper, Jr., compares the lives and ideas of the progressive movement's leading national politicians in *The Warrior and the Priest: Woodrow Wilson and Theodore Roosevelt* (1983). John Morton Blum, *The Republican Roosevelt* (1954) is a long-popular brief study. Edmund Morris, *Theodore Rex* (2002) is a popular history of Roosevelt's presidency, and H. W. Brands, *TR* (1997) is a large biography. Donald E. Anderson, *William Howard Taft* (1973) is a useful account of this unhappy presidency. Arthur S. Link is Wilson's most important biographer and the author of *Woodrow Wilson*, 5 vols., (1947–1965). Kendrick A. Clements, *The Presidency of Woodrow Wilson* (1992) is a more recent study. Thomas K. McCraw, *Prophets of Regulation* (1984) is an excellent examination of important figures in the making of modern state capacity. Michael McGerr, *The Decline of Popular Politics* (1986) is a perceptive examination of the decline of public enthusiasm for parties in the North in the late nineteenth and early twentieth centuries. Samuel P. Hays, *The Gospel of Efficiency: The Progressive Conservation Movement, 1890–1920* (1962) makes a pioneering argument about the organizational imperatives behind the conservation movement and Stephen R. Fox, *The American Conservation Movement: John Muir and His Legacy* (1981) is another valuable study. John Opie, *Nature's Nation: An Environmental History of the United States* (1998) is an ambitious synthesis of environmental history. The effects of America's interventionist policies in Latin America are described in John Womack's arresting account of the revolution in *Mexico, Zapata and the Mexican Revolution* (1968). *Theodore Roosevelt*, by David Grubin (1997) is a fine biographical film. *The "Battle for Wilderness"* (1990) is a documentary film about the conservation movement and two of its rival leaders, Gifford Pinchot and John Muir.

23

America and the Great War

(National Archives and Records Administration)

The Great War, as it was known to a generation unaware that another, greater war would soon follow, began quietly in August 1914 when Austria-Hungary invaded the tiny Balkan nation of Serbia. Within weeks, however, it had grown into a conflagration engaging the armies of most of the major nations of Europe. Americans looked on with horror as the war dragged on, murderously and inconclusively, for two and a half years. But Americans also believed at first that the conflict had little to do with them. They were wrong. After nearly three years of attempting to affect the outcome of the conflict without becoming embroiled in it, the United States formally entered the war in April 1917.

THE ROAD TO WAR

By 1914, the European nations had created an unusually precarious international system. It careened into war very quickly on the basis of what most historians agree was a minor series of provocations.

The Collapse of the European Peace

The major powers of Europe were organized by 1914 in two great, competing alliances. The "Triple Entente," which during the war became known as the "Allies," linked Britain, France, and Russia. The "Triple Alliance," later called the "Central Powers," united Germany, the Austro-Hungarian Empire, and Italy, although Italy withdrew when war began and joined the Allies. The chief rivalry, however, was not between the two alliances but between the great powers that dominated them: Great Britain and Germany.

The Anglo-German rivalry was not the immediate cause of the war. The conflict emerged most directly out of a controversy involving nationalist movements within the Austro-Hungarian Empire. On June 28, 1914, the Archduke Franz Ferdinand, heir to the throne of the tottering empire, was assassinated while paying a state visit to Sarajevo. Sarajevo is the capital of Bosnia, then a province of Austria-Hungary, which Slavic nationalists wished to annex to neighboring Serbia; the archduke's assassin was a Serbian nationalist.

This local controversy quickly escalated through the workings of the system of alliances that the great powers had constructed. Germany supported Austria-Hungary's decision to launch a punitive assault on Serbia. The Serbians called on Russia to help with their defense. The Russians began mobilizing their army on July 30. By August 3, Germany had declared war on both Russia and France and had invaded Belgium. On August 4, Great Britain declared war on Germany. Russia and the Austro-Hungarian Empire formally began hostilities on August 6. Within months, other smaller nations joined the fighting. By early 1915, virtually the entire European continent (and part of Asia) was embroiled in a major war.

> Mobilization for War

Wilson's Neutrality

Wilson called on his fellow citizens in 1914 to remain "impartial in thought as well as deed." But that was impossible, for several reasons. For one thing, many Americans were not, in fact, genuinely impartial. Some sympathized with the German cause; many more sympathized with Britain. Lurid reports of German atrocities in Belgium and France, skillfully exaggerated by British propagandists, strengthened the hostility of many Americans toward Germany.

> Sympathy with Britain

Economic realities also made it impossible for the United States to deal with the belligerents on equal terms. The British had imposed a naval blockade on Germany. As a neutral, the United States had the right, in theory, to trade with whomever it wished. A truly neutral response to the blockade would be either to defy it or to stop trading with Britain as well. But while the United States could survive an interruption of its relatively modest trade with Germany and its allies, it could not easily weather an embargo on its much more extensive trade with Britain and France. So America tacitly

1914	1915	1916	1917
World War I begins	*Lusitania* torpedoed Wilson supports preparedness	Wilson reelected	German unrestricted submarine warfare U.S. enters World War I Selective Service Act War Industries Board created

1918	1919	1920	1927
Sedition Act Wilson's Fourteen Points Armistice ends war Paris Peace Conference	Senate rejects Treaty of Versailles Race riots in Chicago and other cities Steel strike and other labor actions	19th Amendment ratified Palmer Raids and Red Scare Harding elected president	Sacco and Vanzetti executed

accepted the blockade of Germany and continued trading with Britain. By 1915, the United States had gradually transformed itself from a neutral power into the arsenal of the Allies.

The Germans, in the meantime, were resorting to a new and, in American eyes, barbaric tactic: subma-

Submarine Warfare

rine warfare. Unable to challenge British domination on the ocean's surface, the Germans announced early in 1915 that enemy vessels would be sunk on sight. Months later, on May 7, 1915, a German submarine sank the British passenger liner *Lusitania* without warning, causing the deaths of 1,198 people, 128 of them Americans. The ship was carrying not only passengers but munitions; but most Americans considered the attack an unprovoked act on civilians.

Wilson angrily demanded that Germany promise not to repeat such outrages, and the Germans finally agreed to his demands. But early in 1916, in response to an announcement that the Allies were now arming merchant ships to sink submarines, Germany proclaimed that it would fire on such vessels without warning. A few weeks later, it attacked the unarmed French steamer *Sussex*, injuring several American passengers. Again, Wilson demanded that Germany abandon its "unlawful" tactics; again, the German government relented.

Preparedness versus Pacifism

The question of whether America should make military and economic preparations for war provided a preliminary issue over which pacifists and interventionists could debate. Wilson at first

Pacifists and Interventionists

denounced the idea of an American military buildup as needless and provocative. In the fall of 1915, however, he endorsed an ambitious proposal by American military leaders for a large and rapid increase in the nation's armed forces.

Still, the peace faction wielded considerable political strength, as became clear at the Democratic Convention in the summer of 1916. The convention became almost hysterically enthusiastic when the keynote speaker punctuated his list of the president's diplomatic achievements with the chant, "What did we do? What did we do? . . . We didn't go to war! We didn't go to war!" That speech helped produce one of the most prominent slogans of Wilson's reelection campaign: "He kept us out of war." During the campaign, Wilson did nothing to discourage those who argued that the Republican candidate, the progressive New York governor Charles Evans Hughes, was more likely than he to lead the nation into war. Wilson ultimately won reelection by fewer than 600,000 popular votes and only 23 electoral votes.

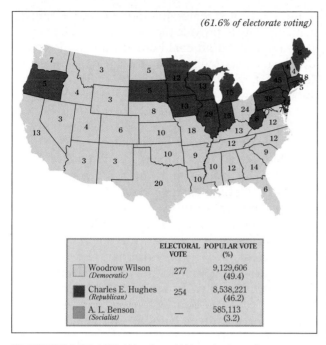

(61.6% of electorate voting)

	ELECTORAL VOTE	POPULAR VOTE (%)
Woodrow Wilson (Democratic)	277	9,129,606 (49.4)
Charles E. Hughes (Republican)	254	8,538,221 (46.2)
A. L. Benson (Socialist)	—	585,113 (3.2)

ELECTION OF 1916 Woodrow Wilson had good reason to be concerned about his reelection prospects in 1916. He had won only about 42 percent of the vote in 1912, and the Republican party—which had been divided four years earlier—was now reunited around the popular Charles Evans Hughes. In the end, Wilson won a narrow victory. Note the striking regional character of his victory. ▮ *How did Wilson use the war in Europe to bolster his election prospects?*

A War for Democracy

Tensions between the United States and Germany remained high. But Wilson still required a justification for American intervention that would unite public opinion. In the end, he created that rationale himself. The United States, Wilson insisted, was committed to using the war as a vehicle for constructing a new world order. In a speech before a joint session of Congress in January 1917, he presented a plan for a postwar order in which the United States would help maintain peace through a permanent league of nations—a "peace without victory." These were, Wilson believed, goals worth fighting for.   **"Peace without Victory"** ▮

In January, the military leaders of Germany decided on a dramatic gamble: a series of major assaults on the enemy's lines in France. At the same time, they would begin unrestricted submarine warfare (against American as well as Allied ships) to cut Britain off from vital supplies. Then, on February 25, the British gave Wilson an intercepted telegram sent by the German foreign minister, Arthur Zimmermann, to the government of Mexico. It   **Zimmermann Telegram** ▮ proposed that in the event of war between Germany and the United States, the Mexicans should join with Germany against the Americans. In return,

MARCHING FOR VICTORY
One of the great tasks facing the United States government as it entered World War I in 1917 was to generate popular support for a war that most Americans had been reluctant to enter. Here, President Wilson marches in a Red Cross parade in Washington shortly after the declaration of war. *(Bettmann/Corbis)*

they would regain their "lost provinces" in the north when the war was over. Widely publicized by British propagandists and in the American press, the Zimmermann telegram inflamed public opinion. Meanwhile in March 1917 a revolution in Russia toppled the czarist regime and replaced it with a republican government. The United States would now be spared the embarrassment of allying itself with a despotic monarchy.

On the rainy evening of April 2, two weeks after German submarines had torpedoed three American ships, Wilson appeared before a joint session of Congress and asked for a declaration of war. Even then, opposition remained. For four days, pacifists in Congress carried on their futile struggle. When the declaration of war finally passed on April 6, fifty representatives and six senators had voted against it.

"WAR WITHOUT STINT"

Armies on both sides in Europe were decimated and exhausted by the time of Woodrow Wilson's declaration of war. The Allies looked desperately to the United States for help in breaking the stalemate.

The Military Struggle

By the spring of 1917, Great Britain was suffering such vast losses from attacks by German submarines that its ability to continue receiving vital supplies from across the Atlantic was in jeopardy. Within weeks of joining the war the United States had begun to alter the balance. A fleet of American destroyers aided the British navy in its assault on the U-boats. Other American warships escorted merchant vessels across the Atlantic. Americans also helped plant antisubmarine mines in the North Sea. The results were dramatic.

Many Americans had hoped that providing naval assistance alone would be enough to turn the tide in the war, but it quickly became clear that a major commitment of American ground forces would be necessary as well. Britain and France had few remaining reserves; and after the Bolshevik Revolution in November 1917, a new communist government, led by V. I. Lenin, negotiated a hasty and costly peace between Russia and the Central Powers, thus freeing German troops to fight on the western front.

Bolshevik Revolution

But the United States did not have a large enough standing army to provide the necessary ground forces. Only a national draft could provide the needed men. Despite protests, Wilson won passage of the Selective Service Act, which brought nearly 3 million men into the army.

The engagement of these forces in combat was brief but intense. Not until the spring of 1918 were significant numbers of American troops available for battle. Under the command of General John J. Pershing, the American troops joined the existing Allied forces in turning back a series of new German assaults. In early June, they assisted the French in repelling a bitter German offensive at Château-Thierry, near Paris. Six weeks later, the American Expeditionary Force (AEF) helped turn away another assault, at Rheims, farther south. By July 18, the German advance had been halted. On September 26, an American fighting force of over 1 million soldiers advanced against the Germans in the Argonne Forest. By the end of October, the force had helped push the Germans back toward their own border.

Argonne Forest

Faced with an invasion of their own country, German military leaders now began to seek an armistice. Pershing wanted to drive on into Germany itself; but other Allied leaders, after first insisting on terms that made the agreement (in their eyes at least) little different from a surrender, accepted the German proposal. On November 11, 1918, more than four years after it began, the Great War shuddered to a close.

The New Technology of Warfare

World War I was a proving ground for a range of military and other technologies. The trench warfare that characterized the conflict was necessary because of the enormous destructive power of newly improved machine guns and higher-powered artillery. Trenches sheltered troops while allowing limited, and usually inconclusive, fighting. But technology overtook the trenches, too, as mobile weapons—tanks and flamethrowers—proved capable of piercing entrenched positions. Most terrible of all, perhaps, poisonous mustard gas, which required troops to carry gas masks at all times, made it possible to attack entrenched soldiers without direct combat.

Trench Warfare

AMERICA IN WORLD WAR I: THE WESTERN FRONT, 1918 These maps show the principal battles in which the United States participated in the last year of World War I. The small map on the upper right helps locate the area of conflict within the larger European landscape. The larger map at left shows the long, snaking red line of the western front in France—stretching from the border between France and southwest Germany all the way to the northeast border between Belgium and France. Along that vast line, the two sides had been engaged in murderous, inconclusive warfare for over three years by the time the Americans arrived. American troops, as this map makes clear, were decisive along the southern part of the front. ▌ *At what point did the Germans begin to consider putting an end to the war?*

 For an interactive version of this map go to www.mhhe.com/unfinishedinteractive

The new forms of technological warfare required elaborate maintenance. Faster machine guns required more ammunition. Motorized vehicles required fuel and spare parts and mechanics capable of servicing them. The logistical difficulties of providing so many supplies became a major factor in planning tactics and strategy. Once supplies were unloaded and stored, the process of repacking and moving them forward when troops advanced was hopelessly time-consuming. Late in the war, when Allied armies were advancing toward Germany, they frequently had to stop for days at a time to wait for their equipment.

World War I was the first conflict in which airplanes played a significant role. The planes themselves were not very maneuverable; but anti-aircraft technology was not yet highly developed either, so their effectiveness was still considerable. Planes began to be constructed to serve various functions: bombers, fighters, and reconaissance aircraft.

The most "modern" part of the military during World War I was the navy. Battleships made use of new technologies such as turbine propulsion, hydraulic gun controls, electric light and power, wireless telegraphy, and advanced navigational aids. Submarines, which had made a brief appearance in the American Civil War, now became significant weapons. The new submarines were driven by diesel engines, which had the advantage of being more compact than steam engines and whose fuel was less explosive than that of gasoline engines.

The new technologies were to a large degree responsible for the most stunning and horrible

LIFE IN THE TRENCHES For most British, French, German, and ultimately American troops in France, the most debilitating part of World War I was the seeming endlessness of life in the trenches. Some young men lived in these cold, wet, muddy dugouts for months, even years, surrounded by filth, sharing their space with vermin, eating mostly rotten food. Occasional attacks to try to dislodge the enemy from its trenches usually ended in failure and became scenes of terrible slaughter. *(The National Archives and Records Administration)*

Appalling Casualties characteristic of World War I—its appalling level of casualties. A million men representing the British Empire (Britain, Canada, Australia, India, and others) died. France lost 1.7 million men; Germany 2 million; the former Austro-Hungarian Empire 1.5 million; Italy 460,000; and Russia 1.7 million. The United States, which entered the war near its end, suffered very light casualties in contrast— 112,000 dead, half of them victims of influenza, not battle. But the American casualties were very high in the battles in which U.S. troops were centrally involved.

Organizing the Economy for War

By the time the war ended, the federal government had appropriated $32 billion for expenses directly related to the conflict—a staggering sum at the time. To raise the money, the government relied on two devices. First, it launched a major drive to solicit loans from the American people by selling "Liberty Bonds" to the "Liberty Bonds" public. By 1920, the sale of bonds, accompanied by elaborate patriotic appeals, had produced $23 billion. At the same time, new taxes were bringing in an additional sum of nearly $10 billion—some from levies on the "excess profits" of corporations, much from new, steeply graduated income and inheritance taxes that ultimately rose as high as 70 percent in some brackets.

An even greater challenge was organizing the economy to meet war needs. In 1916, Wilson established the Council of National Defense, composed of members of his cabinet, and the Civilian Advisory Commission, which set up local defense councils in every state and locality. But this early administrative structure soon proved completely unworkable, and members of the Council of National Defense urged a more centralized approach. Instead of dividing the economy geographically, they proposed dividing it functionally by organizing a series of planning bodies, each to supervise a specific sector of the economy. The administrative structure that slowly emerged from such proposals was dominated by a series of "war boards," one to oversee the railroads (led by Secretary of the Treasury William McAdoo), one to supervise fuel supplies (largely coal), another to handle food (a board that helped elevate to prominence the brilliant young engineer and business executive Herbert Hoover). The boards were not without weaknesses, but they generally succeeded in meeting essential war needs without paralyzing the domestic economy.

At the center of the effort to rationalize the economy was the War Industries Board (WIB), an agency cre- War Industries Board ated in July 1917 to coordinate government purchases of military supplies. Casually organized at first, it stumbled badly until March 1918, when Wilson restructured it and placed it under the control of the Wall Street financier Bernard Baruch.

WOMEN INDUSTRIAL WORKERS In World War II, such women were often called "Rosie the Riveter." Their presence in these previously all-male work environments was no less startling to Americans during World War I. These women are shown working with pneumatic hammers in the Midvale Steel and Ordnance factory in Philadelphia in 1918. (*The National Archives and Records Administration*)

Baruch decided which factories would convert to the production of which war materials, and he set prices for the goods they produced. When materials were scarce, Baruch decided to whom they should go. When corporations were competing for government contracts, he chose among them.

The National War Labor Board, established in April 1918, served as the final mediator of labor disputes. It pressured industry to grant important concessions to workers: an eight-hour day, the maintenance of minimal living standards, equal pay for women doing equal work, recognition of the right of unions to organize and bargain collectively. In return, it insisted that workers forgo strikes and that employers not engage in lockouts.

The Search for Social Unity

Government leaders were painfully aware that public sentiment about American involvement in the war was divided. Many believed that a crucial prerequisite for victory was uniting public opinion behind the war effort. The government approached that task in several ways.

The most conspicuous of its efforts was a vast propaganda campaign orchestrated by the Committee on Public Information (CPI),

Committee on Public Information

under the direction of the Denver journalist George Creel. The CPI supervised the distribution of over 75 million pieces of printed material and controlled much of the information available for newspapers and magazines. Creel encouraged journalists to exercise "self-censorship" when reporting war news, and most complied. By 1918, however, government-distributed posters and films were offering exaggerated portrayals of the savagery of the Germans.

The government also soon began efforts to suppress dissent. CPI-financed advertisements implored citizens to report to the authorities any evidence among their neighbors of disloyalty, pessimism, or yearning for peace. The Espionage Act of 1917 gave the government new tools with

Espionage and Sedition Acts

which to combat spying, sabotage, or obstruction of the war effort. More repressive were two measures of 1918: the Sabotage Act of April 20 and the Sedition Act of May 16. These bills made illegal any public expression of opposition to the war; in practice, they allowed officials to prosecute anyone who criticized the president or the government.

The most frequent targets of the new legislation were anticapitalist groups such as the Socialist Party and the Industrial Workers of the World (IWW).

Many Americans had favored the repression of socialists and radicals even before the war; the wartime policies now made it possible to move against them with full legal sanction. Eugene V. Debs, the humane leader of the Socialist Party and an opponent of the war, was sentenced to prison in 1918. Big Bill Haywood and members of the IWW were especially energetically prosecuted. Only by fleeing to the Soviet Union did Haywood avoid imprisonment. In all, more than 11,500 people were arrested in 1918 for the crime of criticizing the government or the war.

State and local governments, corporations, universities, and private citizens contributed as well to the climate of repression. A cluster of citizens'

Suppressing Dissent

groups emerged to mobilize "respectable" members of their communities to root out disloyalty. The greatest target of abuse was the German-American community. While most German Americans supported the American war effort once it began, public opinion turned bitterly hostile. A campaign to purge society of all things German quickly gathered speed, at times assuming ludicrous forms. Performances of German music were frequently banned. Courses in the German language were dropped from school curricula. Germans were routinely fired from jobs in war industries, lest they "sabotage" important tasks.

THE SEARCH FOR A NEW WORLD ORDER

On January 8, 1918, Woodrow Wilson appeared before Congress to present the principles for which he claimed the nation was fighting. He grouped the war aims under fourteen headings, widely known as

The Fourteen Points

the Fourteen Points. They fell into three broad categories. First, Wilson's proposals contained a series of eight specific recommendations for adjusting postwar boundaries and for establishing new nations to replace the defunct Austro-Hungarian and Ottoman Empires. Second, there was a set of five general principles to govern international conduct in the future: freedom of the seas, open covenants instead of secret treaties, reductions in armaments, free trade, and impartial mediation of colonial

claims. Finally, there was a proposal for a "League of Nations" that would help implement these new principles and territorial adjustments and resolve future controversies.

Wilson's international vision reflected his belief that the world was as capable of just and efficient government as were individual nations—that once the international community accepted certain basic principles of conduct, and once it constructed modern institutions to implement them, the human race could live in peace.

Despite Wilson's confidence, the leaders of the Al-

Allied Resistance

lied powers were preparing to resist him even before the armistice was signed. Britain and France in particular were in no mood for a benign and generous peace. At the same time, Wilson was encountering problems at home. In 1918, with the war almost over, Wilson unwisely appealed to the American voters to support his peace plans by electing Democrats to Congress in the November elections. Days later, the Republicans captured majorities in both houses. Domestic economic troubles, more than international issues, had been the most important factor in the voting; but the results damaged his ability to claim broad popular support for his peace plans.

Wilson further antagonized the Republicans when he refused to appoint any important member of their party to the negotiating team that would represent the United States at the peace conference in Paris.

The Paris Peace Conference

Wilson arrived in Europe to a welcome such as few men in history have experienced. When he entered Paris on December 13, 1918, he was greeted, some claimed, by the largest crowd in the history of France. The peace conference itself, however, proved less satisfying.

The principal figures in the negotiations were the

Negotiating the Peace

leaders of the victorious Allied nations: David Lloyd George, the prime minister of Great Britain; Georges Clemenceau, the president of France; Vittorio Orlando, the prime minister of Italy; and Wilson, who hoped to dominate them all.

From the beginning, the atmosphere of idealism Wilson had sought to create competed with a spirit of national self-interest. There was also a pervasive sense of unease about the unstable situation in eastern Europe and the threat of communism. Russia, whose new Bolshevik government was still fighting "White" counterrevolutionaries, was unrepresented in Paris; but the radical threat it seemed to pose to Western governments was never far from the minds of the delegates.

In this tense and often vindictive atmosphere, Wilson was unable to win approval of many of the broad principles he had espoused. He was also unable to prevent the other allies from imposing high reparations on the defeated Central Powers. Wilson did manage to win some important victories in Paris in setting boundaries and dealing with former colonies. But his most visible triumph, and the one of most importance to him, was the creation of a permanent international organization to oversee world affairs and prevent future wars. On January 25, 1919, the Allies voted to accept the "covenant" of the League of Nations.

The League of Nations

The Ratification Battle

Wilson presented the Treaty of Versailles (which took its name from the former royal palace outside Paris where the final negotiating sessions had taken place) to the Senate on July 10, 1919. But members of the Senate had many objections to the treaty. Some—the so-called irreconcilables—opposed the agreement in principle. But many other opponents were principally concerned with constructing a winning issue for the Republicans in 1920. Most notable of these was Senator Henry Cabot Lodge of Massachusetts, the powerful chairman of the Foreign Relations Committee, who loathed the president. He used every possible tactic to obstruct the treaty.

Henry Cabot Lodge

Public sentiment clearly favored ratification, so at first Lodge could do little more than play for time. Gradually, however, Lodge's general opposition to the treaty crystallized into a series of "reservations"—amendments to the League covenant further limiting American obligations to the organization. Wilson might still have won approval at this point if he had agreed to some relatively minor changes in the language of the treaty. But the president refused to yield. When he realized the Senate would not budge, he decided to appeal to the public.

He embarked on a grueling, cross-country speaking tour to arouse public support for the treaty. For more than three weeks, he traveled over 8,000 miles by train, speaking as often as four times a day, resting hardly at all. Finally, he reached the end of his strength. After speaking at Pueblo, Colorado, on September 25, 1919, he collapsed with severe headaches.

Canceling the rest of his itinerary, he rushed back to Washington, where, a few days later, he suffered a major stroke. For two weeks, he was close to death; for six weeks more, he was so seriously ill that he could conduct virtually no public business. His wife and his doctor formed an almost impenetrable barrier around him, shielding the president from any official pressures that might impede his recovery.

Wilson ultimately recovered enough to resume a limited official schedule, but he was essentially an invalid for the remaining eighteen months of his presidency. His condition only intensified his tendency to resist any attempts at compromise. When the Foreign Relations Committee finally sent the treaty to the Senate, recommending nearly fifty amendments and reservations, Wilson refused to consider any of them. The effort to win ratification failed.

League Membership Rejected

In the aftermath of this defeat, Wilson became convinced that the 1920 national election would serve as a "solemn referendum" on the League. By now, however, public interest in the peace process had begun to fade.

A SOCIETY IN TURMOIL

Even during the peace conference, many Americans were concerned less about international matters than about events at home. Some of this unease was a legacy of the hysterical atmosphere of the war years; some was a response to issues that surfaced after the armistice.

The Unstable Economy

The war ended sooner than almost anyone had anticipated; and the nation lurched into the difficult task of economic reconversion. At first, the boom continued, but accompanied by raging inflation. Through

Postwar Recession

most of 1919 and 1920, prices rose at an average of more than 15 percent a year. Finally, late in 1920, the economic bubble burst. Between 1920 and 1921, the gross national product declined nearly 10 percent; 100,000 businesses went bankrupt; and nearly 5 million Americans lost their jobs.

Well before this severe recession began, there was a dramatic increase in labor unrest. The raging inflation of 1919 wiped out the modest wage gains workers had achieved during the war; many laborers were worried about job security as veterans returned to the work force; arduous working conditions continued to be a source of discontent. Employers aggravated the resentment by using the end of the war to rescind benefits they had been forced to concede to workers in 1917 and 1918—most notably recognition of unions.
The year 1919, therefore, saw

Labor Unrest

an unprecedented wave of strikes. In January, a walkout by shipyard workers in Seattle evolved into a general strike that brought the city to a virtual standstill. In September, there was a strike by the Boston police force, which was demanding recognition of its union. Seattle had remained generally calm; but with its police off the job, Boston erupted in violence and looting.

These and other strikes aroused widespread middle-class hostility to the unions, a hostility that played a part in defeating the greatest strike of 1919: a steel strike that began in September, when 350,000 steelworkers in several midwestern cities demanded an eight-hour day and recognition of their union. The steel strike was long and bitter and climaxed in a riot in Gary, Indiana, in which eighteen strikers were killed. Steel executives managed to keep most plants running with nonunion labor, and by January, the strike—like most of the others in 1919—had collapsed.

The Demands of African Americans

The black men who had served in the armed forces during the war came home in 1919 and marched down the main streets of the industrial cities with other returning troops. And then they marched again through the streets of black neighborhoods such as Harlem, cheered by thousands of African Americans, who believed that the glory of black heroism in the war would make it impossible for white society ever again to treat African Americans as less than equal citizens.

In truth, the fact that black soldiers had fought in the war had almost no impact at all on white attitudes. But it did have a profound effect on black attitudes: it increased the determination of blacks to fight for their rights. Nearly half a million migrated from the rural South to industrial cities (often enticed by northern "labor agents") in search of the factory jobs the war was rapidly generating. This was the beginning of what became known as the "Great Migration." Within a few years, the nation's racial

"Great Migration"

demographics were transformed; suddenly there were large black communities crowding into northern cities.

By 1919, however, the racial climate had become savage. In the South, there was a sudden increase in lynchings: more than seventy blacks died at the hands of white mobs in 1919 alone. In the North, black factory workers faced widespread layoffs as returning white veterans displaced them. And as whites became convinced that black workers with lower wage demands were hurting them economically, animosity grew rapidly.

Wartime riots in East St. Louis and elsewhere were a prelude to a summer of much worse racial violence in 1919. In Chicago, a black teenager swimming in Lake Michigan on a hot July day happened to drift toward a white beach. Whites on shore allegedly stoned him unconscious; he sank and drowned. Angry blacks gathered in crowds and marched into white neighborhoods to retaliate; whites formed even larger crowds and roamed into black neighborhoods. For more than a week, Chicago was virtually at war. In the end, 38 people died and 537 were injured.

Chicago Race Riot

The Chicago riot was not the only racial violence during the so-called red summer of 1919; in all, 120 people died in such racial outbreaks in the space of little more than three months.

Racially motivated urban riots were not new. But the 1919 riots were different in one respect: they did not just involve white people attacking blacks; they also involved blacks fighting back. The NAACP signaled this change by urging blacks not just to demand government protection

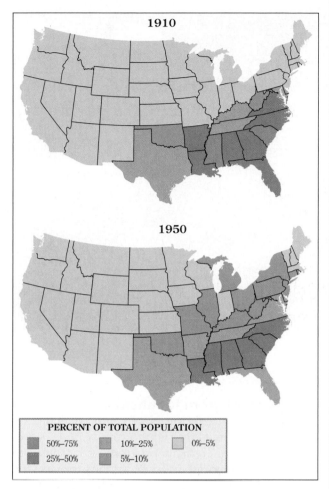

1910

1950

PERCENT OF TOTAL POPULATION

50%–75%	10%–25%	0%–5%
25%–50%	5%–10%	

AFRICAN-AMERICAN MIGRATION, 1910–1950 Two great waves of migration produced a dramatic redistribution of the African-American population in the first half of the twentieth century—one around the time of World War I, the other during and after World War II. The map on the bottom shows both the tremendous increase of black populations in northern states by 1950, and the relative decline of black populations in parts of the South. ▌ *Why did the wars produce such significant migration out of the South?*

but also to defend themselves. The poet Claude McKay wrote a poem after the Chicago riot called "If We Must Die":

Like men we'll face the murderous cowardly pack.
Pressed to the wall, dying, but fighting back.

At the same time, a black Jamaican, Marcus Garvey, began to attract a wide following in the United States. Garvey encouraged African Americans to reject assimilation into white society and develop pride in their own race and culture. His Universal Negro Improvement Association (UNIA) launched a chain of black-owned grocery stores. Eventually, Garvey began urging his supporters Marcus Garvey to leave America and return to Africa, where they could create a new society. In the 1920s, the Garvey movement experienced explosive growth for a time. It began to decline, however, after Garvey was indicted in 1923 on charges of business fraud. He was deported to Jamaica two years later. But the allure of black nationalism survived in black culture long after Garvey himself was gone.

The Red Scare

Much of the public considered the industrial warfare and the racial violence in 1919 a frightening omen of instability and radicalism. This was in part because after the Russian Revolution of November 1917, communism was no longer simply a theory; it was now the basis of an important regime. Concerns about the communist threat grew in 1919 when the Soviet government announced the formation of the Communist International (or Comintern), whose purpose was to export revolution around the world.

In America, meanwhile, there was, in addition to the great number of imagined radicals, a modest number of real ones. These small groups of radicals were presumably responsible for a series of bombings in the spring of 1919. In April, the post office intercepted several dozen parcels addressed to leading businessmen and politicians that were triggered to explode when opened. Two months later, eight bombs exploded in eight cities within minutes of one another, suggesting a nationwide conspiracy.

In response to these and other provocations, what became known as the Red Scare began. Nearly thirty states enacted new peacetime sedition laws imposing harsh penalties on those who promoted revolution. There were spontaneous acts of violence against supposed radicals in some communities, and more calculated efforts by universities and other institutions to expel radicals

SACCO AND VANZETTI The artist Ben Shahn painted this view of the anarchists Nicola Sacco and Bartolomeo Vanzetti, handcuffed together in a courtroom in 1927 waiting to hear if the appeal of their 1921 verdicts for murdering a Boston paymaster would succeed. It did not, and the two men were executed later that year. *(Sacco & Vanzetti, Ben Shahn. © Estate of Ben Shahn/Licensed by VAGA, New York, NY/ © The Museum of Modern Art/SCALA/Art Resource, NY)*

from their midst. But the greatest contribution to the Red Scare came from the federal government. On New Year's Day, 1920, Attorney General A. Mitchell Palmer and his ambitious young assistant, J. Edgar Hoover, orchestrated a series of raids on alleged radical centers and arrested more than 6,000 people. Most of those arrested were ultimately released, but about 500 who were not American citizens were deported.

| A. Mitchell Palmer |

The ferocity of the Red Scare soon abated, but its effects lingered well into the 1920s. In May of 1920, two Italian immigrants, Nicola Sacco and Bartolomeo Vanzetti, were charged with the murder of a paymaster in Braintree, Massachusetts. The case against them was weak; but because both men were confessed anarchists, they faced a widespread presumption of guilt. They were convicted and sentenced to death. Over the next several years, public support for Sacco and Vanzetti grew to formidable proportions. But on August 23, 1927, amid widespread protests around the world, Sacco and Vanzetti, still proclaiming their innocence, died in the electric chair.

| Sacco and Vanzetti |

The Retreat from Idealism

On August 26, 1920, the Nineteenth Amendment, guaranteeing women the right to vote, became part of the Constitution. To many progressives it seemed to promise new support for reform. Yet the passage of the Nineteenth Amendment marked not the beginning of an era of progressive reform but the end of one.

Economic problems, labor unrest, racial tensions, and the intensity of the antiradicalism they helped create—all combined in the years immediately following the war to produce a general sense of disillusionment. That became particularly apparent in the election of 1920. Woodrow Wilson wanted the campaign to be a referendum on the League of Nations, and the Democratic candidates, Governor James M. Cox of Ohio and Assistant Secretary of the Navy Franklin D. Roosevelt, dutifully tried to keep Wilson's ideals alive. The Republican presidential nominee, however, offered a different vision. He was Warren Gamaliel Harding, an obscure Ohio senator. Harding offered no ideals, only a vague promise of a return, as he later phrased it, to "normalcy." He won in a landslide. To many Americans it seemed that, for better or worse, a new era had begun.

| Disillusionment and Reaction |

For a time after the outbreak of war in Europe in 1914, most Americans wanted to stay out of the conflict. Gradually, however, as the tactics of Britain and Germany began to impinge on American trade and on freedom of the seas, the United States found itself drawn into the conflict. In April 1917 Congress agreed to the president's request that the United States enter the war as an ally of Britain.

American forces quickly broke the stalemate that had bogged the European forces down in years of inconclusive trench warfare. Within a few months of the arrival of substantial numbers of American troops in Europe, Germany agreed to an armistice. American casualties were negligible compared to the millions suffered by the European combatants.

The social experience of the war in the United States was, on the whole, dismaying to reformers. Although the war enhanced some reform efforts—most notably prohibition and woman suffrage—it also introduced an atmosphere of intolerance and repression into American life. The aftermath of the war was even more disheartening to progressives, both because of a brief recession and because of a wave of repression directed against labor, radicals, African Americans, and immigrants.

At the same time, Woodrow Wilson's dream of a peace based on the principles of democracy and justice suffered a painful death. The Treaty of Versailles was far from what Wilson had hoped. It did, however, contain a provision for a League of Nations. But the League quickly became controversial in the United States; and despite strenuous efforts by the president—efforts that hastened his own physical collapse—the treaty was defeated in the Senate. In the aftermath of that traumatic battle, the American people turned away from Wilson and his ideals and prepared for a very different era.

CONCLUSION

INTERACTIVE LEARNING

On the *Primary Source Investigator CD-ROM,* check out a number of valuable tools for further exploration of the content of this chapter.

Interactive Maps
- America in World War I (Map M23)
- Influenza Epidemic (Map M24)

Primary Sources
Documents, images, and maps related to U.S. involvement in the Great War and the significant postwar problems. Highlights include:

- The text of Woodrow Wilson's famous Fourteen Points
- The 1918 Sedition Act, which criminalized speech critical of the United States

- Images that depict a widespread fear of radicalism, such as soldiers destroying a Socialist flag, and a portrait of Nicola Sacco and Bartolomeo Vanzetti, two Italian immigrants whose controversial murder trial ended in their execution

 Online Learning Center (www.mhhe.com/unfinishedinteractive)
Explore this rich website, providing additional exploration of the material covered in this chapter, online versions of the interactive maps included on the Primary Source Investigator CD-ROM, as well as several study aids, including a multiple-choice quiz, essay questions, a glossary, and other valuable tools.

FOR FURTHER REFERENCE

Ernest R. May, *The World War and American Isolation* (1959), is an authoritative account of America's slow and controversial entry into the Great War. Frank Freidel provides a sweeping account of the American soldier's battlefield experience during World War I in *Over There: The Story of America's First Great Overseas Crusade* (1964). David Kennedy, *Over Here: The First World War and American Society* (1980) is an important study of the domestic impact of the war. Robert D. Cuff, *The War Industries Board: Business-Government Relations During World War I* (1973) is a good account of mobilization for war in the United States. Ronald Schaffer, *America in the Great War: The Rise of the War Welfare State* (1991) examines the ways in which mobilization for war created new public benefits for various groups, including labor. Maureen Greenwald, *Women, War, and Work* (1980) describes the impact of World War I on women workers. John Keegan, *The First World War* (1998) is a superb military history. Thomas Knock, *To End All Wars: Woodrow Wilson and the Quest for a New World Order* (1992) is a valuable recent study of the battle for peace. Arno Mayer, *Wilson vs. Lenin* (1959) and *Politics and Diplomacy of Peacemaking: Containment and Counterrevolution* (1965) are important revisionist accounts of the peacemaking process. America's stormy debate over immigration and national identity before, during, and after World War I is best captured by John Higham, *Strangers in the Land: Patterns of American Nativism* (1955). William M. Tuttle, Jr., in *Race Riot: Chicago in the Red Summer of 1919* (1970) recounts the terrible riots of 1919 that showed America violently divided along racial and ideological lines. Paul L. Murphy, *World War I and the Origins of Civil Liberties* (1979) shows how wartime efforts to quell dissent created new support for civil liberties. *The Great War—1918* (1997) is a documentary film chronicling the experiences of American soldiers in the closing battles of World War I through their letters and diaries.

24

The New Era

(Culver Pictures, Inc.)

MINI-DOCUMENTARY Route 66

T he 1920s are often remembered as an era of affluence, conservatism, and cultural frivolity. In reality, however, the decade was a time of significant, even dramatic social, economic, and political change. It was an era in which the American economy not only enjoyed spectacular growth but developed new forms of organization. It was a time in which American popular culture reshaped itself to reflect the increasingly urban, industrial, consumer-oriented society of the United States. And it was a decade in which American government experimented with new approaches to public policy. That was why contemporaries liked to refer to the 1920s as the "New Era."

At the same time, however, the decade saw the rise of a series of spirited and at times effective rebellions against the modern developments that were transforming American life. The intense cultural conflicts that characterized the 1920s were evidence of how much of American society remained unreconciled to the modernizing currents of the New Era.

THE NEW ECONOMY

After the recession of 1921–1922, the United States began a long period of prosperity and economic expansion. Less visible but equally significant was the survival of inequalities and imbalances.

Technology, Organization, and Economic Growth

No one could deny the remarkable feats of the American economy in the 1920s. The nation's manufacturing output rose by more than 60 percent. Per capita income grew by a third. Inflation was negligible. A mild recession in 1923 interrupted the pattern of growth; but when it subsided early in 1924, the economy expanded with even greater vigor.

The economic boom was a result of many things, but one of the most important causes was technology. The automobile industry became one of the most important industries in the nation. It stimulated growth in other, related industries as well. Auto manufacturers purchased the products of steel, rubber, glass, and tool companies. Auto owners bought gasoline. Road construction became an important industry. The increased mobility that the automobile made possible increased the demand for suburban housing, fueling a boom in the construction industry.

Rise of the Automobile Industry

MINI-DOCUMENTARY: Route 66

Other new industries contributed to the economic growth. Radio began to become popular. Early radio had been able to broadcast little beside pulses, which meant that radio communication could occur only through the Morse Code. But with the discovery of the theory of modulation, pioneered by the Canadian scientist Reginald Fessenden, it became possible to transmit speech and music. Many people built their own radio sets for very little money, benefiting from the discovery that inexpensive crystals could receive signals over long distances. These "short wave" radios, which allowed individual owners to establish contact with each other, marked the beginning of what later became known as "ham radio." Once commercial broadcasting began, families flocked to buy more conventional radio sets, which could receive high-quality signals over short and medium distances. By 1925, there were two million sets in American homes, and by the end of the 1920s almost every family had one.

Commercial aviation developed slowly in the 1920s, beginning with the use of planes to deliver mail. On the whole, airplanes remained curiosities and sources of entertainment. But technological advances—the development of the radial engine and the creation of pressurized cabins—were laying the groundwork for the great increase in commercial

Commercial Aviation

1914–1920	1920	1922	1923
Great Migration of blacks to the North	Prohibition begins Harding elected president	Lewis's *Babbitt*	Harding dies; Coolidge becomes president Harding administration scandals revealed

1924	1925	1927	1928
National Origins Act passed Coolidge elected president Ku Klux Klan membership peaks	Fitzgerald's *The Great Gatsby* Scopes trial	Lindbergh's solo transatlantic flight First sound motion picture, *The Jazz Singer*	Hoover elected president

TIME LINE

travel in the 1930s and beyond. Trains became faster and more efficient as well with the development of the diesel-electric engine. Electronics, home appliances, plastics and synthetic fibers such as nylon, aluminum, magnesium, oil, electric power, and other industries fueled by technological advances—all grew dramatically. Telephones continued to proliferate.

The seeds of future technological breakthroughs were also visible in the 1920s and 1930s. In both England and America, scientists and engineers were working to transform primitive calculating machines into devices capable of performing more complicated tasks. By the early 1930s, researchers at MIT, led by Vannevar Bush, had created such a device—the first analog computer. A few years later, Howard Aiken built a much more complex computer with memory, capable of multiplying eleven-digit numbers in three seconds.

Genetic Research

Genetic research had begun in Austria in the mid-nineteenth century through the work of Gregor Mendel, a monk who performed experiments on the hybridization of vegetables in the garden of his monastery. His findings attracted little attention during his lifetime, but in the early twentieth century they were discovered by several investigators and helped shape modern genetic research. Among the American pioneers was Thomas Hunt Morgan of Columbia University and later Cal Tech, whose experiments with fruit flies revealed how several genes could be transmitted together. His work helped open the path to understanding how genes could recombine—a critical discovery that led to more advanced experiments in hybridization and genetics.

Large sectors of American business were accelerating their drive toward national organization and consolidation. Certain industries— **Growing Industrial Consolidation** notably those dependent on large-scale mass production, such as steel and automobiles—seemed naturally to move toward concentrating production in a few large firms. Others proved more resistant to consolidation.

The strenuous efforts by industrialists throughout the economy to find ways to curb competition reflected a strong fear of overcapacity. Even in the booming 1920s, industrialists remembered how too-rapid expansion and overproduction had helped produce recessions in 1893, 1907, and 1920. The great, unrealized dream of the New Era was to find a way to stabilize the economy so that such collapses would never occur again.

Workers in an Age of Capital

Despite the remarkable economic growth, more than two-thirds of the American people in 1929 lived at no better than what one major study described as the "minimum comfort level." Half of those were at or below the level of "subsistence and poverty."

American labor experienced both the successes and the failures of the 1920s as much as any other group. On the one hand, most workers saw their standard of living rise during the decade. Some employers adopted paternalistic techniques that came to be known as "welfare capitalism." Henry Ford, for example, shortened the workweek, raised wages, and instituted paid vacations. When labor grievances surfaced despite these efforts, workers could voice them through the so-called company unions that were emerging in many industries—workers' councils and shop committees, organized by the corporations themselves. But company unions were feeble vehicles, and welfare capitalism survived only as long as industry prospered. After 1929, with the economy in crisis, the entire system collapsed.

Welfare capitalism affected only a relatively small number of workers in any case. Most laborers worked for employers interested primarily in keeping their labor costs low. Workers as a whole, therefore, received wage increases that were proportionately far below the growth of the economy as a whole. At the end of the decade, the average annual income of a worker remained below $1,500 a year, when $1,800 was considered necessary to maintain a minimally decent standard of living.

The New Era was a bleak time for labor organization, in part because many unions themselves were relatively conservative and failed to adapt to the realities of the modern economy. The American Federation of Labor (led by the cautious William Green) remained wedded to the concept of the craft union, in which workers were organized on the basis of particular skills. The AFL sought peaceful cooperation with employers. In the meantime, the number of unskilled industrial workers was rising rapidly.

But whatever the weaknesses of the unions, the strength of the corporations was the principal reason for the absence of effective labor organization in the 1920s. After the turmoil of 1919, corporate leaders worked hard to spread the doctrine that a crucial element of democratic capitalism was the protection of the "open shop" (a shop in which no worker could be required to join a union). The crusade for the open shop, euphemistically titled the "American Plan," became a pretext for a harsh campaign of union-busting. As a result, union membership fell from more than 5 million in 1920 to under 3 million in 1929.

"American Plan"

Women and Minorities in the Work Force

A growing proportion of the work force consisted of women, who were concentrated in what have since become known as "pink-collar" jobs—low-paying service occupations. Large numbers of women worked as secretaries, salesclerks, and telephone operators and in other nonmanual service capacities. Because technically such positions were not industrial jobs, the AFL and other labor organizations were uninterested in organizing these workers. Similarly, the half-million African Americans who had migrated from the rural South into the cities during the Great Migration after 1914 had few opportunities for union representation. Most blacks worked as janitors, dishwashers, garbage collectors, domestics, and other service capacities. A. Philip Randolph's Brotherhood of Sleeping Car Porters was one of the few important unions dominated and led by African Americans.

Brotherhood of Sleeping Car Porters

In the West and the Southwest, the ranks of the unskilled included considerable numbers of Asians and Hispanics. In the wake of the Chinese Exclusion Acts, Japanese immigrants increasingly took the place of the Chinese in menial jobs in California. They worked on railroads, construction sites, and farms and in many other low-paying workplaces. Some Japanese managed to escape the ranks of the unskilled by forming their own small businesses or setting themselves up as truck farmers; and many of the Issei (Japanese immigrants) and Nisei (their American-born children) enjoyed significant economic success. Other Asians—most notably Filipinos—also swelled the unskilled work force and generated considerable hostility. Anti-Filipino riots in California beginning in 1929 helped produce legislation in 1934 virtually eliminating immigration from the Philippines.

Mexican immigrants formed a major part of the unskilled work force throughout the Southwest and California. Nearly half a million Mexicans entered the United States in the 1920s, and by 1930, most lived in cities. Large Mexican barrios grew up in Los Angeles, El Paso, San Antonio, Denver, and many other cities and towns. Some of the residents found work locally in factories and shops; others traveled to mines or did migratory labor on farms but returned to the cities between jobs. Mexican workers, too, faced hostility and discrimination, but there were few efforts actually to exclude them. Employers in the relatively underpopulated West needed this ready pool of low-paid workers.

Rising Mexican Immigration

Agricultural Technology and the Plight of the Farmer

Like industry, American agriculture in the 1920s was embracing new technologies. The number of tractors on American farms quadrupled during the 1920s. They helped to open 35 million new acres to cultivation. Increasingly sophisticated combines and harvesters were proliferating, helping to make it possible to produce more crops with fewer workers.

Agricultural researchers were already at work on other advances: the invention of hybrid corn, which became available to farmers in 1921 but was not grown in great quantities for a decade or more; and the creation of chemical fertilizers and pesticides, which also began to have limited use in the 1920s but proliferated quickly in the 1930s and 1940s.

The new technologies greatly increased agricultural productivity, but the demand for agricultural goods was not rising as fast as production. The results were substantial surpluses, a disastrous decline in food prices, and a severe drop in farmers' income beginning early in the 1920s. More than 3 million people left agriculture altogether in the course of the decade. Of those who remained, many lost ownership of their lands and had to rent instead.

Declining Food Prices

In response, some farmers began to demand relief in the form of government price supports. One price-raising scheme in particular came to dominate agrarian demands: the idea of "parity." Parity was a complicated formula for setting an adequate price for farm goods and ensuring that farmers would

BREAKING DOWN RURAL ISOLATION: THE EXPANSION OF TRAVEL HORIZONS IN OREGON, ILLINOIS This map uses the small town of Oregon, Illinois—west of Chicago—to illustrate the way in which first railroads and then automobiles reduced the isolation of rural areas in the first decades of the twentieth century. The gold and purple areas of the two maps show the territory that residents of Oregon could reach within two hours. ▌ *Why did automobile travel do so much more than railroads to expand the travel horizons of small towns?*

OLC **For an interactive version of this map go to** www.mhhe.com/unfinishedinteractive

earn back at least their production costs. Champions of parity urged high tariffs against foreign agricultural goods and a government commitment to buy surplus domestic crops at parity and sell them abroad.

McNary-Haugen Bill The legislative expression of the demand for parity was the McNary-Haugen Bill, named after its two principal sponsors in Congress. In 1926 and again in 1928, Congress approved a bill requiring parity for grain, cotton, tobacco, and rice, but President Coolidge vetoed it both times.

THE NEW CULTURE

The urban and consumer-oriented culture of the 1920s helped Americans in all regions to live their lives and perceive their world in increasingly similar ways. But different parts of American society experienced the new culture in very different ways.

Consumerism and Communications

Growing Consumer Culture The United States of the 1920s was a consumer society. Many more people than ever before could buy items not just because of need but for convenience and pleasure. Middle-class families purchased electric refrigerators, washing machines, and vacuum cleaners. People wore wristwatches and smoked cigarettes. Women purchased cosmetics and mass-produced fashions. Above all, Americans bought automobiles. By the end of the decade, there were more than 30 million cars on American roads.

No group was more aware of the emergence of consumerism (or more responsible for creating it) than the advertising industry. In the 1920s, advertising came of age. Publicists no longer simply conveyed information; they sought to identify products with a particular lifestyle. They also encouraged the public to absorb the values of promotion and salesmanship and to admire effective "boosters" and publicists. One of the most successful books of the 1920s was *The Man Nobody Knows*, by advertising executive Bruce Barton. It por- **Bruce Barton** trayed Jesus Christ as not only a religious prophet but also a "super salesman." Barton's message was that Jesus had been a man concerned with living a full and rewarding life in this world and that twentieth-century men and women should be concerned with doing the same.

The advertising industry could never have had the impact it did without the emergence of new vehicles of communication that made it possible to reach large audiences quickly and easily. Newspapers were being absorbed into national chains. Mass-circulation magazines attracted broad, national audiences. The movies were becoming an ever more popular and powerful form of mass

THE ELECTRIC REFRIGERATOR The development of new appliances for the home was an important part of the boom in the production and sale of consumer goods in the 1920s. Executives of the Delcom Light Company, a subsidiary of General Motors, pose here in front of the first Frigidaire electric refrigerator as it is readied for shipping from Dayton, Ohio, in 1921. *(Bettmann/Corbis)*

communication. The most important communications vehicle, however, was radio. The first commercial radio station in America, KDKA in Pittsburgh, began broadcasting in 1920, and the first national radio network, the National Broadcasting Company, was formed in 1927.

Psychology and Psychiatry

The growing consumerism of the 1920s produced new psychological challenges. The rise of anxiety and alienation as characteristic ailments of the consumer age coincided with the rise of new theories of psychology and psychiatry. Together these two phenomena helped entrench important emerging fields in medicine and science.

Psychiatry had been spreading in the United States since the early twentieth century, driven in part by the growing awareness of the theories of Sigmund Freud and Carl Jung. Although Freud and Jung differed sharply on many points, they both helped legitimize the idea of exploring the unconscious as a way of discovering the roots of mental problems. Psychoanalysis, which Freud pioneered, began to attract American adherents as early as 1912 and spread significantly in the 1920s.

John B. Watson of Johns Hopkins University challenged the Freudian belief in the exploration of the unconscious. Instead, he argued that mental ailments, like physical ones, should be treated by observation and treatment of symptoms—of behavior. The

Behavioralism

point of therapy was to modify behavior—to discourage undesirable behavior and reinforce "acceptable" actions. Although many psychiatrists dismissed behavioralism as treating symptoms rather than causes, it demonstrated significant success in treating such disorders as alcoholism, drug addiction, and phobias.

Although psychoanalysis and other forms of therapy could be performed by psychologists without medical training, the biggest growth in psychiatry was as a field of medicine. At first, medical psychiatrists worked mostly in mental institutions. But as mental hospitals evolved from places where patients came for treatment and then were discharged to places where chronically ill people (many of them aged) resided indefinitely, psychiatrists began to move into conventional hospitals and into private practice. Psychiatry began to offer services not just to the mentally ill, but to otherwise stable individuals experiencing difficulties with everyday life. A new theory of "dynamic" psychiatry helped psychiatrists to offer therapy for ordinary anxieties, not just severe mental disturbance.

Psychology and psychiatry were, from the beginning, fields in which women played a much larger role than in most areas of medicine. That was in part because training in psychology was considered valuable for occupations in which women had been traditionally dominant—teaching, social work, nursing. Women who had medical training often found it easier to establish

Opportunities for Women

themselves in psychiatry than in other, more traditionally male-dominated areas of medicine.

Women in the New Era

College-educated women were no longer pioneers in the 1920s. There were now two and even three generations of graduates of women's or coeducational colleges and universities, and some were making their presence felt in the professions. The "new professional woman" was a vivid and widely publicized image in the 1920s. In reality, however, most employed women were nonprofessional, lower-class workers. Middle-class women, in the meantime, remained largely in the home.

Yet the 1920s constituted a new era for middle-class women nonetheless. In particular, the decade saw a redefinition of motherhood. Shortly after World

Motherhood Redefined

War I, John B. Watson and other behavioralists began to challenge the long-held assumption that women had an instinctive capacity for motherhood. Maternal affection was not, they claimed, sufficient preparation for child rearing. Instead, mothers should rely on the advice and assistance of experts and professionals: doctors, nurses, and trained educators.

For many middle-class women, these changes devalued what had been an important and consuming activity. Many attempted to compensate by devoting new attention to their roles as wives and companions. And many women now openly considered their sexual relationships with their husbands not simply as a means of procreation but as an important and pleasurable experience in its own right.

One result was growing interest in birth control. The pioneer of the American birth-control movement, Margaret Sanger, began her career as a promoter

Margaret Sanger

of the diaphragm and other birth-control devices out of a concern for working-class women; she believed that large families were among the major causes of poverty and distress in poor communities. By the 1920s, she was becoming more effective in persuading middle-class women to see the benefits of birth control. Nevertheless, some birth-control devices remained illegal in many states (and abortion remained illegal nearly everywhere).

Some women concluded that in the New Era it was no longer necessary to maintain a rigid, Victorian female "respectability." They could smoke, drink, dance, wear seductive clothes and makeup, and attend lively parties. Those assumptions became the basis of the "flapper"—

"Flappers"

the modern woman whose liberated lifestyle found expression in dress, hairstyle, speech, and behavior. The flapper lifestyle had a particular impact on lower-middle-class and working-class single women. At night, such women flocked to clubs and dance halls in search of excitement and companionship.

Despite all the changes, most women remained highly dependent on men and relatively powerless when men exploited that dependence. The National Woman's Party, under the leadership of Alice Paul, attempted to fight that powerlessness through its campaign for the Equal Rights Amendment. Responding to the suffrage victory, women organized the League of Women Voters and the women's auxiliaries of both the Democratic and Republican Parties. Female-dominated consumer groups grew rapidly and increased the range and energy of their efforts.

The Disenchanted

Many artists and intellectuals coming of age in the 1920s were becoming disenchanted with modern America. One result of this alienation was a series of savage critiques of modern

Modern Society Critiqued

society by a wide range of writers, some of whom were known as the "debunkers." Among them was the Baltimore journalist H. L. Mencken, who delighted in ridiculing religion, politics, the arts, even

democracy itself. Sinclair Lewis published a series of savage novels—*Main Street* (1920), *Babbitt* (1922), *Arrowsmith* (1925), and others—in which he lashed out at modern bourgeois society. Intellectuals of the 1920s claimed to reject the "success ethic" that they believed dominated American life. The novelist F. Scott Fitzgerald, for example, attacked the American obsession with material success in *The Great Gatsby* (1925). The roster of important American writers active in the 1920s may have no equal in any other period. It included Fitzgerald, Lewis, Ernest Hemingway, Thomas Wolfe, John Dos Passos, Ezra Pound, T. S. Eliot, Gertrude Stein, Edna Ferber, William Faulkner, and Eugene O'Neill.

It also included a remarkable group of black artists. In New York City, a new generation of African-American intellectuals created a flourishing artistic life widely described as the "Harlem Renaissance."

"Harlem Renaissance"

The Harlem poets, novelists, and artists drew heavily from their African roots in an effort to prove the richness of their own racial heritage. The poet Langston Hughes captured much of the spirit of the movement in a single sentence: "I am a Negro—and beautiful." Other black writers in Harlem and elsewhere—James Weldon Johnson, Countee Cullen, Zora Neale Hurston, Claude McKay, Alain Locke—as well as black artists and musicians helped to establish a thriving, and at times highly politicized, culture rooted in the historical legacy of their race.

A CONFLICT OF CULTURES

The modern, secular culture of the 1920s did not go unchallenged. It grew up alongside an older, more traditional culture, with which it continually and often bitterly competed.

Prohibition

When the prohibition of the sale and manufacture of alcohol went into effect in January 1920, it had the support of most members of the middle class and most progressives. Within a year, however, it had become clear that the "noble experiment," as its defenders called it, was not working well. Prohibition

Failure of Prohibition

did substantially reduce drinking, but it also produced conspicuous violations. Before long, it was almost as easy to acquire illegal alcohol as it had once been to acquire legal alcohol. And since an enormous, lucrative industry was now barred to legitimate businessmen, organized-crime figures took it over.

Many middle-class progressives who had originally supported prohibition soon soured on the experiment. But an enormous constituency of provincial, largely rural, Protestant Americans continued vehemently to defend it. To them, prohibition represented the effort of an older America to defend traditional notions of morality. Drinking, which they associated with the modern city and with Catholic immigrants, became a symbol of the new culture they believed was displacing them.

As the decade proceeded, opponents of prohibition (or "wets," as they **"Wets" versus "Drys"** came to be known) gained steadily in influence. Not until 1933, however, when the Great Depression added weight to their appeals, were they finally able to effectively challenge the "drys" and win repeal of the Eighteenth Amendment.

Nativism and the Klan

The fear of immigrants that many prohibitionists expressed found other expressions as well. Agitation for a curb on foreign immigration to the United States had begun in the nineteenth century and had gathered strength largely because of the support of middle-class progressives. After the war, when immigration began to be associated with radicalism, popular sentiment on behalf of restriction grew rapidly.

In 1921, Congress passed an emergency immigration act, establishing a quota system by which annual immigration from any country could not exceed 3 percent of the number of persons of that nationality who had been in the United States in 1910. The new law cut immigration from 800,000 to 300,000 in any single year, but the nativists remained unsatisfied. The National **National Origins Act of 1924** tional Origins Act of 1924 banned immigration from east Asia entirely. It also reduced the quota for Europeans from 3 to 2 percent. The quota would be based, moreover, not on the 1910 census, but on the census of 1890, a year in which there had been far fewer southern and eastern Europeans in the country. What immigration there was, in other words, would heavily favor northwestern Europeans. Five years later, a further restriction set a rigid limit of 150,000 immigrants a year.

To defenders of an older, more provincial America, the growth of large communities of foreign peoples came to seem a direct threat to their way of life. Among other things, this provincial nativism helped instigate the rebirth of the Ku Klux Klan as a major **Rise of the New Klan** force in American society. The first Klan, founded during Reconstruction, had died in the 1870s. But in 1915, a new group of white southerners met on Stone Mountain near Atlanta and established a modern version of the society. Nativist passions had swelled in response to the case of Leo Frank, a Jewish factory manager in Atlanta convicted in 1914 (on very flimsy evidence) of murdering a female employee; a mob stormed Frank's jail and lynched him. The premiere (also in Atlanta) of D. W. Griffith's film *The Birth of a Nation*, which glorified the early Klan, also helped inspire white southerners to join a new one.

At first the new Klan, like the old, was largely concerned with intimidating blacks. After World War I, however, concern about blacks gradually became secondary to concern about Catholics, Jews, and foreigners. At that point, membership in the Klan expanded rapidly, not just in the South but in industrial cities in the North and Midwest. By 1924, there were reportedly 4 million members, including many women, organized in separate, parallel units. Beginning in 1925, a series of scandals involving the organization's leaders precipitated a slow but steady decline in the Klan's influence.

Most Klan units (or "klaverns") tried to present their members as patriots and defenders of morality, and some did nothing more menacing than stage occasional parades and rallies. Often, however, the Klan also operated as a brutal opponent of "alien" groups. Klansmen terrorized blacks, Jews, Catholics, and foreigners. At times, they did so through public whipping, tarring and feathering, arson, and lynching. What the Klan feared, however, was not simply "foreign" or "racially impure" groups; it feared anyone who challenged traditional values.

DARROW AND BRYAN IN DAYTON Although the Scopes trial was chiefly significant for the issues it raised, it attracted national attention in 1925 at least as much because of its two celebrated attorneys: Clarence Darrow, the best-known defense attorney in America and a personification of the modern, skeptical, secular intellect; and William Jennings Bryan, the great political leader who had become, in the last years of his life, an ardent defender of Christian fundamentalism. *(Bettmann/CORBIS)*

Religious Fundamentalism

Fundamentalists and Modernists

Another cultural controversy of the 1920s was the result of a bitter conflict over the place of religion in contemporary society. By 1921, American Protestantism was already divided into two warring camps. On one side stood the modernists: mostly urban, middle-class people who were attempting to adapt religion to the realities of their modern, secular society. On the other side stood the fundamentalists: provincial, largely rural men and women fighting to preserve traditional faith. The fundamentalists insisted the Bible was to be interpreted literally. Above all, they opposed the teachings of Charles Darwin, whose theory of evolution had openly challenged the biblical story of the Creation.

By the mid-1920s, to the great alarm of modernists, fundamentalism was gaining political strength in some states with its demands for legislation to forbid the teaching of evolution in public schools. In Tennessee in March 1925, the legislature actually adopted a measure making it illegal for any public school teacher "to teach any theory that denies the story of the divine creation of man as taught in the Bible."

When the fledgling American Civil Liberties Union (ACLU) offered free counsel to any Tennessee educator willing to defy the law and become the defendant in a test case, a twenty-four-year-old biology teacher in the town of Dayton, John T. Scopes,

Scopes Trial

agreed to have himself arrested. And when the ACLU decided to send the famous attorney Clarence Darrow to defend Scopes, the aging William Jennings Bryan announced that he would assist the prosecution. Journalists from across the country flocked to Tennessee to cover the trial. Scopes had, of course, clearly violated the law; and a verdict of guilty was a foregone conclusion, especially when the judge refused to permit "expert" testimony by evolution scholars. Scopes was fined $100, and the case was ultimately dismissed in a higher court because of a technicality. Nevertheless, Darrow scored an important victory for the modernists by calling Bryan himself to the stand to testify as an "expert on the Bible." In the course of the cross-examination, which was broadcast by radio to much of the nation, Darrow made Bryan's stubborn defense of biblical truths appear foolish and finally tricked Bryan into admitting the possibility that not all religious dogma was subject to only one interpretation.

The Scopes trial put fundamentalists on the defensive and discouraged many of them from participating openly in politics. But it did not resolve the conflict between fundamentalists and modernists.

The Democrats' Ordeal

The anguish of provincial Americans attempting to defend an embattled way of life proved particularly troubling to the Democratic Party during the 1920s. More than the Republicans, the Democrats consisted of a diverse coalition of interest groups, including prohibitionists, Klansmen, and fundamentalists on one side and Catholics, urban workers, and immigrants on the other.

Divided Democrats

At the 1924 Democratic National Convention in New York, a bitter conflict broke out over the platform when the party's urban wing attempted to win approval of planks calling for the repeal of prohibition and a denunciation of the Klan. Both planks narrowly failed. More serious was a deadlock in the balloting for a presidential candidate. Urban Democrats supported Alfred E. Smith, the Irish Catholic governor of New York; rural Democrats backed William McAdoo, Woodrow Wilson's Treasury secretary. For 103 ballots, the convention dragged on, until finally both Smith and McAdoo withdrew and the party settled on a compromise: the corporate lawyer John W. Davis.

A similar schism plagued the Democrats again in 1928, when Al Smith finally secured his party's nomination for president. He was not, however, able to unite his divided party—in part because of widespread anti-Catholic sentiment, especially in the South. Smith's opponent, and the victor in the presidential election, was a man who perhaps more than any other personified the modern, prosperous, middle-class society of the New Era: Herbert Hoover.

Al Smith

REPUBLICAN GOVERNMENT

For twelve years, beginning in 1921, both the presidency and the Congress rested in the hands of the Republican Party. For most of those years, the federal government enjoyed a warm and supportive relationship with the American business community. Yet the government of the New Era was more than the passive, pliant instrument that critics often described. It attempted to serve in many respects as an agent of economic change.

Harding and Coolidge

Nothing seemed more clearly to illustrate the unadventurous character of 1920s politics than the characters of the two men who served as president during most of the decade: Warren G. Harding and Calvin Coolidge.

Harding, who was elected to the presidency in 1920, was an undistinguished senator from Ohio. He had received the Republican presidential nomination as a result of an agreement among leaders of his party, who considered him, as one noted, a "good second-rater." Harding appointed capable men to the most important cabinet offices, and he attempted to stabilize the nation's troubled foreign policy. But he seemed baffled by his responsibilities. "I am a man of limited talents from a small town," he reportedly told friends on one occasion. Harding's intellectual limits were compounded by his penchant for gambling, illegal alcohol, and attractive women.

Warren Harding

Harding lacked the strength to abandon the party hacks who had helped create his political success. One of them, Ohio party boss Harry Daugherty, he appointed attorney general. Another, New Mexico Senator Albert B. Fall, he made secretary of the interior. Members of the so-called Ohio Gang filled important offices throughout the administration. Unknown to the public, Daugherty, Fall, and others were engaged in fraud and corruption. The most spectacular scandal involved the rich naval oil reserves at Teapot Dome, Wyoming, and Elk Hills, California. At the urging of Fall, Harding transferred control of those reserves from the Navy Department to the Interior Department. Fall then secretly leased them to two wealthy businessmen and received in return nearly half a million dollars in "loans." Fall was ultimately convicted of bribery and sentenced to a year in prison.

Teapot Dome Scandal

In the summer of 1923, a tired and depressed Harding left Washington for a speaking tour in the West. In Seattle late in July, he suffered severe pain, which his doctors wrongly diagnosed as food poisoning. A few days later, in San Francisco, he died. He had suffered two major heart attacks.

In many ways, Calvin Coolidge, who succeeded Harding in the presidency, was utterly different from his predecessor. Where Harding was genial,

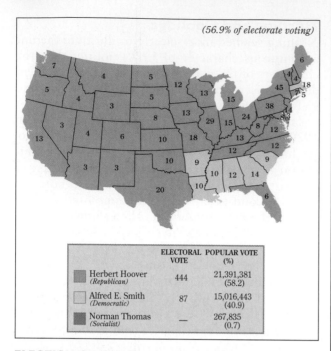

(56.9% of electorate voting)

		ELECTORAL VOTE	POPULAR VOTE (%)
	Herbert Hoover *(Republican)*	444	21,391,381 (58.2)
	Alfred E. Smith *(Democratic)*	87	15,016,443 (40.9)
	Norman Thomas *(Socialist)*	—	267,835 (0.7)

ELECTION OF 1928 The election of 1928 was, by almost any measure, highly one-sided. Herbert Hoover won over 58 percent of the vote to Alfred Smith's 41. Smith carried only Massachusetts, Rhode Island, and some traditionally Democratic states in the South. ▮ *Why did Smith do so poorly even in traditionally Democratic areas of the country in 1928?*

garrulous, and debauched, Coolidge was dour, silent, even puritanical. In other ways, however, Harding and Coolidge were similar figures. Both took essentially passive approaches to their office.

Elected governor of Massachusetts in 1919, Coolidge had won national attention with his laconic response to the Boston police strike that year: "There is no right to strike against the public safety." That was enough to make him his party's vice presidential nominee in 1920. Three years later, after Harding's death, he took the oath of office from his father, a justice of the peace, by the light of a kerosene lamp.

Calvin Coolidge

If anything, Coolidge was even less active as president than Harding, partly as a result of his conviction that government should interfere as little as possible in the life of the nation. In 1924, he received his party's presidential nomination virtually unopposed. Running against John W. Davis, he won

a comfortable victory. Coolidge probably could have won renomination and reelection in 1928. Instead, he walked into a press room one day and handed each reporter a slip of paper containing a single sentence: "I do not choose to run for president in 1928."

Government and Business

However passive the New Era presidents may have been, much of the federal government was working effectively and efficiently during the 1920s to adapt public policy to the widely accepted goal of the time: helping business and industry operate with maximum efficiency and productivity. Secretary of the Treasury Andrew Mellon, a wealthy steel and aluminum tycoon, devoted himself to working for substantial reductions in taxes on corporate profits and personal incomes and inheritances. Largely because of his efforts, Congress cut them all by more than half. Mellon also worked closely with President Coolidge after 1924 on a series of measures to trim dramatically the already modest federal budget.

Sharp Tax Reductions

The most prominent member of the cabinet was Commerce Secretary Herbert Hoover. During his eight years in the Commerce Department, Hoover constantly encouraged voluntary cooperation in the private sector as the best avenue to stability. But the idea of voluntarism did not require that the government remain passive; on the contrary, public institutions, Hoover believed, had a duty to play an active role in creating the new, cooperative order. Above all, Hoover became the champion of the concept of business "associationalism"—a concept that envisioned the creation of national organizations of businessmen in particular industries. Through these trade associations, private entrepreneurs could, Hoover believed, stabilize their industries and promote efficiency in production and marketing.

"Associationalism"

Some progressives derived encouragement from the election of Herbert Hoover to the presidency in 1928. Hoover entered office promising bold new efforts to solve the nation's remaining economic problems. But Hoover had few opportunities to prove himself. Less than a year after his inauguration, the nation plunged into the severest and most prolonged economic crisis in its history—a crisis that brought many of the optimistic assumptions of the New Era crashing down and launched the nation into a period of unprecedented social innovation and reform.

The remarkable prosperity of the 1920s shaped much of what exuberant contemporaries liked to call the "New Era." In the years after World War I, America built a vibrant and extensive national culture. Its middle class moved increasingly into the embrace of the growing consumer culture. Its politics reorganized itself around the needs of a booming, interdependent industrial economy—rejecting many of the reform crusades of the previous generation, but also creating new institutions to help promote economic growth and stability.

Beneath the glittering surface of the New Era, however, were great controversies and injustices. Although the prosperity of the 1920s was more widely spread than at any time in the nation's industrial history, more than half the population failed to achieve any real benefits from the growth. A new, optimistic, secular culture was attracting millions of urban, middle-class people. But many other Americans looked at it with alarm and fought against it with great fervor. The unprepossessing conservative presidents of the era suggested a time of stability, but in fact few eras in modern American history have seen so much political and cultural conflict.

The 1920s ended in a catastrophic economic crash that has colored the image of those years ever since. The crises of the 1930s should not obscure the real achievements of the New Era economy. Neither, however, should the prosperity of the 1920s obscure the inequity and instability in those years that helped produce the difficult years to come.

INTERACTIVE LEARNING

On the *Primary Source Investigator CD-ROM,* check out a number of valuable tools for further exploration of the content of this chapter.

Mini-Documentary Movie
- **Route 66.** A look at the planning behind the most famous American highway, and how it served to transform the country (Doc D16)

Interactive Maps
- Breaking Down Rural Isolation: The Expansion of Travel Horizons in Oregon, Illinois (Map M22)
- Areas of Population Growth (Map M25)
- U.S. Elections (Map M7)

Primary Sources
Documents, images, and maps related to America in the 1920s. Some highlights include:

- A text excerpt from the Ku Klux Klan's Constitution and a speech given by their former leader, Hiram Wesley Evans

- Letters written by Sacco and Vanzetti to their family, friends, and supporters

 Online Learning Center (www.mhhe.com/unfinishedinteractive)
Explore this rich website, providing additional exploration of the material covered in this chapter, online versions of the interactive maps included on the Primary Source Investigator CD-ROM, as well as several study aids, including a multiple-choice quiz, essay questions, a glossary, and other valuable tools.

FOR FURTHER REFERENCE

Frederick Lewis Allen, *Only Yesterday* (1931) is a classic popular history of the 1920s. Michael Parrish, *Anxious Decades: America in Prosperity and Depression, 1920–1941* (1992) is a good recent survey. Ellis Hawley, *The Great War and the Search for a Modern Order* (1979) describes the effect of World War I on American ideas, culture, and society. William E. Leuchtenburg, *The Perils of Prosperity* (rev. ed. 1994) reveals the class divisions and culture dislocation that accompanied economic prosperity in the 1920s. David Brody, *Workers in Industrial America* (1980) includes important essays on welfare capitalism and other labor systems of the 1920s. T. J. Jackson Lears, *Fables of Abundance: A Cultural History of Advertising in America* (1994) and Roland Marchand, *Advertising the American Dream* (1985) are valuable inquiries into the role of advertising in the new consumer culture. James J. Flink, *The Car Culture* (1975) examines ways in which the automobile transformed American life. Susan Smulyan, *Selling Radio: The Commercialization of American Broadcasting, 1920–1934* (1994) chronicles the emergence of commercial radio. Robert Lynd and Helen Merrell Lynd, *Middletown* (1929) is a classic sociological study of how an American city encountered the consumer culture and economy of the 1920s. Ann Douglas, *Terrible Honesty: Mongrel Manhattan in the 1920s* (1995) examines the cultural and political history of the New Era in New York City. Lynn Dumenil, *The Modern Temper: America in the 1920s* (1995) examines the reactions of Americans to modern culture. George Chauncey, *Gay New York: Gender, Urban Culture, and the Making of the Gay Male World, 1890–1940* (1994) is an excellent work in a relatively new field of history. The decline of the feminist movement in the 1920s is explored in Nancy Cott, *The Grounding of American Feminism* (1987). Gary Gerstle, *American Crucible* (2000) is an important study of the changing role of race and ethnicity in defining American nationhood in the twentieth century. Andrew Gyory, *Closing the Gate: Race, Politics, and the Chinese Exclusion Act* (1998) examines an early chapter in immigration restriction. Nathan I. Huggins chronicles the cultural and political efflorescence of black Harlem during these years in *Harlem Renaissance* (1971), as does David Levering Lewis in *When Harlem Was in Vogue* (1981). George Marsden, *Fundamentalism and American Culture* (1980) is a good study of some of the religious battles that came to a head in the 1920s. Grant Wacker, *Heaven Below: Early Pentecostals and American Culture* (2001) examines the emergence of modern pentecostalism. Edward J. Larson, *Summer for the Gods: The Scopes Trial and America's Continuing Debate Over Science and Religion* (1997) is a valuable analysis of the Scopes trial. Leonard Moore, *Citizen Klansmen: The Ku Klux Klan in Indiana, 1921–1928* (1991) is a challenging view of the Klan. Kathleen M. Blee, *Women and the Klan: Racism and Gender in the 1920s* (1991) recreates the female world of the Klan. David Burner, *The Politics of Provincialism* (1967) is a good study of the ordeal of the Democratic Party in the 1920s. Morton Keller, *Regulating a New Economy: Public Policy and Economic Change in America, 1900–1933* (1990) and *Regulating a New Society: Public Policy and Social Change in America, 1900–1933* (1994) are important studies of New Era public policy. *Coney Island* (1990) is a documentary film recreating the drama and fantasy of Coney Island. *That Rhythm, Those Blues* (1997) is a film documenting the one-night stands, makeshift housing, and poor transportation that were all a step toward the big time at the famed Apollo Theatre on Harlem's 125th Street. *Mr. Sears' Catalogue* (1997) is a film exploring how the Sears catalog became a symbol for the ambitions and dreams of a sprawling, fast developing America.

25

The Great Depression

MINI-DOCUMENTARY
Documenting the Depression

(Franklin Delano Roosevelt Library)

W e in America today," Herbert Hoover proclaimed in August 1928, "are nearer to the final triumph over poverty than ever before in the history of any land." Only fifteen months later, those words would return to haunt him, as the nation plunged into the severest and most prolonged economic depression in its history—a depression that continued in one form or another for a full decade.

THE COMING OF THE DEPRESSION

The sudden financial collapse in 1929 came as an especially severe shock because it followed so closely a period in which the New Era seemed to be performing another series of economic miracles— miracles that seemed especially evident in the remarkable performance of the stock market.

In February 1928, stock prices began a steady ascent that continued, with only a few temporary lapses, for a year and a half. Between May 1928 and September 1929, the average price of stocks rose over 40 percent. Trading mushroomed from 2 or 3 million shares a day to over 5 million, and at times to as many as 10 or 12 million. There was, in short, a widespread speculative fever that grew steadily more intense, particularly once brokerage firms began offering absurdly easy credit to those buying stocks.

The Great Crash

"Black Tuesday"   In the autumn of 1929, the market began to fall apart. On October 29, "Black Tuesday," after a week of steadily rising instability, all efforts to save the market failed. Sixteen million shares of stock were traded; the industrial index dropped 43 points (or nearly 10 percent), wiping out all the gains of the previous year; stocks in many companies became virtually worthless. Within a month stocks had lost half their September value, and despite occasional, short-lived rallies, they continued to decline for several years after that.

Popular folklore has established the stock market crash as the beginning, and even the cause, of the Great Depression. But the Depression had earlier beginnings and more important causes.

Causes of the Depression

Economists, historians, and others have argued for decades about the causes of the Great Depression. But most agree that what is remarkable about the crisis is not that it occurred, but that it was so severe and that it lasted so long. Most observers agree, too, that a number of different factors account for the severity of the crisis. One of those factors was a lack of diversification in the American economy in the 1920s. Prosperity had depended excessively on a few basic industries, notably construction and automobiles. In the late 1920s, those industries began to decline. Expenditures on construction fell from $11 billion to under $9 billion between 1926 and 1929. Automobile sales fell by more than a third in the first nine months of 1929. Newer industries were emerging to take up the slack—among them petroleum, chemicals, electronics, and plastics—but had not yet developed enough strength to compensate for the decline in other sectors.

A second important factor was the maldistribution of purchasing power and, as a result, a weakness in consumer demand. As industrial and agricultural production increased, the proportion of the profits going to potential consumers was too small to create an adequate market for the goods the economy was producing. Even in 1929, after nearly a decade of economic growth, more than half the families in America lived on the edge of or below the minimum subsistence level.

A third major problem was the credit structure of the economy. Farmers were deeply in debt, and small banks were in constant trouble as their customers defaulted on loans; large banks were in trouble, too. Although most American bankers were very conservative, some of the nation's biggest

Uneven Distribution of Wealth

MINI-DOCUMENTARY: Documenting the Depression

1929	1930	1931	1932
Stock market crash; Great Depression begins Agricultural Marketing Act	Hawley-Smoot Tariff Drought begins in Dust Bowl	Scottsboro defendants arrested	Reconstruction Finance Corporation established Bonus Army in Washington Franklin D. Roosevelt elected president

1934	1935	1936	1939	1940
Southern Tenant Farmers Union organized	American Communist Party proclaims Popular Front	Mitchell's *Gone with the Wind*	Steinbeck's *The Grapes of Wrath*	Wright's *Native Son*

banks were investing recklessly in the stock market or making unwise loans. When the market crashed and the loans went bad, some banks failed and others made the crisis worse by calling in loans that borrowers could not pay.

A fourth factor contributing to the Depression was America's position in international trade. Late in the 1920s, European demand for American goods began to decline. That was partly because European industry and agriculture were becoming more productive and partly because some European nations were having financial difficulties of their own. But it was also because the European economy was being destabilized by the international debt structure that had emerged in the aftermath of World War I.

International Debt Structure

The international debt structure, therefore, was a fifth factor contributing to the Depression. When the war came to an end in 1918, all the European nations that had been allied with the United States owed large sums of money to American banks, sums much too large to be repaid out of their shattered economies. That was one reason why the Allies had insisted on reparation payments from Germany and Austria. Reparations, they believed, would provide them with a way to pay off their own debts. But Germany and Austria were unable to pay the reparations.

The American government refused to forgive or reduce the debts. Instead, American banks began making large loans to European governments, which used them to pay off their earlier loans. Thus debts (and reparations) were being paid only by piling up new and greater debts. At the same time, American protective tariffs were making it difficult for Europeans to sell their goods in American markets. Without any source of foreign exchange with which to repay their loans, they began to default. The collapse of the international credit structure was one of the reasons the Depression spread to Europe after 1931.

Visit Chapter 25 of the book's Online Learning Center for a Where Historians Disagree essay on "Causes of the Great Depression."

Progress of the Depression

The stock market crash of 1929 did not so much cause the Depression, then, as help trigger a chain of events that exposed larger weaknesses in the American economy. During the next three years, the crisis grew steadily worse.

The most serious problem at first was the collapse of much of the banking system. Over 9,000

**THE UNEMPLOYED,
1930** Thousands of
unemployed men wait to
be fed outside the
Municipal Lodgers House
in New York City. *(The
Library of Congress)*

Banking Crisis   American banks either went
bankrupt or closed their
doors to avoid bankruptcy between 1930 and 1933.
Partly as a result, the nation's money supply shrank
by a third or more. The declining money supply
meant a decline in purchasing power, and thus deflation. Manufacturers and merchants began reducing prices, cutting back on production, and laying
off workers. Some economists argue that a severe
depression could have been avoided if the Federal
Reserve system had acted responsibly. But late in
1931, in a misguided effort to build international
confidence in the dollar, it raised interest rates,
which contracted the money supply even further.

Plunging GNP   The American gross national product plummeted
from over $104 billion in 1929 to $76.4 billion in
1932—a 25 percent decline. By 1932, an estimated
25 percent of the American work force was unemployed. For the rest of the decade, unemployment
averaged nearly 20 percent, never dropping below
15 percent. Up to another one-third of the work
force was "underemployed"—experiencing major
reductions in wages, hours, or both.

THE AMERICAN PEOPLE IN HARD TIMES

Someone asked the British economist John May-
nard Keynes in the 1930s whether he was aware of
any historical era comparable to the Great Depression. "Yes," Keynes replied. "It was called the Dark
Ages, and it lasted 400 years." The Depression did
not last 400 years. It did, however, bring unprecedented despair to the economies of the United
States and much of the Western world.

Unemployment and Relief

In the industrial Northeast and Midwest, cities
were becoming virtually paralyzed by unemployment. Unemployed workers walked through the
streets day after day looking for jobs that did not exist. An increasing number of families were turning
to state and local public relief systems. But those
systems, which in the 1920s had served only a small
number of indigents, were totally unequipped to
handle the new demands being placed on them. In
many cities, therefore, relief simply collapsed. Private charities attempted to supplement the public

relief efforts, but the problem was far beyond their capabilities as well.

In rural areas conditions were in many ways worse. Farm income declined by 60 percent between 1929 and 1932. A third of all American farmers lost their land. In addition, a large area of the Great Plains was suffering from one of the worst droughts in the history of the nation. Beginning in 1930, the region, which came to be known as **"Dust Bowl"** the "Dust Bowl" and which stretched north from Texas into the Dakotas, experienced a steady decline in rainfall. The drought continued for a decade, turning what had once been fertile farm regions into virtual deserts.

Many farmers left their homes in search of work. In the South, in particular, many dispossessed farmers—black and white—wandered from town to town. Hundreds of thousands of families from the Dust Bowl (often known as "Okies," since many came from Oklahoma) traveled to California and other states. Many worked as agricultural migrants, traveling from farm to farm picking fruit and other crops at starvation wages.

African Americans and the Depression

Soaring Black Unemployment As the Depression began, over half of all black Americans still lived in the South. Most were farmers. The collapse of prices for cotton and other staple crops left some with no income at all. Many left the land altogether—either by choice or because they had been evicted by landlords who no longer found the sharecropping system profitable. Some migrated to southern cities. But there, unemployed whites believed they had first claim to what work there was, and some now began to take positions as janitors, street cleaners, and domestic servants, displacing the blacks who formerly occupied those jobs. By 1932, over half the blacks in the South were without employment.

Unsurprisingly, therefore, many black southerners—perhaps 400,000 in all—left the South in the 1930s and journeyed to the cities of the North. But conditions there were little better than those in the South. In New York, black unemployment was nearly 50 percent. In other cities, it was higher. Two million African Americans—half the total black population of the country—were on some form of relief by 1932.

Traditional patterns of segregation and disenfranchisement in the South survived the Depression largely unchallenged. But a few particularly notorious examples of racism did attract the attention of the nation. The most celebrated was the Scottsboro case. In March 1931, nine black teenagers were taken off a freight train in northern Alabama (in a small town near Scottsboro) and arrested for vagrancy and disorder. Later, two white women who

BLACK MIGRANTS The Great Migration of blacks from the rural South into the cities had begun before World War I. But in the 1930s and 1940s the movement accelerated. Jacob Lawrence, an eminent African-American artist, created a series of paintings entitled, collectively, *The Migration of the Negro,* to illustrate this major event in the history of African Americans. (*The Phillips Collection, Washington, DC. Artwork Copyright 2005 Gwendolyn Knight Lawrence, courtesy of the Jacob and Gwendolyn Lawrence Foundation*)

had also been riding the train accused them of rape. In fact, there was overwhelming evidence, medical and otherwise, that the women had not been raped at all; they may have made their accusations out of fear of being arrested themselves. Nevertheless, an all-white jury in Alabama quickly convicted all nine

"Scottsboro Boys"

of the "Scottsboro boys" (as they were known to both friends and foes) and sentenced eight of them to death.

The Supreme Court overturned the convictions in 1932, and a series of new trials began. The International Labor Defense, an organization associated with the Communist Party, came to the aid of the accused youths and began to publicize the case. Although the white southern juries who sat on the case never acquitted any of the defendants, all of the accused eventually gained their freedom—although the last of the Scottsboro defendants did not leave prison until 1950.

Hispanics and Asians in Depression America

Similar patterns of discrimination confronted many Mexicans and Mexican Americans. The Hispanic population of the United States had been growing steadily since early in the century, largely through immigration from Mexico. Chicanos (as Mexican Americans are sometimes known) filled many of the same menial jobs there that blacks had traditionally filled. Some farmed small, marginal tracts; some became agricultural migrants. It had always been a precarious existence, and the Depression made things significantly worse. Unemployed whites in the Southwest demanded jobs held by Hispanics. Thus Mexican unemployment rose quickly to levels far higher than those for whites. Some officials arbitrarily removed Mexicans from relief rolls or simply rounded them up and transported them across the border. Perhaps half a million Chicanos left the United States for Mexico in the first years of the Depression.

Hispanic Resistance

There were, occasionally, signs of organized resistance by Mexican Americans themselves, most notably in California, where some formed a union of migrant farmworkers. But harsh repression by local growers and the public authorities allied with them prevented such organizations from having much

impact. As a result, many Hispanics began to migrate to cities such as Los Angeles, where they lived in a poverty comparable to that of urban blacks in the South and Northeast.

For Asian Americans, too, the Depression reinforced

Asians Marginalized

longstanding patterns of discrimination and economic marginalization. In California, where the largest Japanese-American and Chinese-American populations were, even educated Asians had always found it difficult, if not impossible, to move into mainstream professions. For those who found jobs in the industrial or service economy, employment was precarious; like blacks and Hispanics, Asians often lost jobs to white Americans desperate for work. Japanese farmworkers, like Chicano farmworkers, suffered from the increasing competition for even these low-paying jobs from white migrants from the Great Plains.

Chinese Americans fared no better. Those who moved outside the Asian community could rarely find jobs above the entry level. Chinese women, for example, might find work as stock girls in department stores but almost never as salesclerks. Educated Chinese men and women could hope for virtually no professional opportunities outside the world of the Chinatowns.

Women and Families in the Great Depression

The economic crisis served in many ways to strengthen the widespread belief that a woman's proper place was in the home. There was a particularly strong belief that no woman whose husband was employed should accept a job. Indeed, from 1932 until 1937, it was illegal for more than one member of a family to hold a federal civil service job.

But the widespread assumption that married women, at least, should not work outside the home did not stop them from doing so. Both single and married women worked in the 1930s because they or their families needed the money. By the end of the Depression, 25 percent more women were working than had been doing so at the beginning. This occurred despite considerable obstacles. Professional opportunities for women declined because un-

Growing Female Employment

employed men began moving into professions that had previously been considered women's fields. Female industrial workers were more likely to be laid off or to experience wage reductions than their male counterparts. But white women also had certain advantages in the workplace. The nonprofessional jobs that women traditionally held—salesclerks, stenographers, and other service positions—were less likely to disappear than the predominantly male jobs in heavy industry.

Black women suffered massive unemployment, particularly in the South, because of a great reduction of domestic service jobs. As many as half of all black working women lost their jobs in the 1930s. Even so, at the end of the 1930s, 38 percent of black women were employed, as compared with 24 percent of white women. That was because black women—both married and unmarried—had always been more likely to work than white women, less out of preference than out of economic necessity.

The economic hardships of the Depression years placed great strains on American families. Middle-class families found themselves plunged suddenly into uncertainty. Some working-class families had achieved a precarious prosperity in the 1920s but saw their gains disappear in the 1930s. Such circumstances caused many families to change the way they lived. Some women returned to sewing clothes for themselves and their families and to preserving their own food. Others engaged in home businesses such as taking in laundry or boarders.

| Declining Marriage and Birth Rates | But the Depression also worked to erode the strength of many family units. There |

was a decline in the divorce rate, but largely because divorce was now too expensive for some. More common was the informal breakup of families, particularly the desertion of families by unemployed men. The marriage rate and the birth rate both declined for the first time since the early nineteenth century. For an

 America in the World feature essay on "The Global Depression," visit Chapter 25 of the book's Online Learning Center.

THE DEPRESSION AND AMERICAN CULTURE

The Great Depression was a traumatic experience for millions of Americans. Out of the crisis emerged probing criticisms of American life. But the Depression also produced powerful confirmations of more traditional values and reinforced many traditional goals.

Depression Values

Prosperity and industrial growth had done much to shape American values in the 1920s. Mainstream culture, at least, had celebrated affluence and consumerism. Many Americans assumed, therefore, that the experience of hard times would have profound effects on the nation's social values. In general, however, American social values seemed to change relatively little. Instead, many people responded to hard times by redoubling their commitment to familiar ideas and goals.

No assumption would seem to have been more vulnerable to erosion during the Depression than the belief that anyone displaying sufficient talent and industry could become a success. And in some respects, the economic crisis did work to undermine the traditional "success ethic" in America. Many people began to look to government for assistance; many learned to blame corporate moguls and others for their distress. Yet the Depression did not destroy the success ethic.

The survival of the ideals of work and individual responsibility was evident in many ways, not least in the reactions of people who suddenly found themselves without employment. Some expressed anger and struck out at the economic system. Many, however, seemed to blame themselves. At the same time, millions responded eagerly to reassurances that they could restore themselves to prosperity and success. Dale Carnegie's *How to Win Friends and Influence People* | Dale Carnegie | (1936), a self-help manual preaching individual initiative, was one of the best-selling books of the decade.

Artists and Intellectuals in the Great Depression

Not all Americans, of course, responded to the crisis of the Depression so passively. Artists and intellectuals engaged in a broad effort to dramatize the problem of rural poverty. Among those involved in this venture was a group of documentary photographers, many of them employed by the federal Farm Security Administration in the late 1930s, who traveled through the South recording the nature of agricultural life. Men such as Walker Evans, Arthur Rothstein, Russell Lee, and Ben Shahn and women such as Margaret Bourke-White and Dorothea Lange produced memorable studies of farm families and their surroundings, studies designed to show the savage impact of a hostile environment on its victims. Many writers, similarly, devoted themselves to exposés of social injustice. Erskine Caldwell's *Tobacco Road* (1932), which later became a long-running play, was an exposé of poverty in the rural South. Richard Wright, a major African-American writer, exposed the plight of residents of the urban ghetto in novels such as *Native Son* (1940).

But the cultural products of the 1930s that attracted the widest popular audiences were those that diverted attention away from the Depression. And they came to Americans primarily through the two most powerful instruments of popular culture in the 1930s—radio and the movies.

Radio

| Radio's Mass Popularity | Almost every American family had a radio in the 1930s. In cities and towns, radio consoles were as familiar a part of the furnishing of parlors and kitchens as tables and chairs. Even in remote rural areas without access to electricity, many families purchased radios and hooked them up to car batteries when they wished to listen.

Listening to radio is generally considered a private experience—something people do in their homes. But in some communities, radio was often a community experience. Young people would place radios on their front porches and invite friends by to sit, talk, or dance. In poor urban neighborhoods, people would gather to listen to sporting events or concerts. Within families, the radio often drew parents and children together to listen to favorite programs.

What did Americans hear on the radio? Although radio stations occasionally carried socially and politically provocative programs, the staple of broadcasting was escapism: comedies such as *Amos n' Andy* (with its humorous if demeaning picture of urban blacks); adventures such as *Superman, Dick Tracy,* and *The Lone Ranger;* and other entertainment programs. Radio brought a new kind of comedy to a wide audience. Jack Benny, George Burns, and Gracie Allen

| Escapist Programming |

developed broad followings. Soap operas were enormously popular as well, especially with women who were alone in the house during the day. (That was why they became known as soap operas; soap companies—whose advertising was targeted at women—generally sponsored them.)

Radio provided Americans with their first direct access to important public events, and radio news and sports divisions grew rapidly to meet the demand. Some of the most dramatic moments of the 1930s were a result of radio coverage of celebrated events: the World Series, the Academy Awards, political conventions. When the German dirigible the *Hindenburg* crashed in flames in Lakehurst, New Jersey, in 1937, it produced an enormous national reaction largely because of the live radio account by a broadcaster overcome with emotion who cried out, as he watched the terrible crash, "Oh the humanity! Oh the humanity!" The actor/director Orson Welles created another memorable event on Halloween night, 1938, when he broadcast a radio play about aliens whose spaceship landed in central New Jersey and who had set off toward New York armed with terrible weapons. The play took the form of a news broadcast, and it created panic among millions of people who believed for a while that the events it described were real.

The Movies

In the first years of the Depression, movie attendance dropped significantly. By the mid-1930s, however, most Americans had resumed their moviegoing habits to at least some extent in part because the movies were becoming more appealing.

| Hollywood's Self-Censorship | Hollywood continued to exercise tight control over its products in the 1930s through its resilient censor Will Hays, who ensured that most movies carried no sensational or controversial messages. The studio system—through which a few large movie companies exercised iron control over actors, writers, and directors—also worked to ensure that Hollywood films avoided controversy.

Neither the censor nor the studio system, however, could (or wished to) prevent films from exploring social questions altogether. A few films, such as King Vidor's *Our Daily Bread* (1932) and John Ford's adaptation of *The Grapes of Wrath* (1940), did explore political themes. Gangster movies such as

Little Caesar (1930) and *The Public Enemy* (1931) portrayed a dark, gritty, violent world with which few Americans were familiar, but their desperate stories were popular nevertheless.

But the most effective presentation of a social message, even if a muted one, came from the brilliant Italian-born director Frank

| Frank Capra |

Capra. Capra had a deep and somewhat romanticized love for his adopted country, and he translated that love into a vaguely populistic admiration for ordinary people. He contrasted the decency of small-town America and the common man with what he considered the grasping opportunism of the city and the greedy capitalist marketplace. In *Mr. Deeds Goes to Town* (1936), a simple man from a small town inherits a large fortune, moves to the city, and—not liking the greed and dishonesty he finds there—gives the money away and moves back home. In *Mr. Smith Goes to Washington* (1939), a decent man from a western state is elected to the United States Senate, refuses to join in the self-interested politics of Washington, and dramatically exposes the corruption and selfishness of his colleagues. Capra's films, outstandingly popular in the 1930s, helped audiences find solace in a vision of an imagined American past.

More often, however, the commercial films of the 1930s, like most radio programs, were deliberately and explicitly escapist: lavish musicals such as *Gold Diggers of 1933*, "screwball" comedies (such as Capra's *It Happened One Night*), or the many films of the Marx Brothers—films designed to divert audiences from their troubles and, often, indulge their fantasies about quick and easy wealth.

The 1930s saw the beginning of Walt Disney's long

| Walt Disney |

reign as the champion of animation and children's entertainment. After producing cartoon shorts for theaters in the late 1920s, many of them starring the newly created character of Mickey Mouse, Disney began to produce feature-length animated films, starting in 1937 with *Snow White*. Other enormously popular films of the 1930s were adaptations of popular novels: *The Wizard of Oz* and *Gone with the Wind*, both released in 1939.

Hollywood did little to challenge the conventions of popular culture on issues of gender and race. Women in movies were portrayed overwhelmingly as wives and mothers, or if not, as sexually attractive people engaged in elaborate flirtations with men. Mae West portrayed herself in a series of successful films as an overtly sexual woman manipulating men through her attractiveness. Few films included important African-American characters. Most of the black men and women who did appear in movies were portrayed as servants or farmhands or entertainers.

Popular Literature and Journalism

The social and political strains of the Great Depression found voice much more successfully in print than they did on the airwaves or the screen. Much literature and journalism in the 1930s dealt with the tremendous disillusionment, and the increasing radicalism, of the time.

Not all literature, of course, was challenging or controversial. The most popular books and magazines of the 1930s, in fact, were as escapist and romantic as the most popular radio shows and movies. Two of the best-selling novels of the decade were romantic sagas set in earlier eras: Margaret Mitchell's *Gone with the Wind* (1936) and Hervey Allen's *Anthony Adverse* (1933). Leading magazines focused more on fashions, stunts, scenery, and the arts than on the social conditions of the nation. The enormously popular new photographic journal *Life*, which began publication in 1936, devoted some attention to politics and to the economic conditions of the Depression, but it was best known for stunning photographs of sporting and theater events, natural landscapes, impressive public projects, and even celebrated parties.

Other Depression writing, however, was frankly and openly challenging to the dominant values of American popular culture. Some of the most significant literature offered corrosive portraits of the harshness and emptiness of American life: John Dos Passos's *U.S.A.* trilogy (1930–1936), which

| John Dos Passos |

attacked what he considered the materialistic madness of American culture; Nathanael West's *Miss Lonelyhearts* (1933), the story of an advice columnist overwhelmed by the sadness he encounters in the lives of those who consult him; Jack Conroy's *The Disinherited* (1933), a harsh portrait of the lives of coalminers; and James T. Farrell's *Studs Lonigan* (1932), a portrait of a lost, hardened working-class youth.

The Popular Front and the Left

In the later 1930s, much of the political literature adopted a more optimistic approach to society. This was in part a result of the rise of the Popular Front, a broad coalition of "antifascist" groups on the left, of which the most important was the American Communist Party. The party had long been a harsh and unrelenting critic of American capitalism and the government it claimed was controlled by it. But in 1935, under instructions from the Soviet Union, the party softened its attitude toward Franklin Roosevelt and formed loose alliances with many other "progressive" groups. The party began to praise the New Deal and John L. Lewis, a powerful (and strongly anticommunist) labor leader, and it adopted the slogan "Communism is twentieth-century Americanism." In its heyday, the Popular Front did much to enhance the reputation and influence of the Communist Party. It also helped mobilize writers, artists, and intellectuals behind a critical, democratic sensibility.

The importance to many American intellectuals of the Spanish Civil War of the mid-1930s was a good example of how the left helped give meaning and purpose to individual lives. The war in Spain pitted the reactionary forces of Francisco Franco against the existing republican government. It attracted a substantial group of young Americans—more than 3,000 in all—who formed the Abraham Lincoln Brigade and traveled to Spain to join in the fight against the fascists. The American Communist Party was instrumental in creating the Lincoln Brigade, and directed many of its activities.

Abraham Lincoln Brigade

The party was active as well in organizing the unemployed in the early 1930s and staged a hunger march in Washington, D.C., in 1931. Party members were among the most effective union organizers in some industries. And the party was virtually alone among political organizations in taking a firm stand in favor of racial justice; its active defense of the Scottsboro defendants was but one example of its efforts to ally itself with the aspirations of African Americans.

The American Communist Party was not, however, the open, patriotic organization it tried to appear. It was always under the close and rigid supervision of the Soviet Union. Most members obediently followed the "party line." The subordination of the party leadership to the Soviet Union was most clearly demonstrated in 1939, when Stalin signed a nonaggression pact with Nazi Germany. Moscow then sent orders to the American Communist Party to abandon the Popular Front and return to its old stance of harsh criticism of American liberals; and Communist Party leaders in the United States immediately obeyed—although thousands of disillusioned members left the party as a result.

The Socialist Party of America, under the leadership of Norman Thomas, also cited the economic crisis as evidence of the failure of capitalism and sought vigorously to win public support for its own political program. Among other things, it attempted to mobilize support among the rural poor. The Southern Tenant Farmers Union, organized by a young socialist, H. L. Mitchell, attempted to create a biracial coalition of sharecroppers, tenant farmers, and others to demand economic reform. Neither the STFU nor the party itself, however, made any real progress toward establishing socialism as a major force in American politics.

Southern Tenant Farmers Union

Antiradicalism was a powerful force in the 1930s. Hostility toward the Communist Party, in particular, was intense at many levels of government. Congressional committees chaired by Hamilton Fish of New York and Martin Dies of Texas investigated communist influence wherever they could find (or imagine) it. White southerners tried to drive communist organizers out of the countryside, just as growers in California and elsewhere tried (unsuccessfully) to keep communists from organizing Mexican-American and other workers.

Even so, at few times before (and few since) in American history did being part of the left seem so respectable. Thus the 1930s witnessed an impressive, if temporary, widening of the ideological range of mainstream art and politics. The New Deal, for example, sponsored artistic work through the Works Projects Administration that was frankly challenging to the capitalist norms of the 1920s. The filmmaker Pare Lorentz, with funding from New Deal agencies, made a series of powerful documentaries—*The Plow that Broke the Plains* (1936), *The River* (1937)—that combined a celebration of New Deal programs with a harsh critique of the exploitation of people and the environment that industrial capitalism had produced.

A less confrontational grappling with the social misery of the 1930s was a remarkable book by the novelist James Agee and the photographer Walker Evans, *Let Us Now Praise Famous Men* (1941). Agee and Walker had traveled to rural

Let Us Now Praise Famous Men

Alabama in the mid-1930s on an assignment from *Fortune* magazine to produce an article about sharecropping and rural poverty. The long, rambling, highly emotional text that Agee produced, accompanied by extraordinary photographs of three families of white southern sharecroppers, was too long and too unconventional for *Fortune*. But the book that eventually appeared is a passionate tribute to the strength and even nobility of the struggling people he had come to know.

Perhaps the most successful chronicler of social conditions in the 1930s was the novelist John Steinbeck, particularly in his celebrated novel *The Grapes of Wrath*, published in 1939. In telling the story of

The Grapes of Wrath

the Joad family, migrants from the Dust Bowl to California who encounter an unending string of calamities and failures, he offered a harsh portrait of the exploitive features of agrarian life in the West, but also a tribute to the endurance of his main characters—and to the spirit of community they represent.

THE ORDEAL OF HERBERT HOOVER

Herbert Hoover began his presidency in March 1929 believing, like most Americans, that the nation faced a bright and prosperous future. For the first six months of his administration, he attempted to expand the policies he had advocated during his eight years as secretary of commerce. The economic crisis that began before the year was out forced the president to deal with a new set of problems, but for most of the rest of his term, he continued to rely on the principles that had always governed his public life.

The Hoover Program

Hoover's first response to the Depression was to attempt to restore public confidence in the economy. He summoned leaders of business, labor, and agriculture to the White House and urged them to adopt a program of voluntary cooperation for recovery. He implored businessmen not to

Failure of Voluntary Cooperation

cut production or lay off workers; he talked labor leaders into forgoing demands for higher wages or better hours. But by mid-1931, economic conditions had deteriorated so much that the structure of voluntary cooperation he had erected collapsed.

Hoover also attempted to use government spending as a tool for fighting the Depression. The president proposed to Congress an increase in federal public works programs, and he exhorted state and local governments to fund public construction. But the spending was not nearly enough in the face of such devastating problems. And when economic conditions worsened, he became less willing to increase spending, worrying instead about keeping the budget balanced.

Even before the stock market crash, Hoover had begun to construct a program to assist the already troubled agricultural economy. In April 1929, he proposed the Agricultural Marketing Act, which established the first

Agricultural Marketing Act

major government program to help farmers maintain prices. A federally sponsored Farm Board would make loans to national marketing cooperatives or establish corporations to buy surpluses and thus raise prices. At the same time, Hoover attempted to protect American farmers from international competition by raising agricultural tariffs. The Hawley-Smoot Tariff of 1930 contained increased protection on seventy-five farm products. But neither the Agricultural Marketing Act nor the Hawley-Smoot Tariff ultimately helped American farmers significantly.

By the spring of 1931, Hoover's political position had deteriorated. In the 1930 elections, Democrats won control of the House and made substantial inroads in the Senate. Many Americans blamed the president for the crisis and began calling the shantytowns that unemployed people established on the outskirts of cities "Hoovervilles." Democrats urged the president to support more vigorous programs of relief and public spending. Hoover, instead, seized on a slight improvement in economic conditions early in 1931 as proof that his policies were working.

The international financial panic of the spring of 1931 destroyed the illusion that the

International Economic Collapse

economic crisis was coming to an end. Throughout the 1920s, European nations had depended on loans from American banks to allow them to make payments on their debts. After 1929, when they could no longer get such loans, the financial fabric of several European nations began to unravel. In May 1931, the largest bank in Austria collapsed. Over the next several months, panic gripped the financial institutions of neighboring countries. The American economy rapidly declined to new lows.

By the time Congress convened in December 1931, conditions had grown so desperate that Hoover supported a series of measures designed to keep endangered banks afloat and protect homeowners from foreclosure on their mortgages. Most important was a bill passed in January 1932 establishing the Reconstruction Finance Corporation (RFC), a government agency whose purpose was to provide federal loans to troubled banks, railroads, and other businesses. Unlike some earlier Hoover programs, the RFC operated on a large scale.

Failure of the RFC Nevertheless, the new agency failed to deal directly or forcefully enough with the real problems of the economy to produce any significant recovery. The RFC lent funds only to financial institutions with sufficient collateral; it helped finance only those public works projects that promised ultimately to pay for themselves (toll bridges, public housing, and others). Above all, the RFC did not have enough money to make any real impact on the Depression, and it did not even spend all the money it had.

Popular Protest

For the first several years of the Depression, most Americans were either too stunned or too confused to raise any effective protest. By the middle of 1932, however, dissident voices began to be heard.

In the summer of 1932, a group of unhappy farm owners gathered in Des Moines, Iowa, to establish a new organization: the Farmers' Holiday Association, which endorsed the withholding of farm products from the market— **Farmers' Holiday Association** in effect a farmers' strike. The strike began in August in western Iowa, spread briefly to a few neighboring areas, and succeeded in blockading several markets, but in the end it dissolved in failure.

A more celebrated protest movement emerged from American veterans. In 1924, Congress had approved the payment of a $1,000 bonus to all those who had served in World War I, the money to be paid beginning in 1945. By 1932, however, many

CLEARING OUT THE BONUS MARCHERS In July 1932, President Hoover ordered the Washington, D.C. police to evict the Bonus Marchers from some of the public buildings and land they had been occupying. The result was a series of pitched battles (one of them visible here), in which both veterans and police sustained injuries. Such skirmishes persuaded Hoover to call out the army to finish the job. *(Bettmann/Corbis)*

veterans were demanding that the bonus be paid immediately. Hoover, concerned about balancing the budget, rejected their appeal. In June, more than 20,000 veterans, members of the self-proclaimed Bonus Expeditionary Force, or "Bonus Army," marched into Washington, built crude camps around the city, and promised to stay until Congress approved legislation to pay the bonus. Some of the veterans departed in July, after Congress had voted down their proposal. Many, however, remained where they were.

Their continued presence in Washington embarrassed President Hoover. Finally, in mid-July, he ordered police to clear the marchers out of several abandoned federal buildings in which they had been staying. A few marchers threw rocks at the police, and someone opened fire; two veterans fell dead. Hoover called the incident evidence of uncontrolled violence and radicalism, and he ordered the United States Army to assist the police in clearing out the buildings.

Demise of the "Bonus Army" General Douglas MacArthur, the army chief of staff, carried out the mission himself. He led the Third Cavalry, two infantry regiments, a machine-gun detachment, and six tanks down Pennsylvania Avenue in pursuit of the Bonus Army. The veterans fled in terror. MacArthur followed them across the Anacostia River, where he ordered the soldiers to burn their tent city to the ground. More than 100 marchers were injured.

The incident served as perhaps the final blow to Hoover's already battered political standing. The Great Engineer, the personification of the optimistic days of the 1920s, had become a symbol of the nation's failure to deal effectively with its startling reversal of fortune.

The Election of 1932

As the 1932 presidential election approached, few people doubted the outcome. The Republican Party dutifully renominated Herbert Hoover for a second term of office, but few delegates believed he could win. The Democrats, in the meantime, gathered jubilantly in Chicago to nominate the governor of New York, Franklin Delano Roosevelt.

Franklin Delano Roosevelt Roosevelt had been a well-known figure in the party for many years already. A distant

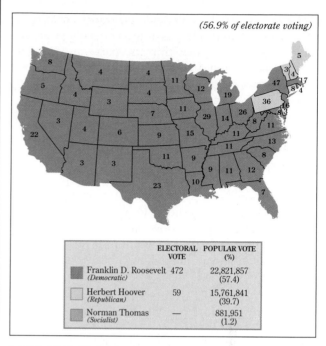

(56.9% of electorate voting)

	ELECTORAL VOTE	POPULAR VOTE (%)
Franklin D. Roosevelt *(Democratic)*	472	22,821,857 (57.4)
Herbert Hoover *(Republican)*	59	15,761,841 (39.7)
Norman Thomas *(Socialist)*	—	881,951 (1.2)

ELECTION OF 1932 Like the election of 1928, the election of 1932 was exceptionally one-sided. But this time, the landslide favored the Democratic candidate, Franklin Roosevelt, who overwhelmed Herbert Hoover in all regions of the country except New England. Roosevelt obviously benefited primarily from popular disillusionment with Hoover's response to the Great Depression. ▌ *But what characteristics of Roosevelt himself contributed to his victory?*

For an interactive version of this map go to www.mhhe.com/unfinishedinteractive

cousin of Theodore Roosevelt, and a handsome, charming, aristocratic young man, he progressed rapidly: from the New York State legislature to assistant secretary of the navy under Woodrow Wilson during World War I to his party's vice presidential nomination in 1920 on the ill-fated ticket with James M. Cox. Less than a year later, he was stricken with polio. Although he never regained use of his legs, he built up sufficient strength to return to politics in 1928. When Al Smith received the Democratic nomination for president that year, Roosevelt was elected to succeed him as governor. In 1930, he easily won reelection.

Roosevelt worked no miracles in New York, but he did initiate enough positive programs of government assistance to be able to present himself as a more energetic and imaginative leader than Hoover. In national politics, he avoided divisive cultural issues and emphasized the economic grievances that most Democrats shared. He was able as a result to assemble a broad coalition within the party and win his party's nomination. In a break with tradition, he flew to Chicago to accept the nomination. In his acceptance speech, he aroused the delegates with his ringing promise: "I pledge you, I pledge myself, to a new deal for the American people." Neither then nor in the campaign did Roosevelt give much indication of what that program would be. But Hoover's unpopularity virtually ensured Roosevelt's election.

FDR Elected

Roosevelt won by a landslide. He received 57.4 percent of the popular vote to Hoover's 39.7. In the electoral college, the result was even more overwhelming. Democrats won majorities in both houses of Congress. It was a convincing mandate, but it was not yet clear what Roosevelt intended to do with it.

The "Interregnum"

The period between the election and the inauguration was a season of growing economic crisis. Presidents-elect traditionally do not involve themselves directly in government. But in a series of brittle exchanges, Hoover tried to exact from Roosevelt a pledge to maintain policies of economic orthodoxy. Roosevelt genially refused.

In February, only a month before the inauguration, a new crisis developed when the collapse of the banking system accelerated. Depositors were withdrawing their money in panic; and one bank after another was declaring bankruptcy. Hoover again asked Roosevelt to give prompt public assurances that there would be no tinkering with the currency, no heavy borrowing, no unbalancing of the budget. Roosevelt again refused.

Banking Collapse

March 4, 1933, was, therefore, a day of both economic crisis and considerable personal bitterness. On that morning, Herbert Hoover rode glumly down Pennsylvania Avenue with a beaming, buoyant Franklin Roosevelt, who would shortly be sworn in as the thirty-second president of the United States.

CONCLUSION

The Great Depression created unemployment on a scale never before experienced in the nation's history. It put enormous pressures on families, on communities, on state and local governments, and ultimately on Washington—which during the presidency of Herbert Hoover was unable to produce policies capable of dealing effectively with the crisis. In the nation's politics and culture, there were strong currents of radicalism and protest; and many middle-class Americans came to fear that a revolution might be approaching.

In reality, while the Great Depression shook much of American society and culture, it actually toppled very little. The capitalist system survived, damaged for a time but never truly threatened. The values of materialism and personal responsibility were shaken, but never overturned. The American people in the 1930s were more receptive than they had been in the 1920s to evocations of community, generosity, and the dignity of common people. They were more open to experiments in government and business and even private lives, but belief in the "American way of life" remained strong throughout the long years of economic despair.

INTERACTIVE LEARNING

On the *Primary Source Investigator CD-ROM,* check out a number of valuable tools for further exploration of the content of this chapter.

Mini-Documentary Movie

- **Documenting the Depression.** A look at the 1930s documentary film *The River,* and its ties to New Deal ideas about society (Doc D17)

Interactive Maps

- U.S. Elections (Map M7)
- Unemployment Relief (Map M26)

Primary Sources

Documents, images, and maps related to the onset of the Great Depression, the suffering of the people, and the ordeal of President Herbert Hoover. Some highlights include:

- "Migrant Mother" and other striking images by Farm Security Administration photographer Dorothea Lange
- An image of the Depression-era shantytowns dubbed "Hoovervilles"

- Photographs of a Texas dust storm and other images of Dust Bowl life

Online Learning Center
(www.mhhe.com/unfinishedinteractive)

Explore this rich website, providing additional exploration of the material covered in this chapter, online versions of the interactive maps included on the Primary Source Investigator CD-ROM, as well as several study aids, including a multiple-choice quiz, essay questions, a glossary, and other valuable tools. Also in the Online Learning Center for this chapter, look for *Interactive Feature Essays* **on:**

- **Where Historians Disagree: Causes of the Great Depression**
- **America in the World: The Global Depression**

FOR FURTHER REFERENCE

Donald Worster scathingly indicts agricultural capitalism for its destruction of the plains environment in *Dust Bowl: The Southern Plains in the 1930s* (1979). In *The Great Depression: Delayed Recovery and Economic Change in America, 1929–1939* (1987), Michael Bernstein argues that we should ask not so much why the economy crashed in 1929 but rather why the expected recovery from the crash was so slow. Richard Pells, *Radical Visions and American Dreams: Culture and Social Thought in the Depression Years* (1973) is an important survey of the cultural and intellectual history of the 1930s. Studs Terkel, *Hard Times* (1970) is an excellent oral history of the Depression. Susan Ware analyzes the effect of the Great Depression on women in *Holding Their Own: American Women in the 1930s* (1982). The Communist Party's most popular period in the United States is the subject of Harvey Klehr's *The Heyday of American Communism: The Depression Decade*

(1984) and, from quite different viewpoints, Robin D. G. Kelley, *Hammer and Hoe: Alabama Communists During the Great Depression* (1990) and Michael Denning, *The Cultural Front: The Laboring of American Culture in the Twentieth Century* (1997). Joan Hoff Wilson, *Herbert Hoover: Forgotten Progressive* (1975) argues that President Hoover was in many ways a surprisingly progressive thinker about the American social order.

The Great Depression (1993), a multipart film by Blackside Productions, is an eloquent picture of many aspects of the depression decade. *Union Maids* (1997) is a vivid film history of women organizing in the 1930s. *The Lemon Grove Incident* (1985) is a film providing a rare glimpse of Mexican-American civil rights activism over school integration in the early 1930s.

The New Deal

26

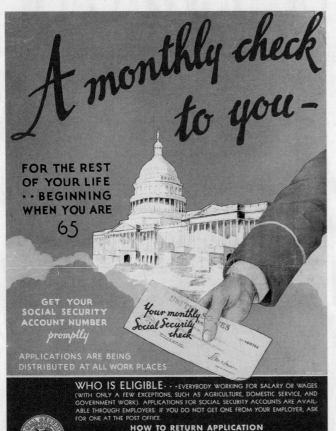

(Library of Congress)

During his twelve years in office Franklin Roosevelt constructed a series of programs that permanently altered the federal government and its relationship to society. By the end of the 1930s, the New Deal (as the Roosevelt administration was called) had not ended the Great Depression; only World War II did that. But it had created many of the broad outlines of the political world we know today.

LAUNCHING THE NEW DEAL

Roosevelt's first task was to alleviate the panic that was creating chaos in the financial system. He did so in part by force of personality and in part by constructing an ambitious and diverse program of legislation.

Restoring Confidence

Much of Roosevelt's early success was a result of his ebullient personality. He was the first president to make regular use of the radio; and his friendly "fireside chats," during which he explained in simple terms his programs and plans to the people, helped build public confidence in the administration. But Roosevelt could not rely on image alone. On March 6, two days after taking office, he issued a proclamation closing all American banks for four days until Congress could meet in special session to consider banking reform legislation. So great was the panic about bank failures that the "bank holiday" created a general sense of relief and hope.

"Bank Holiday" Declared

Three days later, Roosevelt sent to Congress the Emergency Banking Act, a bill designed primarily to protect the larger banks from being dragged down by the weakness of smaller ones. The bill provided for Treasury Department inspection of all banks before they would be allowed to reopen, for federal assistance to some troubled institutions, and for a thorough reorganization of those banks in the greatest difficulty. Congress passed the bill within a few hours of its introduction. Whatever else the new law accomplished, it helped dispel the panic. Three-quarters of the banks in the Federal Reserve system reopened within the next three days, and $1 billion in hoarded currency and gold flowed back into them within a month.

Emergency Banking Act

On the morning after passage of the Emergency Banking Act, Roosevelt sent to Congress another measure—the Economy Act—designed to convince the public that the federal government was in safe, responsible hands. The act proposed to balance the federal budget by cutting the salaries of government employees and reducing pensions to veterans by as much as 15 percent. Like the banking bill, this one passed through Congress almost instantly. Later that spring, Roosevelt signed the Glass-Steagall Act of June 1933, which gave the government authority to curb irresponsible speculation by banks. More important, perhaps, it established the Federal Deposit Insurance Corporation, which guaranteed all bank deposits up to $2,500. In

THE RADIO PRESIDENT Franklin D. Roosevelt was the first American president to master the use of radio. Beginning in his first days in office, he regularly bypassed the newspapers (many of which were hostile to him) and communicated directly with the people through his famous "Fireside Chats." He is shown here speaking in 1938, urging communities to continue to provide work relief for the unemployed. *(Franklin Delano Roosevelt Library)*

TIME LINE

1933	1934	1935
"First New Deal" legislation Prohibition ends	American Liberty League founded Long's Share-Our-Wealth Society established	Supreme Court invalidates NRA "Second New Deal" legislation, including Social Security and Wagner Acts Lewis breaks with AFL

1936	1937	1938	1939
Supreme Court invalidates Agricultural Adjustment Act CIO established Roosevelt reelected Sit-down strikes	Roosevelt's "Court-packing" plan Supreme Court upholds Wagner Act Severe recession	Fair Labor Standards Act	Marian Anderson sings at Lincoln Memorial

other words, even if a bank should fail, small depositors would be able to recover their money.

To restore confidence in the stock market, Congress passed the so-called Truth in Securities Act of 1933, requiring corporations issuing new securities to provide full and accurate information about them to the public. Another act, of June 1934, established the Securities and Exchange Commission (SEC) to police the stock market.

Securities and Exchange Commission

Roosevelt also signed a bill to legalize the manufacture and sale of beer with a 3.2 percent alcohol content—an interim measure pending the repeal of prohibition, for which a constitutional amendment (the Twenty-first) was already in process. The amendment was ratified later in 1933.

Agricultural Adjustment

These initial actions were stopgaps, to buy time for more comprehensive programs. The first was the Agricultural Adjustment Act, which Congress passed in May 1933. Under the provisions of the act, producers of seven basic commodities would decide on production limits for their crops. The government, through the Agricultural Adjustment Administration (AAA), would then tell individual farmers how much they should produce and would pay them subsidies for leaving some of their land idle. A tax on food processing (for example, the milling of wheat) would provide the funds for the new payments. Farm prices were to be subsidized up to the point of parity.

The AAA helped bring about a rise in prices for farm commodities in the years after 1933. Gross farm income increased by half in the first three years of the New Deal, and the agricultural economy as a whole emerged from the 1930s much more stable and prosperous than it had been in many years. But by distributing payments to landowners, not those who worked the land, the government did little to discourage planters who were reducing their acreage from evicting tenants and sharecroppers and firing field hands.

In January 1936, the Supreme Court struck down the crucial provisions of the Agricultural Adjustment Act, arguing that the government had no constitutional authority to require farmers to limit production. But within a few weeks the administration had secured passage of new legislation (the Soil Conservation and Domestic Allotment Act), which permitted the government to pay farmers to reduce production so as to "conserve soil," prevent erosion, and accomplish other secondary goals.

The administration launched several efforts to assist poor farmers as well. The Resettlement Administration, established in 1935, and its successor,

Farm Security Administration

the Farm Security Administration, created in 1937, provided loans to help farmers relocate to better lands. But the programs moved no more than a few thousand farmers. More effective was the Rural Electrification Administration, created in 1935, which worked to make electric power available to thousands of farmers through utility cooperatives.

Industrial Recovery

Ever since 1931, leaders of the United States Chamber of Commerce and many others had been urging the government to adopt an antideflation scheme that would permit trade associations to cooperate in stabilizing prices within their industries. Existing antitrust laws clearly forbade such practices, and Herbert Hoover had refused to endorse suspension of the laws. The Roosevelt administration was more receptive. In exchange for relaxing antitrust provisions, however, business leaders would have to recognize workers' right to bargain collectively through unions—to ensure that the incomes of workers would rise along with prices. And to help create jobs and increase consumer buying power, the administration added a major program of public works spending. The result was the National Industrial Recovery Act, which Congress passed in June 1933.

National Recovery Administration Established

At its center was a new federal agency, the National Recovery Administration (NRA), under the direction of the flamboyant and energetic Hugh S. Johnson. Johnson called on every business establishment in the nation to accept a temporary "blanket code": a minimum wage of between 30 and 40 cents an hour, a maximum workweek of thirty-five to forty hours, and the abolition of child labor. At the same time, Johnson negotiated another, more specific set of codes with leaders of the nation's major industries. These industrial codes set floors below which no company would lower prices or wages, and they included provisions for maintaining employment and production. He quickly won agreements from almost every major industry in the country.

From the beginning, however, the NRA encountered serious difficulties. Large producers consistently dominated the code-writing process and ensured that the new regulations would work to their advantage and to the disadvantage of smaller firms. And the codes at times did more than simply set floors under prices; they artificially raised them—sometimes to levels higher than the market could sustain.

Other NRA goals did not progress as quickly as the efforts to raise prices. Section 7(a) of the National Industrial Recovery Act promised workers the right to form unions and engage in collective bargaining. But it contained no enforcement mechanisms. The Public Works Administration (PWA), established to administer the National Industrial Recovery Act's spending programs, only gradually allowed the $3.3 billion in public works funds to trickle out.

Perhaps the clearest evidence of the NRA's failure

Failure of the NRA

was that industrial production actually declined despite the rise in prices that the codes had helped to create. By the spring of 1934, the NRA was besieged by criticism. That fall, Roosevelt pressured Johnson to resign and established a new board of directors to oversee the NRA. Then the Supreme Court intervened.

In 1935, a case came before the Court involving alleged NRA code violations by the Schechter brothers, who operated a wholesale poultry business confined to Brooklyn, New York. The Court ruled unanimously that the Schechters were not engaged in interstate commerce (and thus not subject to federal regulation) and, further, that Congress had unconstitutionally delegated legislative power to the president to draft the NRA codes. The justices struck down the legislation. Roosevelt denounced the justices for their "horse-and-buggy" interpretation of the interstate commerce clause. He was rightly concerned, for the reasoning in the Schechter case threatened many other New Deal programs as well.

Regional Planning

The AAA and the NRA largely reflected the beliefs of New Dealers who favored economic planning but wanted private interests (farmers or business leaders) to dominate the planning process. Other reformers believed that the government itself should be the chief planning agent. Their most conspicuous success was an unprecedented experiment in regional planning: the Tennessee Valley Authority (TVA).

| Tennessee Valley Authority |

Progressive reformers had agitated for years for public development of the nation's water resources as a source of cheap electric power. In particular, they had urged completion of a great dam at Muscle Shoals on the Tennessee River in Alabama—a dam begun during World War I but left unfinished when the war ended. But opposition from the utilities companies had been too powerful to overcome.

In 1932, however, one of the great utility empires—that of the electricity magnate Samuel Insull—collapsed amid widely publicized exposés of corruption. Hostility to the utilities soon grew so intense that the companies were no longer able to block the public power movement. The result was legislation supported by the president and enacted by Congress in May 1933 creating the Tennessee Valley Authority. The TVA was authorized to complete the dam at Muscle Shoals and build others in the region, and to generate and sell electricity from them at reasonable rates. It was also intended to be an agent for redevelopment of the region: encouraging the growth of local industries, supervising a substantial program of reforestation, and helping farmers improve productivity.

Opposition by conservatives ultimately blocked many of the ambitious social planning projects proposed by the more visionary TVA administrators, but the | Benefits of the TVA | Authority revitalized the region in numerous ways.

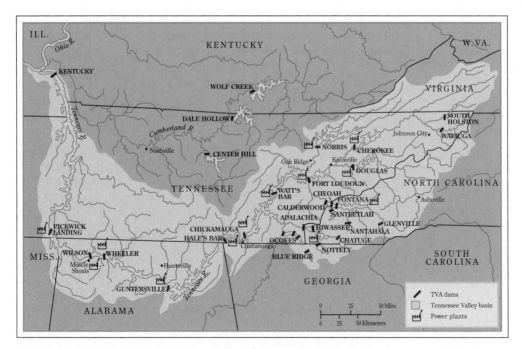

THE TENNESSEE VALLEY AUTHORITY The Tennessee Valley Authority was one of the largest experiments in government-funded public works and regional planning in American history to that point. The federal government had helped fund many projects in its history—canals, turnpikes, railroads, bridges, dams, and others. But never before had it undertaken a project of such great scope, and never before had it maintained such close control and ownership over the public works it helped create. This map illustrates the broad reach of the TVA within the Tennessee Valley region, which spanned seven states. TVA dams throughout the region helped control floods and also provided a source for hydroelectric power, which the government sold to consumers. Note the dam near Muscle Shoals, Alabama, in the bottom left of the map. It was begun during World War I, and efforts to revive it in the 1920s helped create the momentum that produced the TVA. ▌ *Why were progressives so eager to see the government enter the business of hydroelectric power in the 1920s?*

It improved water transportation. It virtually eliminated flooding in the region. It provided electricity to thousands who had never before had it. Throughout the country, largely because of the "yardstick" provided by the TVA's cheap production of electricity, private power rates declined. The Tennessee Valley itself, however, remained a generally impoverished region despite the TVA's efforts.

The Growth of Federal Relief

The Roosevelt administration did not consider relief to the unemployed its most important task, but it recognized the necessity of doing something to help impoverished Americans survive. Among Roosevelt's first acts as president was the establishment of the Federal Emergency Relief Administration (FERA), which provided cash grants to states to prop up bankrupt relief agencies. To administer the program, he chose the director of the New York State relief agency, Harry Hopkins. Both Hopkins and Roosevelt had misgivings about establishing a government "dole." They felt somewhat more comfortable with another form of government assistance: work relief. Thus when it became clear that the FERA grants were not enough, the administration established a second program: the Civil Works Administration (CWA). Between November 1933 and April 1934, it put more than 4 million people to work on temporary projects such as the construction of roads, schools, and parks, thus pumping money into an economy badly in need of it and providing assistance to people with nowhere else to turn.

Roosevelt's favorite relief project was the Civilian Conservation Corps (CCC). The CCC created camps in national parks and forests and in other rural and wilderness settings. There young unemployed men from the cities worked in a semimilitary environment on such projects as planting trees, building reservoirs, developing parks, and improving agricultural irrigation.

Mortgage relief was a pressing need for millions of farm owners and homeowners. The Farm Credit Administration, which within two years refinanced one-fifth of all farm mortgages in the United States, was one response to that problem. The Frazier-Lemke Farm Bankruptcy Act of 1933 was another.

It enabled some farmers to regain their land even after the foreclosure of their mortgages. Despite such efforts, however, 25 percent of all American farm owners had lost their land by 1934. Homeowners were similarly troubled, and in June 1933 the administration established the Home Owners' Loan Corporation, which by 1936 had refinanced the mortgages of more than 1 million householders. A year later, Congress established the Federal Housing Administration to insure mortgages for new construction and home repairs.

THE NEW DEAL IN TRANSITION

Seldom has an American president enjoyed such remarkable popularity as Franklin Roosevelt did during his first two years in office. But by early 1935, the New Deal found itself the target of fierce public criticism. In the spring of 1935, Roosevelt responded by launching a new program of legislation that has often been called the "Second New Deal."

Critics of the New Deal

Some of the most strident attacks on the New Deal came from critics on the right. In August 1934, a group of the most fervent (and wealthiest) Roosevelt opponents formed the American Liberty League, designed specifically to arouse public opposition to the New Deal's "dictatorial" policies. But the new organization was never able to expand its constituency much beyond the northern industrialists who had founded it.

Roosevelt's critics on the far left also managed to produce alarm among some supporters of the administration. The Communist Party, the Socialist Party, and other radical and semiradical organizations were at times harshly critical of the New Deal. But they too failed ever to attract genuine mass support.

More menacing to the New Deal than either the far right or the far left was a group of dissident political movements that defied easy ideological classification. Some gained substantial public support within particular states and regions. And three men succeeded in mobilizing genuinely national followings.

"AN ATTACK ON THE NEW DEAL" This cartoon by William Gropper appeared in *Vanity Fair* in 1935 to illustrate a long excerpt from an anti-New Deal editorial that had appeared a few weeks before in the Republican newspaper, the New York *Herald Tribune*. The cartoon echoes the newspaper's references to Jonathan Swift's famous satire, *Gulliver's Travels*. In this case, Gulliver is Uncle Sam, and the Lilliputians who tie him down with a thousand tiny cords are New Deal agencies and laws. *(Courtesy Vanity Fair © 1935 (renewed 1963, 1991) by The Condé Nast Publications, Inc.)*

Dr. Francis Townsend Dr. Francis E. Townsend, an elderly California physician, rose from obscurity to lead a movement of more than 5 million members with his plan for federal pensions for the elderly. According to the Townsend Plan, all Americans over the age of sixty would receive monthly government pensions of $200, provided they retired (thus freeing jobs for younger, unemployed Americans) and spent the money in full each month (which would pump needed funds into the economy). By 1935, the Townsend Plan had attracted the support of many older men and women.

Father Charles Coughlin Father Charles E. Coughlin, a Catholic priest in the Detroit suburb of Royal Oak, Michigan, achieved even greater renown through his weekly sermons broadcast nationally over the radio. He proposed a series of monetary reforms—remonetization of silver, issuing of greenbacks, and nationalization of the banking system—that he insisted would restore prosperity. At first a warm supporter of Franklin Roosevelt, by late 1934 he had become disheartened by what he claimed was the president's failure to deal harshly enough with the "money powers." In

the spring of 1935, he established his own political organization, the National Union for Social Justice.

Most alarming of all to the administration was the growing national popularity of Senator Huey P. Long of Louisiana. Long had risen to power in his home state through his strident attacks on the banks, oil companies, and utilities and on the conservative political oligarchy allied with them. Elected governor in 1928, he launched an assault on his opponents so thorough and forceful that they were soon left with virtually no political power whatsoever. But he also maintained the overwhelming support of the Louisiana electorate, in part because of his flamboyant personality and in part because of his solid record of conventional progressive accomplishments: building roads, schools, and hospitals; revising the tax codes; distributing free textbooks; lowering utility rates. Barred by law from succeeding himself as governor, he ran in 1930 for a seat in the United States Senate and won easily.

Long, like Coughlin, supported Franklin Roosevelt for president in 1932. But within six months of Roosevelt's inauguration he had broken with the president. As an alternative to the New Deal, he advocated a drastic program of wealth redistribution, a program he ultimately named the Share-Our-Wealth Plan. The government, he claimed, could end the Depression easily by using the tax system to confiscate the surplus riches of the wealthiest men and women in America and distribute these surpluses to the rest of the population. That would, he claimed, allow the government to guarantee every family a minimum "homestead" of $5,000 and an annual wage of $2,500. In 1934, Long established his own national organization: the Share-Our-Wealth Society, which soon attracted a large following through much of the nation.

| Long's Share-Our-Wealth Plan |

Members of the Roosevelt administration considered dissident movements—and the broad popular discontent they represented—a genuine threat to the president. An increasing number of advisers were warning Roosevelt that he would have to do something dramatic to counter their strength.

The "Second New Deal"

Roosevelt launched the so-called Second New Deal in the spring of 1935 in response both to the growing political pressures and to the continuing economic crisis. The new proposals represented a shift in the emphasis of New Deal policy. Perhaps the most conspicuous change was in the administration's attitude toward big business. Symbolically at least, the president was now willing to attack corporate interests openly. In March, for example, he proposed to Congress an act designed to break up the utility holding companies.

| Holding Company Act |

The Holding Company Act of 1935 was the result, although furious lobbying by the utilities led to amendments that limited its effects.

Equally alarming to affluent Americans was a series of tax reforms proposed by the president in 1935. Apparently designed to undercut the appeal of Huey Long's Share-Our-Wealth Plan, the Roosevelt proposals called for establishing the highest and most progressive peacetime tax rates in history—although the actual impact of these rates was limited.

The Supreme Court decision in 1935 to strike down the National Industrial Recovery Act also invalidated Section 7(a) of the act, which had guaranteed workers the right to organize and bargain collectively. A group of progressives in Congress led by Senator Robert E. Wagner of New York introduced what became the National Labor Relations Act of 1935. The new law, popularly known as the Wagner Act, established the National Labor Relations Board (NLRB), which would have power to compel employers to recognize and bargain with legitimate unions. The president was not entirely happy with the bill, but he signed it anyway. That was in large part because American workers themselves had by 1935 become so important a force that Roosevelt realized his own political future would depend in part on responding to their demands.

| National Labor Relations Board |

Labor Militancy

The emergence of a powerful trade union movement in the 1930s occurred partly in response to government efforts to enhance the power of unions, but it was also a result of the increased militancy of American workers. During the 1920s, most workers had displayed relatively little militancy. In the 1930s, however, many of the factors that had impeded militancy vanished or grew weaker. Business leaders and industrialists lost the ability to control government policies. Equally important, new and more militant labor organizations emerged.

The American Federation of Labor remained committed to the idea of the craft union: organizing workers on the basis of their skills. But that concept had little to offer unskilled laborers, who now constituted the bulk of the industrial work force. During the 1930s, therefore, a newer concept of labor organization challenged the craft union ideal: industrial unionism. Advocates of this approach argued that all workers in a particular industry should be organized in a single union, regardless of what functions the workers performed. United in this way, workers would greatly increase their power.

Leaders of the AFL craft unions for the most part opposed the new concept. But industrial unionism found a number of important advocates, most prominent among them John L. Lewis, the leader of the United Mine Workers. At first, Lewis and his allies attempted to work within the AFL, but friction between the new industrial organizations Lewis was promoting and the older craft unions grew rapidly. At the 1935 AFL convention, Lewis became embroiled in a series of angry confrontations with craft union leaders before finally walking out. A few

CIO Founded

weeks later, he created the Committee on Industrial Organization. When the AFL expelled the new committee and all the industrial unions it represented, Lewis renamed the committee the Congress of Industrial Organizations (CIO) and became its first president.

The CIO was more receptive to women and to blacks than the AFL had been, in part because CIO organizing drives targeted previously unorganized industries such as textiles, where women and minorities constituted much of the work force. The CIO was also more militant than the AFL. By the time of the 1936 schism, it was already engaged in major organizing battles in the automobile and steel industries.

Organizing Battles

Out of several competing auto unions, the United Auto Workers (UAW) was gradually emerging preeminent in the early and mid-1930s. But although it was gaining recruits, it was making little progress in winning recognition from the corporations. In December 1936, however, autoworkers employed a controversial new technique:

Sit-down Strike

the sit-down strike. Employees in several General Motors plants in Detroit simply sat down inside the plants, refusing either to work or to leave, thus preventing the company from using strikebreakers. The tactic spread to other locations, and by February 1937 strikers had occupied seventeen GM plants. The strikers ignored court orders and local police efforts to force them to vacate the buildings. When Michigan's governor refused to call up the National Guard to clear out the strikers, and when the federal government also refused to intervene on behalf of employers, General Motors relented. In February 1937 it became the first major manufacturer to recognize the UAW; other automobile companies soon did the same.

In the steel industry, the battle for unionization was less easily won. In 1936, the Steel Workers' Organizing Committee began a major organizing drive involving thousands of workers and frequent, at times bitter, strikes. In March 1937, United States Steel, the giant of the industry, recognized the union rather than risk a costly strike. But the smaller companies (known collectively as "Little Steel") were less accommodating. On Memorial Day 1937, a group of striking workers from Republic Steel gathered with their families for a demonstration in South Chicago. When they attempted to march peacefully (and legally) toward the steel plant, police opened fire on them. Ten demonstrators were killed; another ninety were wounded. Despite a public outcry against the "Memorial Day Massacre," the harsh tactics

"Memorial Day Massacre"

of Little Steel companies succeeded. The 1937 strike failed.

But the victory of Little Steel was one of the last gasps of the kind of brutal strikebreaking that had proved so effective in the past. In 1937 alone, there were 4,720 strikes—over 80 percent of them settled in

Rapid Union Growth

favor of the unions. By the end of the year, more than 8 million workers were members of unions recognized as official bargaining units by employers (as compared with 3 million in 1932). By 1941, that number had expanded to 10 million.

Social Security

From the first moments of the New Deal, important members of the administration had been lobbying for a system of federally sponsored social insurance for the elderly and the unemployed. In 1935, Roosevelt gave public support to what became the Social Security Act, which Congress passed the same year. It established several distinct programs. For the elderly, there were two types of assistance. Those who were presently destitute could receive up to $15 a month in federal assistance. More important for the future, many Americans presently working were incorporated into a pension system, to which they and their employers would contribute through a payroll tax. Pension payments would not begin until 1942 and even then would provide only $10 to $85 a month to recipients. But the act was a crucial first step in building the nation's most important social program for the elderly.

In addition, the Social Security Act created a system of unemployment insurance, which employers alone would finance. It also established a system of federal aid to people with disabilities and a program of aid to dependent children.

The framers of the Social Security Act wanted to create a system of "insurance," not "welfare." And the largest programs (old-age pensions and unemployment insurance) were in many ways similar to private insurance programs. But the act also

Need-based Direct Assistance

provided considerable direct assistance based on need—to the elderly poor, to those with disabilities, to dependent children and their mothers. These groups were widely perceived to be small and genuinely unable to support themselves. But in later generations the programs for these groups would expand until they assumed dimensions that the planners of Social Security had not foreseen.

New Directions in Relief

Social Security was designed primarily to fulfill long-range goals. But millions of unemployed Americans had immediate needs. To help them, the Roosevelt administration established in 1935 the Works Progress Administration (WPA). Under the

Harry Hopkins

direction of Harry Hopkins, the WPA was responsible for building or renovating 110,000 public buildings and for constructing almost 600 airports, more than 500,000 miles of roads, and over 100,000 bridges. In the process, the WPA kept an average of 2.1 million workers employed and pumped needed money into the economy.

The WPA also displayed remarkable flexibility and imagination. The Federal Writers Project of the WPA, for example, gave unemployed writers a chance to do their work and receive a government salary. The Federal Arts Project, similarly, helped painters, sculptors, and others to continue their careers. The Federal Music Project and the Federal Theater Project oversaw the production of concerts and plays, creating work for unemployed musicians, actors, and directors. Other relief agencies emerged alongside the WPA. The National Youth Administration (NYA) provided work and scholarship assistance to high-school and college-age men and women. The Emergency Housing Division of the Public Works Administration began federal sponsorship of public housing.

The new welfare system dealt with men and women in very different ways. For men, the government concentrated mainly on work relief. The principal government aid to women was cash assistance—most notably through the Aid to Dependent Children program of Social Security, which was designed largely to assist single mothers. This disparity

WPA MURAL ART The Federal Arts Project of the Works Progress Administration commissioned an impressive series of public murals from the artists it employed. Many of these murals adorned post offices, libraries, and other public buildings constructed by the WPA. William Gropper, the same artist who drew the cartoon on p. 408, painted *Construction of the Dam*, a detail of which is seen here. *(Detail, Construction of the Dam by William Gropper (Mural Study, Department of the Interior), c. 1937. Oil on canvas, overall: 27$^{1}/_{4}$ × 87$^{1}/_{4}$ inches. Smithsonian American Art Museum, Washington, DC/Art Resource, NY)*

in treatment reflected a widespread assumption that men should constitute the bulk of the paid work force. In fact, millions of women were already employed by the 1930s.

The 1936 "Referendum"

By the middle of 1936—with the economy visibly reviving—there could be little doubt that Roosevelt would win a second term. The Republican Party nominated the moderate governor of Kansas, Alf M. Landon. Roosevelt's dissident challengers now appeared powerless. One reason was the death of their most effective leader, Huey Long, who was assassinated in Louisiana in September 1935. Another reason was the ill-fated alliance among Father Coughlin, Dr. Townsend, and Gerald L. K. Smith (an intemperate henchman of Huey Long), who joined forces that summer to establish a new political movement—the Union Party, which nominated an undistinguished North Dakota congressman, William Lemke.

The result was the greatest landslide in American history to that point. Roosevelt polled just under 61 percent of the vote to Landon's 36 percent and carried every state except Maine and Vermont. The Democrats increased their already large majorities in both houses of Congress.

The election results demonstrated the party realignment that the New Deal had produced. The Democrats now controlled a broad coalition of western and southern farmers, the urban working classes, the poor and unemployed, and the black communities of northern cities, as well as traditional progressives and committed new liberals—a coalition that constituted a substantial majority of the electorate. It would be decades before the Republican Party could again create a lasting majority coalition of its own.

Electoral Realignment

THE NEW DEAL IN DISARRAY

Roosevelt emerged from the 1936 election at the zenith of his popularity. Within months, however, the New Deal was mired in serious new difficulties.

The Court Fight

The 1936 mandate, Franklin Roosevelt believed, made it possible for him to do something about the Supreme Court. No program of reform, he had become convinced, could long survive the conservative justices, who had already struck down the NRA and the AAA.

In February 1937, Roosevelt sent a surprise message to Capitol Hill proposing a general overhaul of the federal court system; included among the many provisions was one to add up to six new justices to the Supreme Court. The courts were "overworked," he claimed, and needed additional manpower to cope with their increasing burdens. But Roosevelt's real purpose was to give himself the opportunity to appoint new, liberal justices and change the ideological balance of the Court.

Conservatives were outraged at the "Court-packing plan," and even many Roosevelt supporters were disturbed by what they considered evidence of the president's hunger for power. Still, Roosevelt might well have persuaded Congress to approve at least a compromise measure had not the Supreme Court itself intervened. Of the nine justices, three reliably supported the New Deal, and four reliably opposed it. Of the remaining two, Chief Justice Charles Evans Hughes often sided with the progressives and Associate Justice Owen J. Roberts usually voted with the conservatives. On March 29, 1937, Roberts, Hughes, and the three progressive justices voted together to uphold a state minimum-wage law, thus reversing a 5-to-4 decision of the previous year invalidating a similar law. Two weeks later, again by a 5-to-4 margin, the Court upheld the Wagner Act, and in May it validated the Social Security Act. Whatever the reasons for the decisions, the Court's newly moderate position made the Court-packing bill seem unnecessary. Congress ultimately defeated it.

"Court-Packing Plan" Defeated

On one level, Franklin Roosevelt had achieved a victory. The Court was no longer an obstacle to New Deal reforms. But the Court-packing episode did lasting political damage to the administration. From 1937 on, southern Democrats and other conservatives voted against Roosevelt's measures much more often than they had in the past.

Retrenchment and Recession

By the summer of 1937, the national income, which had dropped from $82 billion in 1929 to $40 billion in 1932, had risen to nearly $72 billion. Other economic indices showed similar advances. Roosevelt seized on these improvements as a justification for trying to balance the federal budget. Between January and August 1937, for example, he cut the WPA in half, laying off 1.5 million relief workers. A few weeks later, the fragile boom collapsed. Four million additional workers lost their jobs. Economic conditions were soon almost as bad as they had been in the bleak days of 1932–1933.

| Sources of "Roosevelt Recession" | The recession of 1937, known to the president's critics as the "Roosevelt recession," was a result of many factors. But to many observers at the time, it seemed to be a result of the administration's decision to reduce spending. And so in April 1938, the president asked Congress for an emergency appropriation of $5 billion for public works and relief programs, and government funds soon began pouring into the economy once again. Within a few months, another recovery seemed to be under way.

At about the same time, Roosevelt sent a stinging message to Congress, vehemently denouncing what he called an "unjustifiable concentration of economic power" and asking for the creation of a commission to examine that concentration with an eye to major reforms in the antitrust laws. In response, Congress established the Temporary National Economic Committee (TNEC), whose members included representatives of both houses of Congress and officials from several executive agencies. Later in 1938, it passed the Fair Labor Standards Act, which for the first time established a national minimum wage and a forty-hour work week, and which also placed strict limits on child labor.

| End of the New Deal | Despite these achievements, however, by the end of 1938 the New Deal had essentially come to an end. Congressional opposition now made it difficult for the president to enact any major new programs. Moreover, Roosevelt was gradually growing more concerned with persuading a reluctant nation to prepare for war than with pursuing new avenues of reform. Visit Chapter 26 of the book's Online Learning Center for a Where Historians Disagree essay on "The New Deal."

LIMITS AND LEGACIES OF THE NEW DEAL

The New Deal made major changes in American government, some of them still controversial today. It also left important problems unaddressed.

African Americans and the New Deal

One group the New Deal did relatively little to assist was African Americans. The administration was not hostile to black aspirations. Eleanor Roosevelt spoke throughout the 1930s on behalf of racial justice and put continuing pressure on her husband and others in the federal government to ease discrimination against blacks. The president himself appointed a number of blacks to significant second-level positions in his administration, creating an informal network of officeholders that became known as the "Black Cabinet."

Eleanor Roosevelt, Interior | The "Black Cabinet" |
secretary Harold Ickes, and WPA director Harry Hopkins all made efforts to ensure that New Deal relief programs did not exclude blacks, and by 1935 an estimated 30 percent of all African Americans were receiving some form of government assistance. One result was a historic change in black electoral behavior. As late as 1932, most American blacks were voting Republican, as they had been doing since the Civil War. By 1936, more than 90 percent of them were voting Democratic.

Blacks supported Franklin Roosevelt, but they had few illusions that the New Deal represented a major turning point in American race relations. The president was, for example, never willing to risk losing the support of southern Democrats by supporting legislation to make lynching a federal crime or to ban the poll tax, one of the most potent tools by which white southerners kept blacks from voting.

New Deal relief agencies | Discrimination Reinforced |
did not challenge, and indeed reinforced, existing patterns of discrimination. The Civilian Conservation Corps established separate black camps. The NRA codes tolerated paying blacks less than whites doing the same jobs. The WPA routinely relegated black and Hispanic workers to the least-skilled and lowest-paying jobs; when funding ebbed, African Americans, like women, were among the first to be dismissed.

The New Deal and the "Indian Problem"

New Deal policy toward the Indian tribes marked a significant break from the approach in the years before Roosevelt, largely because of the efforts of the extraordinary commissioner of Indian affairs in the 1930s, John Collier. Collier was greatly influenced by the work of twentieth-century anthropologists

ELEANOR ROOSEVELT AND MARY MCLEOD BETHUNE
Mrs. Roosevelt was a leading champion of racial equality within her husband's administration, and her commitment had an important impact on the behavior of the government even though she held no official post. She is seen here meeting in 1937 with Aubrey Williams, executive director of the National Youth Administration, and Mary McLeod Bethune, the agency's Director of Negro Affairs. *(Bettmann/ CORBIS)*

who advanced the idea of cultural relativism—the theory that every culture should be accepted and respected on its own terms.

Collier favored legislation that would, he hoped, reverse the pressures on Native Americans to assimilate. He effectively promoted legislation—which became the Indian Reorganization Act of 1934—to advance his goals. Among other things, it restored to the tribes the right to own land collectively and to elect tribal governments. In the thirteen years after passage of the 1934 bill, tribal land increased by nearly 4 million acres, and Indian agricultural income increased dramatically (from under $2 million in 1934 to over $49 million in 1947). Even with the redistribution of lands under the 1934 act, however, Indians continued to possess only territory whites did not want—much of it arid, some of it desert. And as a group, they continued to constitute the poorest segment of the population.

> Indian Reorganization Act

Women and the New Deal

Symbolically, at least, the New Deal marked a breakthrough in the role of women in public life. Roosevelt appointed the first female member of the cabinet in the nation's history, Secretary of Labor Frances Perkins. He also named more than 100 other women to positions at lower levels of the federal bureaucracy. But the administration was concerned

> Frances Perkins

not so much about achieving gender equality as about obtaining special protections for women.

The New Deal generally supported the widespread belief that in hard times women should withdraw from the workplace to open up more jobs for men. Frances Perkins, for example, spoke out against what she called the "pin-money worker"—the married woman working to earn extra money for the household. New Deal relief agencies offered relatively little employment for women. The Social Security program excluded domestic servants, waitresses, and other predominantly female occupations.

As with African Americans, so also with women: The New Deal was not actively hostile to feminist aspirations, but it accepted prevailing cultural norms. There was not yet sufficient political pressure from women themselves to persuade the administration to do otherwise.

The New Deal and the West

One part of American society that did receive special attention from the New Deal was the American West. The West received more government funds per capita through relief programs than any other region.

The largest New Deal public works programs—the great dams and power stations—were mainly in the West. The Grand Coulee Dam on the Columbia River was the largest public works project in American history to that point, and it provided cheap electric power for much of the Northwest. Its construction, and the construction of other, smaller dams and water projects, created a basis for economic development in the region. Without this enormous public investment by the federal government, much of the economic growth that transformed the West after World War II would have been much more difficult, if not impossible, to achieve.

The New Deal, the Economy, and Politics

The most frequent criticisms of the New Deal involve its failure genuinely to revive or reform the American economy. New Dealers never fully recognized the value of government spending as a vehicle for recovery. The economic boom sparked by World War II, not the New Deal, finally ended the crisis. Nor did the New Deal substantially alter the distribution of power within American capitalism, and it had only a small impact on the distribution of wealth among the American people.

The New Deal's Economic Legacy

Nevertheless, the New Deal did have a number of important and lasting effects on both the behavior and the structure of the American economy. It helped elevate new groups—workers, farmers, and others—to positions from which they could at times effectively challenge the power of the corporations. It increased the regulatory functions of the federal government in ways that helped stabilize previously troubled areas of the economy: the stock market, the banking system, and others. And the administration helped establish the basis for new forms of federal fiscal policy, which in the postwar years would give the government tools for promoting and regulating economic growth.

The New Deal also created the rudiments of the American welfare state, through its

American Welfare State Established

many relief programs and above all through the Social Security system. The welfare system that ultimately emerged would be limited in its impact, would reinforce some traditional patterns of gender and racial discrimination, and would be expensive and cumbersome to administer. But for all its limits, the new system marked a historic break with the nation's traditional reluctance to offer any public assistance whatsoever to its neediest citizens.

Finally, the New Deal had a dramatic effect on the character of American politics. It took a weak and divided Democratic Party and turned it into a mighty coalition that would dominate national party competition for more than thirty years. It turned the attention of many voters away from some of the cultural issues that had preoccupied them in the 1920s and awakened in them an interest in economic matters of direct importance to their lives.

From the time of Franklin Roosevelt's inauguration in 1933 to the beginning of World War II eight years later, the federal government engaged in a broad and diverse series of experiments designed to relieve the distress of unemployment and poverty; to reform the economy to prevent future crises; and to bring the Great Depression itself to an end. It had only partial success in all those efforts.

Unemployment and poverty remained high throughout the New Deal, although many federal programs provided assistance to millions of people. The structure of the American economy remained essentially the same, although there were by the end of the New Deal some important new regulatory agencies in Washington—and an important new role for organized labor. Nothing the New Deal did ended the Great Depression, but some of its policies kept it from getting worse—and some of them pointed the way toward more effective economic policies.

Perhaps the most important legacy of the New Deal was to create a sense of possibilities among many Americans, to persuade them that the fortunes of individuals need not be left entirely to chance or to the workings of an unregulated market. Many Americans emerged from the 1930s convinced that individuals deserved some protections from the unpredictability and instability of the modern economy, and that the New Deal—for all its limitations—had demonstrated the value of enlisting government in the effort to provide those protections.

CONCLUSION

government in the region without questioning the means it had used to obtain power. He even repudi-

Roosevelt Corollary Repudiated

ated the Roosevelt Corollary to the Monroe Doctrine by refusing to permit American intervention when several Latin American countries defaulted on debt obligations to the United States in October 1931.

In Europe, the administration enjoyed few successes. When Hoover's proposed moratorium on debts failed to attract broad support or produce financial stability, he refused to cancel all war debts to the United States as many economists advised him to do. Several European nations promptly went into default. Efforts to extend the 1921 limits on naval construction fell victim to French and British fears of German and Japanese militarism.

The ineffectiveness of American diplomacy in Europe was particularly troubling in light of the new governments on the Continent. Benito Mussolini's Fascist Party had been in control of Italy since the early 1920s and had become increasingly nationalistic and militaristic. Still more ominous was the growing power of the National Socialist (or Nazi) Party in Germany. By the late 1920s, the Weimar Republic, the nation's government since the end of World War I, had been largely discredited by, among other things, a ruinous inflation. Adolf Hitler, the leader of the Nazis, was growing rapidly in popular favor and would take power in 1933. Hitler believed in the genetic superiority of the Aryan (German) people and in extending German territory to provide *Lebensraum* (living space) for the German "master race." He also displayed a pathological anti-Semitism.

More immediately alarming to the Hoover administration was a major crisis in Asia. The Japanese were concerned about the increasing power of the Soviet Union and about the insistence of the Chinese leader Chiang Kai-Shek on expanding his government's power in Manchuria, officially a part of China but over which the Japanese had maintained informal economic control since 1905. In 1931, Japan's military leaders staged what was, in effect, a coup in Tokyo. Weeks later, they launched an invasion of northern Manchuria.

Manchuria Invaded

Hoover permitted Secretary of State Henry Stimson to issue stern warnings to the Japanese but barred him from cooperating with

HITLER AND MUSSOLINI The German and Italian dictators, shown here reviewing troops together in Berlin in the mid-1930s, acted publicly as if they were equals. Privately, however, Hitler viewed Mussolini with contempt, and the Italian dictator complained frequently of being treated as a junior partner by his ally. *(Culver Pictures, Inc.)*

the League of Nations to impose economic sanctions against them. Early in 1932, Japan moved further into China, attacking the city of Shanghai and killing thousands of civilians.

ISOLATIONISM AND INTERNATIONALISM

The administration of Franklin Roosevelt faced a dual challenge as it entered office in 1933. It had to deal with the worst economic crisis in the nation's history, and it had to deal as well with the effects of a decaying international structure.

Depression Diplomacy

Hoover had argued that only by resolving the question of war debts and reinforcing the gold standard could the American economy hope to recover. He had, therefore, agreed to participate in the World

Economic Conference, to be held in London in June 1933. By the time the conference assembled, however, Roosevelt had already become convinced that the gold value of the dollar had to be allowed to fall in order for American goods to be able to compete in world markets. Shortly after the conference convened, he released what became known as the "bombshell message," rejecting any agreement on currency stabilization. The conference quickly dissolved.

At the same time, Roosevelt abandoned the commitments of the Hoover administration to settle the issue of war debts through international agreement. In April 1934 he signed a bill that prohibited American banks from making loans to any nation in default on its debts. The legislation ended the old, circular system by which debt payments continued only by virtue of increasing American loans; within months, war-debt payments from every nation except Finland stopped for good.

Sixteen years after the Bolshevik Revolution of 1917, the American government still had not officially recognized the government of the Soviet Union. But a growing number of influential Americans were urging a change in policy—largely because the Soviet Union appeared to be a possible source of trade. The Russians, for their part, were hoping for American cooperation in containing Japan. In November 1933, the United States and the Soviet Union agreed to open formal diplomatic relations. American trade failed to establish a foothold in Russia, however, and the American government did little to reassure the Soviets that it was interested in stopping Japanese expansion in Asia. By the end of 1934, the Soviet Union and the United States were once again viewing each other with considerable mistrust.

Soviet Union Recognized

The Roosevelt administration was also taking a new approach toward Latin America, an approach which became known as the "Good Neighbor Policy." At an Inter-American Conference in Montevideo, Uruguay, in December 1933, Secretary of State Cordell Hull signed a formal convention declaring: "No state has the right to intervene in the internal or external affairs of another."

"Good Neighbor Policy"

The Rise of Isolationism

With the international system of the 1920s now beyond repair, the United States faced a choice between more active efforts to stabilize the world and more energetic attempts to isolate itself from it. Most Americans unhesitatingly chose the latter. Support for isolationism emerged from many quarters. Some Wilsonian internationalists had grown disillusioned with the League of Nations. Other Americans were listening to the argument that powerful business interests had tricked the United States into participating in World War I. An investigation by a Senate committee chaired by Senator Gerald Nye of North Dakota claimed to have produced evidence of exorbitant profiteering and tax evasion by many corporations during the war, and it suggested that bankers had pressured Wilson to intervene in the war so as to protect their loans abroad. (Few historians now lend much credence to these charges.)

Sources of Isolationism

Roosevelt continued to hope for at least a modest American role in maintaining world peace. In 1935, he proposed to the Senate a treaty to make the United States a member of the World Court—a largely symbolic gesture. Isolationists aroused popular opposition to the agreement, and the Senate voted it down.

In the summer of 1935, Italy was preparing to invade Ethiopia. Fearing the invasion would provoke a new European war, American legislators sought ways to prevent the United States from being dragged into the conflict. The Neutrality Act of 1935 established a mandatory arms embargo against both sides in any military conflict and directed the president to warn American citizens against traveling on the ships of warring nations. Thus, isolationists believed, the "protection of neutral rights" could not again become an excuse for American intervention in war. A 1937 law established the so-called cash-and-carry policy, by which warring nations could purchase only nonmilitary goods from the United States and could do so only by paying cash and shipping their purchases themselves.

Neutrality Acts

Isolationist sentiment showed its strength again in 1936–1937 in response to the civil war in Spain. The Falangists of General Francisco Franco, a group much like the Italian fascists, revolted in July 1936 against the existing republican government.

Hitler and Mussolini supported Franco. Some Americans, mostly communists and adventurers, traveled to Spain to assist the republican cause, but the United States government joined with Britain and France in an agreement to offer no assistance to either side.

In the summer of 1937, Japan intensified its six-year-old assault on Manchuria and attacked China's five northern provinces. Roosevelt responded in a speech in Chicago in October 1937. He warned of the dangers of the Japanese actions and argued that aggressors should be "quarantined" by the international community to prevent the contagion of war from spreading. He was deliberately vague about

"Quarantine" Speech what such a "quarantine" would mean. Even so, public response to the speech was hostile, and Roosevelt drew back. On December 12, 1937, Japanese aviators bombed and sank the United States gunboat *Panay* as it sailed the Yangtze River in China. But so reluctant was the Roosevelt administration to antagonize the isolationists that it eagerly seized on Japanese claims that the bombing had been an accident, accepted Japan's apologies, and overlooked the attack. For an America in the World feature

 essay on "The Sino-Japanese War," visit Chapter 27 of the book's Online Learning Center.

The Failure of Munich

In 1936, Hitler had moved the revived German army into the Rhineland, rearming an area that had been off-limits to German troops since World War I. In March 1938, German forces marched without opposition into Austria, and Hitler proclaimed a union (or *Anschluss*) between Austria, his native land, and Germany, his adopted one. Neither in America nor in most of Europe was there much more than a murmur of opposition.

The Austrian invasion, however, soon created another crisis. Germany had by now occupied territory surrounding three sides of western Czechoslovakia, a region Hitler dreamed of annexing. In September 1938, he demanded that Czechoslovakia cede him the Sudetenland, an area in which many ethnic Germans lived. Although Czechoslovakia was prepared to fight to stop Hitler, it needed assistance from other nations. But most Western governments were willing to pay almost any price to settle the crisis

THE BLITZ, LONDON The German Luftwaffe terrorized London and other British cities in 1940–1941 and again late in the war by bombing civilian areas indiscriminately in an effort to break the spirit of the English people. The effort failed, and the fortitude of the British did much to arouse support for their cause in the United States. *(Brown Brothers)*

peacefully. On September 29, Hitler met with the leaders of France and Great Britain in Munich in an effort to resolve the crisis. The French and British agreed to accept the German demands in Czechoslovakia in return for Hitler's promise to expand no farther.

The Munich agreement, which Roosevelt applauded at the time, was the most prominent element of a policy that came to be known as "appeasement" and identified largely with British Prime **"Appeasement"** Minister Neville Chamberlain. Whoever was to blame, the policy was a failure. In March 1939, Hitler occupied the remaining areas of Czechoslovakia and in April, he began issuing threats against Poland.

At that point, both Britain and France assured the Polish government that they would come to its assistance in case of an invasion; they even tried, too late, to draw the Soviet Union into a mutual defense agreement. But Stalin had decided he could expect no protection from the West. He signed a nonaggression pact with Hitler in August 1939, freeing the Germans for the moment from the danger of a two-front war. Shortly after that, Hitler staged an incident on the Polish border to allow him to claim that Germany had been attacked, and on September 1, 1939, he launched a full-scale invasion of Poland. Britain and France declared war on Germany two days later. World War II had begun.

FROM NEUTRALITY TO INTERVENTION

"This nation will remain a neutral nation," the president declared shortly after the hostilities began in Europe, "but I cannot ask that every American remain neutral in thought as well." There was never any question that both he and the majority of the American people favored Britain, France, and the other Allied nations in the contest. The question was how much the United States was prepared to do to assist them.

Neutrality Tested

At the very least, Roosevelt believed, the United States should make armaments available to the Allied armies to help them counter the military advantage the large German munitions industry gave Hitler. In September 1939, he asked Congress to revise the Neutrality Acts and lift the arms embargo against any nation engaged in war. Congress maintained the prohibition on American ships entering war zones. But the 1939 law did permit belligerents to purchase arms on the same cash-and-carry basis that the earlier Neutrality Acts had established for the sale of nonmilitary materials.

Cash-and-Carry

After the German armies quickly subdued Poland, the war in Europe settled into a long, quiet lull that lasted through the winter and spring. But in the spring of 1940, Germany launched a massive invasion known as the "blitzkrieg," to the west—first attacking Denmark and Norway, sweeping next across the Netherlands and Belgium, and driving finally deep into the heart of France. On June 10, Mussolini invaded France from the south as Hitler was attacking from the north. On June 22, finally, France fell, and Nazi troops marched into Paris. A new

Fall of France

French regime assembled in Vichy, largely controlled by the German occupiers.

On May 16, in the midst of the offensive, Roosevelt asked Congress for an additional $1 billion for defense and received it quickly. That was one day after Winston Churchill, the new British prime minister, had sent Roosevelt the first of many long lists of requests for armaments, without which, he insisted, England could not long survive. Some Americans (including the United States ambassador to London, Joseph P. Kennedy) argued that the British plight was already hopeless, but the president was determined to make war materials available to Britain. He even circumvented the cash-and-carry provisions of the Neutrality Acts by giving England fifty American destroyers in return for the right to build American bases on British territory in the Caribbean and he returned to the factories a number of new airplanes purchased by the American military so that the British could buy them instead.

Roosevelt was able to take such steps in part because of a major shift in American public opinion. By July 1940, more than 66 percent of the public believed that Germany posed a direct threat to the United States. Congress was, therefore, more willing to permit expanded American assistance to the Allies. Congress also approved the Burke-Wadsworth Act, inaugurating the first peacetime military draft in American history.

Burke-Wadsworth Act

But a powerful new isolationist lobby—the America First Committee, whose members included such prominent Americans as Charles Lindbergh and Senators Gerald Nye and Burton Wheeler—joined the debate over American policy toward the war. The lobby had at least the indirect support of a large proportion of the Republican Party. Through the summer and fall of 1940, the debate was complicated by a presidential campaign.

The Campaign of 1940

The biggest political question of 1940 was whether Franklin Roosevelt would break with tradition and run for an unprecedented third term. The president himself did not reveal his own wishes. But by refusing to withdraw from the contest, he made it impossible for any rival Democrat to establish a claim to the nomination. And when, just before the

Democratic Convention in July, he let it be known that he would accept a "draft" from his party, the issue was virtually settled. The Democrats quickly renominated him and even reluctantly swallowed his choice for vice president: Agriculture secretary Henry A. Wallace, a man too liberal and too controversial for the taste of many party leaders.

The Republicans nominated for president a politically inexperienced Indiana businessman, Wendell Willkie. Both the candidate and the party platform took positions little different from Roosevelt's: they would keep the country out of war but would extend generous assistance to the Allies. Willkie was an appealing figure, and he managed to evoke more public enthusiasm than any Republican candidate in decades. But Roosevelt still won decisively. He received 55 percent of the popular vote to Willkie's 45 percent, and he won 449 electoral votes to Willkie's 82.

FDR Reelected

Neutrality Abandoned

In the last months of 1940, Great Britain was virtually bankrupt and could no longer meet the cash-and-carry requirements imposed by the Neutrality Acts. The president, therefore, proposed a new system for supplying Britain: "lend-lease." It would allow the government not only to sell but also to lend or lease armaments to any nation deemed "pivotal to the defense of the United States." In other words, America could funnel weapons to England on the basis of no more than Britain's promise to return them when the war was over. Congress enacted the bill by wide margins.

"Lend-lease"

Attacks by German submarines had made shipping lanes in the Atlantic extremely dangerous. The British navy was losing ships more rapidly than it could replace them. Roosevelt argued that the western Atlantic was a neutral zone and the responsibility of the American nations. By July 1941, therefore, American ships were patrolling the ocean as far east as Iceland.

At first Germany did little to challenge these obviously hostile American actions. By September 1941, however, the situation had changed. Nazi forces had invaded the Soviet Union in June of that year. When the Soviets did not surrender, as many had predicted they would, Roosevelt persuaded Congress to extend lend-lease privileges to them. Now American industry was providing vital assistance to Hitler's foes on two fronts, and the American navy was protecting the flow of those goods to Europe. In September, Nazi submarines began a concerted campaign against American vessels. Roosevelt ordered American ships to fire on German submarines "on sight." In October, Nazi submarines hit two American destroyers and sank one of them, the *Reuben James*, killing many American sailors. Congress now voted to allow the United States to arm its merchant vessels and to sail all the way into belligerent ports. The United States had, in effect, launched a naval war against Germany.

In August 1941, Roosevelt met with Churchill aboard a British vessel off the coast of Newfoundland. The president made no military commitments, but he did join with the prime minister in releasing a document that became known as the Atlantic Charter, in which the two nations set out "certain common principles" on which to base "a better future for the world." It called openly for "the final destruction of the Nazi tyranny" and for a new world order in which every nation controlled its own destiny.

The Atlantic Charter

The Road to Pearl Harbor

Japan, in the meantime, extended its empire in the Pacific. In September 1940, the Japanese signed the Tripartite Pact, a loose defensive alliance with Germany and Italy. In July 1941, Japanese troops moved into Indochina and seized the capital of Vietnam, a colony of France. The United States, having broken Japanese codes, knew Japan's next target was to be the oil-rich Dutch East Indies; and when Tokyo failed to respond to Roosevelt's stern warnings, the president froze all Japanese assets in the United States, severely limiting Japan's ability to purchase needed American supplies.

Japanese Assets Frozen

Tokyo now faced a choice. Either it would have to repair relations with the United States to restore the flow of supplies or it would have to find those supplies elsewhere, most notably by seizing British and Dutch possessions in the Pacific. In October, militants in Tokyo forced the moderate prime minister out of office and replaced him with the leader of the war party, General Hideki Tojo.

By late November, the State Department had given up on the possibility of a peaceful settlement. American intelligence, meanwhile, had decoded Japanese messages that made clear a Japanese attack was imminent. But most U.S. officials continued to

PEARL HARBOR, DECEMBER 7, 1941 The destroyer U.S.S. *Shaw*, immobilized in a floating drydock in Pearl Harbor in December 1941, survived the first wave of Japanese bombers unscathed. But in the second attack, the Japanese scored a direct hit and produced this spectacular explosion, which blew off the ship's bow. Damage to the rest of the ship, however, was slight. Just a few months later the *Shaw* was fitted with a new bow and rejoined the fleet. *(U.S. Navy Photo)*

believe that the Japanese would move first not against American territory but against British or Dutch possessions to their south. A combination of confusion and miscalculation caused the government to overlook indications that Japan intended a direct attack on American forces.

At 7:55 A.M. on Sunday, December 7, 1941, a wave of Japanese bombers attacked the United States naval base at Pearl Harbor in Hawaii. A second wave came an hour later. Within two hours, the United States lost 8 battleships, 3 cruisers, 4 other vessels, 188 airplanes, and several vital shore installations. More than 2,400 soldiers and sailors died, and another 1,000 were injured. The Japanese suffered only light losses.

Pearl Harbor Attacked

American forces were now greatly diminished in the Pacific (although by a fortunate accident, no American aircraft carriers—the heart of the Pacific fleet—had been at Pearl Harbor on December 7). Nevertheless, the raid on Hawaii unified the American people behind war. On December 8, after a stirring speech by the president, the Senate voted unanimously and the House voted 388 to 1 to approve a declaration of war against Japan. Three days later, Germany and Italy, Japan's European allies, declared war on the United States; on the same day, December 11, Congress reciprocated without a dissenting vote. Visit Chapter 27 of the book's Online Learning Center for a Where Historians Disagree essay on "The Question of Pearl Harbor."

CONCLUSION

American foreign policy in the years after World War I attempted something that ultimately proved impossible. The United States was determined to be a major power in the world and to influence other nations in ways Americans believed would be beneficial to their own, and the world's, interests. But the United States was also determined to do nothing that would limit its own freedom of action. It would not join the League of Nations. It would not join the World Court. It would not form alliances with other nations. It would operate powerfully—and alone.

But forces were at work that would push the United States into greater engagement with other nations. The economic disarray that the Great Depression created around the globe, the rise of totalitarian regimes, the expansionist ambitions of powerful new leaders: all worked to destroy the uneasy stability of the post–World War I international system. America's own interests were imperiled. And America's go-it-alone foreign policy seemed powerless to change the course of events.

Franklin Roosevelt tried throughout the later years of the 1930s to push the American people slowly into a greater involvement in international affairs. In particular, he tried to nudge the United States toward taking a more forceful stand against dictatorship and aggression. A powerful isolationist movement helped stymie him for a time, even after war broke out in Europe. Gradually, however, public opinion shifted toward support of the Allies (Britain, France, and the Soviet Union) and against the Axis (Germany, Italy, and Japan). The nation began to mobilize for war, to supply ships and munitions to Britain, even to engage in naval combat with German forces in the Atlantic. Finally, on December 7, 1941, the surprise Japanese attack on the American base at Pearl Harbor in Hawaii eliminated the last elements of uncertainty and drove the United States—now united behind the war effort—into the greatest and most terrible conflict in human history.

INTERACTIVE LEARNING

On the *Primary Source Investigator CD-ROM,* check out a number of valuable tools for further exploration of the content of this chapter.

Primary Sources

Documents, images, and maps related to the rising world tensions in the 1920s and 1930s, and the outbreak of World War II. Some highlights include:

- Excerpt from the Lend-Lease Act of 1941 providing U.S. aid to Britain

- A 1941 "Fireside Chat" in which President Roosevelt makes the case for expanded powers during wartime

Online Learning Center
(www.mhhe.com/unfinishedinteractive)

Explore this rich website, providing additional exploration of the material covered in this chapter, online versions of the interactive maps included on the Primary Source Investigator CD-ROM, as well as several study aids, including a multiple-choice quiz, essay questions, a glossary, and other valuable tools. Also in the Online Learning Center for this chapter look for *Interactive Feature Essays* **on:**

- **America in the World: The Sino-Japanese War**

- **Where Historians Disagree: The Question of Pearl Harbor**

FOR FURTHER REFERENCE

Robert Dallek, *Franklin D. Roosevelt and American Foreign Policy, 1932–1945* (1979) is a comprehensive study of Roosevelt's foreign policy. Akira Iriye, *The Cambridge History of American Foreign Relations, vol. 3: The Globalizing of America, 1913–1945* (1993) is another important study. In *Inevitable Revolutions* (1983), Walter LaFeber recounts America's attempts to halt revolutionary movements throughout the world. James MacGregor Burns, *Roosevelt: The Soldier of Freedom* (1970) and Warren F. Kimball, *The Juggler: Franklin Roosevelt as Wartime Statesman* (1991) are two important studies of the president. Wayne S. Cole, *Charles A. Lindbergh and the Battle Against American Intervention in World War II* (1974) and *Roosevelt and the Isolationists, 1932–1945* (1983) examine prewar isolationism. A. Scott Berg, *Lindbergh*

(1998) is an excellent biography of the aviation hero who became such a controversial figure in the 1930s. Charles DeBenedetti, *Origins of the Modern American Peace Movement, 1915–1929* (1978) and *The Peace Reform in American History* (1980) examine antiwar movements in American history, including prior to World War II. Joseph Lash's *Roosevelt and Churchill* (1976) explores the dynamic relationship between the two leaders of the United States and England. Akira Iriye, *The Origins of the Second World War in Asia and the Pacific* (1988) examines the conflict between China and Japan that preceded American intervention in the Pacific War. Gordon Prange, *At Dawn We Slept* (1981) examines the controversial attack on Pearl Harbor from both the Japanese and American sides.

(Library of Congress)

MINI-DOCUMENTARY Dawn of the Nuclear Age

T he attack on Pearl Harbor had thrust the United States into the greatest and most terrible war in the history of humanity, a war that changed the world as profoundly as any event of the twentieth century, perhaps of any century. World War II also transformed the United States in profound, if not always readily visible, ways.

WAR ON TWO FRONTS

Whatever political disagreements and social tensions there may have been among the American people during World War II, there was striking unity of opinion about the conflict itself. But both unity and confidence faced severe tests in the first, troubled months of 1942.

Containing the Japanese

Ten hours after the strike at Pearl Harbor, Japanese airplanes attacked the American airfields at Manila in the Philippines, destroying much of America's remaining air power in the Pacific. Three days later Guam, an American possession, fell to Japan; Wake Island and Hong Kong followed. The great British fortress of Singapore in Malaya surrendered in February 1942, the Dutch East Indies in March, Burma in April. In the Philippines, exhausted Filipino and American troops gave up their defense of the islands on May 6.

Japanese Victories

American strategists planned two broad offensives to turn the tide against the Japanese. One, under the command of General Douglas MacArthur, would move north from Australia, through New Guinea, and eventually to the Philippines. The other, under Admiral Chester Nimitz, would move west from Hawaii toward major Japanese island outposts in the central Pacific. Ultimately, strategists predicted, the two offensives would come together to invade Japan itself.

Battle of Midway

The Allies achieved their first important victory in the Battle of the Coral Sea, just northwest of Australia, on May 7–8, 1942, when American forces turned back the previously unstoppable Japanese navy. A month later, an enormous battle raged for four days, June 3–6, 1942, near the small American outpost at Midway Island, at the end of which the United States, despite great losses, was clearly victorious. The American navy destroyed four Japanese aircraft carriers and lost only one of its own; the action regained control of the central Pacific for the United States.

The Americans took the offensive for the first time several months later in the southern Solomon Islands, to the east of New Guinea. In August 1942, American forces assaulted three of the islands: Gavutu, Tulagi, and Guadalcanal. A struggle of terrible ferocity developed at Guadalcanal and continued for six months, inflicting heavy losses on both sides. In the end, however, the Japanese were forced to abandon the island. The Americans, with aid from the Australians and the New Zealanders, now began the slow, arduous process of moving toward the Philippines and Japan itself.

Holding Off the Germans

In the European war, the United States was fighting in cooperation with, among others, Britain and the exiled "Free French" forces in the west; and it was trying also to conciliate its new ally, the Soviet Union, which was now fighting Hitler in the east. The army chief of staff, General George C. Marshall, supported a plan for a major Allied invasion of France across the English Channel in the spring of 1943, and he placed a previously little-known general, Dwight D. Eisenhower, in charge of Dwight Eisenhower planning the operation. But the Soviet Union, which was absorbing the brunt of the German war effort, wanted the Allied invasion to begin at the earliest possible moment. The British, on the other hand, wanted first to launch a series of Allied offensives around the edges of the Nazi empire—in northern Africa and southern Europe.

Roosevelt ultimately decided to support the British plan. At the end of October 1942, the British opened a counteroffensive against General Erwin

1942	1943
Battle of Midway	Americans capture Guadalcanal
Campaign in Northern Africa	Allied invasion of Italy
Japanese Americans interned	Soviet victory at Stalingrad
Manhattan Project begins	Detroit Race Riot
CORE founded	L. A. Zoot-Suit Riots

1944	1945
Allies invade Normandy	Roosevelt dies; Truman becomes president
Roosevelt reelected	Germany surrenders
Americans capture Philippines	U.S. drops atomic bombs on Hiroshima, Nagasaki
	Japan surrenders

T I M E   L I N E

Rommel and the Nazi forces in North Africa. In a major battle at El Alamein, they forced the Germans to retreat from Egypt. On November 8, Anglo-American forces landed at Oran and Algiers in Algeria and at Casablanca in Morocco—areas under the Nazi-controlled French government at Vichy—and began moving east toward Rommel. The Germans threw the full weight of their forces in Africa against the inexperienced Americans and inflicted a serious defeat on them at the Kasserine Pass in Tunisia. General George S. Patton, however, regrouped the American troops. With the help of Allied air and naval power and of British forces attacking from the east under Field Marshall Bernard Montgomery, the American offensive finally drove the last Germans from Africa in May 1943.

The North African campaign had tied up a large proportion of Allied resources. That was one reason why the planned May 1943 cross-Channel invasion of France had to be postponed, despite angry complaints from the Soviet Union. By now, however, the threat of a Soviet collapse seemed much diminished, for during the winter of 1942–1943, the Red Army had successfully held off a major German assault at Stalingrad in southern Russia. Hitler had committed such enormous forces to the battle, and had suffered such appalling losses, that he could not continue his eastern offensive.

Battle of Stalingrad

The Soviet successes persuaded Roosevelt to agree, in a January 1943 meeting with Churchill in Casablanca, to a British plan for an Allied invasion of Sicily. On the night of July 9, 1943, American and British armies landed in southeast Sicily; thirty-eight days later, they had conquered the island and were moving onto the Italian mainland. In the face of these setbacks, Mussolini's government collapsed and the dictator himself fled north toward Germany. (He was later captured by Italian insurgents and hanged.) Although Mussolini's successor, Pietro Badoglio, quickly committed Italy to the Allies, Germany moved eight divisions into the country and established a powerful defensive line south of Rome. The Allied offensive on the Italian peninsula, which began on September 3, 1943, soon bogged down. Not until May 1944 did the Allies break through the German defenses. On June 4, 1944, they captured Rome.

Italy Invaded

WORLD WAR II IN THE PACIFIC This map illustrates the changing fortunes of the two combatants in the Pacific phase of World War II. The long red line stretching from Burma around to Manchuria represents the eastern boundary of the vast areas of the Pacific that had fallen under Japanese control by the summer of 1942. The blue lines illustrate the advance of American forces back into the Pacific beginning in May 1942 and accelerating in 1943 and after, which drove the Japanese forces back. By the summer of 1945, American forces were approaching the Japanese mainland and were bombing Tokyo itself. The dropping of two American atomic bombs, on Hiroshima and Nagasaki, finally brought the war to an end. ▌ *Why did the Soviet Union enter the Pacific War in August 1945, as shown in the upper left corner of the map?*

The invasion of Italy contributed to postponing the invasion of France by as much as a year, deeply embittering Stalin and giving the Soviets time to begin moving toward the countries of eastern Europe.

America and the Holocaust

In the midst of this intensive fighting, the leaders of the American government found themselves confronted with one of history's great tragedies: the Nazi campaign to exterminate Jews—the Holocaust. As early as 1942, high officials in Washington had incontrovertible evidence that Hitler's forces were rounding up Jews and others (including Poles, homosexuals, and communists) from all over Europe, transporting them to concentration camps in eastern

Germany and Poland, and systematically murdering them. (The death toll would ultimately reach 6 million Jews and at least 4 million others.) News of the atrocities was reaching the public as well, and pressure began to build for an Allied effort to end the killing or at least to rescue some of the surviving Jews.

The American government consistently resisted almost all such entreaties. Although by mid-1944 Allied bombers were flying missions within a few miles of the most notorious death camp, at Auschwitz in Poland, the War Department rejected as militarily unfeasible pleas that the planes try to destroy the crematoria at the camp. American officials also refused requests that the Allies try to destroy railroad lines leading to the camp. And the United States resisted

WORLD WAR II IN NORTH AFRICA AND ITALY: THE ALLIED COUNTEROFFENSIVE, 1942–1943 This map shows the Anglo-American offensive in Europe that preceded the great Normandy Invasion of 1944. Eight months after landing in North Africa, U.S. and British forces established their first foothold in Europe when they landed in Sicily in July 1943. ▌ *Why did Stalin have so little enthusiasm for the North African invasion?*

THE *ST. LOUIS* Many people consider the fate of the German liner *St. Louis* to be a powerful symbol of the indifference of the United States and other nations to the fate of European Jews during the Holocaust, even though its forlorn journey preceded both the beginning of World War II and the beginning of systematic extermination of Jews by the Nazi regime. The *St. Louis* carried a group of over 900 Jews fleeing from Germany in 1939. It became a ship without a port as it sailed from country to country where its passengers were refused entry time and again. Most of the passengers were hoping for a haven in the United States, but the American State Department refused to allow the ship even to dock as it sailed up the American eastern seaboard. Eventually, the *St. Louis* returned to Europe and distributed its passengers among Britain, France, Holland, and Belgium (where this photograph was taken showing refugees smiling and waving as they prepared to disembark in Antwerp in June 1939). Less than a year later, all those nations except Britain fell under Nazi control. *(Bettmann/Corbis)*

pleas that it admit large numbers of Jewish refugees attempting to escape Europe.

Moral Failure

After 1941, there was probably little American leaders could have done, other than defeat Germany in the war, to save most of Hitler's victims. But more forceful action might well have saved at least some lives. That they did not take such action, it seems clear in retrospect, constituted a considerable moral failure. But policymakers justified their inaction by insisting that they needed to focus exclusively on the larger goal of winning the war. Any diversion of energy and attention to other purposes, they believed, would distract them from the overriding goal of victory.

THE AMERICAN ECONOMY IN WARTIME

Not since the Civil War had the United States been involved in so prolonged and consuming a military experience as World War II. American armed forces engaged in combat around the globe for nearly four years. American society, in the meantime, experienced changes that reached into virtually every corner of the nation.

Prosperity and the Rights of Labor

World War II had its most profound impact on American domestic life by ending the Great Depression. By the middle of 1941, the economic problems of the 1930s—unemployment, deflation, industrial sluggishness—had virtually vanished before the great wave of wartime industrial expansion.

Massive Government Spending

The most important agent of the new prosperity was government spending, which after 1939 was pumping more money into the economy each year than all the New Deal relief agencies combined had done. In 1939, the federal budget had been $9 billion; by 1945, it had risen to $100 billion. Largely as a result, the gross national product soared: from $91 billion in 1939 to $166 billion in 1945. Personal incomes in some regions grew by as much as 100 percent.

The impact of government spending was perhaps most dramatic in the West. The government created large manufacturing facilities in California and elsewhere to serve the needs of its military.

Altogether, the government made almost $40 billion worth of capital investments (factories, military and transportation facilities, highways, power plants) in the West during the war, more than in any other region. By the end of the war, the Pacific Coast had become the center of the growing American aircraft industry and an important center of the shipbuilding industry. Los Angeles, formerly a medium-sized city notable chiefly for its film industry, now became a major industrial center as well.

The war created a serious labor shortage. The armed forces took over 15 million men and women out of the civilian work force at the same time that the demand for labor was rising rapidly. Nevertheless, the supply of workers increased by almost 20 percent during the war—largely through the employment of the very young, the elderly, minorities, and, most important, several million women.

Union Membership Boosted

The war gave a substantial boost to union membership, which rose from about 10.5 million in 1941 to over 13 million in 1945. That was in part a result of a "maintenance-of-membership" agreement, which ensured that the thousands of new workers pouring into unionized defense plants would be automatically enrolled in the unions. But the government also managed to win two important concessions from union leaders. One was the "no-strike" pledge, by which unions agreed not to stop production in wartime. Another was the so-called Little Steel formula, which set a 15 percent limit on wage increases.

Despite the no-strike pledge, there were nearly 15,000 work stoppages during the war, mostly wildcat strikes (strikes unauthorized by the union leadership). When the United Mine Workers defied the government by striking in May 1943, Congress reacted by passing, over Roosevelt's veto, the Smith-Connally Act (the War Labor Disputes Act), which required that unions wait thirty days before striking and which empowered the president to seize a struck war plant.

Stabilizing the Boom and Mobilizing Production

The fear of deflation, the central concern of the 1930s, gave way during the war to a fear of inflation. Holding the line against inflation was the task of the Office of Price Administration (OPA). The

| Office of Price Administration |

OPA was successful enough that inflation was a much less serious problem during World War II than it had been during World War I. Even so, the agency was never popular. Black-marketing and overcharging grew in proportions far beyond OPA policing capacity.

From 1941 to 1945, the federal government spent a total of $321 billion—twice as much as it had spent in the entire 150 years of its existence to that point, and ten times as much as the cost of World War I. The government borrowed about half the revenues it needed by selling $100 billion worth of bonds. Much of the rest it raised by radically increasing income-tax rates, through the Revenue Act of 1942. To simplify collection, Congress enacted a withholding system of payroll deductions.

In January 1942, the president responded to widespread criticism of earlier efforts to mobilize the economy for war by creating the War Pro-

| War Production Board |

duction Board (WPB), under the direction of former Sears Roebuck executive Donald Nelson. Throughout its troubled history, the WPB was never able to win complete control over military purchases; the army and navy often circumvented the board. It was never able to satisfy the complaints of small business, which charged (correctly) that most contracts were going to large corporations. Gradually, the president transferred much of the WPB's authority to a new office located within the White House: the Office of War Mobilization (OWM). But the OWM was only slightly more successful than the WPB.

Despite the administrative problems, however, the war economy managed to meet almost all of the nation's critical war needs. By the beginning of 1944, American factories were, in fact, producing more than the government needed. Their output was twice that of all the Axis countries combined.

Wartime Science and Technology

More than any previous American war, World War II was a watershed for technological and scientific innovation. That was partly because the American government poured substantial funds into research and development beginning in 1940. In that year

| National Defense Research Committee |

the government created the National Defense Research Committee, headed by the

MIT scientist Vannevar Bush, who had been a pioneer in the early development of the computer. By the end of the war, the new agency had spent more that $100 million on research, more than four times the amount spent by the government on military research and development in the previous forty years.

In the first years of the war, all the technological advantages seemed to lie with the Germans and Japanese. Germany had made great advances in tanks and other mechanized armor in the 1930s. It used its armor effectively during its blitzkrieg in Europe in 1940 and again in North Africa in 1942. German submarine technology was significantly advanced compared to British and American capabilities in 1940. Japan had developed extraordinary capacity in its naval-air technology. Its highly sophisticated fighter planes, launched from distant aircraft carriers, conducted the successful raid on Pearl Harbor in December 1941.

But Britain and America had advantages of their own. American techniques of mass production were converted efficiently to military production in 1941 and 1942 and soon began producing airplanes, ships, tanks, and other armaments in much greater numbers than the Germans and Japanese could produce. Allied scientists and engineers moved quickly as well to improve Anglo-American aviation and naval technology, and particularly to improve the performance of submarines and tanks. By late 1942, Allied weaponry was at least as advanced as that of the enemy.

In addition, each technological innovation by the enemy produced a corresponding innovation to limit the damage of the new techniques. American and British physicists made rapid advances in improving radar and sonar,

| Sonar |

which helped Allied naval forces decimate German U-boats in 1943 and effectively end their effectiveness in the naval war. Particularly important was the creation in 1940 of "centimetric radar," whose narrow beams of short wavelength made radar more efficient and effective than ever before—as the British navy discovered in April 1941 when the instruments on one of its ships detected a surfaced submarine 10 miles away at night and, on another occasion, spotted a periscope at three-quarters of a mile range. This new radar could also be effectively miniaturized, which was critical to its use on airplanes and submarines in particular. The Allies also learned early how to detect and disable German naval mines; and when the Germans tried to counter this progress by introducing an "acoustic" mine, which detonated when a ship came near it, not necessarily just on contact, the Allies developed acoustical countermeasures of their own, which transmitted sounds through the water to detonate mines before ships came near them. Anglo-American antiaircraft technology—both on land and on sea—also improved.

Germany made substantial advances in the development of rocket technology in the early years of the war, and it managed to launch some rocket-propelled bombs (the V1s and V2s) across the English Channel, aimed at London. The psychological effects of the rockets on the British people were considerable. But the Germans were never able to create a production technology capable of building enough such rockets to make a real difference in the balance of military power.

Beginning in 1942, British and American forces seized the advantage in the air war by producing new and powerful four-engine bombers in great numbers.

Long-range Bombing

Because they were able to fly higher and longer than the German equivalents, they were able to conduct extensive bombing missions over Germany (and later Japan) with much less danger of being shot down. But the success of the bombers rested heavily as well on new electronic devices capable of guiding their bombs to their targets. The Gee navigation system used electronic pulses to help pilots plot their exact location, something that in the past only a highly skilled navigator could do. In March 1942, eighty Allied bombers fitted with Gee systems staged a devastatingly effective bombing raid on German industrial and military installations in the Ruhr Valley. Also effective was the Oboe system, a radio device that sent a sonic message to airplanes to tell them when they were within 20 yards of their targets, first introduced in December 1942.

The area in which the Allies had perhaps the greatest advantage was the gathering of intelligence, much of it through Britain's top-secret Ultra project. Some of the advantages the Allies enjoyed came from successful efforts to capture or steal German and Japanese intelligence devices. More important, however, were the

Importance of Code Breaking

efforts of cryptologists to puzzle out the enemy's systems, and advances in computer technology that helped the Allies decipher coded messages sent by the Japanese and the Germans. Much of Germany's coded communication made use of the so-called Enigma machine, which was effective because it constantly changed the coding systems it used. In the first months of the war, Polish intelligence had developed an electro-mechanical computer, which it called the "Bombe," which could decipher some Enigma messages. After the fall of Poland, British scientists, led by the brilliant computer pioneer Alan Turing, took the Bombe and greatly improved it. On April 15, 1940, the new, high-speed Bombe broke the coding of a series of German messages within hours rather than days. A few weeks later, it began decrypting German messages at the rate of 1,000 a day, providing a constant flow of information about enemy operations that continued until the end of the war. Later in the war, British scientists working for the intelligence services built the first real programmable, digital computer—the Colossus II, which became operational less than a week before the beginning of the Normandy invasion.

The United States also had some important intelligence breakthroughs, including, in 1941, a dramatic success by the American Magic operation (the counterpart to the British Ultra) in breaking a Japanese coding system not unlike the German Enigma. The result was that Americans had access to intercepted information that, if properly interpreted, could have alerted them to the Japanese raid on Pearl Harbor in December 1941. But because such a raid had seemed entirely inconceivable to most American officials prior to its occurrence, those who received the information failed to understand or disseminate it in time.

RACE AND GENDER IN WARTIME AMERICA

In most ways, the war loosened traditional barriers that had restricted the lives of minorities and women. There was too much demand for fighting men, too much demand for labor, and too much fluidity and mobility in society for rigid, traditional barriers to survive intact.

African Americans and the War

A. Philip Randolph

In the summer of 1941, A. Philip Randolph, president of the Brotherhood of Sleeping Car Porters, an important union with a primarily black membership, began to insist that the government require companies receiving defense contracts to integrate their work forces. To mobilize support for the demand, Randolph planned a massive march on Washington. Roosevelt finally persuaded Randolph to cancel the march in return for a promise to establish what became the Fair Employment Practices Commission (FEPC) to investigate discrimination against African Americans in war industries.

Wartime Race Riots

The need for labor in war plants greatly increased the migration of African Americans from the rural areas of the South into industrial cities. The migration bettered the economic condition of many African Americans, but it also created urban tensions and occasionally violence. The most serious conflict occurred in Detroit in 1943, when racial friction in the city produced a major riot in which thirty-four people died, twenty-five of them black.

Despite such tensions, the leading black organizations redoubled their efforts to challenge segregation. The Congress of Racial Equality (CORE) mobilized mass popular resistance to discrimination. Randolph and other, younger African-American leaders helped organize sit-ins and demonstrations in segregated theaters and restaurants.

Pressure for change was also growing within the military. The armed forces maintained their traditional practice of limiting blacks to the most menial assignments, keeping them in segregated training camps and units, and barring them entirely from the Marine Corps and the Army Air Force. But there were signs of change. By the end of the war, the number of black servicemen had increased sevenfold, to 700,000; some training camps were being at least partially integrated; African Americans were being allowed to serve on ships with white sailors; and more black units were being sent into combat. The changes did not come easily. In some of the partially integrated army bases, riots occasionally broke out when black soldiers protested having to serve in segregated divisions.

Native Americans and the War

Approximately 25,000 Indians performed military service during World War II. Many Native Americans served in combat. Others (mostly Navajos) became "code-talkers," working in military communica-
Navajo "Code-Talkers"
tions and speaking their own language (which enemy forces would be unlikely to understand) over the radio and the telephones. The war brought Indians into intimate contact (often for the first time) with white society, and it awakened among some of them a taste for the material benefits of life in capitalist America. Some never returned to the reservations, but chose to remain in the non-Indian world and assimilate to its ways.

The war had important effects, too, on those Native Americans who stayed on the reservations. Talented young people left the reservations to serve in the military or work in war production, creating manpower shortages in some tribes. The wartime emphasis on national unity undermined support for the revitalization of tribal autonomy that the Indian Reorganization Act of 1934 had launched. New pressures emerged to eliminate the reservation system and require the tribes to assimilate into white society—pressures so severe that John Collier, the energetic director of the Bureau of Indian Affairs, resigned in 1945.

Mexican-American War Workers

Large numbers of Mexican workers entered the United States during the war in response to labor shortages on the Pacific coast and in the Southwest. The American and Mexican governments agreed in 1942 to a program by which
braceros (contract laborers)
Braceros Program
would be admitted to the United States for a limited time. Some worked as migrant farm laborers, but many Mexicans were able for the first time to find factory jobs. They were concentrated mainly in the West, but there were significant Mexican communities in Chicago, Detroit, and other industrial cities.

The sudden expansion of Mexican-American neighborhoods created tensions and occasionally conflict in some American cities. White residents of Los Angeles became alarmed at the activities of Mexican-American teenagers, many of whom were joining street gangs *(pachucos)*. The youths were particularly distinctive because of their style of

ZOOT-SUITER The baggy pants, the long, loose jacket, the big collar, the exaggerated watch chain, the slicked-back hair—all were features of the outfit known as the zoot suit, which was popular among young Mexican Americans in Los Angeles and elsewhere. The "zoot-suit riots" in Los Angeles in June 1943 were a product of the suspicion with which Anglos (in this case servicemen stationed nearby) looked at the culture of the Chicano communities that were growing rapidly throughout the Southwest. *(Bettmann/CORBIS)*

dress. They wore long, loose jackets with padded shoulders, baggy pants tied at the ankles, long watch chains, broad-brimmed hats, and greased, ducktail hairstyles. The outfit was known as a "zoot suit." In June 1943, animosity toward the "zoot-suiters" produced a four-day riot in Los Angeles, during which white sailors stationed at a base in Long Beach invaded Mexican-American communities and attacked zoot-suiters. The police did little to restrain the sailors, who grabbed Hispanic teenagers, tore off and burned their clothes, cut off their ducktails, and beat them. When Mex-

icans tried to fight back, the police moved in and arrested them. In the aftermath of the "zoot-suit riots," Los Angeles passed a law prohibiting the wearing of zoot suits.

"Zoot-Suit Riots"

The Internment of Japanese Americans

Although World War II, unlike World War I, produced little popular animosity toward Germans, it created considerable animosity toward the Japanese. After the attack on Pearl Harbor, government propaganda and popular culture combined to create an image of the Japanese as a devious, malign, and savage people.

Predictably, this racial animosity soon extended to Americans of Japanese descent. There were not many Japanese Americans in the United States—about 127,000, most of them concentrated in a few areas in California. About a third of them were unnaturalized, first-generation immigrants (Issei); two-thirds were naturalized or native-born citizens of the United States (Nisei). Because they generally kept to themselves and preserved traditional Japanese cultural patterns, it was easy for some to imagine that the Japanese Americans were engaged in conspiracies on behalf of their ancestral homeland. (There is no evidence that they actually were.)

In February 1942, in response to pressure from military officials and political leaders on the West Coast, the president authorized the army to "intern" the Japanese Americans. More than 100,000 people were rounded up and taken to what the government called "relocation centers." In fact,

"Relocation Centers"

they were facilities little different from prisons, many of them located in the western mountains and desert. Thus a group of innocent, hardworking people (many of them citizens of the United States) were forced to spend up to three years in grim, debilitating isolation, provided with only minimal medical care, and deprived of decent schools for their children. The Supreme Court upheld the evacuation in a 1944 decision; and although most of the Japanese Americans were released later that year, they were unable to win any significant compensation for their losses until Congress finally acted to redress the wrongs in the late 1980s.

Chinese Americans and the War

The American alliance with China during World War II significantly enhanced both the legal and social status of Chinese Americans. In 1943, partly to improve relations with the government of China, Congress finally repealed the Chinese Exclusion Acts, which had barred almost all Chinese immigration since 1892. The new quota for Chinese immigrants was minuscule (105 a year), but a substantial number of Chinese women managed to gain entry into the country through other provisions covering war brides and fiancées. Permanent residents of the United States of Chinese descent were finally permitted to become citizens.

Declining Prejudice toward Chinese Americans Racial animosity toward the Chinese did not disappear, but it did decline—in part because government propaganda began presenting positive images of the Chinese (partly to contrast them with the Japanese); in part because Chinese Americans began taking jobs in war plants and other booming areas suffering from labor shortages and hence moving out of the relatively isolated world of the Chinatowns. A higher proportion of Chinese Americans (22 percent of all adult males) were drafted than of any other national group, and the entire Chinese community in most cities worked hard and conspicuously for the war effort.

Women and Children in Wartime

The number of women in the work force increased by nearly 60 percent during the war. These wage-earning women were more likely to be married and were, on the whole, older than most of those who had entered the work force in the past.

Many factory owners continued to categorize jobs by gender, reserving the most lucrative positions for men. (Female work, like male work, was also categorized by race: black women were usually assigned more menial tasks, and paid at a lower rate, than their white counterparts.) But some women began now to take on heavy industrial jobs that had long been considered "men's work." The famous wartime image of **"Rosie the Riveter"** "Rosie the Riveter" symbolized the new importance of the female industrial worker. Women joined unions in substantial numbers, and they helped erode at least some of the prejudice that had previously kept many of them from paid employment.

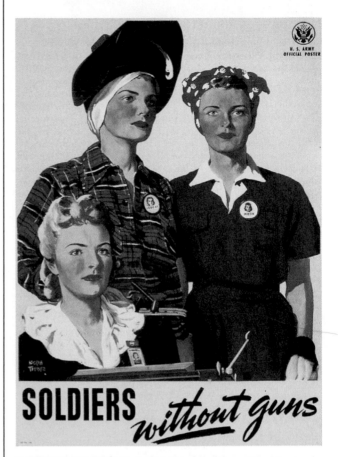

WOMEN AT WAR Many American women enlisted in the army and navy women's corps during World War II, but an equally important contribution of women to the war effort was their work in factories and offices—often in jobs that would have been considered inappropriate for them in peacetime but that they were now encouraged to assume because of the absence of so many men. *(The Library of Congress)*

Most women workers during the war, however, were employed not in factories but in service-sector jobs. Above all, they worked for the government, whose bureaucratic needs expanded dramatically alongside its military and industrial needs. Even within the military, which enlisted substantial numbers of women as WAACs (army) and WAVEs (navy), **WAACs and WAVEs** most female work was clerical.

Many mothers whose husbands were in the military had to combine working with caring for their children. The scarcity of child-care services meant that some women had to leave young children—often known as "latchkey children" or "eight-hour orphans"—at home alone (or sometimes locked in cars in factory parking lots) while they worked.

Perhaps in part because of the family dislocations the war produced, juvenile crime rose markedly. Young boys were arrested at rapidly increasing rates for car theft and other burglary, vandalism, and vagrancy. The arrest rate for prostitutes rose too, as did the incidence of venereal disease. For many children, however, the distinctive experience of the war years was not crime but work. More than a third of all teenagers between the ages of fourteen and eighteen were employed in the last years of the war.

The return of prosperity helped increase the marriage rate and lower the age at which people married, but many marriages were unable to survive the pressures of wartime separation. The divorce rate rose rapidly. The rise in the birth rate that accompanied the increase in marriages was the

Start of the "Baby Boom"

first sign of what would become the great postwar "baby boom."

ANXIETY AND AFFLUENCE IN WARTIME CULTURE

The war created considerable anxiety in American lives. Families worried about loved ones at the front and, as the war continued, many mourned relatives who had died in combat. Women struggled to support families in the absence of husbands and fathers, who had been the principal breadwinners in peacetime. Businesses and communities struggled with shortages of goods and shortages of labor. People living on the two coasts, in particular, worried about enemy invasions and sabotage.

Consumerism Reborn

But the abundance of the war years also created a striking buoyancy in American life. Suddenly people had money to spend again and at least some things to spend it on. In fact, consumerism became, as it had in the 1920s, one of the most powerful forces in American culture and, for many, one of the features of American life that the war was being fought to defend.

Wartime Entertainment and Leisure

The book, theater, and movie industries did record business during the war. Audiences equal to about half the nation's population attended movies each week. Magazines reached the peak of their popularity by providing pictures of and stories about the war. Radio ownership and listenership also increased, for the same reason.

Fuel rationing and rubber shortages limited travel by car, but many people traveled nevertheless—by train or bus, or to places relatively close to their homes. Resort hotels, casinos, and racetracks were jammed with customers. More often, however, people sought entertainment in their own communities. Dance halls were packed with young people; soldiers and sailors were especially attracted to the dances and the big bands, which became to many of them a symbol of the life they believed they were fighting to defend.

By far the most popular music in dance halls, and on

Popularity of Swing

radio, was the relatively new jazz form known as swing, which had emerged from the African-American musical world. During the heyday of swing, band leaders such as Benny Goodman, Duke Ellington, Tommy Dorsey, and Glenn Miller were among the most recognized and popular figures in American popular culture. Swing sold more records than any other kind of music. And it became one of the first forms of popular music to challenge racial taboos. Benny Goodman hired the black pianist Teddy Wilson to play with his band in 1935; other white bandleaders followed.

Women and Men in the Armed Services

For men at the front, the image of home was a powerful antidote to the rigors of wartime. They dreamed of music, food, movies, and other material comforts. Many also dreamed of women—wives and girlfriends, but also movie stars and others, who became the source of one of the most popular icons of the front: the pinup. Sailors pasted pinups inside their lockers. Infantrymen carried them in their knapsacks. Fighter pilots gave their planes female names and painted bathing beauties on their nosecones.

For the servicemen who remained in America during the war, and for soldiers and sailors in cities far from home in particular, the company of friendly, "wholesome" women was, the military believed, critical to sustaining morale. The branches of the United Servicemen's Organization (known as USOs) recruited thousands of young women

Importance of USOs

to serve as hostesses in their clubs. They were expected to dress nicely, dance well, and chat happily with lonely men. Other women joined "dance brigades" and traveled by bus to military bases for social evenings with servicemen. They too were expected to be pretty, to dress attractively, and to interact comfortably with men they had never met before and would likely never see again. The "USO girls" and the members of the dance brigades were forbidden to have any contact with men except at parties at the clubs or during dances. Clearly such regulations were often violated. But while the military took elaborate measures to root out gay men and lesbians from their ranks—vigilantly searching for evidence of homosexuality and unceremoniously dismissing gay people with undesirable discharges—the services quietly tolerated illicit heterosexual relationships, which they believed were both natural and, for many men, necessary.

As during World War I, the armed services virtually took over many American colleges and universities. Emptied of male students and professors (and many females as well), who left to join the war effort, they turned themselves into training camps for military officers.

WORLD WAR II IN EUROPE: THE ALLIED COUNTEROFFENSIVE, 1943–1945 This map illustrates the final, climatic movements in the war in Europe—the two great offensives against Germany that began in 1943 and culminated in 1945. From the east, the armies of the Soviet Union, having halted the Germans at Stalingrad and Moscow, swept across eastern Europe toward Germany. From the west and the south, American, British, and other Allied forces moved toward Germany through Italy and—after the Normandy invasion in June 1944—through France. The two offensives met in Berlin in May 1945. ▌ *What problems did the position of the Allied forces at the end of the war help to produce?*

For an interactive version of this map go to www.mhhe.com/unfinishedinteractive

Retreat from Reform

Late in 1943, Franklin Roosevelt publicly suggested that "Dr. New Deal," as he called it, had served its purpose and should now give way to "Dr. Win-the-War." The statement reflected the president's own genuine shift in concern, but it also reflected the political reality that had emerged during the first two years of war.

Conservative Assault on the New Deal
The greatest assault on New Deal reforms came from conservatives in Congress, who seized on the war as an excuse to dismantle many of the achievements of the New Deal. They were assisted by the end of mass unemployment, which decreased the need for such relief programs as the Civilian Conservation Corps and the Works Progress Administration. They were assisted, too, by their own increasing numbers. In the congressional elections of 1942, Republicans gained 47 seats in the House and 10 in the Senate.

Republicans approached the 1944 election determined to exploit what they believed was resentment of wartime regimentation and unhappiness with Democratic reform. They nominated as their candidate the young and vigorous governor of New York, Thomas E. Dewey. Roosevelt was unopposed within his party, but Democratic leaders pressured him to abandon Vice President Henry Wallace, an advanced New Dealer, and replace him with a more moderate figure. Roosevelt acquiesced in the selection of Senator Harry S. Truman of Missouri, who had won acclaim as chairman of the Senate committee, which compiled an impressive record uncovering waste and corruption in wartime production.

Roosevelt Reelected
The election revolved around domestic economic issues and, indirectly, the president's health. The president was, in fact, gravely ill, suffering from, among other things, advanced arteriosclerosis. But the campaign seemed momentarily to revive him. He made several strenuous public appearances late in October, which dispelled popular doubts about his health and ensured his reelection. He captured 53.5 percent of the popular vote to Dewey's 46 percent. He won 432 electoral votes to Dewey's 99. Democrats lost 1 seat in the Senate, gained 20 in the House, and maintained control of both.

THE DEFEAT OF THE AXIS

By the middle of 1943, America and its allies had succeeded in stopping the Axis advance both in Europe and in the Pacific. In the next two years, the Allies themselves seized the offensive and launched a series of powerful drives that rapidly led the way to victory.

The Liberation of France

By early 1944, American and British bombers were attacking German targets almost around the clock, drastically cutting production and impeding transportation. Especially devastating was the massive bombing of German cities. A February 1945 incendiary raid on Dresden created a firestorm that destroyed three-fourths of the city and killed approximately 135,000 people, almost all civilians.

D-Day
An enormous offensive force had been gathering in England for two years before the spring of 1944: almost 3 million troops, and perhaps the greatest array of naval vessels and armaments ever assembled in one place. On the morning of June 6, 1944, this vast invasion force moved into action. The landing came not at the narrowest part of the English Channel, where the Germans had expected and prepared for it, but along sixty miles of the Cotentin Peninsula on the coast of Normandy. While airplanes and battleships offshore bombarded the Nazi defenses, 4,000 vessels landed troops and supplies on the beaches. (Three divisions of paratroopers had been dropped behind the German lines the night before.) Fighting was intense along the beach, but the superior manpower and equipment of the Allied forces gradually prevailed. Within a week, the German forces had been dislodged from virtually the entire Normandy coast.

For the next month, further progress remained slow. But in late July in the Battle of Saint-Lô, General Omar Bradley's First Army smashed through the German lines. George S. Patton's Third Army moved through the hole Bradley had created and began a drive into the heart of France. On August 25, Free French forces arrived in Paris and liberated the city. By mid-September the Allied armies had driven the Germans almost entirely out of France and Belgium.

The great Allied drive came to a halt, however, at the Rhine River against a firm line of Nazi defenses. In mid-December, German forces struck in desperation along fifty miles of front in the

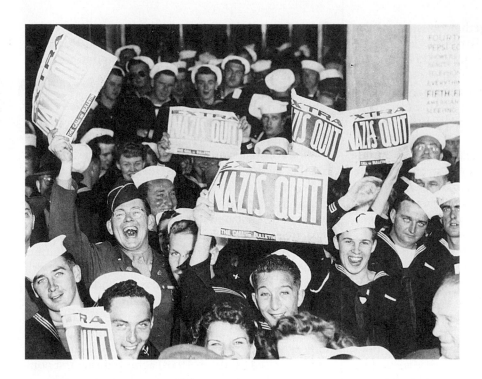

A VICTORY CELEBRATION IN SAN FRANCISCO Soldiers and sailors in San Francisco react jubilantly to the news that the war in Europe has ended. But the news they were celebrating was, in fact, one of the many false rumors of surrender circulating in the spring of 1945. The actual V-E Day occurred several weeks later. *(Bettmann/CORBIS)*

Battle of the Bulge Ardennes Forest. In the Battle of the Bulge (named for a large bulge that appeared in the American lines as the Germans pressed forward), they drove fifty-five miles toward Antwerp before they were finally stopped at Bastogne.

While the western Allies were fighting their way through France, Soviet forces were sweeping westward into central Europe. In late January 1945, the Russians launched a great offensive toward the Oder River, inside Germany. By **Germany Invaded** early spring, they were ready to launch a final assault against Berlin. General Omar Bradley, in the meantime, was pushing toward the Rhine from the west. Early in March, his forces captured the city of Cologne. The next day, he seized an undamaged bridge over the river at Remagen; Allied troops were soon pouring across the Rhine. In the following weeks the British commander, Montgomery, with a million troops, pushed into Germany in the north while Bradley's army completed the encirclement of 300,000 German soldiers in the Ruhr.

The German defense was now broken on both fronts. American forces were moving eastward faster than they had anticipated and could have beaten the Russians to Berlin and Prague. The American and British high commands decided, instead, to halt the advance along the Elbe River in central Germany to await the Russians. That decision enabled the Soviets to occupy eastern Germany and Czechoslovakia.

On April 30, with Soviet forces on the outskirts of Berlin, Adolf Hitler killed himself in his bunker in the capital. And on May 8, 1945, the remaining German forces surrendered unconditionally.

The Pacific Offensive

In February 1944, American naval forces under Admiral Chester Nimitz won a series of victories in the Marshall Islands. Within a month, the navy had destroyed other vital Japanese bastions. American submarines, in the meantime, were decimating Japanese shipping and crippling Japan's domestic economy.

In mid-June 1944, an enormous American armada struck the heavily fortified Mariana Islands and, after some of the bloodiest operations of the war, captured Tinian, Guam, and Saipan, 1,350 miles from Tokyo. In September, American forces landed on the western Carolines. And on October 20, General MacArthur's troops landed on Leyte Island in the Philippines. The Japanese now employed virtually their entire fleet against the Allied invaders in three major encounters—which together constituted the

Battle of Leyte Gulf

decisive Battle of Leyte Gulf. American forces held off the Japanese onslaught and sank four Japanese carriers. In February 1945, American marines seized the tiny volcanic island of Iwo Jima, only 750 miles from Tokyo, but only after the costliest battle in the history of the Marine Corps.

The battle for Okinawa, an island only 370 miles south of Japan, gave evidence of the strength of the Japanese resistance in these last desperate days. Week after week, the Japanese sent kamikaze (suicide) planes against American and British ships. Japanese troops on shore launched desperate nighttime attacks on the American lines. The United States and its allies suffered nearly 50,000 casualties before finally capturing Okinawa in late June 1945. Over 100,000 Japanese died in the siege.

It seemed likely that the same kind of bitter fighting would await the Americans when they invaded Japan. But there were also some signs early in 1945 that such an invasion might not be necessary. The Japanese had almost no ships or planes left with which

Tokyo Firebombed

to fight. The firebombing of Tokyo in March, in which over 80,000 people died, further weakened the Japanese will to resist. Moderate Japanese leaders, who had long since concluded the war was lost, were looking for ways to bring the fighting to an end, although they continued to face powerful opposition from military leaders. Whether the moderates could ultimately have prevailed is a question about which historians and others continue to disagree. In any case, their efforts became superfluous in August 1945, when the United States made use of a terrible new weapon it had been developing throughout the war.

The Manhattan Project and Atomic Warfare

Reports had reached the United States in 1939 that Nazi scientists had taken the first step toward the creation of an atomic bomb, a weapon more powerful than any ever previously devised. The United States and Britain immediately began a race to develop the weapon before the Germans did.

The search for the new weapon emerged from theories developed by atomic physicists, particularly Albert Einstein. Einstein's famous theory of relativity had revealed the relationships between mass and energy. More precisely, he had argued that, in theory at least, matter could be converted into a tremendous

force of energy. Einstein himself, who was by then living in the United States, warned Franklin Roosevelt that the Germans were developing atomic weapons and that the United States must begin trying to do the same. The effort to build atomic weapons centered on the use of uranium, whose atomic structure made possible the creation of a nuclear chain reaction.

MINI-DOCUMENTARY: Dawn of the Nuclear Age

The construction of atomic weapons had become feasible by the 1940s because of the discovery of the radioactivity of uranium in the 1930s by Enrico Fermi in Italy. In 1939, the great Danish physicist Niels Bohr, sent news of German experiments in radioactivity to the United States, where experiments began in many places. In 1940, scientists at Columbia University began chain-reaction experiments with uranium and produced persuasive evidence of the feasibility of using uranium as fuel for a weapon. The Columbia experiments stalled in 1941, and the work moved to Berkeley and the University of Chicago, where Enrico Fermi (who had emigrated to the United States in 1938) achieved the first controlled fission chain reaction in December 1942.

By then, the army had taken control of the research and appointed General Leslie Groves to reorganize the project—which soon became known as the Manhattan Project. Over the next three years, the government secretly poured nearly $2 billion into the Manhattan Project—a massive scientific and technological effort conducted at hidden laboratories in Oak Ridge, Tennessee; Los Alamos, New Mexico; Hanford, Washington; and other sites. Scientists in Oak Ridge, who were charged with finding a way to create a nuclear chain reaction that could be feasibly replicated within the confined space of a bomb, began experimenting with plutonium—a derivative of uranium first discovered by scientists at Berkeley. Plutonium proved capable of providing a practical fuel for the weapon. Scientists in Los Alamos, under the direction of J. Robert Oppenheimer, were charged

J. Robert Oppenheimer

with the construction of the actual atomic bomb.

By 1944, the government was secretly funneling over $1 billion a year to the Manhattan Project, and despite many unforeseen problems, the scientists pushed ahead much faster than anyone had predicted. Even so, the war in Europe ended before they were ready to test the first weapon. Just before dawn on July 16, 1945, in the desert near Alamogordo, New Mexico, the scientists gathered to witness the first atomic explosion in history. The explosion—a blinding flash of light, probably brighter than any ever seen on earth, followed by a huge, billowing mushroom cloud—created a vast crater in the barren desert.

News of the explosion reached President Harry S. Truman (who had taken office in April on the death of Roosevelt) in Potsdam, Germany, where he was attending a conference of Allied leaders. He issued an ultimatum to the Japanese (signed jointly by the British) demanding that they surrender by August 3 or face utter devastation. When the Japanese failed to meet the deadline, Truman ordered the air force to use the new atomic weapons against Japan.

Persistent Controversy Controversy has continued for decades over whether Truman's decision to use the bomb was justified and what his motives were. Some have argued that the atomic attack was unnecessary—that had the United States agreed to the survival of the emperor (which it ultimately did agree to in any case), or had it waited only a few more weeks, the Japanese would have surrendered. Others argue that nothing less than the atomic bombs could have persuaded the Japanese to surrender without a costly American invasion.

The nation's military and political leaders, however, seemed little concerned about such matters. Truman was, apparently, making what he believed to be a simple military decision. A weapon was available that would end the war quickly; he could see no reason not to use it.

Hiroshima Destroyed On August 6, 1945, an American B-29, the *Enola Gay*, dropped an atomic weapon on the Japanese industrial center at Hiroshima. With a single bomb, the United States completely incinerated a four-square-mile area at the center of the city. More than 80,000 civilians died, according to later American estimates. Many more suffered the crippling effects of radioactive fallout or passed those effects on to their children in the form of birth defects.

The Japanese government, stunned by the attack, was at first unable to agree on a response. Two days later, on August 8, the Soviet Union declared war on Japan. And the following day, another American plane dropped another atomic weapon—this time on the city of Nagasaki—inflicting 100,000 deaths and horrible damage. Finally, the emperor intervened to break the stalemate in the cabinet, and on August 14 the government announced that it was ready to give up. On September 2, 1945, on board the American battleship *Missouri*, anchored in Tokyo Bay, Japanese officials signed the articles of surrender. **Surrender of Japan**

The greatest war in the history of mankind had come to an end, and the United States had emerged from it not only victorious but in a position of unprecedented power, influence, and prestige. It was a victory, however, that few could greet with unambiguous joy. Fourteen million combatants had died in the struggle. Many more civilians had perished. The United States had suffered only light casualties in comparison with some other nations, but the cost had still been high: 322,000 dead, another 800,000 injured. And the world continued to face an uncertain future, menaced by the threat of nuclear warfare and by an emerging antagonism between the world's two strongest nations—the United States and the Soviet Union. Visit Chapter 28 of the book's Online Learning Center for a Where Historians Disagree essay on "The Decision to Drop the Atomic Bomb."

The United States played a critical, indeed decisive, role in the war against Germany and Italy; and it defeated Imperial Japan in the Pacific largely alone. But Britain, France, and above all the Soviet Union paid a staggering price—in lives, treasure, and social unity—that had no counterpart in the United States. Most American citizens experienced a booming prosperity during the conflict. There were, of course, jarring social changes during the war that even prosperity could not entirely offset: shortages, restrictions, regulations, family dislocations, and perhaps most of all the absence of millions of men, and considerable numbers of women, who went overseas to fight.

American fighting men and women had very different experiences from those of the people who remained at home. They endured tremendous hardships, substantial casualties, and great loneliness. They helped liberate North Africa and Italy from German occupation. And in June 1944, finally, they joined British, French, and other forces in a great invasion of France, which led less than a year later to the destruction of the Nazi regime and the end of the European war. In the Pacific, they turned

CONCLUSION

back the Japanese offensive. Ultimately, however, it was not the American army and navy that brought the war against Japan to a close. It was the unleashing of the most destructive weapon mankind had ever created—the atomic bomb—on the people of Japan that finally persuaded the leaders of that nation to surrender.

INTERACTIVE LEARNING

 On the ***Primary Source Investigator CD-ROM,*** check out a number of valuable tools for further exploration of the content of this chapter.

Mini-Documentary Movie
- **Dawn of the Nuclear Age.** This mini-documentary explores the secret Manhattan Project and the ultimate decision to use the atomic bombs against Japan (Doc D18)

Interactive Maps
- U.S. Elections (Map M7)

- World War II (Map M27)

Primary Sources
Documents, images, and maps related to the massive U.S. effort in World War II and the effects of the war on the home front. Some highlights include:

- Significant documents related to the development of the atomic bomb, including Albert Einstein's letter to President Roosevelt warning

of the possible German development of this new weapon

- Images of women war workers immortalized in Norman Rockwell's illustration of "Rosie the Riveter"

- Government posters that encouraged women to join the wartime work force

 Online Learning Center (www.mhhe.com/unfinishedinteractive)
Explore this rich website, providing additional exploration of the material covered in this chapter, online versions of the interactive maps included on the Primary Source Investigator CD-ROM, as well as several study aids, including a multiple-choice quiz, essay questions, a glossary, and other valuable tools. Also in the Online Learning Center for this chapter, look for an *Interactive Feature Essay*:

- **Where Historians Disagree: The Decision to Drop the Atomic Bomb**

FOR FURTHER REFERENCE

John Morton Blum, *V Was for Victory: Politics and American Culture During World War II* (1976) and Richard Polenberg, *War and Society* (1972) are important studies of the home front during World War II. David Kennedy, *Freedom from Fear: The American People in Depression and War, 1929–1945* (1999) is an important narrative of both the American military experience in the war and the war's impact on American politics and society. Alan Brinkley, *The End of Reform: New Deal Liberalism in Recession and War* (1995) examines the impact of the war on liberal ideology and political economy. Doris Kearns Goodwin, *No Ordinary Time: Franklin and*

Eleanor Roosevelt: The Home Front in World War II (1994) is an engaging portrait of the Roosevelts during the war. Susan Hartmann examines the transformation in women's work and family roles during and after the war in *The Homefront and Beyond: American Women in the 1940s* (1982). Richard M. Dalfiume, *Desegregation of the U.S. Armed Forces: Fighting on Two Fronts, 1939–1953* (1969) discusses race relations in the military during World War II and beyond. Barbara Dianne Savage, *Broadcasting Freedom: Radio, War, and the Politics of Race, 1938–1948* (1999) reveals the role of African-American radio in tying the war to the struggle for black freedom.

Maurice Isserman, *Which Side Were You On? The American Communist Party During World War II* (1982) portrays the dramatic shifts in Communist Party strategy and status during the war. John W. Dower, *War Without Mercy: Race and Power in the Pacific War* (1986) examines the intense racism that shaped both sides of the war between the United States and Japan. Peter Irons, *Justice at War* (1983) and Roger Daniels, *Concentration Camps USA: Japanese-Americans and World War II* (1981) examine the internment of Japanese Americans. John Keegan, *Six Armies in Normandy: From D-Day to the Liberation of Paris, June 6–August 25, 1944* (1982) is a superb account of the Normandy Invasion. David S. Wyman, *The Abandonment of the Jews: America and the Holocaust, 1941–1945* (1984) is sharply critical of American policy toward the victims of the Holocaust. Richard Rhodes, *The Making of the Atomic Bomb* (1987) is an excellent account of one of the great scientific projects of the twentieth century. Gar Alperovitz, *The Decision to Use the Atomic Bomb and the Architecture of an American Myth* (1995) is an exhaustive and highly critical study of why the United States used atomic weapons in 1945. A sharply different view is visible in Herbert Feis, *The Atomic Bomb and the End of World War II* (1966). John Hersey's *Hiroshima* (1946) reconstructs in minute detail the terrifying experience of the American atomic bomb attack on that Japanese city.

The Cold War

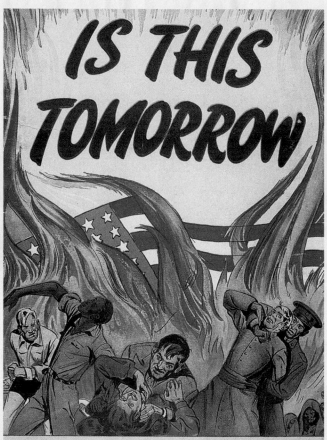

IS THIS TOMORROW

AMERICA UNDER COMMUNISM!

(From Red Scared! by Michael Barson and Steven Heller)

Even before World War II ended, there were signs of tension between the United States and the Soviet Union. Once the hostilities were over, those tensions quickly grew to create what became known as the "Cold War"—a tense and dangerous rivalry between the two former allies that would cast its shadow over international affairs and American domestic life for decades.

ORIGINS OF THE COLD WAR

No issue in twentieth-century American history has aroused more debate than the question of the origins of the Cold War. Some have claimed that Soviet expansionism created the international tensions, others that American global ambitions were at least equally to blame.

Sources of Soviet-American Tension

At the heart of the rivalry between the United States and the Soviet Union was a fundamental difference in the ways the great powers envisioned the postwar world. One vision, outlined in the Atlantic Charter in 1941, was of a world in which nations abandoned their traditional beliefs in military alliances and spheres of influence and governed their relations with one another through democratic processes, with an international organization serving as the arbiter of disputes and the protector of every nation's right of self-determination. That vision appealed to many Americans, including Franklin Roosevelt.

America's Postwar Vision

The other vision was that of the Soviet Union and to some extent of Great Britain. Both Stalin and Churchill had signed the Atlantic Charter. But Britain had always been uneasy about the implications of the self-determination ideal for its own enormous empire. And the Soviet Union was determined to create a secure sphere for itself in Central and Eastern Europe as protection against possible future aggression from the West. Both Churchill and Stalin, therefore, tended to envision a postwar structure in which the great powers would control areas of strategic interest to them. Gradually, the differences between these two positions would turn the peacemaking process into a form of warfare.

Wartime Diplomacy

Serious strains had already begun to develop in the alliance with the Soviet Union in January 1943, when Roosevelt and Churchill met in Casablanca, Morocco, to discuss Allied strategy. The two leaders could not accept Stalin's most important demand—the immediate opening of a second front in western Europe. But they tried to reassure Stalin by announcing that they would accept nothing less than the unconditional surrender of the Axis powers, thus indicating that they would not negotiate a separate peace with Hitler and would not leave the Soviets to fight on alone.

In November 1943, Roosevelt and Churchill traveled to Teheran, Iran, for their first meeting with Stalin. By now, however, Roosevelt's most effective bargaining tool—Stalin's need for American assistance in his struggle against Germany—had been largely removed. The German advance against Russia had been halted. Nevertheless, the Teheran Conference seemed in most respects a success. Roosevelt and Stalin established a cordial personal relationship. Stalin agreed to an American request that the Soviet Union enter the war in the Pacific soon after the end of hostilities in Europe. Roosevelt, in turn, promised that an Anglo-American second front would be established within six months.

Teheran Conference

On other matters, however, the origins of future disagreements were already visible. Most important was the question of the future of Poland. Roosevelt and Churchill were willing to agree to a movement of the Soviet border westward. But on the nature of the postwar government in the portion of Poland that would remain independent, there were sharp differences. Roosevelt and Churchill supported the claims of the Polish government-in-exile that had been functioning in London since 1940; Stalin wished to install another, pro-communist exiled

TIME LINE	1945	1946	1947	1948
	Yalta and Potsdam Conferences United Nations founded	Atomic Energy Commission established Iran crisis	Truman Doctrine Marshall Plan proposed National Security Act Taft-Hartley Act	Berlin blockade Truman elected president Hiss case begins
	1949	**1950**	**1951**	**1952**
	NATO established Soviet Union explodes A-bomb Mao victorious in China	NSC-68 Korean War begins McCarthy's anticommunism campaign begins	Truman fires MacArthur	American occupation of Japan ends Eisenhower elected president

government that had spent the war in Lublin, in the Soviet Union. The three leaders left the Teheran Conference with the issue unresolved.

Yalta

More than a year later, in February 1945, Roosevelt joined Churchill and Stalin for a great peace conference in the Soviet city of Yalta. In return for Stalin's renewed promise to enter the Pacific war, Roosevelt agreed that the Soviet Union should receive some of the territory in the Pacific that Russia had lost in the 1904 Russo-Japanese War.

The negotiators also agreed to a plan for a new international organization, a plan that had been hammered out the previous summer at a conference in Washington, D.C. The new United Nations would contain a General Assembly, in which every member would be represented, and a Security Council, with permanent representatives of the five major powers (the United States, Britain, France, the Soviet Union, and China), each of which would have veto power. The Security Council would also have temporary delegates from several other nations. These agreements became the basis of the United Nations charter, drafted at a

United Nations Established

conference of fifty nations beginning April 25, 1945, in San Francisco. The United States Senate ratified the charter in July by a vote of 80 to 2.

On other issues, however, the Yalta Conference produced no real accord. Basic disagreement remained about the postwar Polish government. Stalin, whose armies now occupied Poland, had already installed a government composed of the pro-communist "Lublin" Poles. Roosevelt and Churchill insisted that the pro-Western "London" Poles must be allowed a place in the Warsaw regime. Roosevelt envisioned a government based on free, democratic elections. Stalin agreed only to a vague compromise by which an unspecified number of pro-Western Poles would be granted a place in the government. He reluctantly consented to hold "free and unfettered elections" in Poland on an unspecified future date. They did not take place for more than forty years.

Disagreements over Poland

Nor was there agreement about the future of Germany. Roosevelt seemed to want a reconstructed and reunited Germany. Stalin wanted to impose heavy reparations on Germany and to ensure a permanent dismemberment of the nation. The final agreement was, like the Polish accord,

YALTA, 1945 Churchill *(left)* and Stalin *(right)* were shocked at the physical appearance of Franklin Roosevelt *(center)* when he arrived for their critical meeting at Yalta. Roosevelt had enough energy to perform capably at the conference, but he was in fact gravely ill. Two months later, not long after he gave Congress what turned out to be an unrealistically optimistic report of the prospects for postwar peace, he died. *(Bettmann/Corbis)*

vague and unstable. The decision on reparations would be referred to a future commission. The United States, Great Britain, France, and the Soviet Union would each control its own "zone of occupation" in Germany. Berlin, the German capital, was already well inside the Soviet zone, but because of its symbolic importance it would itself be divided into four sectors, one for each nation to occupy. At an unspecified date, Germany would be reunited. As for the rest of Europe, the conference produced a murky accord on the establishment of governments "broadly representative of all democratic elements" and "responsible to the will of the people."

| Problems of the Yalta Accords

The Yalta accords, in other words, were less a settlement of postwar issues than a set of loose principles that sidestepped the most difficult questions. Roosevelt, Churchill, and Stalin returned home from the conference each apparently convinced that he had signed an important agreement. But the Soviet interpretation of the accords differed so sharply from the Anglo-American interpretation that the illusion endured only briefly. In the weeks following the Yalta Conference, Roosevelt watched with growing alarm as the Soviet Union moved systematically to establish pro-communist governments in one Central or Eastern European nation after another and as Stalin refused to make the changes in Poland that the president believed he had promised. Still believing the differences could be settled, Roosevelt left Washington early in the spring for a vacation at his retreat in Warm Springs, Georgia. There, on April 12, 1945, he suffered a sudden, massive stroke and died.

THE COLLAPSE OF THE PEACE

Harry S. Truman, who succeeded Roosevelt in the presidency, had almost no familiarity with international issues. Nor did he share Roosevelt's apparent faith in the flexibility of the Soviet Union. Truman sided instead with those in the government who considered the Soviet Union untrustworthy and viewed Stalin himself with suspicion and even loathing.

The Failure of Potsdam

Truman had been in office only a few days before he decided to "get tough" with the Soviet Union. Stalin had made what the new president considered solemn agreements with the United States at Yalta. Truman met on April 23 with Soviet Foreign Minister Molotov and sharply chastised him for violations of the Yalta accords.

In fact, Truman had little leverage with which to compel the Soviet Union to carry out its agreements. Russian forces already occupied Poland and much of the rest of Central and Eastern Europe. Germany was already divided among the conquering nations. The United States was still engaged in a war in the Pacific and was neither able nor willing to enter into a second conflict in Europe. Truman insisted that the United States should be able to get "85 percent" of what it wanted, but he was ultimately forced to settle for much less.

Limited American Leverage |

He conceded first on Poland. When Stalin made a few minor concessions to the pro-Western exiles,

Truman recognized the Warsaw government, hoping that noncommunist forces might gradually expand their influence there. Until the 1980s, they did not. To settle other questions, Truman met in July at Potsdam, in Russian-occupied Germany, with Churchill and Stalin. Truman reluctantly accepted the adjustments of the Polish-German border that Stalin had long demanded; he refused, however, to permit the Russians to claim any reparations from the American, French, and British zones of Germany. This stance effectively confirmed that Germany would remain divided. The western zones ultimately united into one nation, friendly to the United States, and the Russian zone survived as another nation, with a pro-Soviet, communist government.

The China Problem

American hopes for an open, peaceful world "policed" by the great powers required a strong, independent China. But those hopes faced a major obstacle: the Chinese government of Chiang Kai-shek.

`Chiang Kai-shek`

Chiang was generally friendly to the United States, but his government was corrupt and incompetent with feeble popular support. Ever since 1927, the nationalist government he headed had been engaged in a bitter rivalry with the communist armies of Mao Zedong. By 1945, Mao was in control of one-fourth of the population.

Some Americans urged the government to try to find a "third force" to support as an alternative to either Chiang or Mao. Truman, however, decided reluctantly that he had no choice but to continue supporting Chiang. For the next several years the United States continued to pump money and weapons to Chiang, even as it was becoming clear that the cause was lost. But Truman was not prepared to intervene militarily.

Instead, the American government was beginning to consider an alternative to China as the strong, pro-Western force in Asia: a revived Japan. Abandoning the strict occupation policies of the first years after the war (when General Douglas MacArthur had governed the nation), the United States lifted all restrictions on industrial development. The vision of an open, united world was giving way in Asia, as it was in Europe, to an acceptance of a divided world with a strong, pro-American sphere of influence.

The Containment Doctrine

By the end of 1945, a new American foreign policy was slowly emerging. It became known as containment. Rather than attempting to create a unified, "open" world, the United States and its allies would work to "contain" the threat of further Soviet expansion.

The new doctrine emerged in part as a response to events in Europe in 1946. In Turkey, Stalin was trying to win control over the vital sea lanes to the Mediterranean. In Greece, communist forces were threatening the pro-Western government. Faced with these challenges, Truman decided to enunciate a firm new policy. In doing so, he drew from the ideas of the influential American diplomat George F. Kennan, who had warned not long after the war that the only viable policy toward the Soviet Union was "a long-term, patient but firm and vigilant containment of Russian expansive tendencies." On March 12, 1947, Truman appeared before Congress and used Kennan's warnings as the basis of what became known as the Truman Doctrine. "I believe," he argued,

`Truman Doctrine`

"that it must be the policy of the United States to support free peoples who are resisting attempted subjugation by armed minorities or by outside pressures." In the same speech he requested $400 million—for aid to Greece and Turkey. Congress quickly approved the measure.

The American commitment ultimately helped ease Soviet pressure on Turkey and helped the Greek government defeat the communist insurgents. More important, it established a basis for American foreign policy that would survive for more than thirty years.

The Marshall Plan

An integral part of the containment policy was a proposal to aid in the economic reconstruction of Western Europe. There were many motives: humanitarian concern; a fear that Europe would remain an economic drain on the United States if it could not quickly rebuild; a desire for a strong European market for American goods. But above all, American policymakers believed that unless something could be done to strengthen the shaky pro-American governments in Western Europe, those governments might fall under the control of domestic communist parties.

In June 1947, Secretary of State George C. Marshall announced a plan to provide economic assistance to all European nations (including the Soviet Union) that would join in drafting a program for recovery. Although Russia and its Eastern satellites rejected the plan, sixteen Western European nations participated. Whatever opposition there was in the United States largely vanished after a sudden coup in Czechoslovakia in February 1948 that established a Soviet-dominated communist government there. In April, Congress approved the creation of the Economic Cooperation Administration, the agency that would administer the Marshall Plan, as it became known. Over the next three years, the Marshall Plan channeled over $12 billion of American aid into Europe. By the end of 1950, European industrial production had risen 64 percent, communist strength in the member nations had declined, and opportunities for American trade had revived.

Rebuilding Europe

Mobilization at Home

In 1948, at the president's request, Congress approved a new military draft and revived the Selective Service System. In the meantime, the United States, having failed to reach agreement with the Soviet Union on international control of nuclear weapons, redoubled its own efforts in atomic research. The Atomic Energy Commission, established in 1946, became the supervisory body charged with overseeing all nuclear research, civilian and military alike. And in 1950, the Truman administration approved the development of the new hydrogen bomb, a nuclear weapon far more powerful than the bombs the United States had used in 1945.

The National Security Act of 1947

The National Security Act of 1947 reshaped the nation's major military and diplomatic institutions. A new Department of Defense would oversee all branches of the armed services, combining functions previously performed separately by the War and Navy departments. A National Security Council (NSC), operating out of the White House, would govern foreign and military policy. A Central Intelligence Agency (CIA) would replace the wartime Office of Strategic Services and would be responsible for collecting information through both open and covert methods; as the Cold War continued, the CIA would also engage secretly in political and military operations on behalf of American goals. The National Security Act, in other words, gave the president expanded powers with which to pursue the nation's international goals.

The Road to NATO

The United States was also moving to strengthen the military capabilities of Western Europe. Convinced that a reconstructed Germany was essential to the hopes of the West, Truman reached an agreement with Great Britain and France to merge the three western zones of occupation into a new West German republic (which would include the American, British, and French sectors of Berlin, even though that city lay within the Soviet zone). Stalin responded quickly. On June 24, 1948, he imposed a tight blockade around the western sectors of Berlin. If Germany was to be officially divided, he was implying, then the country's Western government would have to abandon its outpost in the heart of the Soviet-controlled eastern zone. Unwilling to risk war through a military challenge to the blockade, Truman ordered a massive airlift to supply the city with food, fuel, and other **Berlin Airlift** needed goods. The airlift continued for more than ten months, transporting nearly 2.5 million tons of material, keeping a city of 2 million people alive. In the spring of 1949, Stalin lifted the now ineffective blockade. And in October, the division of Germany into two nations—the Federal Republic in the west and the Democratic Republic in the East—became official.

The crisis in Berlin accelerated the consolidation of what was already in effect an alliance among the United States and the countries of Western Europe. On April 4, 1949, twelve nations signed an agreement establishing the North Atlantic Treaty Organization (NATO) and declaring that an armed attack against one member would be considered an attack against all. The NATO countries would, moreover, maintain a standing military force in Europe to defend against what many believed was the threat of a Soviet invasion. The formation of NATO eventually spurred the Soviet Union to create an alliance of its own with the communist governments in Eastern Europe—an alliance formalized in 1955 by the Warsaw Pact.

DIVIDED EUROPE AFTER WORLD WAR II This map shows the sharp division that emerged in Europe after World War II between the area under the control of the Soviet Union, and the area allied with the United States. The small map in the upper right shows the division of Berlin among the various occupying powers at the end of the war. Eventually, the American, British, and French sectors were combined to create West Berlin, a city governed by West Germany but entirely surrounded by communist East Germany. ▮ *How did the West prevent East Germany from absorbing West Berlin?*

Reevaluating Cold War Policy

In September 1949, the Soviet Union successfully exploded its first atomic weapon, years earlier than predicted, an event that shocked and frightened many Americans. So did the collapse of Chiang Kai-shek's nationalist government in China, which occurred with startling speed in the last months of 1949. Chiang fled with his political allies and the remnants of his army to the offshore island of Formosa (Taiwan), and the entire Chinese mainland came under the control of a communist government that many Americans believed to be an extension of the Soviet Union. The United States refused to recognize the new communist regime.

In this atmosphere of escalating crisis, Truman called for a thorough review of American foreign policy. The result was a National Security Council report, issued in 1950 and commonly known as NSC-68, which outlined a shift in the American position. The first statements of the containment doctrine   `Containment Expanded` had made at least some distinctions between areas of vital interest to the United States and areas of less importance to the nation's foreign policy and called on America to share the burden of containment with its allies. But the April 1950 document argued that the United States must move on its own to stop communist expansion virtually anywhere it occurred,

HARRY AND BESS TRUMAN AT HOME Senator Harry Truman and his wife Bess pose for photographers in the kitchen of their Washington apartment, suggesting the "common man" image that Truman retained throughout his public life. The picture was taken shortly before the 1944 Democratic National Convention, which would nominate Truman for vice president. Less than a year later, the Trumans would be living in the White House. *(UPI/Corbis-Bettmann)*

regardless of the intrinsic strategic or economic value of the lands in question. Among other things, the report called for a major expansion of American military power. Visit Chapter 29 of the book's Online Learning Center for a Where Historians Disagree essay on "The Origins of the Cold War."

AMERICA AFTER THE WAR

The crises overseas were not the only frustrations the American people encountered after the war. The nation also faced economic difficulties in adapting to the peace. And it suffered from a heated political climate that produced a new wave of insecurity and repression.

The Problems of Reconversion

Despite widespread predictions that the end of the war would return America to depression conditions, economic growth continued after 1945. Pent-up consumer demand from workers who had accumulated substantial savings during the war helped spur the boom. So did a $6 billion tax cut. The Servicemen's Readjustment Act of 1944, better known as the GI Bill of Rights, provided housing, education,

and job training subsidies to veterans and increased spending even further.

This flood of consumer demand contributed to more than two years of serious inflation, during which prices rose at rates of 14 to 15 percent annually. Compounding the economic difficulties was a sharp rise in labor unrest. By the end of 1945, there had been major strikes in the automobile, electrical, and steel industries. In April 1946, John L. Lewis led the United Mine Workers out on strike, shutting down the coal fields for forty days. Truman finally forced coal production to resume by ordering government seizure of the mines.

> Inflation and Labor Unrest

But in the process, he pressured mine owners to grant the union most of its demands. Almost simultaneously, the nation's railroads suffered a total shutdown—the first in the nation's history—as two major unions walked out on strike. By threatening to use the army to run the trains, Truman pressured the strikers back to work after only a few days.

Reconversion was particularly difficult for the millions of women and minorities who had entered the work force during the war. Employers tended to push women, African Americans, Hispanics, and others out of the plants to make room for returning veterans. Some of the war workers, particularly women, left the work force voluntarily. But as many as 80 percent of women workers, and virtually all black and Hispanic males, wanted to continue working. The postwar inflation, the pressure to meet the growing expectations of a high-consumption society, the rising divorce rate—all combined to create a high demand for paid employment among women. As they found themselves excluded from industrial jobs, therefore, women workers moved increasingly into other areas of the economy (above all, the service sector).

The Fair Deal Rejected

Days after the Japanese surrender, Truman submitted to Congress a twenty-one-point domestic program outlining what he later named the "Fair Deal." It called for expansion of Social Security benefits, the raising of the legal minimum wage from 40 to 65 cents an hour, a program to ensure full employment, a permanent Fair Employment Practices Act, public housing and slum clearance, long-range environmental and public works planning, and government promotion of scientific research. Weeks later he added other proposals: federal aid to education, government health insurance and prepaid medical care, funding for the St. Lawrence Seaway, and nationalization of atomic energy.

But most of Truman's programs fell victim to the same public and congressional conservatism that had crippled the last years of the New Deal. Indeed, that conservatism seemed to be intensifying, as the November 1946 congressional elections suggested. Using the simple but devastating slogan "Had Enough?" the Republican Party won control of both houses of Congress. The new Republican Congress quickly moved to reduce government spending and chip away at New Deal reforms. Its most notable action was its assault on the Wagner Act of 1935, in the form of the Labor-Management Relations Act of 1947, better known as the Taft-Hartley Act. It made illegal the closed shop (a workplace in which no one can be hired without first being a member of a union). And although it continued to permit the creation of union shops (in which workers must join a union after being hired), it permitted states to pass "right-to-work" laws prohibiting even that. The Taft-Hartley Act also empowered the president to call for a ten-week "cooling-off" period before a strike by issuing an injunction

Taft-Hartley Act

against any work stoppage that endangered national safety or health. Truman vetoed the bill, but both houses easily overruled him the same day. The Taft-Hartley Act did not destroy the labor movement. But it did damage weaker unions in relatively lightly organized industries such as chemicals and textiles, and it made much more difficult the organizing of workers who had never been union members at all, especially in the South and the West.

The Election of 1948

Truman and his advisers believed that the American public was not ready to abandon the achievements of the New Deal, despite the 1946 election results. As they planned their strategy for the 1948 campaign,

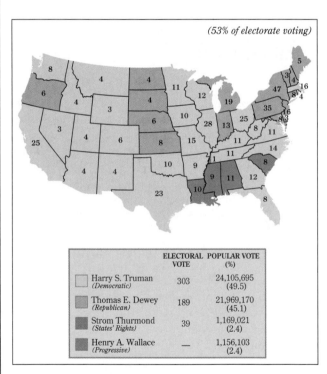

(53% of electorate voting)

	ELECTORAL VOTE	POPULAR VOTE (%)
Harry S. Truman *(Democratic)*	303	24,105,695 (49.5)
Thomas E. Dewey *(Republican)*	189	21,969,170 (45.1)
Strom Thurmond *(States' Rights)*	39	1,169,021 (2.4)
Henry A. Wallace *(Progressive)*	—	1,156,103 (2.4)

ELECTION OF 1948 Despite the widespread expectation that the Republican candidate, Thomas Dewey, would easily defeat Truman in 1948, the president in fact won a substantial reelection victory that year. This map shows the broad geographic reach of Truman's victory. Dewey swept most of the Northeast, but Truman dominated almost everywhere else. Strom Thurmond, the States' Rights candidate, carried four states in the South. ▌ *What had prompted Thurmond to desert the Democratic Party and run for president on his own?*

ⓄⒼ **For an interactive version of this map go to** www.mhhe.com/unfinishedinteractive

therefore, they placed their hopes in an appeal to enduring Democratic loyalties. Throughout 1948, Truman proposed one reform measure after another. To no one's surprise, Congress ignored or defeated them all, but the president was building campaign issues for the fall.

There remained, however, the problem of Truman's personal unpopularity and the deep divisions within the Democratic Party. At the Democratic

| Divided Democratic Party |

Convention that summer, two factions abandoned the party altogether. Southern conservatives were angered by the approval at the convention of a civil rights plank in the platform. They walked out and formed the States' Rights (or "Dixiecrat") Party, with Governor Strom Thurmond of South Carolina as its nominee. At the same time, some members of the party's left wing joined the new Progressive Party, whose candidate was Henry A. Wallace. Wallace supporters objected to what they considered the slow and ineffective domestic policies of the Truman administration, but they resented even more the president's confrontational stance toward the Soviet Union.

Many Democratic liberals who were unhappy with Truman were unwilling to leave the party. The Amer-

| Americans for Democratic Action |

icans for Democratic Action (ADA), a coalition of anticommunist liberals, tried to entice Dwight D. Eisenhower, the popular war hero, to contest the nomination. Only after Eisenhower had refused did liberals concede the nomination to Truman. The Republicans, in the meantime, once again nominated Governor Thomas E. Dewey of New York. Austere, dignified, and competent, he seemed to offer an unbeatable alternative to the president.

Only Truman, it seemed, believed he could win. As the campaign gathered momentum, he became ever more aggressive, turning the fire away from himself and toward Dewey and the "do-nothing, good-for-nothing" Republican Congress. To dramatize his point, he called Congress into special session in July to give it a chance, he said, to enact the liberal measures the Republicans had recently written into their platform. Congress met for two weeks and, predictably, did almost nothing.

| Truman's Stunning Victory |

On election night, to the surprise of almost everyone, he won a narrow but decisive and dramatic victory: 49.5 percent of the popular vote to Dewey's 45.1 percent, and an electoral margin of 303 to 189. Democrats also regained both houses of Congress by substantial margins.

The Fair Deal Revived

Despite the Democratic victories, the Eighty-first Congress was little more hospitable to Truman's Fair Deal reform than its Republican predecessor had been. Truman did win some important victories, to be sure. Congress raised the legal minimum wage from 40 cents to 75 cents an hour. It approved an important expansion of the Social Security system, increasing benefits by 75 percent and extending them to 10 million additional people. And it passed the National Housing Act of 1949, which provided for the construction of 810,000 units of low-income housing accompanied by long-term rent subsidies.

But on other issues—national health insurance and aid to education among them—Truman made little progress. Nor was he able to persuade Congress to accept the civil rights legislation he proposed in 1949, legislation that would have made lynching a federal crime, provided federal protection of black voting rights, abolished the poll tax, and established a new Fair Employment Practices Commission to curb discrimination in hiring.

Truman did proceed on his own to battle several forms of racial discrimination. He ordered an end to discrimination in the hiring of government employees. He began to dismantle segregation within the armed forces. And he allowed the Justice Department to become actively involved in court battles against discriminatory statutes. The Supreme Court, in the meantime, signaled its own growing awareness of the issue by ruling, in *Shelley* v. *Kraemer* (1948), that the courts could not be used to enforce private "covenants" meant to bar blacks from residential neighborhoods.

The Nuclear Age

Looming over the political, economic, and diplomatic struggles of the postwar years was the issue of atomic weapons. Americans greeted the introduction of these terrible new instruments of destruction with fear and awe, but also with expectation. Postwar culture was torn between a dark image of the nuclear war that many Americans feared would be a result of the rivalry with the Soviet Union, and the bright image of a dazzling technological future that atomic power might help to produce.

The fear of nuclear weapons appeared widely in popular culture, but it was often disguised. The late 1940s and early 1950s were the heyday of the *film noir*, a kind of filmmaking that had originated in France and had been named for the dark lighting that was characteristic of the genre. American *film noir* portrayed the loneliness of individuals in an impersonal world—a staple of American culture for many decades—but also suggested the menacing character of the age, the looming possibility of vast destruction. Sometimes, films and television programs addressed nuclear fear explicitly—for example, the celebrated television show of the 1950s and early 1960s, *The Twilight Zone*, which featured dramatic portrayals of the aftermath of nuclear war; or postwar comic books, which depicted powerful superheroes saving the world from destruction.

| Film Noir |

Such images resonated with the public because awareness of nuclear weapons was increasingly built into their daily lives. Schools and office buildings had regular air raid drills. Radio stations regularly tested the emergency broadcast systems. Fallout shelters sprang up in public buildings and private homes, stocked with water and canned goods. America was a nation filled with anxiety.

And yet at the same time, the United States was dazzled by its own prosperity and excited by the technological innovations that were transforming the world. Among those innovations was nuclear power. The same scientific knowledge that could destroy the world, many believed, might also lead it into a dazzling future. The *New York Times*, only days after Hiroshima, expressed its own rosy view of the nuclear future:

> The atomic bomb was perfected for war, but the knowledge which made it possible came out of . . . the deathless yearning to know and to use the gifts of nature for the common good. . . . This new knowledge . . . can bring to this earth not death but life, not tyranny and cruelty, but a divine freedom.

That kind of optimism soon became widespread. The "secret of the atom," many Americans soon predicted, would bring "prosperity and a more complete life." A public opinion poll late in 1948 revealed that approximately two-thirds of those who had an opinion on

the subject believed that, "in the long run," atomic energy would "do more good than harm." Nuclear power plants began to spring up in many areas of the country, their potential dangers scarcely even discussed by those who celebrated their creation.

| Atomic Optimism |

THE KOREAN WAR

On June 24, 1950, the armies of communist North Korea swept across their southern border and invaded the pro-Western half of the Korean peninsula to the south. Within days, they had occupied much of South Korea, including Seoul, its capital. Almost immediately, the United States committed itself to the conflict.

The Divided Peninsula

When World War II ended, both the United States and the Soviet Union had troops in Korea fighting the Japanese; neither army was willing to leave. Instead, they divided the nation, supposedly temporarily, along the 38TH parallel. The Russians finally departed in 1949, leaving behind a communist government in the north with a strong, Soviet-equipped army. The Americans left a few months later, handing control to the pro-Western government of Syngman Rhee, who was anticommunist but only nominally democratic. He had a relatively small military.

| Syngman Rhee |

The relative weakness of the south offered a strong temptation to nationalists in the North Korean government who wanted to reunite the country. The temptation grew stronger when the American government implied that it did not consider South Korea within its own "defense perimeter." The Soviets may not have approved the invasion in advance, but they supported the offensive once it began.

Almost immediately on June 27, 1950, the president ordered limited American military assistance to South Korea, and on the same day he appealed to the United Nations to intervene. The Soviet Union was boycotting the Security Council at the time (to protest the council's refusal to recognize the new communist government of China) and was thus unable to exercise its veto power. As a

THE KOREAN WAR, 1950–1953 These two maps illustrate the changing fortunes of UN forces (which were mostly American) in Korea during the 1950–1953 war. The map at the left shows the extent of the North Korean invasion of the South in 1950; communist forces for a time controlled all of Korea except a small area around Pusan in the southeast. On September 15, 1950, UN troops under Douglas MacArthur landed in force at Inchon and soon drove the North Koreans back across the border. MacArthur then pursued the North Koreans well into their own territory. The map at right shows the very different circumstances once the Chinese entered the war in November 1950. Chinese forces drove the UN army back below the 38th parallel and, briefly, deep into South Korea, below Seoul. The UN troops fought back to the prewar border between North and South Korea late in 1951, but the war then bogged down into a stalemate that continued for a year and a half. ▮ *What impact did the Korean War have on American politics in the early 1950s?*

result, American delegates were able to win UN agreement to a resolution calling for international assistance to the Rhee government. On June 30, the United States ordered its own ground forces into Korea, and Truman appointed General Douglas MacArthur to command the UN operations there.

Inchon

After a surprise American invasion at Inchon in September had routed the North Korean forces from the south and sent them fleeing back across the 38TH parallel, Truman gave MacArthur permission to pursue the communists into their own territory. The president's aim was to create "a unified, independent and democratic Korea." He was moving beyond simple containment and envisioning a rollback of communist power.

From Invasion to Stalemate

For several weeks, MacArthur's invasion of North Korea proceeded smoothly. On October 19, the capital, Pyongyang, fell to the UN forces. Victory seemed near—until the Chinese government intervened. By November 4, eight divisions of the Chinese army had en-

China Intervenes

tered the war. The UN offensive stalled and then collapsed. Within weeks, communist forces had pushed the Americans back below the 38TH parallel once again and had recaptured the South Korean capital of Seoul. By mid-January 1951 the rout had ceased; and by March the UN armies had managed to regain much of the territory they had recently lost, taking back Seoul and pushing the communists north of the 38TH parallel for the second time. With that, the war degenerated into a protracted stalemate.

WINTER IN KOREA, 1950 An American soldier trudges to the crest of an icy and embattled ridge during the bitter fighting in North Korea between American divisions and Chinese communist forces, who had entered the war as the United Nations forces approached the Korean-Chinese border. *(The National Archives and Records Administration)*

From the start, Truman had been determined to avoid a direct conflict with China. Once China entered the war, he began seeking a negotiated solution to the struggle. But General MacArthur argued that the United States was really fighting the Chinese. It should, therefore, attack China itself, if not through an actual invasion, then at least by bombing communist forces massing north of the Chinese border. In March 1951, he indicated his unhappiness in a public letter to House Republican leader Joseph W. Martin that concluded: "There is no substitute for victory." The release of the Martin letter struck the president as intolerable insubordination. On April 11, 1951, he relieved MacArthur of his command.

Sixty-nine percent of the American people supported MacArthur, a Gallup poll reported. When the general returned to the United States later in 1951, he was greeted with wild enthusiasm. Public criticism of Truman finally abated

Truman-MacArthur Controversy

somewhat when a number of prominent military figures, including General Omar Bradley, publicly supported the president's decision. But substantial hostility toward Truman remained. In the meantime, the Korean stalemate continued. Negotiations between the opposing forces began at Panmunjom in July 1951, but the talks—and the war—dragged on until 1953.

Limited Mobilization

Just as the war in Korea produced only a limited American military commitment abroad, so it created only a limited economic mobilization at home.

Truman set up the Office of Defense Mobilization to fight inflation by holding down prices and discouraging high union wage demands. When these cautious regulatory efforts failed, the president took more drastic action. Railroad workers walked off the job in 1951, and Truman ordered the government to seize control of the railroads. In 1952, during a nationwide steel strike, Truman seized the steel mills, citing his powers as commander in chief. But in a 6-to-3 decision, the Supreme Court ruled that the president had exceeded his authority.

The Korean War gave a significant boost to economic growth by pumping new government funds into the economy. But the war had other, less welcome effects. It came at a time of rising insecurity about America's position in the world. As the long stalemate continued, producing 140,000 American dead and wounded, frustration turned to anger. The United States, which had recently won the greatest war in history, seemed unable to conclude what many Americans considered a minor border skirmish in a small country. Many began to believe that something must be deeply wrong—not only in Korea but within the United States as well. Such fears contributed to the rise of the second major campaign of the century against domestic communism.

Rising Insecurity and Frustration

THE CRUSADE AGAINST SUBVERSION

Why did the American people develop a growing fear of internal communist subversion—a fear that by the early 1950s had reached the point of near hysteria? There are many possible answers, but no single definitive explanation.

One factor was obvious. Communism was not an imagined enemy. It had tangible shape, in Josef Stalin and the Soviet Union. Adding to the concern were the Korean stalemate, the "loss" of China, the Soviet development of an atomic bomb. Searching for someone to blame, many were attracted to the idea of a communist conspiracy within American borders. But there were other factors as well, rooted in domestic politics.

HUAC and Alger Hiss

Much of the anticommunist furor emerged out of the search by the Republican Party for an issue with which to attack the Democrats. Beginning in 1947, the House Un-American Activities Committee (HUAC) held widely publicized investigations to prove that, under Democratic rule, the government had tolerated communist subversion. The committee turned first to the movie industry, arguing that communists had infiltrated Hollywood and tainted American films with propaganda. Writers and producers, some of them former communists, were called to testify; and when some of them ("the Hollywood Ten")

The "Hollywood Ten"

refused to answer questions about their own political beliefs and those of their colleagues, they were sent to jail for contempt. Others were barred from employment in the industry when Hollywood adopted a "blacklist" of those of "suspicious loyalty."

More alarming to the public was HUAC's investigation into charges of disloyalty leveled against a former high-ranking member of the State Department: Alger Hiss. In 1948, Whittaker Chambers, a former communist agent, now a conservative editor at *Time* magazine, told the committee that Hiss had passed classified State Department documents to him in 1937 and 1938. When Hiss sued him for slander, Chambers produced microfilms of the documents. Hiss could not be tried for espionage because of the statute of limitations (which protects individuals from prosecution for most crimes after seven years have passed). But largely because of the relentless efforts of Richard M. Nixon, a freshman Republican congressman from California and a member of HUAC, Hiss was convicted of perjury and served several years in prison. The Hiss case cast suspicion on a generation of liberal Democrats. It also transformed Nixon into a national figure and helped him win a seat in the United States Senate in 1950.

The Federal Loyalty Program and the Rosenberg Case

Partly to protect itself against Republican attacks, the Truman administration in 1947 initiated a widely publicized program to review the "loyalty" of federal employees. By 1951, more than 2,000 government employees had resigned under pressure and 212 had been dismissed.

The employee loyalty program became a signal throughout the executive branch to launch a major assault on subversion. The attorney general established a widely cited list of supposedly subversive organizations. The director of the Federal Bureau of Investigation (FBI), J. Edgar Hoover, investigated and harassed alleged radicals. In 1950, Congress passed the McCarran Internal Security Act, which required that all communist organizations register with the government and publish their records. Truman vetoed the bill. Congress easily overrode his veto.

McCarran Internal Security Act

The successful Soviet detonation of an atomic bomb in 1949, earlier than generally expected, suggested to some people that there had been a conspiracy to pass American atomic secrets to the Russians. In 1950, Klaus Fuchs, a young British scientist, seemed to confirm those fears when he testified that he had delivered to the Russians details of the manufacture of the bomb. The case ultimately moved to an obscure New York couple, Julius and Ethel Rosenberg, members of the Communist Party. The government claimed the Rosenbergs had received secret information from Ethel's brother, a machinist on the Manhattan Project, and had passed it on to the Soviet Union. The Rosenbergs were convicted and, on April 5, 1951, sentenced to death. After two years of appeals and public protests, they died in the electric chair on June 19, 1953.

All these factors—the HUAC investigations, the Hiss trial, the loyalty investigations, the McCarran Act, the Rosenberg case—combined with other concerns by the early 1950s to create a fear of communist subversion that seemed to grip the entire country. State and local governments, the judiciary, schools and universities, labor unions—all sought to purge themselves of real or imagined subversives. It was a climate that made possible the rise of an extraordinary public figure.

McCarthyism

Joseph McCarthy was an undistinguished, first-term Republican senator from Wisconsin when, in government beginning in 1955. After 1960, an oral vaccine developed by Albert Sabin made widespread vaccination even easier. By the early 1960s, these vaccines had virtually eliminated polio from American life.

As a result of these and many other medical advances, both infant mortality and the death rate among young children declined significantly in the first twenty-five years after the war. Average life expectancy in that same period rose by five years, to seventy-one.

Pesticides

Scientists were also developing new kinds of chemical pesticides, which they hoped would protect crops from destruction by insects and protect humans from such insect-carried diseases as typhus and malaria. Perhaps the most famous of the new pesticides was dichlorodiphenyltrichloroethane, generally known as DDT, a compound discovered in 1939 by a Swiss chemist.

DDT

Although DDT seemed harmless to human beings and other mammals, it was extremely toxic to insects. American scientists learned of DDT in 1942, just as the army was grappling with the insect-borne tropical diseases—especially malaria and typhus—that threatened American soldiers.

DDT was first used on a large scale in Italy in 1943–1944 during a typhus outbreak, which it quickly helped end. Soon it was being sprayed in mosquito-infested areas of Pacific islands where American troops were fighting the Japanese. The incidence of malaria dropped precipitously, and it undoubtedly saved thousands of lives. Only later did it become evident that DDT had long-term toxic effects on animals and humans.

Postwar Electronic Research

The 1940s and 1950s saw dramatic new developments in electronic technology. Researchers in the

Television

1940s produced the first commercially viable televisions. In the late 1950s, scientists at RCA's David Sarnoff Laboratories in New Jersey developed the technology for color television, which first became widely available in the early 1960s.

In 1948 Bell Labs, the research arm of AT&T, produced the first transistor, a solid-state device capable of amplifying electrical signals, which was much smaller and more efficient than the cumbersome vacuum tubes that had powered most electronic equipment in the past. Transistors made possible the miniaturization of many devices and were also important in aviation, weaponry, and satellites. They contributed as well to the development of integrated circuitry in the late 1950s.

Integrated circuits combined a number of once-separate electronic elements

Integrated Circuits Invented

(transistors, resistors, diodes, and others) and embedded them into a single, microscopically small device. They made it possible to create increasingly complex electronic devices requiring complicated circuitry that would have been impractical to produce through other means. Most of all, integrated circuits helped advance the development of the computer.

Postwar Computer Technology

Prior to the 1950s, computers had been constructed mainly to perform complicated mathematical tasks, such as those required to break military codes. In the 1950s, they began to perform commercial functions.

The first significant computer of the 1950s was the Universal Automatic Computer (or UNIVAC), which was developed initially for the U.S. Bureau of the Census by the Remington Rand Company. It was the first computer able to handle both alphabetical and numerical information easily. It used tape storage and could perform calculations and other functions much faster than its predecessor, the ENIAC. Searching for a larger market than the census for their very expensive new device, Remington Rand arranged to use a UNIVAC to predict the results of the 1952 election for CBS television news. Analyzing early voting results, the UNIVAC accurately predicted an enormous landslide victory for Eisenhower over Stevenson.

Remington Rand had limited success in marketing the UNIVAC, but in the mid-1950s the International Business Machines Company (IBM) introduced

IBM

its first major data-processing computers and began to find a wide market for them among businesses in the United States and abroad. These early successes, combined with the enormous amount of money IBM invested in research and development, made the company the worldwide leader in computers.

Bombs, Rockets, and Missiles

In 1952, the United States successfully detonated the first hydrogen bomb. Unlike the plutonium and uranium bombs developed during World War II, the hydrogen bomb derives its power not from fission (the splitting of atoms) but fusion (the joining together of lighter atomic elements with heavier ones). It is capable of producing explosions of vastly greater power than the earlier fission bombs.

The development of the hydrogen bomb gave considerable impetus to the effort to develop unmanned rockets and missiles capable of traveling the new weapons to their targets. Both the United States and the Soviet Union began to put tremendous resources into their development. The United States benefited from the emigration to America of some of the scientists who had helped develop rocketry for Germany during World War II.

In the United States, early missile research was conducted almost entirely by the Air Force, and there were significant early successes in developing rockets capable of traveling several hundred miles. But American and Soviet leaders were both struggling to build longer-range missiles that could cross oceans and continents—intercontinental ballistic missiles, or ICBMs.

ICBMs American scientists experimented in the 1950s first with the Atlas and then the Titan ICBM. There were some early successes, but there were also many setbacks. By 1958, scientists had created a solid fuel to replace the volatile liquid fuels of the early missiles; and they had also produced miniaturized guidance systems capable of ensuring that missiles could travel to reasonably precise destinations. Within a few years, a new generation of missile, known as the Minuteman, became the basis of the American atomic weapons arsenal. American scientists also developed a nuclear missile capable of being carried and fired by submarines—the Polaris, which is launched from below the surface of the ocean by compressed air and fires its engines only once it is above the surface. A Polaris was first successfully fired from underwater in 1960.

The Space Program

The American space program eventually developed a rationale of its own. In the beginning, however, it was a byproduct of the rivalry with the Soviet Union. Its origins can perhaps be traced most directly to a dramatic event in 1957, when the Soviet Union announced that it had launched an earth-orbiting satellite— Sputnik—into outer space.

Sputnik

The United States had yet to perform any similar feats, and the American government (and much of American society) reacted to the announcement with alarm. Federal policy began encouraging (and funding) strenuous efforts to improve scientific education in the schools, to create more research laboratories, and, above all, to speed the development of America's own exploration of outer space. The United States launched its own first satellite, Explorer I, in January 1958.

The centerpiece of space exploration, however, soon became the manned space program, established in 1958 along with a new agency, the National Aeronautics and Space Administration (NASA). The first American space pilots, or "astronauts," quickly became the nation's most revered heroes. On May 5, 1961, Alan Shepard became the first American launched into space. But his short, suborbital flight came several months after a Soviet "cosmonaut," Yuri Gagarin, had made a flight in which he had actually orbited the earth. On February 2, 1962, John Glenn became the first American to orbit the globe. NASA later introduced the Gemini program, whose spacecraft could carry two astronauts at once.

Mercury and Gemini were followed by the Apollo program, whose purpose was to land men on the moon. It had some catastrophic setbacks, most notably a fire in January 1967 that killed three astronauts during a training session. But on July 20, 1969, Neil Armstrong, Edwin Aldrin, and Michael Collins successfully traveled in a space capsule into orbit around the moon. Armstrong and Aldrin then detached a smaller craft from the capsule, landed on the surface of the moon, and became the first men to walk on a body other than earth. Six more lunar missions followed, the last in 1972.

Apollo

Eventually, the space program became a relatively modest effort to make travel in near-space easier and more practical through the development of the "space shuttle," an airplane-like device launched by a missile but capable both of navigating in space and landing on earth much like a conventional aircraft. The first space shuttle was successfully launched in 1982. The explosion of one shuttle, *Challenger*, in January 1986 shortly after takeoff, killing all seven astronauts, stalled the program for two years. But missions resumed in the late 1980s. The space shuttle has been used to launch and repair communications satellites, to insert the Hubble Space Telescope into orbit in 1990 (and later to repair its flawed lens), and to service the orbiting Spacelab.

PEOPLE OF PLENTY

Among the most striking social developments of the immediate postwar era was the rapid extension of a middle-class lifestyle and outlook to an expanding portion of the population. The historian David Potter published an influential examination of "economic abundance and American character" in 1954. He called it *People of Plenty*. For the American middle class in the 1950s, at least, it seemed an appropriate label.

The Consumer Culture

At the center of middle-class culture in the 1950s was a growing absorption with consumer goods. That was a result of increased prosperity, of the increasing variety and availability of products, and of the adeptness of advertisers in creating a demand for those products. It was also a result of the growth of consumer credit, which increased by 800 percent between 1945 and 1957. Prosperity fueled such longtime consumer crazes as the automobile, and Detroit responded to the boom with ever-flashier styling and accessories. Consumers also responded eagerly to the development of such new products as dishwashers, garbage disposals, television, hi-fis, and stereos.

| Growing Focus on Consumer Goods |

Because consumer goods were so often marketed (and advertised) nationally, the 1950s were notable for the rapid spread of great national consumer crazes. For example, children, adolescents, and even some adults became entranced in the late 1950s with the hula hoop—a large plastic ring kept spinning around the waist. The popularity of the Walt Disney-produced children's television show *The Mickey Mouse Club* created a national demand for related products such as Mickey Mouse watches and hats.

The Suburban Nation

A third of the nation's population lived in suburbs by 1960. The growth of suburbs was a result not only of increased affluence but of important innovations in home building, which made single-family houses affordable to millions of new people. The most famous of the suburban developers, William Levitt, came to symbolize the new suburban growth with his use of mass-production techniques to construct large housing developments, the first of which was on Long Island, near New York City.

| William Levitt |

Why did so many Americans want to move to the suburbs? One reason was the enormous importance postwar Americans placed on family life after five years of war. Suburbs provided families with larger homes than they could find (or afford) in the cities. They provided privacy. They also provided a sense of security from the noise and dangers of urban living. They offered space for new consumer goods—appliances, cars, boats, outdoor furniture, and other products.

| Segregated Suburbs |

Another factor motivating white Americans to move to the suburbs was race. Most suburbs were restricted to white inhabitants—both because relatively few African Americans could afford to live in them and because formal and informal barriers kept even prosperous blacks out of all but a few. In an era when the black population of most cities was rapidly growing, many white families fled to the suburbs to escape the integration of urban neighborhoods and schools.

The Suburban Family

For professional men (who tended to work in the city, at some distance from their homes), suburban life generally meant a rigid division between their working and personal worlds. For many middle-class women, it meant an increased isolation from the workplace. Many middle-class

| Traditional Gender Norms Reinforced |

husbands considered it demeaning for their wives to be employed. And many women themselves shied away from the workplace when they could afford to, in part because of prevailing ideas about motherhood (popularized by such widely consulted books as Dr. Benjamin Spock's *Baby and Child Care*, first published in 1946) that advised women to stay at home with their children.

Some women, however, had to balance these pressures against other, contradictory ones. As expectations of material comfort rose, many middle-class families needed a second income to maintain the standard of living they desired. As a result, the number of married women working outside the home actually increased in the postwar years.

The Birth of Television

Television was the result of a series of scientific and technological discoveries, but its impact was largely social and cultural. It quickly became perhaps the most powerful medium of mass communication in history. Experiments in broadcasting pictures (along with sound) had begun as early as the 1920s, but commercial television began only shortly after World War II. Its growth was phenomenally rapid. In 1946, there were only 17,000 sets in the country; by 1957, there were 40 million television sets in use—almost as many sets as there were families.

Growing Popularity of Television

The television industry emerged directly out of the radio industry, and all three of the major networks—the National Broadcasting Company, the Columbia Broadcasting System, and the American Broadcasting Company—had started as radio companies. Like radio, the television business was driven by advertising; and in the early days of television, sponsors often played a direct role in determining the content of the programs they chose to sponsor. Many early television shows bore the names of the corporations that were paying for them: the GE Television Theater, the Chrysler Playhouse, the Camel News Caravan, and others. Some daytime serials (known as "soap operas," because their sponsors were almost always companies making household goods targeted at women) were actually written and produced by Procter & Gamble and other companies.

By the late 1950s, television news had replaced newspapers, magazines, and radios as the nation's most important vehicle of information. Television advertising helped create a vast market for new fashions and products. Televised athletic events gradually made college and professional sports one of the most important sources of entertainment (and one of the biggest businesses) in America. Television entertainment programming replaced movies and radio as the principal source of diversion for American families.

Much of the programming of the 1950s and early 1960s created a common image of American life—an image that was predominantly white, middle class, and suburban, and that was epitomized by the popular situation comedies, which showed families in which, as the title of one of the most popular put it, *Father Knows Best*, and in which most women were striving to serve their children and please their husbands.

Yet television also created conditions that could accentuate social conflict. Even those unable to share in the affluence of the era could, through television, acquire a vivid picture of how the rest of their society lived. Thus at the same time that television was celebrating the white middle class, it was also contributing to the sense of alienation and powerlessness among groups excluded from the world it portrayed. And television news conveyed with unprecedented power the social upheavals that gradually spread beginning in the late 1950s.

Travel, Outdoor Recreation, and Environmentalism

Although the idea of a paid vacation for American workers, and the connection of that idea with travel, had entered American culture beginning in the 1920s, it was not until the postwar years that vacation travel became truly widespread among middle-income Americans. The construction of the interstate highway system contributed dramatically to the growth of travel. So did the increasing affluence of workers. Even in the 1950s, there was a healthy market for vacation vehicles—trailers and small vans—that some families used while traveling. But the urge to travel was also an expression of some of the same impulses that produced the move to suburbs: a desire to escape crowding and stress and experience the natural world.

Nowhere was this surge in travel and recreation more visible than in the nation's national parks.

People who traveled to national parks did so for many reasons—some to hike and camp; some to fish and hunt, some simply to look in awe at the landscape. But whatever their motives, most visitors came in search of an experience in the wilderness. The importance of that search became clear in the early 1950s in the first of many battles over development of wilderness areas: the fight to preserve Echo Park.

Echo Park is a spectacular valley in the Dinosaur National Monument, on the border between Utah and Colorado, near the southern border of Wyoming. In the early 1950s, the federal government's Bureau of Reclamation proposed building a dam across the Green River, which runs through Echo Valley, so as to create a lake for recreation and a source of hydroelectric power. The American environmental movement had been relatively quiet since its searing defeat early in the century in its effort to stop a similar dam in the Hetch Hetchy valley at Yosemite National Park. But the Echo Park proposal helped rouse it from its slumber.

In 1950, Bernard DeVoto, a well-known writer, published an essay in *The Saturday Evening Post* entitled "Shall We Let Them Ruin Our National Parks?" It had a sensational impact, arousing opposition to the Echo Valley dam from many areas of the country. The Sierra Club | **Sierra Club Reborn** | sprang into renewed action; the controversy helped elevate a new and aggressive leader, David Brower, who eventually transformed the Club into the nation's leading environmental organization. By the mid-1950s, a large coalition of environmentalists, naturalists, and wilderness vacationers had mobilized in opposition to the dam, and in 1956 Congress blocked the project and preserved Echo Park in its natural state. The controversy was a major victory for those who wished to preserve the national parks, and it was an important spur to the dawning environmental consciousness that would become so important a decade and more later.

Organized Society and Its Detractors

Large-scale organizations and bureaucracies increased their influence over American life in the postwar era. White-collar workers came to outnumber blue-collar laborers for the first time, and an increasing proportion of them worked in corporate settings with rigid hierarchical structures. Industrial workers also confronted large bureaucracies both in the workplace and in their own unions.

The debilitating impact of bureaucratic life on the individual became one of the central themes of popular and scholarly debate. William H. Whyte, Jr., produced *The Organization Man* (1956), which attempted | **The Organization Man** | to describe the special mentality of the worker in a large, bureaucratic setting. Self-reliance, Whyte claimed, was losing place to the ability to "get along" and "work as a team" as the most valuable trait in the modern character. The sociologist David Riesman made similar observations in *The Lonely Crowd* (1950), in which he argued that the traditional "inner-directed man," who judged himself on the basis of his own values and the esteem of his family, was giving way to a new "other-directed man," more concerned with winning the approval of the larger organization or community.

Novelists, too, expressed misgivings in their work about the impersonality of modern society. Saul Bellow produced a series of novels—*The Adventures of Augie March* (1953), *Seize the Day* (1956), *Herzog* (1964), and many others—that chronicled the difficulties American Jewish men had in finding fulfillment in modern urban America. J. D. Salinger wrote in *The Catcher in the Rye* (1951) of a prep-school student, Holden Caulfield, who was unable to find any area of society—school, family, friends, city—in which he could feel secure or committed.

The Beats and the Restless Culture of Youth

The most derisive critics of bureaucracy, and of middle-class society generally, were a group of young poets, writers, and artists known as the "beats" (or, by disapproving critics, as "beatniks"). They wrote harsh critiques of what they considered the sterility and conformity of American life and the banality of popular culture. Allen Ginsberg's dark, bitter poem *Howl* (1955) decried the "Robot apartments! invincible | **Howl** | suburbs! skeleton treasuries! blind capitals! demonic industries!" of modern life. Jack Kerouac produced *On the Road* (1957), an account of a cross-country automobile trip that depicted the rootless, iconoclastic lifestyle of Kerouac and his friends.

The beats were the most visible evidence of a widespread restiveness among young Americans in the 1950s. The phenomenon of "juvenile delinquency" attracted tremendous public attention, and in both politics and popular culture there were dire warnings about the growing criminality of American youth. The 1955 film *Blackboard Jungle*, for example, was a frightening depiction of crime and violence in city schools. Scholarly studies, presidential commissions, and journalistic exposés all contributed to the sense of alarm about the spread of delinquency—although in fact youth crime did not dramatically increase in the 1950s.

"Juvenile Delinquency"

Many young people began to wear clothes and adopt hairstyles that mimicked popular images of juvenile criminal gangs. The culture of alienation that the beats so vividly represented had counterparts even in ordinary middle-class behavior: teenage rebelliousness toward parents, youthful fascination with fast cars and motorcycles, increasing sexual activity, assisted by the greater availability of birth-control devices. The popularity of James Dean, in such movies as *Rebel Without a Cause* (1955), was a particularly vivid sign of youth culture in the 1950s. Both in the roles he played (moody, alienated teenagers and young men with a streak of self-destructive violence) and in the way he lived his own life (he died in 1955, at the age of 24, in an automobile accident), Dean became an icon of American youth.

Rock 'n' Roll

One of the most important cultural developments for American youth in the 1950s was the enormous popularity of rock 'n' roll—and of the greatest early rock star, Elvis Presley. Presley became a symbol of a youthful determination to push at the borders of the conventional and acceptable. Presley's sultry good looks, his self-conscious effort to dress in the vaguely rebellious style of urban gangs, and, most of all, the open sexuality of his music and his public performances—all made him wildly popular among young Americans in the 1950s. His first great hit, "Heartbreak Hotel," established him as a national phenomenon in 1956, and he remained a powerful figure in American popular culture until—and indeed beyond—his death in 1977.

Elvis Presley

Presley's music, like that of many early white rock musicians, drew heavily from black rhythm and blues traditions. Sam Phillips, a record promoter who had recorded some of the important black rhythm and blues musicians of his time (among them B. B. King), reportedly said in the early 1950s: "If I could find a white man with a Negro sound, I could make a billion dollars." Soon after that, he found Presley. But there were others as well—among them Buddy Holly and Bill Haley—who were closely connected to African-American

Rock 'n' Roll's Black Origins

ELVIS IN CONCERT Elvis Presley ended his career performing before wealthy audiences in Las Vegas, wearing garish sequined suits. But in the early years of his career, as this concert in the late 1950s suggests, both he and his fans were younger—and the connection between them was immediate and intense. *(Bettmann/Corbis)*

B y the late 1950s, a growing restlessness was becoming visible beneath the apparently placid surface of American society. Ultimately, that restlessness would make the 1960s one of the most turbulent and divisive eras of the twentieth century. But at first, it contributed to a bold and confident effort by political leaders to attack social and international problems within the framework of conventional liberal politics.

EXPANDING THE LIBERAL STATE

Those who yearned for a more active government in the late 1950s and who accused the Eisenhower administration of allowing the nation to "drift" hoped for vigorous new leadership. The two men who served in the White House through most of the 1960s—John Kennedy and Lyndon Johnson— seemed for a time to be the embodiment of these liberal hopes.

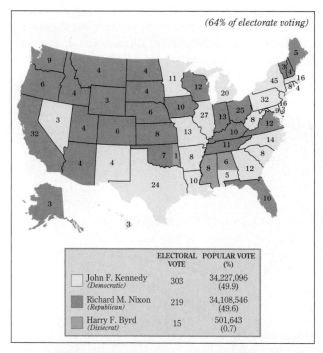

(64% of electorate voting)

	ELECTORAL VOTE	POPULAR VOTE (%)
John F. Kennedy *(Democratic)*	303	34,227,096 (49.9)
Richard M. Nixon *(Republican)*	219	34,108,546 (49.6)
Harry F. Byrd *(Dixiecrat)*	15	501,643 (0.7)

THE ELECTION OF 1960 The election of 1960 was, in the popular vote at least, one of the closest in American history. John Kennedy's margin over Richard Nixon was less than one-third of one percent of the total national vote, but greater in the electoral college. ▮ *What was the significance of this distribution of strength to the future of the two parties?*

OLC For an interactive version of this map go to www.mhhe.com/unfinishedinteractive

John Kennedy

The campaign of 1960 produced two young candidates who claimed to offer the nation active leadership. The Republican nomination went almost uncontested to Vice President Richard Nixon, who

JOHN KENNEDY The new president and his wife, Jacqueline, attend one of the five balls in Washington marking Kennedy's inauguration in 1961. *(Paul Schutzer, Life Magazine, © 1961 Time Warner, Inc./Getty Images)*

1960	1961	1962	1963
Kennedy elected president	Freedom rides Bay of Pigs Berlin Wall erected	Cuban missile crisis	March on Washington Kennedy assassinated; Johnson becomes president Civil rights demonstrations in Birmingham

1964	1965	1967	1968
Johnson launches war on poverty Civil Rights Act Gulf of Tonkin Resolution Johnson elected president	Malcolm X assassinated Voting Rights Act U.S. troops in Vietnam Racial violence in Watts	Antiwar movement grows Racial violence in Detroit	Tet offensive Martin Luther King, Jr. assassinated Robert Kennedy assassinated Nixon elected president

TIME LINE

promised moderate reform. The Democrats, in the meantime, emerged from a spirited primary campaign united, somewhat uneasily, behind John Fitzgerald Kennedy, an attractive and articulate senator from Massachusetts.

John Kennedy was the son of the wealthy, powerful, and highly controversial Joseph P. Kennedy, former American ambassador to Britain. He premised his campaign, he said, "on the single assumption that the American people are uneasy at the present drift in our national course." But his appealing public image

Kennedy Elected

was at least as important as his political positions in attracting popular support. He overcame doubts about his youth (he turned forty-three in 1960) and religion (he was Catholic) to win with a tiny plurality of the popular vote (49.9 percent to Nixon's 49.6 percent) and only a slightly more comfortable electoral majority (303 to 219).

The "New Frontier"

Kennedy had campaigned promising a set of domestic reforms he described as the "New Frontier." But his thin popular mandate and a Congress dominated by a coalition of Republicans and conservative Democrats frustrated many of his hopes. Kennedy did manage to win approval of tariff reductions his administration had negotiated, and he began to build a legislative agenda that he hoped he might eventually see enacted.

More than any other president of the century (except perhaps the two Roosevelts and, later, Ronald Reagan), Kennedy made his own personality an integral part of his presidency and a central focus of national attention. Nothing illustrated that more clearly than the popular reaction to the tragedy of November 22, 1963. Kennedy had traveled to Texas with his wife and Vice President Lyndon Johnson for a series of political appearances. While the presidential motorcade rode slowly through the streets of Dallas, shots rang out. Two bullets struck the president—one in the throat, the other in the head. He was sped to a nearby hospital, where minutes later he was pronounced dead. Lee Harvey Oswald, a confused and embittered Marxist, was arrested for the crime later that day, and then mysteriously murdered by a Dallas nightclub owner, Jack Ruby, two days later as he was being moved from one jail to another. Most Americans at the time accepted the conclusions of a federal commission, chaired by Chief Justice Earl Warren, appointed by President Johnson to investigate the assassination. The commission found that both Oswald and Ruby had acted alone, that there was no larger conspiracy. In later years, however, many Americans came to believe that the Warren Commission report had ignored evidence of a wider conspiracy behind the murders.

Lyndon Johnson

The Kennedy assassination was a national trauma—a defining event for almost everyone old enough to be aware of it. At the time, however, much of the nation took comfort in the personality and performance of Kennedy's successor in the White House, Lyndon Baines Johnson. Johnson was a native of the poor "hill country" of west Texas and had risen to become majority leader of the U.S. Senate by dint of extraordinary, even obsessive effort and ambition. Having failed to win the Democratic nomination for president in 1960, he surprised many who knew him by agreeing to accept the second position on the ticket with Kennedy.

Johnson's rough-edged, even crude personality could hardly have been more different from Kennedy's. But like Kennedy, Johnson was a man who believed in the active use of power. Between 1963 and 1966, he compiled the most impressive legislative record of any president since Franklin Roosevelt. He was aided by the tidal wave of emotion that followed the death of President Kennedy, which helped win support for many New Frontier proposals. But Johnson also constructed a remarkable reform program of his own, one that he ultimately labeled the "Great Society." And he won approval of much of it through the same sort of skillful lobbying in Congress that had made him an effective majority leader.

"Great Society"

Johnson's first year in office was, by necessity, dominated by the campaign for reelection. There was little doubt that he would win—particularly after the Republican Party nominated the very conservative Senator Barry Goldwater of Arizona. In the November 1964 election, the president received a larger plurality, over 61 percent, than any candidate before or since. Goldwater managed to carry only his home state of Arizona and five states in the Deep South. Record Democratic majorities in both houses of Congress ensured that the president would be able to fulfill many of his goals.

The Assault on Poverty

For the first time since the 1930s, the federal government took steps in the 1960s to create important new social welfare programs. The most important of these,

Medicare and Medicaid

perhaps, was Medicare: a program to provide federal aid to the elderly for medical expenses. Its enactment in 1965 came at the end of a bitter, twenty-year debate between those who believed in the concept of national health assistance and those who denounced it as "socialized medicine." But Medicare pacified many critics. For one thing, it avoided the stigma of "welfare" by making Medicare benefits available to all elderly Americans, regardless of need (just as Social Security had done with pensions). The program also defused the opposition of the medical community by allowing doctors serving Medicare patients to practice privately and (at first) to charge their normal fees; Medicare simply shifted responsibility for paying those fees from the patient to the government. In 1966, Johnson steered to passage the Medicaid program, which extended federal medical assistance to welfare recipients and other indigent people of all ages.

Medicare and Medicaid were early steps in a much larger assault on poverty. The centerpiece of this "war on poverty," as Johnson called it, was the Office of Economic Opportunity (OEO), which created an array of new educational, employment, housing, and health-care programs. But the OEO was controversial from the start, in part because of its commitment to the idea of "Community Action."

Community Action was an effort to involve members of poor communities themselves in the planning and administration of the programs designed to help them. The Community Action programs provided jobs for many poor people and gave them valuable experience in administrative and political work. But despite its achievements, the Community Action approach proved impossible to sustain, both because of administrative failures and because the apparent excesses of a few agencies damaged the popular image of the programs.

The OEO spent nearly $3 billion during its first two

Failure of the OEO

years of existence, and it helped reduce poverty in some areas. But it fell far short of eliminating poverty altogether. That was in part because of the weaknesses of the programs themselves and in part because funding for them, inadequate from the beginning, dwindled as the years passed and a costly war in Southeast Asia became the nation's first priority.

Cities, Schools, and Immigration

Closely tied to the antipoverty program were federal efforts to promote the revitalization of decaying cities and to strengthen the nation's schools. The Housing Act of 1961 offered $4.9 billion in federal grants to cities for the preservation of open spaces, the development of mass-transit systems, and the subsidization of middle-income housing. In 1966, Johnson established a new cabinet agency, the Department of Housing and Urban Development. Johnson also inaugurated the Model Cities program, which offered federal subsidies for urban redevelopment pilot programs.

Kennedy had fought for federal aid to public educa-

Federal Aid to Education

tion, but he had failed to overcome two important obstacles: Many Americans feared that aid to education was the first step toward federal control of the schools, and Catholics insisted that federal assistance must extend to parochial as well as public schools. Johnson managed to circumvent both objections with the Elementary and Secondary Education Act of 1965 and a series of subsequent measures. The bills extended aid to both private and parochial schools and based the aid on the economic conditions of the students, not on the needs of the schools themselves.

The Johnson administration also supported the Immigration Act of 1965, one

Immigration Act of 1965

of the most important pieces of legislation of the 1960s. The law maintained a strict limit on the number of newcomers admitted to the country each year (170,000), but it eliminated the "national origins" system established in the 1920s, which gave preference to immigrants from northern Europe over those from other parts of the world. It continued to restrict immigration from some parts of Latin America, but it allowed people from all parts of Europe, Asia, and Africa to enter the United States on an equal basis. By the early 1970s, the character of American immigration had changed dramatically, with members of new national groups—and particularly large groups of Asians—entering the United States.

Legacies of the Great Society

Taken together, the Great Society reforms meant a significant increase in federal spending. For a time, rising tax revenues from the growing economy nearly compensated for the new expenditures. In 1964, Johnson managed to win passage of the $11.5 billion tax cut that Kennedy had first proposed in 1962 to promote economic growth. The cut increased the federal deficit, but substantial economic growth over the next several years made up for much of the revenue initially lost. As Great Society programs began to multiply, however, and particularly as they began to compete with the escalating costs of America's military ventures, the federal budget rapidly outpaced increases in revenues.

The high costs of the Great Society programs, the failures of many of them, and the inability of the government to find the revenues to pay for them contributed to a growing disillusionment with federal efforts to solve social problems. But the Great Society was also responsible for

Achievements of the Great Society

some significant achievements. It significantly reduced hunger in America. It made medical care available to millions of elderly and poor people. It contributed to the greatest reduction in poverty in American history. In 1959, according to the most widely accepted estimates, 21 percent of the American people lived below the officially established poverty line. By 1969, only 12 percent remained below that line.

THE BATTLE FOR RACIAL EQUALITY

The nation's most important domestic initiative in the 1960s was the effort to provide justice and equality to African Americans. It was the most difficult commitment, the one that produced the severest strains on American society. But it was one that could not be avoided. African Americans were themselves ensuring that the nation would have to deal with the problem of race.

Expanding Protests

John Kennedy was sympathetic to the cause of racial justice, but like presidents before him, he feared alienating southern Democratic voters and powerful southern Democrats in Congress. His administration hoped to contain the racial problem by expanding enforcement of existing laws and supporting litigation to overturn segregation statutes.

But the pressure for change was growing uncontainable even before Kennedy took office. In February 1960, black college students in Greensboro, North Carolina, staged a sit-in at a segregated Woolworth's lunch counter; and in the following months, such demonstrations spread throughout the South, forcing many merchants to integrate their facilities. In the fall of 1960, some of those who had participated in the sit-ins formed the Student Nonviolent Coordinating Committee (SNCC)—a student branch of Martin Luther King, Jr.'s Southern Christian Leadership Council; SNCC worked to keep the spirit of resistance alive.

SNCC

In 1961, an interracial group of students, working with the Congress of Racial Equality (CORE), began what they called "freedom rides." Traveling by bus throughout the South, they tried to force the desegregation of bus stations. They were met in some places with such savage violence on the part of whites that the president finally dispatched federal marshals to help keep the peace and ordered the integration of all bus and train stations.

"Freedom Rides"

Events in the Deep South in 1963 helped bring the growing movement to something of a climax. In April, Martin Luther King, Jr., helped launch a series of nonviolent demonstrations in Birmingham, Alabama. Police Commissioner Eugene "Bull" Connor personally supervised a brutal effort to break up the peaceful marches, arresting hundreds of demonstrators and using attack dogs, tear gas, electric cattle prods, and fire hoses—at times even against small children—in full view of television cameras. Two months later, Governor George Wallace stood in the doorway of a building at the University of Alabama to prevent the court-ordered enrollment of several black students. Only after the arrival of federal marshals did he give way. The same night, NAACP official Medgar Evers was murdered in Mississippi. And in September, a bombing of a black church in Birmingham killed four African-American children.

A National Commitment

The president could no longer avoid the issue of race. In an important television address the night of the University of Alabama confrontation, Kennedy spoke eloquently of the "moral issue" facing the nation. Days later, he introduced new legislative proposals prohibiting segregation in "public accommodations" (stores, restaurants, theaters, hotels), barring discrimination in employment, and increasing the power of the government to file suits on behalf of school integration.

To generate support for the legislation, more than 200,000 demonstrators marched down the

THE MARCH ON WASHINGTON, 1963 Martin Luther King, Jr., waves to the vast crowd spreading out from the Lincoln Memorial shortly after delivering his famous "I Have a Dream" speech—the centerpiece of the March on Washington. Initially envisioned as a broad and militant protest against discrimination, it became in the end a moderate, interracial demonstration of support for the civil rights bill President Kennedy had recently proposed to Congress, which passed in 1964. *(Hulton-Deutsch Collection/CORBIS)*

Mall in Washington, D.C., in August 1963 and gathered before the Lincoln Memorial. Martin Luther King, Jr., in one of the greatest speeches of his distinguished oratorical career, aroused the crowd with a litany of images prefaced again and again by the phrase "I have a dream."

The assassination of President Kennedy three months later gave new impetus to the battle for civil rights legislation. The ambitious measure that Kennedy had proposed in June 1963 was stalled in the Senate after having passed through the House of Representatives with relative ease. Early in 1964, after Johnson had applied both public and private pressure, supporters of the measure finally mustered the two-thirds majority necessary to end a filibuster by southern senators; and the Senate passed the most important civil rights bill of the twentieth century.

The Battle for Voting Rights

Having won a significant victory in one area, the civil rights movement shifted its focus to another: voting rights. During the summer of 1964, thousands of civil rights workers, black and white, northern and southern, spread out through the South to work on behalf of black voter registration and participation. The campaign was known as "Freedom Summer," and it produced a violent response from some southern whites. Three of the first freedom workers to arrive in Mississippi—two whites, Andrew Goodman and Michael Schwerner, and one black, James Chaney—were murdered. Local law enforcement officials were involved in the crime.

The "Freedom Summer" also produced the Mississippi Freedom Democratic Party (MFDP), an integrated alternative to the regular state party organization. Under the leadership of Fannie Lou Hamer and others, the MFDP challenged the regular party's right to its seats at the Democratic National Convention that summer. President Johnson, with King's help, managed to broker a compromise by which members of the MFDP could be seated as observers, with promises of party reforms later on, while the regular party retained its official standing.

A year later, in March 1965, King helped organize a major demonstration in Selma, Alabama, to press for the right of blacks to register to vote.

Selma sheriff Jim Clark led local police in a brutal attack on the demonstrators, which was televised nationally. Two northern whites participating in the Selma march were murdered in the course of the effort there. The widespread national outrage that followed the events in Alabama helped push Lyndon Johnson to propose and win passage of the Civil Rights Act of 1965, better known as the Voting Rights Act, which provided federal protection to African Americans attempting to exercise their right to vote. But important as such gains were, they failed to satisfy the rapidly rising expectations of American blacks.

The Changing Movement

By 1966, although the economic condition of most Americans was improving, in many poor urban black communities things were getting significantly worse. More than half of all nonwhite Americans lived in poverty at the beginning of the 1960s.

By the mid-1960s, therefore, the issue of race was moving beyond the issue of formal, legal segregation to an attack on the informal practices that often sustained discrimination. That carried the fight into northern cities, which had no Jim Crow laws but much segregation. African-American leaders began demanding that the battle against job discrimination move to a new level. They argued that the only way for employers to prove that they were not discriminating against African Americans was for them to demonstrate that they were hiring minorities. If necessary, they should adopt positive measures to recruit minorities. Lyndon Johnson gave his support to the concept of "affirmative action" in 1965. Over the next decade, affirmative action guidelines gradually extended to virtually all institutions doing business with or receiving funds from the federal government—and to many others as well.

Urban Violence

The problem of urban poverty had thrust itself into national prominence when riots broke out in black neighborhoods in major cities. There were a few scattered disturbances in the summer of 1964, but the most serious race riot since the end of World War II occurred the following summer in the Watts section of Los Angeles. In the midst of a traffic arrest, a white police officer struck a protesting black bystander with his club. The incident triggered a storm of anger and a week of violence. Thirty-four people died during the uprising, which was eventually quelled by the National Guard. In the summer of 1966, there were forty-three additional outbreaks, the most serious of them in Chicago and Cleveland. And in the summer of 1967, there were eight major disorders, including the largest of them all—a racial clash in Detroit in which forty-three people died.

Televised reports of the violence alarmed millions of Americans and created a growing sense of doubt among some whites who had embraced the cause of racial justice. A special Commission on Civil Disorders created by the president issued a report in the spring of 1968 recommending massive spending to eliminate the abysmal conditions of the ghettoes. To many white Americans, however, the lesson of the riots was the need for stern measures to stop violence and lawlessness.

Black Power

Disillusioned with the ideal of peaceful change through cooperation with whites, an increasing number of African Americans were turning to the philosophy of "black power." Black power meant many different things. But in all its forms, it suggested a shift away from the goal of assimilation and toward increased awareness of racial distinctiveness.

Racial Distinctiveness Emphasized

Perhaps the most enduring impact of the black-power ideology was a social and psychological one: instilling racial pride in African Americans. But black power took political forms as well, and it created a deep schism within the civil rights movement. Traditional black organizations that emphasized cooperation with sympathetic whites—groups such as the NAACP, the Urban League, and King's Southern Christian Leadership Conference—now faced competition from more radical groups. The Student Nonviolent Coordinating Committee and the Congress of Racial Equality had both begun as relatively moderate, interracial organizations. By the mid-1960s, however, these and other groups were calling for more radical and occasionally even violent action against the racism of white society.

The most radical expressions of the black-power idea

Black Panthers

came from such revolutionary organizations as the Black Panthers, based in Oakland, California, and the separatist group, the Nation of Islam, which denounced whites as "devils" and appealed to blacks to embrace the Islamic faith and work for complete racial separation. The most celebrated of the Black Muslims, as whites often termed them, was Malcolm Little, who had adopted the name Malcolm X ("X" to denote his lost African surname). He died in 1965 when black gunmen, presumably under orders from rivals within the Nation of Islam, assassinated him. But he remained a major figure in many black communities long after his death.

"FLEXIBLE RESPONSE" AND THE COLD WAR

In international affairs as much as in domestic reform, the optimistic liberalism of the Kennedy and Johnson administrations dictated a more active and aggressive approach than that of the 1950s.

Diversifying Foreign Policy

The Kennedy administration entered office convinced that the United States needed to be able to counter communist aggression in more flexible ways. In particular, Kennedy was unsatisfied with the nation's ability to meet communist threats in "emerging areas" of the Third World—the areas in which, Kennedy believed, the real struggle against communism would be waged in the future. He gave enthusiastic support to the expansion of the Special Forces (or "Green Berets," as they were soon known)—soldiers trained specifically to fight guerrilla conflicts and other limited wars.

Kennedy also favored expanding American influence through peaceful means. To repair the badly deteriorating relationship with Latin America, he proposed an "Alliance for Progress": a series of projects

"Alliance for Progress"

for peaceful development and stabilization of the nations of that region. Kennedy also inaugurated the Agency for International Development (AID) to coordinate foreign aid. And he established the Peace Corps, which sent young American volunteers abroad to work in developing areas.

Among the first foreign policy ventures of the Kennedy administration was a disastrous assault on the Castro government in Cuba. The Eisenhower administration had started the project; and by the time Kennedy took office, the CIA had been working for months to train a small army of anti-Castro Cuban exiles in Central America. On April 17, 1961, with the approval of the new president, 2,000 of the armed exiles landed at the Bay of Pigs in Cuba, expecting first American air support and then a spontaneous uprising by the Cuban people on their behalf. They received neither. At the last minute, as it became clear that things were going badly, Kennedy withdrew the air support, fearful of involving the United States too directly in the invasion. The expected uprising did not occur. Instead, well-armed Castro forces easily crushed the invaders.

Bay of Pigs

Confrontations with the Soviet Union

In the grim aftermath of the Bay of Pigs, Kennedy traveled to Vienna in June 1961 for his first meeting with Soviet Premier Nikita Khrushchev. Their frosty exchange of views did little to reduce tensions between the two nations—nor did Khrushchev's veiled threat of war unless the United States ceased to support a noncommunist West Berlin in the heart of East Germany.

Khrushchev was particularly unhappy about the mass exodus of residents of East Germany to the West through the easily traversed border in the center of Berlin. But he ultimately found a method short of war to stop it. Before dawn on August 13, 1961, the East German government, complying with directives from Moscow, constructed a wall between East and West Berlin. Guards fired on those who continued to try to escape. For nearly thirty years, the Berlin Wall served as the most potent physical symbol of the conflict between the communist and noncommunist worlds.

The rising tensions culminated the following October in the most dangerous and dramatic crisis of the Cold War. During the summer of 1962, American intelligence agencies had become aware of the arrival of a new wave of Soviet technicians and equipment in Cuba and of military construction in progress. On October 14, aerial reconnaissance photos produced clear evidence that the Soviets were constructing sites on the island for offensive nuclear weapons. To the Soviets, placing missiles in Cuba probably seemed a reasonable—and relatively inexpensive—way to counter the presence of

Cuban Missile Crisis

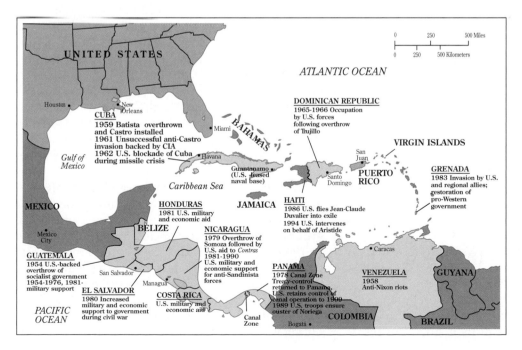

THE UNITED STATES IN LATIN AMERICA, 1954–2001 The Cold War greatly increased the readiness of the United States to intervene in the affairs of its Latin American neighbors. During much of this period, the interventions were driven by fears that communists might take over nations near the United States as they had taken over Cuba in the early 1960s. ■ *What other interests motivated the U.S. to exert influence in Latin America, even after the end of the Cold War?*

American missiles in Turkey (and a way to deter any future American invasion of Cuba). But to Kennedy and most other Americans, the missile sites represented an act of aggression by the Soviets toward the United States. Almost immediately, the president decided that the weapons could not be allowed to remain. On October 22, he ordered a naval and air blockade around Cuba, a "quarantine" against all offensive weapons. Preparations were under way for an American air attack on the missile sites when, late in the evening of October 26, Kennedy received a message from Khrushchev implying that the Soviet Union would remove the missile bases in exchange for an American pledge not to invade Cuba. Ignoring other, tougher Soviet messages, the president agreed. The crisis soon ended.

Johnson and the World

Lyndon Johnson entered the presidency with little prior experience in international affairs. He was eager, therefore, not only to continue the policies of his predecessor but to prove quickly that he too was a strong and forceful leader.

| Intervention in the Dominican Republic |

An internal rebellion in the Dominican Republic gave him an early opportunity to do so. A 1961 assassination had toppled the repressive dictatorship of General Rafael Trujillo, and for the next four years various factions in the country had struggled for dominance. In the spring of 1965, a conservative regime began to collapse in the face of a revolt by a broad range of groups on behalf of the left-wing nationalist Juan Bosch. Arguing (without any evidence) that Bosch planned to establish a pro-Castro, communist regime, Johnson dispatched 30,000 American troops to quell the disorder. Only after a conservative candidate defeated Bosch in a 1966 election were the forces withdrawn.

From Johnson's first moments in office, however, his foreign policy was almost totally dominated by the bitter civil war in Vietnam.

THE AGONY OF VIETNAM

George Kennan, who helped devise the containment doctrine, once called the Vietnam conflict "the most disastrous of all America's undertakings over the whole 200 years of its history." In retrospect, few would now wholly disagree. Yet at first, the conflict in Vietnam seemed simply one more Third World struggle on the periphery of the Cold War.

America and Diem

Having thrown its support to the new leader of South Vietnam, Ngo Dinh Diem, in the aftermath of the 1954 Geneva accords, and having supported Diem in his refusal to hold the elections in 1956 that the accords had required, the United States found itself drawn steadily deeper into the unstable politics of this fractious new nation.

Although Diem was an aristocratic Catholic from central Vietnam, an outsider | Growing Support for Diem | in the south, he was also a nationalist. And he was, for a time, apparently successful. With the help of the CIA, Diem waged an effective campaign against some of the powerful religious sects and the South Vietnamese mafia, which had challenged the authority of the central government. As a result, the United States came to regard Diem as a powerful alternative to Ho Chi Minh. America poured military and economic aid into South Vietnam.

Diem's early successes in suppressing the sects in Vietnam led him in 1959 to begin a similar campaign to eliminate the supporters of Ho Chi Minh, the Vietminh, who had stayed behind in the south after the partition. That campaign persuaded Ho to resume the armed struggle for national unification. In 1959, the Vietminh cadres in the south created the National Liberation Front (NLF), known to many Americans as the Viet Cong—an organization closely allied with the North Vietnamese government. In 1960, under orders from North Vietnam, the NLF began military operations in the south. This marked the beginning of what Americans know as the Vietnam War.

By 1961, NLF forces had established effective control over many areas of the countryside. Diem was also by now losing the support of many other groups in South Vietnam, including his own military. In 1963, the Diem regime precipitated a major crisis by trying to discipline and repress the South Vietnamese Buddhists in an effort to make Catholicism the dominant religion of the country. The Buddhists staged enormous antigovernment demonstrations, during which several monks doused themselves with

THE WAR IN VIETNAM AND INDOCHINA, 1964–1975 Much of the Vietnam War was fought in small engagements in widely scattered areas and did not conform to traditional notions of combat. But as this map shows, there were traditional battles and invasions and supply routes as well. ▐ *What is there in the geography of Indochina, as presented on this map, that helps to explain the great difficulty the American military had in securing South Vietnam against communist attacks?*

gasoline, sat cross-legged in the streets of downtown Saigon, and set themselves on fire—in view of photographers and television cameras.

American officials pressured Diem to reform his now tottering government, but the president made no significant concessions. As a result, in the fall of 1963, Kennedy gave his approval to a plot by a group of South Vietnamese generals to topple Diem. In early November 1963, the generals staged the coup, assassinated Diem along with his brother and principal adviser, Ngo Dinh Nhu, and established the first of a series of new governments, which were, for

Diem Assassinated

over three years, even less stable than the one they had overthrown. A few weeks after the coup, John Kennedy too was dead.

From Aid to Intervention

Lyndon Johnson, therefore, inherited what was already a substantial American commitment to the survival of an anticommunist South Vietnam. During his first months in office, he expanded the American involvement in Vietnam only slightly, sending an additional 5,000 military advisers there and preparing to send 5,000 more. Then, early in August 1964, the president announced that American destroyers on patrol in international waters in the Gulf of Tonkin had been attacked by North Vietnamese torpedo boats. Later information raised serious doubts as to whether the administration reported the attacks accurately. At the time, however, virtually no one questioned Johnson's portrayal of the incident as a serious act of aggression. By a vote of 416 to 0 in the House and 88 to 2 in the Senate, Congress hurriedly passed

Gulf of Tonkin Resolution

the Gulf of Tonkin Resolution, which authorized the president to "take all necessary measures" to protect American forces and "prevent further aggression" in Southeast Asia.

With the South Vietnamese leadership still in disarray, more and more of the burden of opposition to the Viet Cong fell on the United States. In February 1965, after communist forces attacked an American military base at Pleiku, Johnson ordered American bombings of the north, in an attempt to destroy the depots and transportation lines responsible for the flow of North Vietnamese soldiers and supplies into South Vietnam. The bombing continued intermittently until 1972. A month later, in March 1965, two battalions of American marines landed at Da Nang in South Vietnam. There were now more than 100,000 American troops in Vietnam.

Four months later, the president announced that American soldiers would now begin playing an active role in the conflict. By the end of the year, there were more than 180,000 American combat troops in Vietnam; in 1966, that number doubled; and by the end of 1967, there were over 500,000 American soldiers there. In the meantime, the air war intensified.

The Quagmire

"Attrition" Strategy

Central to the American war effort in Vietnam was the strategy known to the military as "attrition," one premised on the belief that the United States could inflict more damage on the enemy than the enemy could absorb. But the attrition strategy failed because the North Vietnamese were willing to commit many more soldiers and resources to the conflict than the United States had predicted.

It failed, too, because the United States was wrong in expecting its bombing of the north to eliminate the communists' war-making capacity. North Vietnam had relatively few of the sort of targets against which bombing is effective. The North

Vietnamese also responded to the bombing with great ingenuity: creating a network of underground tunnels, shops, and factories; securing substantial aid from the Soviet Union and China; and continually moving the Ho Chi Minh Trail to make it elusive to American bombers. Far from breaking the north's resolve, the bombing seemed actually to strengthen popular commitment to the war.

Another important part of the American strategy was the "pacification" pro-gram, whose purpose was to push the Viet Cong from particular regions and then "pacify" those regions by winning the "hearts and minds" of the people. Routing the Viet Cong was often possible, but the subsequent pacification was more difficult. Gradually, the pacification program gave way to a relocation strategy, through which American troops uprooted villagers from their homes, sent them fleeing to refugee camps or into the cities, and then destroyed the vacated villages.

"Pacification"

As the war dragged on and victory remained elusive, some American officers and officials began to urge the president to expand the military efforts. But the Johnson administration resisted—in part because it was beginning to encounter obstacles and frustrations at home.

The War at Home

By the end of 1967, students opposed to the war had become a significant political force. Enormous peace marches in New York, Washington, D.C., and other cities drew broad public attention to the antiwar movement. In the meantime, a growing number of journalists helped sustain the movement with their frank revelations about the brutality and apparent futility of the war.

Growing Antiwar Movement

Senator J. William Fulbright of Arkansas, chairman of the Senate Foreign Relations Committee, also turned against the war and in January 1966 began to stage highly publicized and occasionally televised congressional hearings to air criticisms of it. Other members of Congress joined Fulbright in opposing Johnson's policies—including, in 1967, Robert F. Kennedy, brother of the slain president, now a senator from New York. Even within the administration, the consensus seemed to be crumbling. Robert McNamara, who had done much to help extend the American involvement in Vietnam, left the government in 1968. His successor as secretary of defense, Clark Clifford, became a powerful voice on behalf of a cautious scaling down of that involvement.

In the meantime, Johnson's commitment to fighting the war while continuing his Great Society reforms helped cause a rise in inflation. In August 1967, Johnson asked Congress for a tax increase to avoid even more ruinous inflation. In return, congressional conservatives demanded and received a $6 billion reduction in the funding for Great Society programs.

 Visit Chapter 31 of the book's Online Learning Center for a Where Historians Disagree essay on "The Vietnam Commitment."

War-induced Inflation

THE TRAUMAS OF 1968

By the end of 1967, the twin crises of the war in Vietnam and the deteriorating racial situation at home had produced great social and political tensions. In the course of 1968, those tensions burst to the surface.

The Tet Offensive

On January 31, 1968, the first day of the Vietnamese New Year (Tet), communist forces launched an enormous, concerted attack on American strongholds throughout South Vietnam. A few cities, most notably Hue, fell temporarily to the communists. But what made the Tet offensive so shocking to the American people, who saw vivid reports of it on television, was the sight of communist forces in the heart of Saigon, setting off bombs, shooting down South Vietnamese officials and troops, and holding down fortified areas. The Tet offensive also suggested to the American public something of the brutality of the fighting in Vietnam: Television cameras recorded the sight of a South Vietnamese officer shooting a captured and defenseless young Viet Cong soldier in the head in the streets of Saigon.

American forces soon dislodged the Viet Cong from most of the positions they had seized. The Tet offensive inflicted enormous casualties on the communists and permanently depleted the ranks of the NLF, forcing North Vietnamese troops to take on a much

Political Defeat

larger share of the subsequent fighting. But all that had little impact on American opinion. Tet may have been a military victory for the United States, but it was a political defeat for the administration.

In the following weeks, opposition to the war grew substantially. Leading newspapers and magazines, television commentators, and mainstream politicians began taking public stands against the conflict. Public opposition to the war almost doubled. And Johnson's personal popularity rating had slid to 35 percent, the lowest of any president since Harry Truman.

The Political Challenge

Beginning in the summer of 1967, dissident Democrats tried to mobilize support behind an antiwar candidate who would challenge Lyndon Johnson in the 1968 primaries. When Robert Kennedy turned them down, they recruited Senator Eugene McCarthy of Minnesota. A brilliantly orchestrated campaign by young volunteers in the New Hampshire primary produced a startling showing by McCarthy in March; he nearly defeated the president.

Eugene McCarthy

A few days later, Robert Kennedy entered the campaign, embittering many McCarthy supporters but bringing his own substantial strength among minorities, poor people, and workers to the antiwar cause. Polls showed the president trailing badly in the next scheduled primary, in Wisconsin. On March 31, 1968, Johnson went on television to announce a limited halt in the bombing of North Vietnam and, much more surprising, his withdrawal from the presidential contest.

Robert Kennedy quickly established himself as the champion of the Democratic primaries, winning one election after another. In the meantime, however, Vice President Hubert Humphrey, with the support of President Johnson, entered the contest and began to attract the support of party leaders and of the many delegations that were selected not by popular primaries but by state party organizations. He soon appeared to be the front-runner in the race.

The King Assassination

On April 4, Martin Luther King, Jr., who had traveled to Memphis, Tennessee, to lend his support to striking black sanitation workers in the city, was shot and killed while standing on the balcony of his

JOHNSON AND HUMPHREY, MARCH 27, 1968 Four days before announcing he would not run for reelection, a grim and tired Lyndon Johnson, accompanied by Vice President Hubert Humphrey, receives a briefing on the military situation in Vietnam. *(CORBIS)*

James Earl Ray

motel. The assassin, James Earl Ray, who was captured two months later in London, had no apparent motive. Subsequent evidence suggested that he had been hired by others to do the killing, but he himself never revealed the identity of his employers.

King's tragic death produced a great outpouring of grief. Among African Americans, it also produced anger. In the days after the assassination, major riots broke out in more than sixty American cities. Forty-three people died.

The Kennedy Assassination and Chicago

Late in the night of June 6, Robert Kennedy appeared in the ballroom of a Los Angeles hotel to acknowledge his victory in that day's California primary. As he left the ballroom after his victory statement, Sirhan Sirhan, a young Palestinian apparently enraged by pro-Israeli remarks Kennedy had recently made, emerged from a crowd and shot him in the head. Early the next morning, Kennedy died. The shock of this second tragedy in two months cast a pall over the remainder of the presidential campaign.

When the Democrats finally gathered in Chicago in August, for a convention in which Hubert Humphrey was now the only real contender, even the most optimistic observers were predicting turbulence. Inside the hall, delegates bitterly debated an antiwar plank in the party platform. Miles away,

Democratic National Convention

in a downtown park, thousands of antiwar protesters were staging demonstrations. On the third night of the convention, as the delegates were beginning their balloting, demonstrators and police clashed in a bloody riot in the streets of Chicago. Hundreds of protesters were injured as police attempted to disperse them with tear gas and billy clubs. Aware that the violence was being televised to the nation, the demonstrators taunted the authorities with the chant, "The whole world is watching!" And Hubert Humphrey received a nomination that night which appeared at the time to be almost worthless.

The Conservative Response

The turbulent events of 1968 persuaded some observers that American society was in the throes of revolutionary change. In fact, however, the response of most Americans to the turmoil was a conservative one.

The most visible sign of the conservative backlash was the surprising success of the campaign of George Wallace for the presidency. Wallace had established himself in 1963 as one of the leading spokesmen for the defense of segregation when, as governor of Alabama, he had attempted to block the admission of black students to the University of Alabama. In 1968, he became a third-party candidate for president. He denounced the forced busing of students, the proliferation of government regulations and social programs, and the permissiveness of authorities

George Wallace

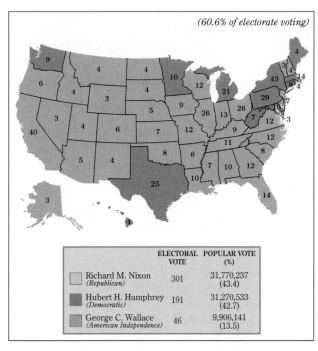

(60.6% of electorate voting)

	ELECTORAL VOTE	POPULAR VOTE (%)
Richard M. Nixon *(Republican)*	301	31,770,237 (43.4)
Hubert H. Humphrey *(Democratic)*	191	31,270,533 (42.7)
George C. Wallace *(American Independence)*	46	9,906,141 (13.5)

THE ELECTION OF 1968 The 1968 presidential election, which Richard Nixon won, was almost as close as the election of 1960, which he lost. ▌ *How does the distribution of Democratic and Republican strength in this election compare to that in 1960?*

OLC **For an interactive version of this map go to** www.mhhe.com/unfinishedinteractive

toward crime, race riots, and antiwar demonstrations. There was never any serious chance that Wallace would win the election, but his standing in the polls rose at times to over 20 percent.

A more effective effort to mobilize the conservative middle in favor of order and stability was under way within the Republican Party. Richard Nixon, whose political career had seemed at an end after his losses in the presidential race of 1960 and a California gubernatorial campaign two years later, reemerged as the spokesman for what he sometimes called the "silent majority." By offering a vision of stability, government retrenchment, and "peace with honor" in Vietnam, he easily captured the nomination of his party for the presidency. And despite a last-minute surge by Humphrey, he hung on to eke out a victory almost as narrow as his defeat in 1960. He received 43.4 percent of the popular vote to Humphrey's 42.7 percent and 301 electoral votes to Humphrey's 191. George Wallace managed to poll 13.5 percent of the popular vote and to carry five southern states. Nixon had hardly won a decisive mandate. But the election made clear that a majority of the electorate was more interested in restoring stability than in promoting social change. For an America in the World feature essay on "1968," visit Chapter 31 of the book's Online Learning Center.

Nixon Elected

Perhaps no decade of the twentieth century created more powerful and enduring images in America than the 1960s. It began with the election—and then the traumatic assassination— of an attractive and energetic young president, John Kennedy, who seemed to symbolize the rising idealism of the time. It produced a dramatic period of political innovation, christened the Great Society by President Lyndon Johnson, which greatly expanded the size and functions of the federal government. It saw the emergence of a sustained and enormously powerful civil rights movement that won a series of important legal victories, including two civil rights acts that dismantled the Jim Crow system constructed in the late nineteenth and early twentieth centuries.

The very spirit of dynamism and optimism that made the early 1960s so productive also helped bring to the surface problems and grievances that had no easy solutions. The civil rights movement awakened expectations of social and economic equality that laws alone could not provide. The peaceful, interracial crusade of the early 1960s gradually turned into a much more militant, confrontational, and increasingly separatist movement. The idealism among white youths that began the 1960s, and played an important role in the political success of John Kennedy, evolved into an angry rebellion against many aspects of American culture and politics and produced a large upsurge of student protest that rocked the nation at the decade's end. Perhaps most of all, a small and largely unnoticed Cold

CONCLUSION

War commitment to defend South Vietnam against communist aggression from the north led to a large and disastrous American military commitment that destroyed the presidency of Lyndon Johnson, shook the faith of millions in their leaders and their political system, sent thousands of young men to their deaths, and showed no signs of producing a victory. A decade that began with soaring ideals ended with deep disillusionment.

INTERACTIVE LEARNING

On the *Primary Source Investigator CD-ROM,* check out a number of valuable tools for further exploration of the content of this chapter.

Interactive Maps
- U.S. Elections (Map M7)
- The Vietnam War (Map M29)
- Patterns of Protest (Map M30)

Primary Sources
Documents, images, and maps related to the turbulent decade of the 1960s, including the Kennedy and Johnson presidencies and the escalation of the Vietnam War. Some highlights include:

- The text of the Gulf of Tonkin Resolution authorizing massive force in Vietnam

- An image of soldiers in the field in Vietnam

- A letter from Ron Ridenhour to government officials, detailing his knowledge of the My Lai Massacre

 Online Learning Center (www.mhhe.com/unfinishedinteractive)
Explore this rich website, providing additional exploration of the material covered in this chapter, online versions of the interactive maps included on the Primary Source Investigator CD-ROM, as well as several study aids, including a multiple-choice quiz, essay questions, a glossary, and other valuable tools. In the Online Learning Center for this chapter look for two *Interactive Feature Essays* on:

- **Where Historians Disagree: The Vietnam Commitment**

- **America in the World: 1968**

FOR FURTHER REFERENCE

Allen J. Matusow, *The Unraveling of America: A History of Liberalism in the 1960s* (1984) is a provocative history of this turbulent decade. David Farber, *The Age of Great Dreams: America in the 1960s* (1994) is an intelligent and lively general history. Arthur M. Schlesinger, Jr., *A Thousand Days* (1965) is a celebrated and celebratory memoir of the Kennedy years. Garry Wills, *The Kennedy Imprisonment* (1982) is an important demystification. Robert Dallek, *Lone Star Rising: Lyndon Johnson and His Times, 1908–1960* (1991) and *Flawed Giant: Lyndon B. Johnson, 1960–1973* (1998) are an important biography. Rick Perlstein, *Before the Storm: Barry Goldwater and the Unmaking of the American Consensus* (2001) is an excellent biography of the first postwar hero of the right, and Matthew Dallek, *The Right Moment: Ronald Reagan's First*

Victory and the Decisive Turning Point in American Politics (2000) is a good study of the rise of Reagan in the 1960s. Robert Weisbrot, *Freedom Bound: A History of America's Civil Rights Movement* (1990) is a good synthetic history of the movement. John Dittmer, *Local People: The Struggle for Civil Rights in Mississippi* (1994) is an important study of the grassroots origins of the movement. William Chafe, *Civilities and Civil Rights: Greensboro, North Carolina, and the Black Struggle for Freedom* (1980) is an excellent study of the southern civil rights movement and the white reaction to it. Taylor Branch, *Parting the Waters: America in the King Years, 1959–1963* (1988) and *Pillar of Fire: America in the King Years, 1963–1965* (1998) are good narrative histories of the movement. Nicholas Lemann, *The Promised Land: The Great Black*

Migration and How it Changed America (1991) is a challenging study of the postwar African-American migration to northern cities and of the Great Society's response to it. Graham T. Allison, *The Essence of Decision: Explaining the Cuban Missile Crisis* (1971) is an important interpretation of the greatest crisis of the Cold War. Ernest R. May and Philip D. Zelikow, *The Kennedy Tapes: Inside the White House during the Cuban Missile Crisis* (1997) provides the annotated transcripts of the taped meetings of Kennedy's inner circle during the crisis. Robert D. Schulzinger, *A Time for War: The United States and Vietnam, 1945–1975* (1997) is a good general history of the war. Neil Sheehan, *A Bright Shining Lie: John Paul Vann and America in Vietnam* (1988) is a compelling picture of the war as experienced by a significant military figure of the 1960s. Frederik Logevall, *Choosing War: The Lost Chance for Peace and the Escalation of War in Vietnam* (1999); David Kaiser, *American Tragedy: Kennedy, Johnson, and the Origins of Vietnam* (2000); A.J. Langguth, *Our Vietnam/Nuoc Viet Ta: A History of the War, 1954–1975* (2000); and James Mann, *A Grand Delusion: America's Descent into Vietnam* (2001) are important recent studies. Christian J. Appy, *Working-Class War: American Combat Soldiers and Vietnam* (1993) examines the class basis of the army that fought in Vietnam. Larry Berman, *Planning a Tragedy* (1982) and *Lyndon Johnson's War*

(1989); Leslie Gelb and Richard Betts, *The Irony of Vietnam: The System Worked* (1979); and David Halberstam, *The Best and the Brightest* (1972) are important interpretations of the American decision to intervene and stay in Vietnam. Dan T. Carter, *The Politics of Rage: George Wallace, The Origins of the New Conservatism, and the Transformation of American Politics* (1995) is a good study of the career of George Wallace. David Farber, *Chicago '68* (1988) examines the turbulent Democratic Convention and, through it, the passions that shaped a traumatic year in recent American history.

Berkeley in the Sixties (1990) is a documentary film portraying the tumultuous student politics at the University of California, Berkeley, and through them larger themes of the decade. *Eyes on the Prize: The American Civil Rights Struggle, 1954–1965* (1986–1987) is a six-part film series by Blackside Productions on the history of the civil rights movement. *Malcolm X: Make it Plain* (1994) is the definitive film biography of Malcolm X. *The Kennedys* (1992) is a film presentation on the lives of President John F. Kennedy and various members of his powerful family. *LBJ* (1991), a film by David Grubin, is a biographical treatment of President Lyndon Johnson. *America's War on Poverty* (1995) is a five-part series on the Kennedy and Johnson administrations' most dramatic welfare initiative.

CHAPTER

The Crisis of Authority

32

(AP/Wide World Photos)

The election of Richard Nixon in 1968 was the result of more than the unpopularity of Lyndon Johnson and the war. It was the result, too, of a broad popular reaction against what many Americans considered a dangerous assault on the foundations of their society and culture. In Richard Nixon such Americans found a man who seemed to match their mood. Himself a product of a hardworking, middle-class family, he projected an image of dedication to traditional values. Yet the presidency of Richard Nixon, far from returning calm and stability to American politics, coincided with, and helped to produce, more years of crisis.

THE YOUTH CULTURE

Perhaps most alarming to many conservatives in the 1960s and 1970s was a pattern of protest by younger Americans, who were giving vent to two related impulses. One was the impulse, emerging from the political left, to create a great new community of "the people," which would rise up to break the power of elites and force the nation to end the war, pursue racial and economic justice, and transform its political life. The other impulse was the vision of personal "liberation." It found expression in part through the efforts of many groups—African Americans, Indians, Hispanics, women, gay people, and others—to define and assert themselves. It also found expression through the efforts of some individuals to create a new culture—one that would allow them to escape from the dehumanizing pressures of the modern "technocracy."

Personal "Liberation"

The New Left

Among the products of the racial crisis and the war in Vietnam was a radicalization of many American students, who in the course of the 1960s formed what became known as the New Left. In 1962, a group of students gathered in Michigan to form Students for a Democratic Society (SDS). Their declaration of beliefs, the Port Huron Statement, expressed their disillusionment with the society they had inherited and their determination to build a new politics. In the following years, SDS became the leading organization of student radicalism.

Campus Unrest

Since most members of the New Left were students, much of their radicalism centered on issues related to the modern university. A 1964 dispute at the University of California at Berkeley over the rights of students to engage in political activities on campus—the Free Speech Movement—was the first outburst of campus protest. The antiwar movement greatly inflamed and expanded the challenge to the universities; and beginning in 1968, campus demonstrations, riots, and building seizures became almost commonplace. At Columbia University in New York, students seized the offices of the president and others and occupied them for several days until local police ejected them. Over the next several years, hardly any major university was immune to some level of disruption. Small groups of especially dogmatic radicals—among them the "Weathermen," an offshoot of SDS—were responsible for a few cases of arson and bombing that destroyed campus buildings and claimed several lives.

Not many people ever accepted the radical political philosophy of the New Left. But many supported the position of SDS and other groups on particular issues, and above all on the Vietnam War. Between 1967 and 1969, student activists organized some of the largest political demonstrations in American history to protest the war.

A related issue that helped fuel the antiwar movement was opposition to the military draft. The gradual abolition of many traditional deferments—for graduate students, teachers, husbands, fathers, and others—swelled the ranks of those faced with conscription. Many draft-age Americans simply refused induction, accepting jail terms as a result. Thousands of others fled to Canada, Sweden, and elsewhere.

Opposition to the Draft

	1963	1964	1966	1968	1969	1970
	Friedan's *The Feminine Mystique*	Free Speech Movement begins	National Organization for Women formed	Turmoil in universities	Antiwar movement's Vietnam "moratoriums" Rock concert in Woodstock, NY	Cambodian incursion

	1971	1972	1973	1974	1975
	Nixon imposes wage-price controls	Nixon visits China SALT I "Christmas bombing" of North Vietnam Watergate burglary Nixon reelected	U.S. withdraws from Vietnam Arab oil embargo Agnew resigns Supreme Court decides *Roe v. Wade*	Nixon resigns; Ford becomes president	South Vietnam falls

The Counterculture

Closely related to the New Left was a new youth culture openly scornful of the values and conventions of middle-class society. The most visible characteristic of the counterculture, as it became known, was a change in personal styles. Young Americans flaunted long hair, shabby or flamboyant clothing, and a rebellious disdain for traditional speech and decorum. Also important to the counterculture were drugs: marijuana and more potent hallucinogens, such as LSD. There was also a new, more permissive view of sex.

Like the New Left, with which it overlapped, the counterculture challenged the structure of modern American society, attacking what it claimed were its banality, hollowness, and artificiality. The most committed adherents of the counterculture—the hippies, who came to dominate the Haight-Ashbury neighborhood of San Francisco and other places, and the social dropouts, many of whom retreated to rural communes—rejected modern society altogether and attempted to find refuge in a simpler, more "natural" existence. But even those whose commitment to the counterculture was less intense shared a commitment to the idea of personal fulfillment.

The counterculture was only an exaggerated expression of impulses that were coursing through the larger society. Long hair and freakish clothing became the badge of an entire generation. The use of marijuana, the freer attitudes toward sex, the iconoclastic language—all spread far beyond the realm of the hippies and radicals.

One of the most pervasive elements of the new youth society was rock music. Its growing influence in the 1960s was a result in part of the phenomenal popularity of the Beatles, the English group whose first visit to the United States in 1964 created a sensation. For a time, most rock musicians—like most popular musicians before them—concentrated largely on uncontroversial romantic themes. By the late 1960s, however, rock had begun to reflect many of the new iconoclastic values of its time. The Beatles, for example, abandoned their once simple and seemingly innocent style for a new, experimental, even mystical approach that reflected the growing popular fascination with drugs and Eastern religions. Other groups, such as the Rolling Stones, turned even more openly to themes of anger, frustration, and rebelliousness. Many popular musicians used their music to express explicit political radicalism as well—especially some of the leading folk singers of the era, such as

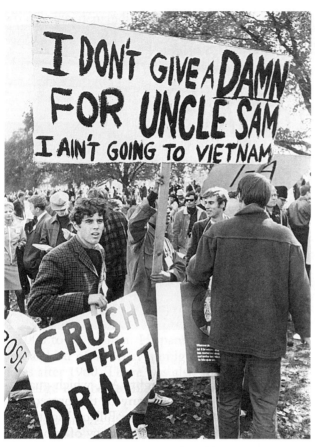

THE WAR AT HOME Demonstrators gather on the Mall in Washington in the fall of 1967 for one of the first of the great antiwar demonstrations of the late 1960s. *(Leif Skoogfors/Woodfin Camp & Associates)*

Bob Dylan and Joan Baez. Rock's driving rhythms, its undisguised sensuality, its often harsh and angry tone—all made it an appropriate vehicle for expressing the social and political unrest of the late 1960s.

A powerful symbol of the fusion of rock music and the counterculture was the music festival at Woodstock, New York, in the summer of 1969, where 400,000 people gathered on a farm for nearly a week. Despite heavy rain, mud, inadequate facilities, and impossible crowding, the crowd remained peaceful and harmonious. Champions of the counterculture spoke rhapsodically of how Woodstock represented the birth of a new youth culture, the "Woodstock nation." Four months later, however, another great rock concert—at the Altamont racetrack near

Woodstock

San Francisco, featuring the Rolling Stones and attended by 300,000 people—became a brutal and violent event at which four people died, several accidentally or from drug overdoses, but one because of injuries received at the hands of members of the Hell's Angels motorcycle gang, who were serving as security guards at the concert.

THE MOBILIZATION OF MINORITIES

The growth of African-American protest encouraged other minorities to demand redress of their grievances. For Indians, Hispanic Americans, gay men and lesbians, and others, the late 1960s and 1970s were a time of growing political activism.

Seeds of Indian Militancy

Few minorities had deeper or more justifiable grievances against the prevailing culture than did American Indians—or Native Americans, as they began to call themselves in the 1960s. Indians were the least prosperous, least healthy, and least stable group in the nation, one that for years had remained largely ignored.

For much of the postwar era, federal policy toward the tribes had been shaped by a determination to incorporate Indians into mainstream American society whether Indians wanted to assimilate or not. Two laws passed in 1953 established the basis of a new policy, which became known as "termination." Through termination, the federal government withdrew all official recognition of the tribes as legal entities and made them subject to the same local jurisdictions as white residents. At the same time, the government encouraged Indians to assimilate into the white world and worked to funnel Native Americans into cities, where, presumably, they would adapt themselves to the larger society and lose their cultural distinctiveness.

"Termination"

The new policies were a failure. Indians fought so bitterly against them that in 1958 the Eisenhower administration barred further "terminations" without the consent of the affected tribes. In the meantime, the struggle against termination mobilized a new generation of Indian militants and breathed life into the National Congress of American Indians, which had been created in 1944.

managed by people who wanted to avoid associations with the radical left, it had an unthreatening quality that made it appealing to many people. According to some estimates, over 20 million Americans joined in some part of the Earth Day observances.

The cautious, centrist character of Earth Day and related efforts to popularize environmentalism helped create a movement that was less divisive than other, more controversial causes. Gradually, environmentalism became more than simply a series of demonstrations and protests. It became part of the consciousness of the vast majority of Americans—absorbed into popular culture, built into primary and secondary education, endorsed by almost all politicians (even if many of them actually opposed some environmental goals).

It also became part of the fabric of public policy. In 1970, Congress passed and President Nixon signed the National Environmental Protection Act, which created a new agency—the Environmental Protection Agency—to en-

EPA Established

force antipollution standards on businesses and consumers. The Clean Air Act, also passed in 1970, and the Clean Water Act, passed in 1972, added additional tools to the government's arsenal of weapons against environmental degradation. The actions of the federal government—and of state and local governments that soon followed its lead—had a measurable impact on many kinds of pollution. Many lakes and rivers that had long been serious environmental hazards became markedly cleaner; restrictions on auto emissions and other air pollutants substantially improved air quality in many cities; industries found it much more difficult to dump toxic wastes in unsafe ways.

But the enlistment of the government behind many of the goals of environmentalists did not put an end to the movement. Different administrations displayed varying levels of support for environmental goals, and advocacy groups remained ready to spring into action to force them to change their positions. And of course new environmental problems continued to emerge even as older ones sometimes found solutions. Environmentalism was simultaneously a movement, a set of public policies, and a broad national ideal—and it was the combination of all those aspects that made it such a continually powerful force in American life.

NIXON, KISSINGER, AND THE WAR

Richard Nixon assumed office in 1969 committed not only to restoring stability at home but to creating a new and more stable order in the world. Central to Nixon's hopes for international stability was a resolution of the stalemate in Vietnam.

Vietnamization

Despite Nixon's own deep interest in international affairs, he brought with him into government a man who at times seemed to overshadow the president himself in the conduct of diplomacy: Henry Kissinger,

Henry Kissinger

a Harvard professor whom Nixon appointed as his special assistant for national security affairs. Kissinger quickly established dominance over Secretary of State William Rogers and Secretary of Defense Melvin Laird, who were both more experienced in public life. Together, Nixon and Kissinger set out to find an acceptable solution to the stalemate in Vietnam.

The new Vietnam policy moved along several fronts. One was the move to "Vietnamize" the conflict—that is, train and equip the South Vietnamese military to assume the burden of combat in place of American forces. In the fall of 1969, Nixon announced the withdrawal of 60,000 American ground troops from Vietnam. By the fall of 1972, relatively few American soldiers remained in Indochina.

Vietnamization (and the decreased draft calls it produced) did help quiet domestic opposition to the war for a time. It did nothing, however, to break the stalemate in the negotiations with the North Vietnamese in Paris. The new administration decided that new military pressures would be necessary to do that.

Escalation

By the end of 1969, Nixon and Kissinger had decided that the most effective way to tip the military balance in America's favor was to destroy the bases in Cambodia and Laos from which the American military believed the North Vietnamese were launching many of their attacks. Very early in his presidency, Nixon secretly ordered the air force to begin bombing Cambodian and Laotian territory to destroy the enemy sanctuaries. On April 30, Nixon went on television to announce that he was ordering American ground troops across the border into Cambodia.

Literally overnight, the Cambodian invasion restored the dwindling antiwar movement to vigorous life. The first days of May saw the most widespread and vocal antiwar demonstrations ever. A mood of crisis was already mounting when, on May 4, four college students were killed and nine others injured after members of the National Guard opened fire on antiwar demonstrators at Kent State University in Ohio.

Kent State

Ten days later, police killed two African-American students at Jackson State University in Mississippi during a demonstration there.

The clamor against the war spread into the government and the press. Congress angrily repealed the Gulf of Tonkin Resolution in December. Then, in June 1971, first the *New York Times* and later other newspapers began publishing excerpts from a secret study of the war prepared by the Defense Department during the Johnson administration. The so-called Pentagon Papers,

Pentagon Papers

leaked to the press by former Defense official Daniel Ellsberg, provided evidence the government had been dishonest, both in reporting the military progress of the war and in explaining its own motives for American involvement. The administration went to court to suppress the documents, but the Supreme Court ruled that the press had the right to publish them.

Morale and discipline among American troops in Vietnam were rapidly deteriorating. The 1971 trial and conviction of Lieutenant William Calley, who was charged with overseeing a massacre of more than 100 unarmed South Vietnamese civilians in 1968 near the village of My Lai, attracted wide public attention to the dehumanizing impact of the war on those who fought it—and to the terrible consequences that dehumanization imposed on the Vietnamese people. Less publicized were other problems among American troops in Vietnam: desertion, drug addiction, racial bias, refusal to obey orders, even the killing of unpopular officers by enlisted men.

By 1971, nearly two-thirds of those interviewed in public opinion polls were urging American withdrawal from Vietnam. President Nixon, however, believed that a defeat in Vietnam would cause unacceptable damage to the nation's (and his own) credibility. The FBI, the CIA, the White House itself, and other federal agencies increased their efforts to discredit and harass antiwar and radical groups, often through illegal means.

In Indochina, meanwhile, the fighting raged on. American bombing in Vietnam and Cambodia increased. In March 1972, the North Vietnamese mounted their biggest offensive since 1968 (the so-called Easter offensive). American and South Vietnamese forces managed to halt the communist

Easter Offensive

advance, but it was clear that without American support the South Vietnamese would not have succeeded. At the same time, Nixon ordered American planes to bomb targets near Hanoi, the capital of North Vietnam, and Haiphong, its principal port, and called for the mining of seven North Vietnamese harbors.

"Peace with Honor"

As the 1972 presidential election approached, the administration stepped up its effort to produce a breakthrough in negotiations with the North Vietnamese. In April 1972, the president dropped his longtime insistence on the removal of North Vietnamese troops from the south before any American withdrawal. Meanwhile, Henry Kissinger met privately in Paris with the North Vietnamese foreign secretary, Le Duc Tho, to work out terms for a cease-fire. On October 26, only days before the presidential election, Kissinger announced that "peace is at hand."

Several weeks later (after the election), negotiations broke down once again. Although both the American and the North Vietnamese governments were ready to accept the Kissinger-Tho plan for a cease-fire, President Nguyen Van Thieu of South Vietnam balked, still insisting on a full withdrawal of North Vietnamese forces from the south. Kissinger tried to win additional concessions from the communists to meet Thieu's objections, but on December 16 talks broke off.

The next day, December 17, American B-52s began the heaviest and most destructive air raids of the entire war on Hanoi, Haiphong, and other North Vietnamese targets. Civilian casualties were high, and fifteen American B–52s were shot down by the

516

On election day, Nixon won reelection by one of the largest margins in history: 60.7 percent of the popular vote compared with 37.5 percent for McGovern, and an electoral margin of 520 to 17. But serious problems, some beyond the president's control and some of his own making, were already lurking in the wings.

The Troubled Economy

Although it was political scandal that would ultimately destroy the Nixon presidency, the most important issue of the early 1970s was the beginning of a long-term transformation of the American economy. For three decades, that economy had been the envy of the world. In fact, however, America's prosperity rested in part on several artificial conditions that were rapidly disappearing by the late 1960s.

The most immediate change was the end of the nation's easy access to cheap raw materials, a change that became a major cause of the serious inflation that plagued the economy through much of the 1970s. For many years, the Organization of Petroleum Exporting Countries (OPEC) had operated as an informal bargaining unit for the sale of oil by Third World nations but had seldom managed to exercise any real strength. But in the early 1970s, OPEC began to assert itself. In 1973, in the midst of the Yom Kippur War, Arab members of OPEC announced that they would no longer ship petroleum to nations supporting Israel. At about the same time, the OPEC nations agreed to raise their prices 500 percent (from $3 to $15 a barrel). These twin shocks produced momentary economic chaos in the West. The United States suffered its first fuel shortage since World War II. And although the crisis eased a few months later, the price of energy continued to skyrocket.

The energy crisis eventually subsided, but another, longer-term change in the American economy was the transformation of the nation's manufacturing sector. Ever since World War II, American industry had enjoyed relatively little competition from the rest of the world. By the end of the 1960s, however, manufacturing in both Western Europe and Japan had recovered, and by the early 1970s they were providing stiff competition to American firms in the sale of automobiles, steel, and many other products. Some American

OPEC

Growing Foreign Competition

corporations failed. Others restructured themselves to become more competitive. In the process, they closed many older plants and eliminated hundreds of thousands of once-lucrative manufacturing jobs. The high-wage, high-employment industrial economy that had been a central fact of American life since the 1940s was gradually disappearing.

The Nixon Response

Nixon's initial answer to these mounting economic problems was to reduce spending and raise taxes, producing a modest budget surplus in 1969. But when those policies proved difficult to sustain, Nixon turned increasingly to control of the currency. Placing conservative economists at the head of the Federal Reserve Board, he ensured sharply higher interest rates and a contraction of the money supply. Even so, the cost of living rose a cumulative 15 percent during Nixon's first two and a half years in office. Economic growth, in the meantime, declined. The United States was encountering a new dilemma: "stagflation," a combination of rising prices and general economic stagnation.

In the summer of 1971, Nixon imposed a ninety-day freeze on all wages and prices at their existing levels. Then, in November, he launched Phase II of his economic plan: mandatory guidelines for some wage and price increases. Inflation subsided temporarily, but the recession continued. Fearful that the recession would be more damaging than inflation

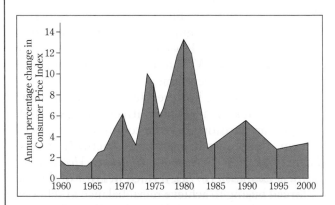

INFLATION, 1960–2000 Inflation was the biggest economic worry of most Americans in the 1970s and early 1980s, and this chart shows why. Having remained very low through the early 1960s, inflation rose slowly in the second half of the decade and then dramatically in the mid- and late 1970s, before beginning a sharp and reasonably steady decline in the early 1980s. ▪ *What caused the great spike in inflation in the 1970s?*

Rising Inflation in an election year, the administration reversed itself late in 1971: interest rates were allowed to drop sharply, and government spending increased. The new tactics helped revive the economy in the short term, but inflation rose substantially. In 1973, prices rose 9 percent; in 1974, after the Arab oil embargo and the OPEC price increases, they rose 12 percent. The new energy crisis, in the meantime, was quickly becoming a national preoccupation. But while Nixon talked often about the need to achieve "energy independence," he offered few concrete proposals.

THE WATERGATE CRISIS

Although economic problems greatly concerned the American people in the 1970s, another stunning development almost entirely preoccupied the nation beginning early in 1973: the fall of Richard Nixon. The president's demise was a result in part of his own personality. But the larger explanation for the crisis lay in Nixon's view of American society and the world. The president believed the United States faced grave dangers from the radicals and dissidents who were challenging his policies. He came increasingly to consider any challenge to his policies a threat to "national security," thus creating a climate in which he could justify almost any tactics to stifle dissent and undermine opposition.

The Scandals

Early on the morning of June 17, 1972, police arrested five men who had broken into the offices of the Democratic National Committee in the Watergate office building in Washington, D.C. Two others were seized a short time later and charged with supervising the break-in. When reporters for the *Washington Post* began researching the backgrounds of the culprits, they discovered that among those involved in the burglary were former employees of the Committee for the Re-Election of the President (CRP). One of them had worked in the White House itself. They had, moreover, been paid for the break-in from a secret fund of the reelection committee, a fund controlled by, among others, members of the White House staff.

Public interest in the disclosures grew slowly in the last months of 1972. Early in 1973, however, the Watergate burglars went on trial; and under prodding from federal judge John J. Sirica, one of the defendants, James W. McCord, agreed to cooperate both with the grand jury and with a special Senate investigating committee recently established under Senator Sam J. Ervin of North Carolina. McCord's testimony opened a floodgate of confessions, and for months a parade of White House and campaign officials exposed one illegality after another. Foremost among them was a member of the inner circle of the White House, John Dean, counsel to the president, who leveled allegations against Nixon himself.

Two different sets of scandals emerged from the investigations. One was a general pattern of abuses of power involving both the White House and the Nixon campaign committee. The other scandal was the way in which the administration tried to manage the investigations of the Watergate break-in and other abuses—a pattern of behavior that became known as the "cover-up." **Watergate "Cover-up"** There was never any conclusive evidence that the president had planned or approved the burglary in advance. But there was mounting evidence that he had been involved in illegal efforts to obstruct investigations of the episode.

Nixon accepted the departure of members of his administration implicated in the scandals. But the president continued to insist on his own innocence. There the matter might have rested had it not been for the disclosure during the Senate hearings of a White House **Watergate Tapes** taping system that had recorded virtually every conversation in the president's office during the period in question. All those investigating the scandals sought access to the tapes; Nixon, pleading "executive privilege," refused to release them. A special prosecutor appointed by the president to handle the Watergate cases, Harvard law professor Archibald Cox, took Nixon to court in October 1973 in an effort to force him to relinquish the recordings. Nixon, now clearly growing desperate, fired Cox and suffered the humiliation of watching both Attorney General Elliot Richardson and his deputy resign in protest. This "Saturday night massacre" made the president's predicament much worse. Not only did public pressure force him to appoint a new special prosecutor, Texas attorney Leon Jaworski, but the episode precipitated an investigation by the House of Representatives into the possibility of impeachment.

The Fall of Richard Nixon

Nixon's situation deteriorated further in the following months. Late in 1973, Vice President Spiro Agnew became embroiled in a scandal of his own when evidence surfaced that he had accepted bribes and kickbacks while serving as governor of Maryland and even as vice president. In return for a Justice Department agreement not to press the case, Agnew pleaded no contest to a lesser charge of income-tax evasion and resigned from the government. With the controversial Agnew no longer in line to succeed to the presidency, the prospect of removing Nixon from the White House became less worrisome to his opponents. The new vice president was House Minority Leader Gerald Ford, an amiable and popular Michigan congressman.

The impeachment investigation quickly gathered momentum. In April 1974, in an effort to head off further subpoenas of the tapes, the president released transcripts of a number of relevant conversations, claiming that they proved his innocence. Investigators and much of the public felt otherwise. Even these edited tapes seemed to suggest Nixon's complicity in the cover-up. In July, the crisis reached a climax. First the Supreme Court ruled unanimously, in *United States v. Richard M. Nixon*, that the president must relinquish the tapes to Special Prosecutor Jaworski. Days later, the House Judiciary Committee voted to recommend three articles of impeachment.

United States v. Richard Nixon

Even without additional evidence, Nixon might well have been impeached by the full House and convicted by the Senate. Early in August, however, he provided at last the "smoking gun"—the concrete proof of his guilt—that his defenders had long contended was missing from the case against him. Among the tapes that the Supreme Court compelled Nixon to relinquish were several that offered apparently incontrovertible evidence of his involvement in the Watergate cover-up. Only three days after the burglary, the recordings disclosed, the president had ordered the FBI to stop investigating the break-in. Impeachment and conviction now seemed inevitable.

For several days, Nixon brooded in the White House, on the verge, some claimed, of a breakdown. Finally, on August 8, 1974, he announced his resignation. At noon the next day, while Nixon and his family were flying west to their home in California, Gerald Ford took the oath of office as president. Visit Chapter 32 of the book's Online Learning Center for a Where Historians Disagree essay on "Watergate."

Nixon's Resignation

OLC

Many Americans expressed relief and exhilaration that, as the new president put it, "our long national nightmare is over." But the wave of good feeling could not obscure the deeper and more lasting damage of the Watergate crisis. In a society in which distrust of leaders and institutions of authority was already widespread, the fall of Richard Nixon confirmed for many Americans their most cynical assumptions about the character of American public life.

CONCLUSION

The victory of Richard Nixon in the 1968 presidential election represented a call for a restoration of order and stability. But order and stability were not the dominant characteristics of Nixon's troubled years in office. American culture and society in the late 1960s and early 1970s were shaped decisively by, and were deeply divided over, the challenges by young people to the norms by which most Americans had lived. They were also the years in which a host of new liberation movements joined the drive for racial equality, and when, above all, women mobilized effectively and powerfully to demand changes in the way their society treated gender differences.

Nixon had run for office attacking the failure of his predecessor to end the war in Vietnam. But for four years under his presidency, the war—and the protests against it—continued. The division of opinion over the war continued to poison the nation's politics and social fabric until the American role in the conflict finally shuddered to a close in 1973.

But much of the controversy and division in the 1970s was a product of the Nixon presidency itself. Nixon was in many ways a dynamic and even visionary leader, who proposed some important domestic reforms and made important changes in American foreign policy, most notably making overtures to communist China and forging a frail détente with the Soviet Union. He was also, however, a devious, secretive, and embittered man whose White House became engaged in a series of covert activities—many of them connected with the president's reelection campaign in 1972—that produced the most dramatic political scandal in American history. Watergate, as it was called, preoccupied much of the nation for nearly two years beginning in 1972; and ultimately, in the summer of 1974, the scandal forced Nixon to become the first president in American history to resign.

INTERACTIVE LEARNING

On the *Primary Source Investigator CD-ROM*, check out a number of valuable tools for further exploration of the content of this chapter.

Interactive Maps
- The Vietnam War (Map M29)
- Patterns of Protest (Map M30)
- Middle East Conflicts (Map M28)

Primary Sources
Documents, images, and maps related to the social changes in the late 1960s and 1970s, the presidency of Richard Nixon, and the Watergate scandal. Some highlights include:

- An excerpt from Betty Friedan's *The Feminine Mystique*
- Documents related to the Watergate scandal, the

ensuing investigation, and the resignation of President Nixon

- Text of the legislation that established the Environmental Protection Agency

 Online Learning Center (www.mhhe.com/unfinishedinteractive)
Explore this rich website, providing additional exploration of the material covered in this chapter, online versions of the interactive maps included on the Primary Source Investigator CD-ROM, as well as several study aids, including a multiple-choice quiz, essay questions, a glossary, and other valuable tools. In the Online Learning Center for this chapter look for an *Interactive Feature Essay* on:

- **Where Historians Disagree: Watergate**

FOR FURTHER REFERENCE

John Morton Blum, *Years of Discord: American Politics and Society, 1961–1974* (1991) is a good overview. James Miller, *"Democracy in the Streets": From Port Huron to the Siege of Chicago* (1987) is a perceptive history of the New Left through its leading organization, SDS. Kristin Luker, *Abortion and the Politics of Motherhood* (1984) is an excellent account of this central battle over the nature of feminism. Daniel Horowitz, *Betty Friedan and the Making of "The Feminine Mystique"* (1998) is a fine study of a major figure in the

feminist movement. Margaret Cruikshank, *The Rise of a Gay and Lesbian Liberation Movement* (1992) recounts another important struggle of the 1960s and beyond. David Allyn, *Make Love Not War: The Sexual Revolution: An Unfettered History* (2000) and Beth Bailey, *Sex in the Heartland* (1999) are studies of a major social change. Ronald Takaki, *Strangers from a Distant Shore: A History of Asian Americans* (1989) examines the growing Asian community in postwar America. Stephen Ambrose, *Nixon: The Triumph of a Politician, 1962–1972*

(1989), and *Nixon, Ruin and Recovery, 1973–1990* (1992) provide a thorough chronicle of this important presidency. Joan Hoff, *Nixon Reconsidered* (1994) is a more sympathetic account of Nixon's presidency before Watergate. Stanley I. Kutler, *The Wars of Watergate* (1990) is a scholarly study of the great scandal, and Jonathan Schell, *The Time of Illusion* (1975) is a perceptive contemporary account. Marilyn Young, *The Vietnam Wars, 1945–1990* (1991) provides, among other things, a full account of the last years of American involvement in Vietnam and of the conflicts in the region that followed the American withdrawal. Larry Berman, *No Peace, No Honor: Nixon, Kissinger, and Betrayal in Vietnam* (2001) is a study of the end of the war.

Chicago 1968 (1995) is a complex and riveting film portrait of the dramatic events around the Democratic National Convention of 1968. The three-part film series *America in 1968* (1979) examines the political, cultural, and international events of that pivotal year. *Nixon* (1990) is a three-hour film biography of one of the most powerful and controversial figures in modern American history. *Watergate* (1994) is a documentary film on the unmaking of the Nixon presidency, including recent interviews with major participants. *In the Spirit of Crazy Horse* (1990) relates the history of the Lakota Indians on the centennial of the Wounded Knee massacre. *Chicano! History of the Mexican-American Civil Rights Movement* (1996) is a four-part series on the Mexican-American movement from 1967.

33

CHAPTER

From "the Age of Limits" to the Age of Reagan

(Dirck Halstead/Getty Images)

The frustrations of the early 1970s—the defeat in Vietnam, the Watergate crisis, the decay of the American economy—inflicted damaging blows to the confident, optimistic nationalism that had characterized so much of the postwar era. Some Americans responded to these problems by announcing the arrival of an "age of limits," in which America would have to learn to live with increasingly constricted expectations. By the end of the decade, however, another response to the challenges was gaining strength—one that combined a conservative retreat from some of the heady visions of the 1960s with a reinforced commitment to the idea of economic growth, international power, and American virtue.

POLITICS AND DIPLOMACY AFTER WATERGATE

In the aftermath of Richard Nixon's ignominious departure from office, many wondered whether faith in the presidency, and in the government as a whole, could easily be restored. The administrations of the two presidents who succeeded Nixon did little to answer those questions.

The Ford Custodianship

Gerald Ford inherited the presidency under unenviable circumstances. He had to try to rebuild confidence in government in the wake of the Watergate scandals. And he had to try to restore prosperity in the face of major economic difficulties.

The new president's effort to establish himself as a symbol of political integrity suffered a setback only a month after he took office, when he granted Richard Nixon "a full, free, **Nixon Pardoned** and absolute pardon" for any crimes he may have committed during his presidency. The pardon caused a decline in Ford's popularity from which he never fully recovered.

In his efforts to curb inflation, the president called for largely ineffective voluntary efforts. After supporting high interest rates, opposing increased federal spending (through liberal use of his veto power), and resisting pressures for a tax reduction, Ford had to deal with a serious recession in 1974 and 1975. Central to the eco-**Economic Problems** nomic problems was the continuing energy crisis. In the aftermath of the Arab oil embargo of 1973, the OPEC cartel raised the price of oil—by 400 percent in 1974 alone—one of the principal reasons why inflation reached 11 percent in 1976.

Ford retained Henry Kissinger as secretary of state and continued the general policies of the Nixon years. Late in 1974, Ford met with Leonid Brezhnev at Vladivostok in Siberia and signed an arms control accord that was to serve as the basis for SALT II, thus achieving a goal the Nixon administration had long sought. Meanwhile, in the Middle East, Henry Kissinger helped produce a new accord by which Israel agreed to return large portions of the occupied Sinai to Egypt, and the two nations pledged not to resolve future differences by force.

As the 1976 presidential election approached, Ford's **1976 Election** policies were coming under attack from both the right and the left. In the Republican primary campaign, Ford faced a powerful challenge from former California governor Ronald Reagan, leader of the party's conservative wing. The president only barely survived the assault to win his party's nomination. The Democrats, in the meantime, were gradually uniting behind a new and, before 1976, almost entirely unknown candidate: Jimmy Carter, a former governor of Georgia. Unhappiness with the economy and a general disenchantment with Ford enabled the Democrat to win a narrow victory. Carter received 50 percent of the popular vote to Ford's 47.9 percent and 297 electoral votes to Ford's 240.

The Trials of Jimmy Carter

Like Ford, Jimmy Carter assumed the presidency at a moment when the nation faced problems of staggering complexity and difficulty. But Carter seemed

TIME LINE

1974	1976	1977	1978–1979	1980	1981	1982	1983
"Stagflation" Ford pardons Nixon	Carter elected president	Panama Canal treaties signed Apple introduces first personal computer	Camp David accords American hostages in Iran Soviet Union invades Afghanistan U.S. and China restore relations Three Mile Island nuclear accident	U.S. boycotts Moscow Olympics Reagan elected president	American hostages in Iran released Reagan wins tax and budget cuts U.S. military buildup begins AIDS first reported in U.S.	Severe recession	U.S. invades Grenada

1984	1985	1986	1987	1988	1989	1990	1991	1992
Reagan reelected	Reagan and Gorbachev meet Crack cocaine appears in U.S. cities	U.S. bombs Libya Iran-contra scandal revealed	Gorbachev visits U.S. Stock market falls	Bush elected president	Berlin Wall dismantled Communist regimes collapse U.S. troops in Panama Human Genome Project launched	Iraq invades Kuwait	Collapse of Soviet regime Persian Gulf War	Los Angeles race riots Clinton elected president

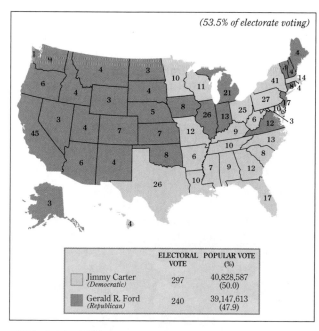

(53.5% of electorate voting)

	ELECTORAL VOTE	POPULAR VOTE (%)
Jimmy Carter (Democratic)	297	40,828,587 (50.0)
Gerald R. Ford (Republican)	240	39,147,613 (47.9)

THE ELECTION OF 1976 Jimmy Carter, a former governor of Georgia, swept the South in the 1976 election and carried enough of the industrial states of the Northeast and Midwest to win a narrow victory over President Gerald R. Ford.

at times to make his predicament worse by a style of leadership that many considered self-righteous and inflexible.

Carter devoted much of his time to the problems of the economy. Entering office in the midst of a recession, he moved first to reduce unemployment by raising public spending and cutting federal taxes. Unemployment declined, but inflation soared—mostly because of the continuing, sharp increases in energy prices by OPEC. During Carter's last two years in office, retail prices rose at well over a 10 percent annual rate. Like Nixon and Ford before him, Carter responded with a combination of tight money and calls for voluntary restraint. The economists he appointed to head the Federal Reserve Board helped push interest rates to the highest levels in American history.

In the summer of 1979, instability in the Middle East produced a second major fuel shortage in the United States. In the midst of the crisis, OPEC announced another major price increase. Faced with increasing pressure to act, Carter retreated to Camp David, the presidential retreat in the Maryland

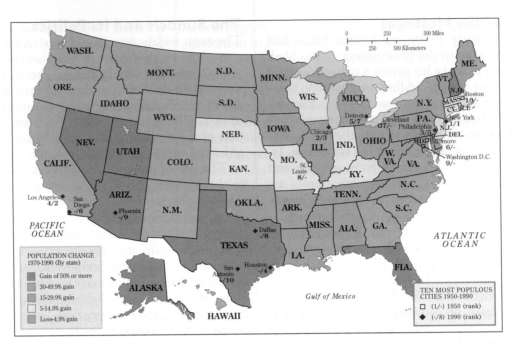

GROWTH OF THE SUNBELT, 1970–1990 One of the most important demographic changes of the last decades of the twentieth century was the shift of population out of traditional population centers in the Northeast and Midwest and toward the states of the so-called "Sunbelt"—most notably the Southwest and the Pacific coast. ▮ *What was the impact of this population shift on the politics of the 1980s?*

Sun Myung Moon; even the tragic People's Temple, whose members committed mass suicide in their jungle retreat in Guyana in 1978. But the most important impulse of the religious revival was the growth of evangelical Christianity.

Surging Evangelicalism Evangelicals have in common a belief in personal conversion (being "born again") through direct communication with God. Evangelical religion had been the dominant form of Christianity in America through much of its history. In its modern form, it became increasingly visible during the early 1950s, when evangelicals such as Billy Graham and Pentecostals such as Oral Roberts began to attract huge followings for their energetic revivalism.

By the late 1970s, more than 70 million Americans described themselves as "born-again" Christians—men and women who had established a "direct personal relationship with Jesus." Christian evangelicals owned their own newspapers, magazines, radio stations, and television networks. They operated their own schools and universities. And one of them

ultimately occupied the White House itself—Jimmy Carter, who during the 1976 campaign had talked proudly of his own "conversion experience" and who continued openly to proclaim his "born-again" Christian faith during his years in office.

For Jimmy Carter and for some others, evangelical Christianity had formed the basis for a commitment to racial and economic justice and world peace. For many evangelicals, however, the message of the new religion was very different—but no less political. In the 1970s, some Christian evangelicals became active on the political and cultural right. They were alarmed by what they considered the spread of immorality and disorder in American life; and they were concerned about the way a secular culture was intruding into their communities and schools and families. Many evangelical men and women feared the growth of feminism and resented the way in which government policies advanced the goals of the women's movement. Particularly alarming to them were Supreme Court decisions eliminating all religious observance from schools and, later, the decision guaranteeing women the right to an abortion.

By the late 1970s, the "Christian right" had become a powerful political force. Jerry Falwell, a fundamentalist minister in Virginia with a substantial television audience, launched a highly visible movement he called Moral Majority. The Pentecostal minister Pat Robertson began a political movement of his own and, in the 1990s, launched an organization known as the Christian

Christian Coalition

Coalition. These and other organizations of the Christian right opposed federal interference in local affairs; denounced abortion, divorce, feminism, and homosexuality; defended unrestricted free enterprise; and supported a strong American posture in the world. Some denied the scientific doctrine of evolution and instead urged the teaching in schools of the biblical story of the Creation.

The Emergence of the New Right

Evangelical Christians were an important part, but only a part, of what became known as the new right—a diverse but powerful movement that enjoyed rapid growth in the 1970s and early 1980s. It had begun to take shape after the 1964 election, in which Barry Goldwater had suffered his shattering defeat. Energetic organizers responded to that disaster by building a new and powerful set of right-wing institutions to help conservatives campaign more effectively in the future. Beginning in the 1970s, largely because of these organizational advances, conservatives found themselves almost always better funded and organized than their opponents.

Another factor in the revival of the right was the emergence of a credible right-wing leadership in the late 1960s and early 1970s in the person of

Ronald Reagan

Ronald Reagan. Once a moderately successful actor, he had moved into politics in the early 1960s and in 1964 delivered a memorable television speech on behalf of Goldwater. After Goldwater's defeat, he worked quickly to seize the leadership of the conservative wing of the party. In 1966, he won the first of two terms as governor of California.

The presidency of Gerald Ford also played an important role in the rise of the right. Ford, probably without realizing it, touched on some of the right's rawest nerves. He appointed as vice president Nelson Rockefeller, the liberal Republican governor of New York and an heir to one of America's great fortunes; he proposed an amnesty program for draft resisters, embraced and even extended the hated Nixon-Kissinger policies of détente, and agreed to cede the Panama Canal to Panama. When Reagan challenged Ford in the 1976 Republican primaries, the president survived, barely, only by dumping Nelson Rockefeller from the ticket and agreeing to a platform largely written by conservatives.

The Tax Revolt

At least equally important to the success of the new right was a new and potent conservative issue: the tax revolt. It had its public beginnings in 1978, when Howard Jarvis, a conservative activist in California, launched the first successful major citizens' tax revolt in California with Proposition 13, a referendum question on

Proposition 13

the state ballot rolling back property tax rates. Similar antitax movements soon began in other states and eventually spread to national politics.

In Proposition 13 and similar initiatives, members of the right succeeded in separating the issue of taxes from the issue of what taxes supported. Instead of attacking popular programs such as Social Security, they attacked taxes themselves and argued that much of the money government raised through taxes was wasted. Virtually no one liked to pay taxes, and as the economy grew weaker and the relative burden of paying taxes grew heavier, that resentment naturally rose.

The Campaign of 1980

By the time of the crises in Iran and Afghanistan, Jimmy Carter was in desperate political trouble. Senator Edward Kennedy, younger brother of John and Robert Kennedy, challenged him in the primaries. And while Carter managed to win his party's nomination, his campaign aroused little popular enthusiasm.

The Republican Party, in the meantime, had rallied enthusiastically behind Ronald Reagan, a sharp critic of the excesses of the federal government. Reagan linked his campaign to the spreading tax revolt by promising substantial tax cuts. He also championed a restoration of American "strength" and "pride" in the world.

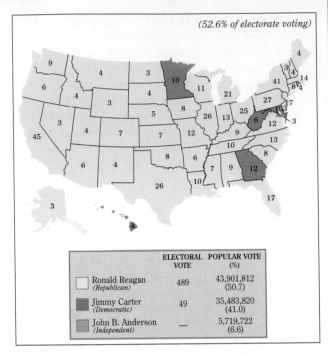

(52.6% of electorate voting)

	ELECTORAL VOTE	POPULAR VOTE (%)
Ronald Reagan *(Republican)*	489	43,901,812 (50.7)
Jimmy Carter *(Democratic)*	49	35,483,820 (41.0)
John B. Anderson *(Independent)*	—	5,719,722 (6.6)

THE ELECTION OF 1980 Although Ronald Reagan won only slightly more than half of the popular vote in the 1980 presidential election, his electoral majority was overwhelming. ▮ *What had made Carter so unpopular?*

ⓆⓁⒸ **For an interactive version of this map go to** www.mhhe.com/unfinishedinteractive

1980 Election   On election day 1980, Reagan swept to victory, winning 51 percent of the vote to 41 percent for Jimmy Carter, and 7 percent for John Anderson—a moderate Republican congressman from Illinois who had mounted an independent campaign. The Republican Party won control of the Senate for the first time since 1952.

On the day of Reagan's inauguration, the American hostages in Iran were released after their 444-day ordeal. The government of Iran, desperate for funds to support its floundering war against neighboring Iraq, had ordered the hostages freed in return for a release of billions in Iranian assets that the Carter administration had frozen in American banks. Americans welcomed the hostages home with demonstrations of joy and patriotism not seen since the end of World War II. But while the celebration in 1945 had marked a great American triumph, the euphoria in 1981 marked something quite different—a troubled nation grasping for reassurance. Ronald Reagan set out to provide it.

THE "REAGAN REVOLUTION"

Ronald Reagan assumed the presidency in January 1981 promising a change in government more fundamental than any since the New Deal of fifty years before. While his eight years in office produced a significant shift in public policy, they brought nothing so fundamental as many of his supporters had hoped or his opponents had feared. But Reagan succeeded brilliantly in making his own engaging personality the central fact of American politics in the 1980s. He also benefited from the power of the diverse coalition that had united behind him.

The Reagan Coalition

The Reagan coalition included a relatively small but highly influential group of wealthy Americans firmly committed to capitalism and to unfettered economic growth. They believed that the market offers the best solutions to most **Free-Market Conservatives** problems, and they shared a deep hostility to most (although not all) government interference in markets. Central to this group's agenda in the 1980s was opposition to what it considered the "redistributive" politics of the federal government (especially its tax structure) and hostility to the rise of what they believed were "antibusiness" government regulations. Reagan courted these free-market conservatives carefully and effectively.

A second element of the Reagan coalition was a small but influential group of intellectuals commonly known as "neo-conservatives," who gave to **"Neo-Conservatives"** the right something it had not had in many years—a firm base among "opinion leaders," people with access to the most influential public forums for ideas. Many of these people had once been liberals and, before that, socialists. But during the turmoil of the 1960s, they had become alarmed by what they considered a dangerous and destructive radicalism. Neo-conservatives were sympathetic to the complaints and demands of capitalists, but their principal concern was to reassert legitimate authority and

RONALD AND NANCY REAGAN The president and the first lady greet guests at a White House social event. Nancy Reagan was most visible in her efforts to make the White House, and her husband's presidency, seem more glamorous than those of most recent administrations. But she also played an important, if quiet, policy role in the administration. *(Dirck Halstead/Getty Images)*

reaffirm Western democratic, anticommunist values and commitments.

These groups formed an uneasy alliance with what became known as the "new right." The new right shared a fundamental distrust of the "eastern establishment." They expressed the kinds of concerns that outsiders, non-elites, have traditionally voiced in American society: an opposition to centralized power and influence, a fear of living in a world where distant, hostile forces are controlling society and threatening individual freedom. It was a testament to Ronald Reagan's political skills and personal charm that he was able to generate enthusiastic support from these populist conservatives while at the same time ap-

pealing to more elite conservative groups whose concerns were in many ways antithetical to those of the new right.

Reagan in the White House

Even many people who disagreed with Reagan's policies found themselves drawn to his attractive public image. He turned seventy a few weeks after taking office and was the oldest man ever to serve as president. But through most of his presidency, he appeared to be vigorous, resilient, even youthful. When he was wounded in an assassination attempt in 1981, he appeared to bounce back from the ordeal with remarkable speed. Even when things went wrong, the blame seldom seemed to attach to Reagan himself (inspiring some Democrats to begin referring to him as the "Teflon president").

Reagan was not much involved in the day-to-day affairs of running the government; he surrounded himself with tough, energetic administrators who insulated him from many of the pressures of the office and who apparently relied on him largely for general guidance, not specific decisions. At times, the president revealed a startling ignorance about the nature of his own policies or the actions of his subordinates. But Reagan did make active use of his office to generate public support for his administration's programs.

"Supply-Side" Economics

Reagan's 1980 campaign for the presidency had promised to restore the economy to health by a bold experiment that became known as "supply-side" economics or, to some, "Reaganomics." Supply-side economics operated from the assumption that the woes of the American economy were in large part a result of excessive taxation, which left inadequate capital available to investors to stimulate growth. The solution, therefore, was to reduce taxes, with particularly generous benefits to corporations and wealthy individuals, in order to encourage new investments.

In its first months in office, the new administration hastily assembled a legislative program based on the supply-side idea. It proposed $40 billion in budget reductions and managed to win congressional approval of almost all of them. In addition, the president proposed a bold three-year, 30 percent reduction on both individual and corporate tax rates. In the summer of 1981, Congress passed it too, after lowering the reductions to 25 percent. Reagan was successful because he had a disciplined Republican majority in the Senate and the Democratic majority in the House was weak.

Men and women whom Reagan appointed fanned out through the executive branch of government committed to reducing the role of government in American economic life. "Deregulation," an idea many Democrats had begun to embrace in the Carter years, became almost a religion in the Reagan administration. Secretary of the Interior James Watt had been a major figure in the Sagebrush Rebellion, a movement among western conservatives to fight federal environmental regulations. Watt opened up public lands and water to development. The Environmental Protection Agency relaxed or entirely eliminated enforcement of major environmental laws and regulations.

By early 1982, however, the nation had sunk into the most severe recession since the 1930s. Unemployment reached 11 percent, its highest level in over forty years. But before the recession could do great damage to Reagan, the economy recovered more

Economic Recovery

rapidly and impressively than almost anyone had expected. By late 1983, unemployment had fallen to 8.2 percent, and it declined steadily for several years after that. The gross national product had grown 3.6 percent in a year, the largest increase since the mid-1970s. Inflation had fallen below 5 percent. The economy continued to grow, and both inflation and unemployment remained low through most of the decade.

The recovery was a result of many things. The years of tight money policies by the Federal Reserve Board had helped lower inflation; perhaps equally important, the Board had lowered interest rates early in 1983 in response to the recession. A worldwide "energy glut" and the virtual collapse of the OPEC cartel had produced at least a temporary end to the inflationary pressures of spiraling fuel costs. And staggering federal budget deficits were pumping billions of dollars into the flagging economy. As a result, consumer spending and business investment both increased.

The Fiscal Crisis

The economic revival did little at first to reduce the federal budget deficits (the gap between revenue Growing Budget Deficits and spending in a single year) or to slow the growth in the national debt (the debt the nation accumulates over time as a result of its annual deficits). By the mid-1980s, this growing fiscal crisis had become one of the central issues in American politics. Having entered office promising a balanced budget within four years, Reagan presided over record budget deficits and accumulated more debt in his eight years in office than the American government had accumulated in its entire previous history. Throughout the 1980s, the annual budget deficit consistently exceeded $100 billion (and in 1991 peaked at $268 billion). The national debt rose from $907 billion in 1980 to nearly $3.5 trillion by 1991.

The enormous deficits had many causes. The budget suffered from enormous increases in the costs of "entitlement" programs (especially Social Security and Medicare), a result of the aging of the population and dramatic increases in the cost of health care. The 1981 tax cuts also contributed to the deficit. The massive increase in military spending on which the Reagan administration insisted added much more to the federal budget than its cuts in domestic spending removed.

In the face of these deficits, the administration proposed further cuts in "discretionary" domestic spending, which included many programs aimed at the poorest (and politically weakest) Americans. By the end of Reagan's third year in office, funding for domestic programs had been cut nearly as far as Congress (and, apparently, the public) was willing to tolerate, and still no end to the rising deficit was in sight. By the late 1980s, many fiscal conservatives were calling for a constitutional amendment mandating a balanced budget.

Reagan and the World

Relations with the Soviet Union, which had been steadily deteriorating in the last years of the Carter administration, grew still chillier in the first years of the Reagan presidency. The president spoke harshly of the Soviet regime (which he once called the "evil empire"), accusing it of sponsoring world terrorism and declaring that any armaments negotiations must

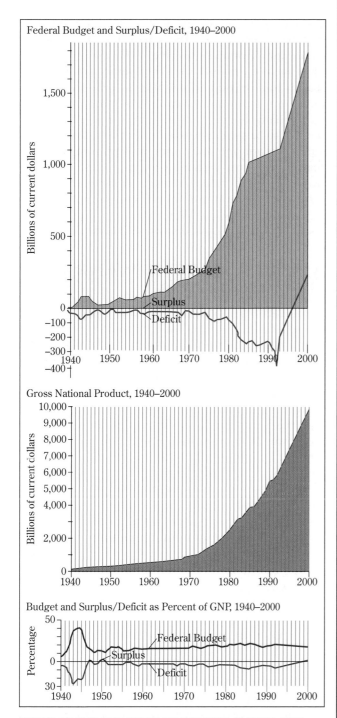

Federal Budget and Surplus/Deficit, 1940–2000

Gross National Product, 1940–2000

Budget and Surplus/Deficit as Percent of GNP, 1940–2000

FEDERAL BUDGET SURPLUS/DEFICIT, 1940 TO 2000
These charts help illustrate why the pattern of federal deficits seemed so alarming to Americans in the 1980s, and also why those deficits proved much less damaging to the economy than many predicted. ▌ *What factors contributed to the increasing deficits of the 1980s? How were those deficits eliminated in the 1990s?*

be linked to negotiations on Soviet behavior in other areas. Although the president had long denounced the SALT II arms control treaty as unfavorable to the United States, he continued to honor its provisions. But the Reagan administration at first made little progress toward arms control in other areas. In fact, the president proposed the most ambitious (and potentially most expensive) new military program in many years: the Strategic Defense Initiative (SDI), widely known as "Star Wars" **"Star Wars"** (after the popular movie of that name). Reagan claimed that SDI, through the use of lasers and satellites, could provide an effective shield against incoming missiles and thus make nuclear war obsolete. The Soviet Union claimed that the new program would elevate the arms race to new and more dangerous levels and insisted that any arms control agreement begin with an American abandonment of SDI.

The escalation of Cold War tensions and the slowing of arms control initiatives helped produce an important popular movement in Europe and the United States calling for an end to nuclear weapons buildups. In America, the principal goal of the movement was a "nuclear freeze," an agreement between the two superpowers not to expand their atomic arsenals. In 1982 nearly a million people rallied in New York City's Central Park to support the freeze. Perhaps partly in response to this growing pressure, the administration began tentative efforts to revive arms control negotiations in 1983.

It also created a new policy, which became known as the Reagan Doctrine, to **Reagan Doctrine** help groups resisting communism in the Third World. The most conspicuous examples of the new activism came in Latin America. In October 1982, the administration sent American soldiers and marines into the tiny Caribbean island of Grenada to oust an anti-American Marxist regime that showed signs of forging a relationship with Moscow. In El Salvador, whose government was fighting left-wing revolutionaries, the administration provided increased military and economic assistance. In neighboring Nicaragua, a pro-American dictatorship had fallen to the revolutionary "Sandinistas" in 1979. The Reagan administration supported the so-called contras, an antigovernment guerrilla movement fighting (without great success) to topple the Sandinista regime.

In other parts of the world, the administration's tough rhetoric seemed to hide an instinctive restraint. In June 1982, the Israeli army launched an invasion of Lebanon in an effort to drive guerrillas of the Palestinian Liberation Organization from the country. An American peacekeeping force entered Beirut to supervise the evacuation of PLO forces from Lebanon. American marines then remained in the city, apparently to protect the fragile Lebanese government. Now identified with one faction in the struggle, Americans became the targets in 1983 of a terrorist bombing of a U.S. military barracks in Beirut that left 241 marines dead. Rather than become more deeply involved in the Lebanese struggle, Reagan withdrew American forces.

The disaster in Lebanon was an example of the changing character of Third World struggles: an increasing reliance on terrorism by otherwise powerless groups to advance their political aims. A series of terrorist acts in the 1980s—attacks on airplanes, cruise ships, commercial and diplomatic posts; the seizing of American and other Western hostages—alarmed and frightened much of the Western world. In 1986, the president ordered American planes to bomb sites in Tripoli, the capital of Libya, whose controversial leader Muammar al-Qaddafi was widely believed to be a leading sponsor of terrorism. In general, however, American leaders had little success in identifying or controlling terrorists.

Terrorism

The Election of 1984

Reagan approached the campaign of 1984 at the head of a united Republican Party firmly committed to his candidacy. The Democrats nominated former vice president Walter Mondale, who fought off challenges from Senator Gary Hart of Colorado and Jesse Jackson, who had established himself as the nation's most prominent spokesman for minorities and the poor. Mondale brought momentary excitement to the Democratic campaign by selecting a woman, Representative Geraldine Ferraro of New York, to be his running mate.

Reagan Reelected

Reagan's triumphant campaign scarcely took note of his opponents and spoke instead of what he claimed was the remarkable revival of American fortunes and spirits under his leadership. He won approximately 59 percent of the vote, and carried every state but Mondale's native Minnesota and the District of Columbia. But the Democrats gained a seat in the Senate and maintained only slightly reduced control of the House of Representatives.

To many Reagan supporters, the 1984 election seemed to be the dawn of a new conservative era. But almost no one anticipated the revolutionary changes that would occur within a very few years. The election of 1984, therefore, was not so much the first of a new era as the last of an old one. It was the final campaign of the Cold War.

AMERICA AND THE WANING OF THE COLD WAR

Many factors contributed to the collapse of the Soviet empire. The long, stalemated war in Afghanistan proved at least as disastrous to the Soviet Union as the Vietnam War had been to America. The government in Moscow had failed to address a long-term economic decline in the Soviet republics and the Eastern-bloc nations. Restiveness with the heavy-handed policies of communist police states was growing throughout much of the Soviet empire. But the most visible factor at the time was the emergence of Mikhail Gorbachev, who succeeded to the leadership of the Soviet Union in 1985 and quickly became the most revolutionary figure in world politics in at least four decades.

Mikhail Gorbachev

The Fall of the Soviet Union

Gorbachev quickly transformed Soviet politics with two dramatic new initiatives. The first he called *glasnost* (openness): the dismantling of many of the repressive mechanisms that had been conspicuous features of Soviet life for over half a century. The other policy Gorbachev called *perestroika* (reform): an effort to restructure the rigid and unproductive Soviet economy by introducing, among other things, such elements of capitalism as private ownership and the profit motive. He also began to transform Soviet foreign policy.

Glasnost and Perestroika

The severe economic problems at home evidently convinced Gorbachev that the Soviet Union could no longer sustain its extended commitments around the world. As early as 1987, he began reducing Soviet influence in Eastern Europe. And in 1989, in the space of a few months, every communist state in Europe—Poland, Hungary, Czechoslovakia, Bulgaria, Romania, East Germany, Yugoslavia, and Albania—either overthrew its government or forced it to transform itself into an essentially noncommunist (and in some cases, actively anticommunist) regime.

In May 1989, students in China launched a mass movement calling for greater democratization. But in June, hard-line leaders seized control of the government and sent military forces to crush the uprising. The result was a bloody massacre on June 3, 1989, in Tiananmen Square in
Tiananmen Square
Beijing. The assault crushed the democracy movement and restored hard-liners to power. It did not, however, stop China's efforts to modernize its economy.

But China was an exception to a widespread movement toward democratization. Early in 1990, the government of South Africa, long an international pariah for its rigid enforcement of "apartheid" (a system designed to protect white supremacy), began a cautious retreat from its traditional policies. Among other things, it legalized the chief black party in the nation, the African National Congress (ANC), which had been banned for decades, and released from prison the leader of the ANC, Nelson Mandela, who had been in jail for twenty-seven years. Over the next several years, the South African government repealed its apartheid laws. And in 1994, there were national elections in which all South Africans could participate. As a result, Nelson Mandela became the first black president of South Africa.

In 1991, communism began to collapse in the
Soviet Union itself. An un-
Collapse of the USSR
successful coup by hard-line Soviet leaders on August 19 precipitated a dramatic unraveling of communist power. Within days, the coup itself collapsed. Mikhail Gorbachev returned to power, but it soon became evident that the legitimacy of both the Communist Party and the central Soviet government had been fatally injured. By the end of August, many of the republics of the Soviet Union had declared independence. Gorbachev himself finally resigned as leader of the Soviet government, and the Soviet Union ceased to exist.

The last years of the Reagan administration coincided with the first years of the Gorbachev regime; and while Reagan was skeptical of Gorbachev at first, he gradually became convinced that the Soviet leader was sincere in his desire for reform. At a summit meeting with Reagan in Reykjavik, Iceland, in 1986, Gorbachev proposed reducing the nuclear arsenals of both sides by 50 percent or more, although continuing disputes over Reagan's commitment to the SDI program prevented agreements. But in 1988, the two superpowers signed a treaty eliminating American and Soviet intermediate-range nuclear forces (INF) from Europe. At about the same time, Gorbachev ended the Soviet Union's long and frustrating military involvement in Afghanistan.

The Fading of the Reagan Revolution

For a time, the dramatic changes around the world and Reagan's personal popularity deflected attention from a series of scandals that might well have destroyed another administration. There were revelations of illegality, corruption, and ethical lapses in the Environmental Protection Agency, the CIA, the Department of Defense, the Department of Labor, the Department of Justice, and the Department of Housing and Urban Development. A more serious scandal emerged within the
savings and loan industry,
Savings and Loan Crisis
which the Reagan administration had helped deregulate in the early 1980s. By the end of the decade the industry was in chaos, and the government was forced to step in to prevent a complete collapse. The cost of the debacle to the public eventually ran to more than half a trillion dollars.

But the most politically damaging scandal of the Reagan years came to light in November 1986, when the White House conceded that it had sold weapons to the revolutionary government of Iran as part of a largely unsuccessful effort to secure the release of several Americans being held hostage by radical Islamic groups. Even more damaging was the revelation that some of the money from the arms deal with Iran had been covertly and illegally funneled into a fund to aid the contras in Nicaragua.

In the months that followed, aggressive reporting and a series of congressional hearings exposed a widespread pattern of covert activities dedicated to advancing the administration's foreign policy aims.

The principal figure in this covert world appeared at first to be an obscure marine lieutenant colonel assigned to the staff of the National Security Council, Oliver North. But gradually it became clear that North was acting in concert with other, more powerful figures in the administration. The Iran-contra scandal, as it became known, did serious damage to the Reagan presidency—even though the investigations were never able decisively to tie the president himself to the most serious violations of the law.

Oliver North

The Election of 1988

The fraying of the Reagan administration helped the Democrats regain control of the United States Senate in 1986 and fueled hopes in the party for a presidential victory in 1988. Michael Dukakis, a three-term governor of Massachusetts, eventually captured the nomination, even though he was a dry, even dull campaigner. But Vice President George Bush, the largely unopposed Republican candidate, had also failed to spark any real public enthusiasm. He entered the last months of the campaign well behind Dukakis.

Bush's Negative Campaign

Beginning at the Republican Convention, however, Bush staged a remarkable turnaround by making his campaign a long, relentless attack on Dukakis, tying him to all the unpopular social and cultural stances associated with "liberals." Bush won a substantial victory in November: 54 percent of the popular vote to Dukakis's 46 percent, and 426 electoral votes to Dukakis's 112. But the Democrats retained secure majorities in both houses of Congress.

The Bush Presidency

The Bush presidency was notable for the dramatic developments in international affairs with which it coincided and at times helped to advance, and for the absence of important initiatives or ideas on domestic issues.

The broad popularity Bush enjoyed during his first three years in office was partly a result of his subdued, unthreatening public image. But it was primarily because of the wonder and excitement with which Americans viewed the dramatic events in the rest of the world. Bush moved cautiously at first in

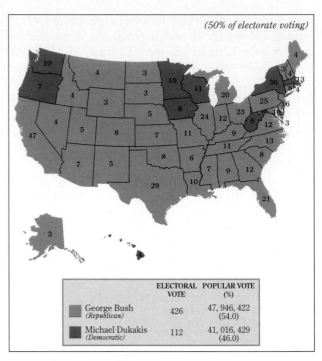

(50% of electorate voting)

	ELECTORAL VOTE	POPULAR VOTE (%)
George Bush (Republican)	426	47, 946, 422 (54.0)
Michael Dukakis (Democratic)	112	41, 016, 429 (46.0)

THE ELECTION OF 1988 Democrats had high hopes going into the election of 1988, but Vice President George Bush won a decisive victory over Michael Dukakis. *What made it so difficult for a Democrat to challenge the Republicans in 1988 after eight years of a Republican administration?*

dealing with the changes in the Soviet Union. But he eventually reached a series of significant agreements with the Soviet Union in its waning years. In the three years after the INF agreement in 1988, the United States and the Soviet Union moved rapidly toward even more far-reaching arms reduction agreements.

On domestic issues, the Bush administration was less successful. It had inherited a staggering burden of debt and a federal deficit that had been out of control for nearly a decade. Any domestic agenda that required significant federal spending was, therefore, incompatible with the president's pledge to reduce the deficit and his 1988 campaign promise of "no new taxes." Concerned about the right wing of his own party, Bush took divisive positions on such cultural issues as abortion and affirmative action that damaged his ability to work with the Democratic Congress.

Despite this political stalemate, Congress and the White House managed on occasion to agree

GORBACHEV AND BUSH
When Bush became president in 1989, the Cold War with the Soviet Union was still in progress. By the time he left office in 1993, the Cold War was over; the once "captive nations" of eastern Europe were free of Soviet domination; and the Soviet Union itself had unravelled and dissolved. Much of the impetus for these changes originated with the last Soviet leader, Mikhail Gorbachev, whose efforts at reform unleashed forces he ultimately could not control. *(Getty Images)*

on significant measures. In 1990, the president bowed to congressional pressure and agreed to a significant tax increase as part of a multiyear "budget package" designed to reduce the deficit—thus violating his own 1988 campaign pledge of "no new taxes."

But the most serious domestic problem facing the Bush administration was a recession that began late in 1990 and became more serious in 1991 and 1992. Because of the enormous level of debt that corporations had accumulated in the 1980s, the recession caused an unusual number of bankruptcies. It also produced fear and frustration among middle- and working-class Americans.

1990 Recession

The Gulf War
The events of 1989–1991 had left the United States in the unanticipated position of being the only real superpower in the world. The Bush administration, therefore, had to consider what to do with America's formidable political and military power in a world in which the major justification for that power—the Soviet threat—was now gone.

The events of 1989–1991 suggested two possible answers. One was that the United States would reduce its military strength and concentrate on press-

ing domestic problems. There was, in fact, considerable movement in that direction both in Congress and within the administration. The other was that America would continue to use its power actively, not to fight communism but to defend its regional and economic interests. In 1989, that led the administration to order an invasion of Panama, which overthrew the unpopular military leader Manuel Noriega and replaced him with an elected, pro American regime. And in 1990, that same impulse drew the United States into the turbulent politics of the Middle East.

On August 2, 1990, the armed forces of Iraq invaded and quickly overwhelmed their small, oil-rich neighbor, the emirate of Kuwait. Saddam Hussein, the militaristic leader of Iraq, soon announced that he was annexing Kuwait. After some initial indecision, the Bush administration agreed to lead other nations in a campaign to force Iraq out of Kuwait—through the pressure of economic sanctions if possible, through military force if necessary. Within a few weeks, Bush had persuaded virtually every important government in the world to join in a United Nations–sanctioned trade embargo of Iraq.

Saddam Hussein

At the same time, the United States and its allies (including the British, French, Egyptians, and

536

Saudis) began deploying a massive military force along the border between Kuwait and Saudi Arabia, a force that ultimately reached 690,000 troops. And on January 16, American and allied air forces began a massive bombardment of Iraqi troops in Kuwait and of military and industrial installations in Iraq itself.

The allied bombing continued for six weeks. On February 23, allied (primarily American) forces un-

| General Norman Schwarzkopf |

der the command of General Norman Schwarzkopf began a major ground offensive— not primarily against the heavily entrenched Iraqi forces along the Kuwait border, as expected, but to the north of them into Iraq itself. The allied armies encountered almost no resistance and suffered only light casualties (141 fatalities). Estimates of Iraqi deaths in the war were 100,000 or more. On February 28, Iraq announced its acceptance of allied terms for a cease-fire.

The quick and (for America) relatively painless victory over Iraq was highly popular in the United States. But the tyrannical regime of Saddam Hussein survived, in a weakened form but showing few signs of retreat from its militaristic ambitions.

The Election of 1992

President Bush's popularity reached a record high in the immediate aftermath of the Gulf War. But the glow of that victory faded quickly as the recession worsened in late 1991, and as the administration failed to produce any effective policies for combating it.

Because the early maneuvering for the 1992 presidential election occurred when President Bush's popularity remained high, many leading Democrats declined to run. That gave Bill Clinton, the young five-term governor of Arkansas, an opportunity to emerge early as the front-runner, as a result of a skillful campaign that emphasized broad economic issues. Clinton survived a bruising primary campaign and a series of damaging personal controversies to win his party's nomination. And George Bush withstood an embarrassing primary challenge from the conservative journalist Pat Buchanan to become the Republican nominee again.

| Ross Perot |

Complicating the campaign was the emergence of Ross Perot, a Texas billionaire who became an independent candidate by promising tough, uncompromising lead-

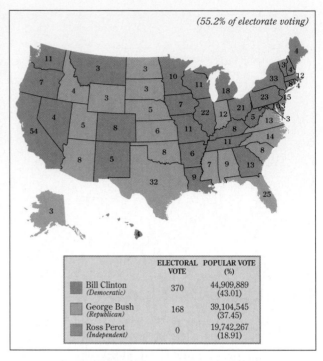

(55.2% of electorate voting)

	ELECTORAL VOTE	POPULAR VOTE (%)
Bill Clinton *(Democratic)*	370	44,909,889 (43.01)
George Bush *(Republican)*	168	39,104,545 (37.45)
Ross Perot *(Independent)*	0	19,742,267 (18.91)

THE ELECTION OF 1992 For the first time since 1976, a Democrat captured the White House in the 1992 election. And although the third party candidacy of Ross Perot deprived Bill Clinton of an absolute majority, he nevertheless defeated George Bush by a decisive margin in both the popular and electoral vote. ▌ *What factors had eroded President Bush's once-broad popularity by 1992? What explained the strong showing of Ross Perot?*

ership to deal with the fiscal crisis and other problems of government. At several moments in the spring, Perot led both Bush and Clinton in public opinion polls. In July, as he began to face hostile scrutiny from the media, he abruptly withdrew from the race. But early in October, he reentered and soon regained much (although never all) of his early support.

After a campaign in which the economy and the president's unpopularity were the principal issues, Clinton won a clear, but hardly overwhelming, vic-

| Clinton Elected |

tory over Bush and Perot. He received 43 percent of the vote, to the president's 38 percent and Perot's 19 percent. Clinton won 370 electoral votes to Bush's 168; Perot won none. Democrats retained control of both houses of Congress.

Amerca in the late 1970s was troubled by the Watergate scandals, the fall of Vietnam, and perhaps most of all the nation's increasing economic difficulties. The presidencies of Gerald Ford and Jimmy Carter provided little relief from these accumulating problems and anxieties. Indeed, in the last year of the Carter presidency, the nation's prospects seemed particularly grim in light of severe economic problems, a traumatic seizure of American hostages in Iran, and a Soviet invasion of Afghanistan.

In the midst of these problems, a coalition of disparate but impassioned groups on the right—including a large movement known as the "new right" with vaguely populist impulses—gained strength from the nation's troubles and from their own success in winning support for a broad-ranging revolt against taxes. Their efforts culminated in the election of 1980, when Ronald Reagan became the most conservative man in more than half a century to be elected president of the United States.

Reagan's first term was a dramatic contrast to the troubled presidencies that had preceded it. He won substantial victories in Congress (cutting taxes, reducing spending on domestic programs, building up the military). Perhaps equally important, he made his own engaging personality one of the central political forces in national life. Easily reelected in 1984, he seemed to have solidified the conservative grip on national political life. In his second term, a series of scandals and misadventures—and the president's own declining energy—limited the administration's effectiveness. Nevertheless, Reagan's personal popularity remained high, and the economy continued to prosper—factors that helped his vice president, George H. W. Bush, to succeed him in 1989.

Bush's presidency was not defined by domestic initiatives, as Reagan's had been. But a colossal historic event often overshadowed domestic concerns during Bush's term in office: the collapse of the Soviet Union and the fall of communist regimes all over Europe and in other parts of the world. The end of the Cold War propelled the United States into unchallenged global pre-eminence—and drew it increasingly into the role of international arbiter and peacemaker. The Gulf War of 1991 was only the most dramatic example of the new global role the United States would now increasingly assume.

INTERACTIVE LEARNING

On the *Primary Source Investigator CD-ROM*, check out a number of valuable tools for further exploration of the content of this chapter.

Interactive Maps
- U.S. Elections (Map M7)
- Middle East Conflicts (Map M28)

Primary Sources
Documents, images, and maps related to politics and society in the late 1970s through the early 1990s, the Reagan presidency and the collapse of the Soviet Union. Some highlights include:

- Text of Ronald Reagan's speech referring to the Soviet Union as an "evil empire"

- An excerpt from the transcripts of the Senate Judiciary Committee hearings into confirming Clarence Thomas to serve on the Supreme Court

- Excerpts from President George H. W. Bush's diary during Operation Desert Storm in 1991

 Online Learning Center
(www.mhhe.com/unfinishedinteractive)
Explore this rich website, providing additional exploration of the material covered in this chapter, online versions of the interactive maps included on the Primary Source Investigator CD-ROM, as well as several study aids, including a multiple-choice quiz, essay questions, a glossary, and other valuable tools.

FOR FURTHER REFERENCE

Bruce J. Schulman, *The Seventies: The Great Shift in American Culture, Society, and Politics* (2001) is a good general history of the period. James M. Cannon, *Time and Chance: Gerald Ford's Appointment with History* (1994) is a journalist's account of the Ford presidency. Charles O. Jones, *The Trusteeship Presidency: Jimmy Carter and the United States Congress* (1988) looks at Carter's frustrations in domestic policy, and Gaddis Smith, *Morality, Reason, and Power* (1986) examines his foreign policy. Steven Gillon, *The Democrats' Dilemma: Walter Mondale and the Liberal Legacy* (1992) is a good discussion of the travails of the Democrats in the 1970s. Jerome L. Himmelstein, *To the Right: The Transformation of American Conservatism* (1990) and Godfrey Hodgson, *The World Turned Upside Down: A History of the Conservative Ascendancy in America* (1996) are good introductions to the subject. Lisa McGirr, *Suburban Warriors: The Origins of the New American Right* (2001) is an excellent grass-roots study. E. J. Dionne, *Why Americans Hate Politics* (1991) is a perceptive discussion of the political discontents of the 1980s and early 1990s. Garry Wills, *Reagan's America* (1987) is an interesting, critical interpretation. Lou Cannon, *President Reagan: The Role of a Lifetime* (1990) and Haynes Johnson, *Sleepwalking Through History* (1991) are accounts by journalists who covered the Reagan White House. Frances Fitzgerald, *Way Out There in the Blue: Reagan, Star Wars, and the End of the Cold War* (2000) is a fine history of the Reagan presidency, and its foreign policy in particular. Hedrick Smith, *The Power Game* (1988) is a sweeping portrait of the culture of political Washington during the Reagan years. John Lewis Gaddis, *The United States and the End of the Cold War* (1992) and *We Now Know: Rethinking Cold War History* (1997) examine the transformation of the world order after 1989. Thomas Crothers, *In the Name of Democracy: U.S. Foreign Policy toward Latin America in the Reagan Years* (1991) examines a controversial area of Reagan's international record, including aspects of the Iran-Contra scandal. Herbert Parmet, *George Bush: The Life of a Lone Star Yankee* (1997) is the first major scholarly study of the 41st president.

The Conservative Resurgence (1991) is a documentary film examining the growing conservative trend in American politics during the late 1970s and the 1980s.

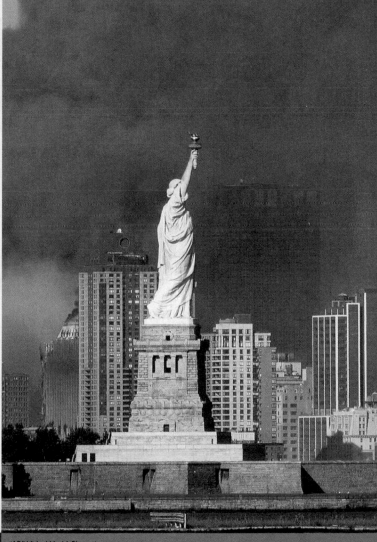

(AP/Wide World Photos)

At 8:45 A.M. on the bright, sunny morning of September 11, 2001, a commercial airliner crashed into the side of one of the two towers of the World Trade Center, the tallest buildings in New York, and exploded in flame. Less than half an hour later, as thousands of workers fled the burning building, another commercial airliner rammed into the companion tower. Little more than an hour after that, both towers—their steel girders buckling in response to the tremendous heat—collapsed. At about the same time, in Washington, another commercial airliner crashed into a side of the Pentagon—the headquarters of the nation's military—turning part of the building's facade into rubble. And several hundred miles away, still another airplane crashed in a field not far from Pittsburgh, after passengers apparently seized the cockpit and prevented the hijackers from taking the plane to its unknown target.

These four almost simultaneous catastrophes were the result of a single orchestrated plan to bring terrorism—for years the bane of such nations as Israel, Lebanon, Turkey, Italy, Germany, Britain, and Ireland—into the United States, which had previously had relatively little recent experience of it. The people who organized the attack on America were Islamic radicals, engaged in what they considered a holy war against "infidels" in the United States. Similarly committed Middle Eastern terrorists had previously attacked American targets overseas—military barracks, a naval vessel, embassies, and consulates.

The events of September 11 and their aftermath produced significant changes in American life. They also seemed to bring to a close an extraordinary period in modern American history—a time of heady prosperity, bitter partisanship, and tremendous social and economic change. And yet there was also at least one great continuity between the world of the 1990s and the world that seemed to begin on September 11, 2001. The United States was becoming more and more deeply entwined in a new age of globalism—an age that combined great promise with great peril.

A RESURGENCE OF PARTISANSHIP

Bill Clinton

Bill Clinton entered office in January 1993 as the first Democratic president since Jimmy Carter. He had a domestic agenda more ambitious than that of any president since the 1960s. But Clinton also had significant political weaknesses. Having won the votes of well under half the electorate, he enjoyed no powerful mandate. Democratic majorities in Congress were frail. The Republican leadership in Congress opposed the president with unusual unanimity on many issues. The president's tendency toward reckless personal behavior gave his many enemies repeated opportunities to discredit him. The Clinton years, therefore, became a time of unusually intense and bitter partisan struggles.

Launching the Clinton Presidency

The new administration compounded its problems with a series of missteps in its first months. The president's effort to end the longtime ban on gay men and women serving in the military met with ferocious resistance, and he was forced to settle for a pallid compromise. Several of his early appointments became so controversial he had to withdraw them. A longtime friend of the president, Vince Foster, serving in the office of the White House counsel, committed suicide in the summer of 1993.

TIME LINE

1993	1994	1995	1996	1997
North American Free Trade Agreement ratified	Health care reform fails Republicans capture Congress	Government shutdown Crime rates decline O. J. Simpson trial	Welfare reform passed Clinton reelected	Microsoft antitrust suit begins Balanced budget agreement

1998	1999	2000	2001	2002
Lewinsky scandal breaks Democrats gain in congressional elections Clinton impeached by House	Clinton acquitted by Senate	George W. Bush wins contested election	Terrorists destroy World Trade Center and attack Pentagon U.S. defeats Taliban regime in Afghanistan	Corporate scandals contribute to economic downturn

His death helped spark an escalating inquiry into some banking and real estate ventures involving the president and his wife in the early 1980s, which became known as the Whitewater affair. An independent counsel began examining these issues in 1993.

Despite its many problems, the Clinton administration could boast of some significant achievements in its first year. The president narrowly won approval of a budget that included a substantial tax increase on the wealthiest Americans, a significant reduction in many areas of government spending, and a major expansion of tax credits to low-income working people.

Clinton was a committed advocate of free trade. After a long and difficult battle, he won approval of the North American Free Trade Agreement (or NAFTA), which eliminated most trade barriers among the United States, Canada, and Mexico. Later he won approval of other far-reaching trade agreements negotiated in the General Agreement on Trade and Tarriffs (or GATT).

NAFTA

The president's most important and ambitious initiative was a major reform of the nation's health-care system. Early in 1993, he appointed a task force chaired by his wife, Hillary Rodham Clinton, which proposed a sweeping reform designed to guarantee coverage to every American and hold down the costs of medical care. The Clinton plan relied heavily on existing institutions, most notably private insurance companies; and some critics complained that the new system would be too closely tied to an undependable market. But the most substantial opposition came from those who believed the reform would transfer too much power to the government. In September 1994, Congress abandoned the health-care reform effort.

The foreign policy of the Clinton administration was at first cautious and even tentative. That was particularly clear in the administration's handling of one of the most troubling international questions of the early 1990s. Yugoslavia, a nation created after World War I out of a group of small Balkan countries, dissolved again into several different nations in the wake of the collapse of its communist government in 1989. Bosnia was among the new nations, and

Bosnia

it quickly became embroiled in a bloody civil war between its two major ethnic groups: one Muslim, the other Serbian and Christian backed by the neighboring Serbian republic. All efforts to negotiate an end to the struggle failed until 1995, when

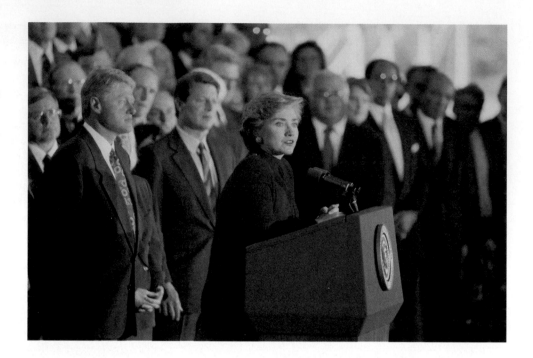

the American negotiator Richard Holbrooke finally brought the warring parties together and crafted an agreement to partition Bosnia.

The Republican Resurgence

The trials of the Clinton administration, and the failure of health-care reform in particular, proved enormously damaging to the Democratic Party as it faced the congressional elections of 1994. For the first time in over forty years, Republicans gained control of both houses of Congress.

Throughout 1995, the Republican Congress worked to construct one of the most ambitious legislative programs in modern times. They proposed a series of measures to transfer important powers from the federal government to the states. They proposed dramatic reductions in federal spending, including a major restructuring of the Medicare program, to reduce costs. They attempted to scale back federal regulatory functions.

President Clinton responded to the 1994 election results by proclaiming that "the era of big government is over" and by announcing his own plan to cut taxes and balance the budget. But because the legislative politics of 1995 was becoming part of the presidential politics of 1996, compromise between

the president and Congress became very difficult. In November 1995 and again in January 1996, the federal government literally shut down for several days because the president and Congress could not agree on a budget. Republican leaders refused to pass a "continuing resolution" (to allow government operations to continue during negotiations) in hopes of pressuring the president to agree to their terms. That proved to be an epic political blunder. Public opinion turned against the Republican leadership. Newt Gingrich, the controversial Republican Speaker of the House, quickly became one of the most unpopular political leaders in the nation, while President Clinton slowly improved his standing in the polls.

The Election of 1996

By the time the 1996 presidential campaign began in earnest, President Clinton was in a commanding position to win reelection. Unopposed for the Democratic nomination, he faced a Republican opponent—Senator Robert Dole of Kansas—who inspired little enthusiasm even within his own party. Clinton's revival was in part a result

Clinton's Renewed Popularity

of his adroitness in taking centrist positions that

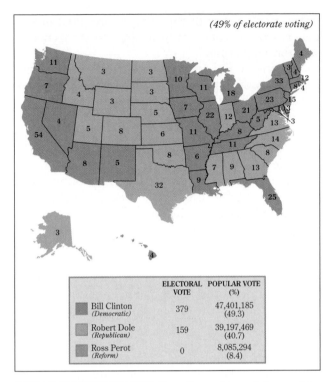

(49% of electorate voting)

	ELECTORAL VOTE	POPULAR VOTE (%)
Bill Clinton *(Democratic)*	379	47,401,185 (49.3)
Robert Dole *(Republican)*	159	39,197,469 (40.7)
Ross Perot *(Reform)*	0	8,085,294 (8.4)

THE ELECTION OF 1996 Rose Perot did much less well in 1996 than he had in 1992, and President Clinton came much closer than he had four years earlier to winning a majority of the popular vote. Once again, Clinton defeated his Republican opponent, this time Robert Dole, by a decisive margin in both the popular and electoral vote. After the 1994 Republican landslide in the congressional elections, Bill Clinton had seemed permanently weakened. ▌ *What explains his political revival?*

For an interactive version of this map go to www.mhhe.com/unfinishedinteractive

undermined the Republicans on one issue after another, and in championing traditional Democratic issues—such as raising the minimum wage—that were broadly popular. But his greatest strength came from the remarkable success of the American economy and the marked reduction in the federal deficit that had occurred during his presidency. Like Reagan in 1984, he could campaign as the champion of peace, prosperity, and national well-being.

As the election approached, both Democrats and Republicans grew uneasy about the failure of the 104th Congress to pass any significant measures. In a flurry of activity in the spring and summer of 1996, the Congress passed several important bills. The most dramatic of them was a welfare reform bill, which President Clinton somewhat uneasily signed, that ended the fifty-year federal guarantee of assistance to families with dependent children and turned most of the responsibility for allocating federal welfare funds (now greatly reduced) to the states. Most of all, it shifted the bulk of welfare benefits away from those without jobs and toward support for low-wage workers. A strong economy in the first few years after the bill passed helped many former welfare recipients move into the paid workforce.

Clinton's buoyant campaign flagged slightly in the last weeks before the election in the face of allegations of improper or illegal fund-raising techniques by the Democrats. But the president nevertheless won a substantial victory. He received just over 49 percent of the popular vote to Dole's 41 percent; Ross Perot generated much less enthusiasm than he had in 1992 but still received over 8 percent of the vote. Clinton won 379 electoral votes to Dole's 159; Perot again won none. But the president's victory did not have much effect on other Democrats, who failed to regain either house of Congress.

Clinton Triumphant and Embattled

Bill Clinton was the first Democrat to win two terms as president since Franklin Roosevelt, and he began his second administration with what appeared to be serene confidence. Facing a somewhat chastened Republican Congress, he proposed a relatively modest domestic agenda. He also negotiated effectively with the Republican leadership on a plan for a balanced budget, which passed with much fanfare late in 1997. By the end of 1998, the federal budget was generating its first surplus in thirty years. The president finished his fifth year in office more popular than he had ever been before.

That popularity would be important to him in the turbulent year that followed, when the most serious crisis of his presidency suddenly erupted. Clinton had been bedeviled by scandals almost from his first weeks in office. Among his problems was a civil suit for sexual harassment filed against the president by a former state employee in Arkansas, Paula Jones, who charged that Clinton, while governor, had made unwanted sexual advances toward her.

In early 1998, inquiries associated with the Paula Jones case led to charges that the president had had a sexual relationship with a young White House intern, Monica Lewinsky; that

Monica Lewinsky

he had lied about it in his deposition before Jones's attorneys; and that he had encouraged Lewinsky to do the same. Those revelations produced a new investigation by the independent counsel in the Whitewater case, Kenneth Starr.

Starr had been investigating the Whitewater matter for nearly four years without any significant results. But he suddenly resurfaced as a major threat to the president with a vigorous effort to prove that the president had lied under oath and had advised others to lie as well. Clinton forcefully denied the charges, and the public strongly backed him. His popularity soared to record levels. In the meantime, a federal judge dismissed the Paula Jones case.

But the scandal revived again in August 1998, when Lewinsky struck a deal with the independent counsel and testified about her relationship with Clinton. Starr then subpoenaed Clinton himself, who—faced with the prospect of speaking to a grand jury—finally admitted that he and Lewinsky had had what he called an "improper relationship." A few weeks later, Starr submitted a report to Congress on the results of his investigation, recommending that Congress impeach the president.

The prospect of impeachment became an issue in the 1998 congressional elections. Democrats believed that the public's strong opposition to impeachment would damage the Republicans, and they turned out to be right. The Republicans lost ten seats in the House and gained no seats in the Senate.

Impeachment, Acquittal, and Resurgence

Despite the polls and the election results, House leaders resisted all calls for compromise or dismissal of the charges. On December 19, 1998, the House,

Clinton Acquitted

voting on strictly partisan lines, narrowly approved two counts of impeachment: lying to the grand jury and obstructing justice. The matter then moved to the Senate, where a trial of the president began in early January. The Senate trial continued for several weeks and ended with a decisive acquittal of the

president. Neither of the charges attracted even a majority of the votes, let alone the two-thirds necessary for conviction.

The investigation into the president's sexual behavior, and the political battle that followed it, illustrated two significant changes in the character of American public life in the 1990s. One was the expanding role of scandal in American politics, driven by an increasingly sensationalist media culture, the legal device of independent counsels, and the intensely adversarial quality of partisan politics. The other was the blurring of the distinction between public and private behavior, which made almost every facet of a politician's life a target of inquiry and exposure.

The last two years of the Clinton presidency were relatively quiet ones domestically. The president had no real hope of major domestic achievements in the face of a hostile Republican Congress. Overseas, however, he was more active than he had ever been before. Beginning in 1998, the United States found itself once again in conflict with Iraqi president Saddam Hussein, who refused to permit international inspectors to examine military sites in his country. Clinton responded by ordering a series of American bombing strikes at military targets in Iraq.

In 1999, the president faced another crisis in the Balkans. This time, the conflict involved a province of

Serbia Bombed

Serbian-dominated Yugoslavia—Kosovo—most of whose residents were Albanian Muslims. A savage civil war erupted there in 1998 between Kosovo nationalists and Serbians. Numerous reports of Serbian atrocities against the Kosovans, and an enormous refugee crisis spurred by Yugoslavian military action in the province, slowly roused world opinion. In May 1999, NATO forces—dominated and led by the United States—began a major bombing campaign against the Serbians, which after little more than a week led the leader of Yugoslavia, Slobodan Milosevic, to agree to a cease-fire. Serbian troops withdrew from Kosovo entirely, replaced by NATO peacekeeping forces. A precarious peace returned to the region.

Clinton finished his eight years in office with his popularity higher than it had been when he had begun. Indeed, public approval of Clinton's presidency—a presidency marked by astonishing prosperity and general world stability as well as persistent scandal—was consistently among the highest of any postwar president.

The Election of 2000

The 2000 presidential election was one of the most extraordinary in American history—not because of the campaign that preceded it, but because of the sensational controversy over its results.

George W. Bush—son of the former president and a second-term governor of Texas—rode his famous name and his enormous campaign war chest to overcome a powerful challenge from Senator John McCain of Arizona, a maverick reformer. Vice President Al Gore, an even more prohibitive favorite in the Democratic race, easily beat back a challenge from former Senator Bill Bradley of New Jersey.

Both men ran cautious, centrist campaigns, making much of their relatively modest differences over how to use the large budget surpluses forecast for the years ahead. Although polls showed an exceptionally tight race right up to the end, no one anticipated how close the election would be. In the congressional races, Republicans maintained control of the House of Representatives by a scant five seats, while the Senate split evenly between Democrats and Republicans. In the presidential race, Gore won the national popular vote by the thin margin of about 540,000 votes out of about 100 million cast (or .5%). But on election night, both candidates remained short of the 270 electoral votes needed for victory because no one could determine who had actually won Florida.

Florida Disputed

After a mandatory recount over the next two days, Bush led Gore in the state by fewer than 300 votes. (Ralph Nader, the presidential candidate of the new Green Party, drew over 90,000 votes in Florida, which almost certainly denied Gore what would otherwise have been a comfortable victory there.) The technology of voting soon became central to the dispute. In a number of Florida counties, including some of the most heavily Democratic ones, votes were cast by punch-card ballots, which were then counted by machines. But punch cards are notoriously inaccurate, and many voters failed to punch out the appropriate holes adequately, leaving the machines unable to read them. In heavily

Democratic Palm Beach County, where the ballot was especially poorly designed, thousands of confused voters punched the wrong hole, or punched two holes when they were supposed to punch one. The Gore campaign asked for hand recounts of punch-card ballots in three critical counties.

The Bush campaign immediately struck back in court and through the Republican Secretary of State, Katherine Harris. As the official responsible for certifying elections in the state, she refused to authorize the recounts and declined to extend a deadline for making an official certification. But the Florida Supreme Court voted unanimously to require Harris to permit the hand recounts and to accept the results after the deadline. Such recounts proceeded in two of those counties, but in the third and largest (Dade County, which includes Miami) the local election board abruptly called off the recount, claiming they could not finish in time.

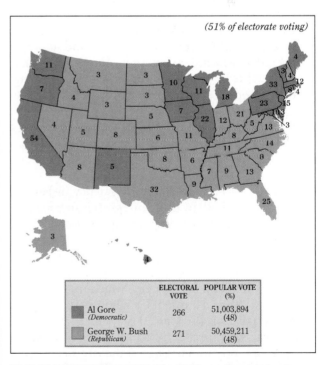

(51% of electorate voting)

	ELECTORAL VOTE	POPULAR VOTE (%)
Al Gore *(Democratic)*	266	51,003,894 (48)
George W. Bush *(Republican)*	271	50,459,211 (48)

THE ELECTION OF 2000 The 2000 presidential election was one of the closest and most controversial in American history. It also starkly revealed a new pattern of party strength, which had been developing over the previous decade. Compare this map to earlier elections, and in particular the election of 1896, and consider how the pattern of party support changed over the course of the twentieth century.

When the new, court-ordered deadline arrived, Harris quickly certified Bush the winner in Florida by a little more than 500 votes. The Gore campaign immediately contested the results in court, asking for the Dade County recount to be reopened. Again they prevailed in the Florida Supreme Court, which ordered hand recounts of all previously uncounted ballots in all Florida counties.

In the meantime, the Bush campaign appealed desperately to the United States Supreme Court to stop the recounts. To the surprise of most observers, the Court issued a stay on Saturday, December 9 (by a vote of 5-4), and late on Tuesday, the Court issued one of the most unusual and controversial decisions in its history. Voting 5-4 again, dividing sharply along party and ideological lines, the conservative majority overruled the

The Supreme Court's Divisive Ruling

Florida Supreme Court's order for a recount, insisted that any revised recount order be completed by December 12 (an obviously impossible demand, since the Court issued its ruling late at night on the 12th), and argued that the standards for evaluating punch-card ballots were too arbitrary and unfair to withstand constitutional scrutiny. The four-member minority bitterly protested the majority's reasoning, and the majority itself appeared deeply divided on some crucial issues. But divided or not, the Court had decided the election. The next day, Gore gave a brief and conciliatory concession speech.

The Second Bush Presidency

George W. Bush assumed the presidency in January 2001 burdened both by the controversies surrounding his election and the widespread perception that he was ill-prepared for the office.

Bush's Tax Cuts

His principal campaign promise had been that he would use the predicted budget surplus to finance a massive tax reduction. By relying on his own party's control of both houses of Congress (Republicans controlled the 50-50 Senate because the Republican vice president, Richard Cheney, broke all ties), he narrowly won passage of the largest tax cut in American history—$1.35 trillion. But a few weeks later, the administration—and the Republican party—suffered a stunning setback when Senator James Jeffords of Vermont, a moderate Republican unhappy with the conservative policies of both the administration and the Republican leadership in

Congress, declared himself an independent and announced he would vote with the Democrats to organize the Senate. Suddenly, Bush's legislative road became much less promising.

In the 2002 midterm elections, however, the Republicans regained control of the Senate and retained a slim majority in the House of Representatives. That enabled the administration and the Republican leadership to move much more aggressively to pursue its ambitious agenda.

Having campaigned as a moderate adept at building coalitions across party lines, Bush spent his first three years as president governing as a staunch conservative, allied with the most determinedly right-wing figures in his party. The administration proposed nothing less than a radical shift in both domestic and foreign policy. Domestically, it sought a series of enormous reductions, and even eliminations, of taxes—especially for wealthy Americans, whom conservatives believed were best suited to promote economic growth through investment. It also sought to reduce government regulation of and interference in the market. Internationally, it proposed a dramatically new foreign policy, which asserted the United States to launch "preemptive" wars to eliminate regimes it considered hostile or dangerous and which committed the nation to working toward a world in which all nations embraced America's commitment to free and open markets.

THE ECONOMIC BOOM

The last twenty years of the twentieth century saw remarkable changes in American life—some a result of the end of the Cold War, some a result of the changing character of the American population, but most a product of the dramatic transformation of the American economy.

From "Stagflation" to Growth

The roots of the economic growth of the 1980s and 1990s lay in part in the troubled years of the 1970s. In the face of the sluggish growth and persistent inflation of those years, many American corporations began making important changes in the way they ran their businesses. Businesses invested heavily in new technology.

Corporate Restructuring

Corporations began to consider mergers with other companies, to provide a more diversified basis for growth. Many enterprises created more energy-efficient plants and offices. Perhaps most of all, American businesses sought to reduce their labor costs, which many believed had made the United States uncompetitive against economies that relied on low-wage workers.

Businesses cut labor costs in many ways. Non-union companies became more successful in staving off unionization drives. Companies already unionized won important concessions from their unions on wages and benefits in exchange for preserving jobs. Some companies moved their operations to areas of the country where unions were weak and wages low. And many companies moved much of their production out of the United States entirely, to such nations as Mexico and China where there were large available labor pools willing to work for much less than American workers earned.

At least as important as the restructuring of existing businesses was the emergence of powerful new sectors of the economy—most notably what became known as the "technol- **"Technology Industries"** ogy industries." The growth of digital technologies made possible an enormous range of new products and services that quickly became central to American economic life: computers, the Internet, cellular phones, digital music, video cameras, personal digital assistants, and many others. The technology industries employed hundreds of thousands of people, created new consumer needs and appetites, and even spawned their own stock exchange—the NASDAQ.

For these and many other reasons, the American economy experienced astonishing growth in the last decades of the twentieth century. The Gross National Product (the total of goods and services produced by the United States) rose from $2.7 trillion in 1980 to over $9.8 trillion in 2000. Inflation was low throughout these decades. Stock prices soared to unprecedented levels, and with few interruptions, from the mid-1980s to the end of the century. The Dow Jones Industrial Average, the most common index of stock performance, stood at 1,000 in late 1980. Late in 1999, it passed 11,000. Economic growth was particularly dramatic in the last years of the 1990s. Most impressive of all was the longevity of the boom. From 1994 to 2000, the economy

recorded growth—at times very substantial growth—in every year, something that had never before happened so continuously in peacetime since modern economic measurements began.

Downturn

The most powerful single figure in the American economy—Alan Greenspan, chairman of the Federal Board—warned in 1999 of the "irrational exuberance" with which Americans were pursuing profits in the stock market. The market justified his concern when, in April 2001, there was a sudden and disastrous collapse of the booming technology sector of the economy. Investors decided that they had greatly overestimated the short-term profitability of Internet-based business. The result was a dramatic sell-off of technology stocks.

The bursting of the "tech bubble" did not have immediate effects on the rest of the market. But in the first months of 2001, the market as a whole began a **Plummetting Stock Market** long slide that continued for more than a year, so that by the summer of 2002 the Dow Jones Industrial Average had lost almost 40 percent of its value.

In the fall of 2001, the economy as a whole slipped into a recession. And although there was a weak recovery in early 2002, many factors continued to depress growth and to threaten long-term economic sluggishness. Among them was a series of major corporate failures that revealed not just weakness, but corruption and dishonesty. The revelations of corruption began in December 2001 when the Enron Corporation, an energy-trading company based in Houston, declared bankruptcy. A model to many managers of bold innovation, it conceded that it had vastly inflated its declared earnings through unorthodox and perhaps illegal accounting methods.

The Enron collapse was only the first of a series of corporate scandals that did grave damage to public con- **Corporate Scandals** fidence in corporate leadership. One major company after another admitted that their reported earnings greatly exaggerated their real income. Major accounting firms—most notably Arthur Andersen, the Enron accountant—came under intense public and legal scrutiny. And the aggressive innovation that had been so lionized in corporate

America in the late nineties suddenly projected a different image—recklessness, occasional lawlessness, and (in the words of Alan Greenspan) "infectious greed."

The Two-Tiered Economy

Although the American economy in the late twentieth century revived triumphantly from the sluggishness of the 1970s and early 1980s, the benefits of the new economy were less widely shared than those of earlier boom times. The increasing abundance created enormous new wealth that enriched those talented, or lucky, enough to profit from the areas of booming growth. The rewards for education increased enormously. In 1995, the average annual income of a person with less than a high-school education was $14,000. A college graduate's average salary was $37,000, and the average salary of someone with an advanced degree was $56,700—four times the level of those who did not graduate from high school. Between 1980 and the mid-1990s, the average family incomes of the wealthiest 20 percent of the population grew by nearly 20 percent (to over $100,000 a year); the average family income of the next 20 percent of the population grew by more than 8 percent. Incomes remained flat for most of the remaining 60 percent of the public, and actually declined for many in the bottom 20 percent.

Poverty in America had declined steadily in the years after World War II, so that by the end of the 1970s the percentage of people living in poverty had declined to 12 percent. But in the 1980s, the poverty rate rose again, at times as high as 18 percent. By the late 1990s, it had dropped to under 13 percent again, but that was about the same as it had been twenty years before.

Rising Poverty Rates

Globalization

The great prosperity of the 1950s and 1960s had rested on, among other things, the relative insulation of the United States from the pressures of international competition. As late as 1970, international trade still played a relatively small role in the American economy as a whole. By the end of the 1970s, however, the world had intruded on the American economy in profound ways. Exports rose from just under $43 billion in 1970 to over $789 billion in 2000. Imports rose even more dramatically: from just over $40 billion in 1970 to over $1.2 trillion in 2000. Most American products, in other words, now faced foreign competition inside the United States. America had made 76 percent of the world's automobiles in 1950 and 48 percent in 1960. By 2000 the American share was only 21.5 percent. The first American trade imbalance in the postwar era occurred in 1971; only twice since then, in 1973 and 1975, has the balance been favorable.

Globalization brought many benefits for the American consumer: new and more varied products, and lower prices for many of them. Most economists, and most national leaders, welcomed the process and worked to encourage it through lowering trade barriers. The North American Free Trade Agreement (NAFTA) and the General Agreement on Trade and Tariffs (GATT) were the boldest of a long series of treaties designed to lower trade barriers stretching back to the 1960s. But globalization had many costs as well. It was particularly hard on industrial workers, who saw industrial jobs disappear as American companies lost market share to foreign competitors and as American companies began exporting work to lower-wage countries to avoid having to pay the high wages workers had won in America.

Costs and Benefits of Globalization

SCIENCE AND TECHNOLOGY IN THE NEW ECONOMY

The "new economy" that emerged in the last decades of the twentieth century was driven by dramatic new scientific and technological discoveries. Much as in the late nineteenth century when technological innovations transformed society, so in the late twentieth century, new technologies had profound effects on the way Americans lived.

The Personal Computer

The most visible element of the technological revolution to most Americans was the dramatic growth in the use of computers in almost every area of life. By the early 1990s, most Americans were doing their banking by computer. Most retail transactions were conducted by computerized credit mechanisms. Most businesses, schools, and

The Computer Revolution

other institutions were using computerized record-keeping, and many areas of manufacturing were revolutionized by computer-driven product design and factory robotics.

Among the most significant innovations was the development of the microprocessor, introduced in 1971 by Intel. A microprocessor miniaturized the central processing unit of a computer, making it possible for a small machine to perform calculations that in the past only very large machines could do. Considerable technological innovation was needed before the microprocessor could actually become the basis of what was first known as a "minicomputer" and then a personal computer. But in 1977, Apple launched its Apple II personal computer, and several years later, IBM entered the personal computer market with the first "PC." IBM had engaged a small software development company, Microsoft, to design an operating system for their new computer. Microsoft produced a program known as MS-DOS (DOS for "disk operating system"). No PC could operate without it. The PC, and its software, made its debut in August 1981 and immediately became enormously successful. Three years later, Apple introduced its Macintosh computer, which marked another major innovation in computer technology, among other things because its software was much easier to use than that of the PC. But Apple could not match IBM's marketing power, and by the mid-1980s the PC had clearly established its dominance in the booming personal computer market—a dominance enhanced by the introduction of a new software package to replace DOS in 1985: Windows, also developed by Microsoft. IBM, however, was not in the end the principal beneficiary of the dominance of its own system, as other companies began marketing their own IBM-compatible personal computers, usually at a lower price than IBMs.

The computer revolution created thousands of new, lucrative businesses: computer manufacturers themselves (IBM, Apple, and many others); makers of the tiny silicon chips that ran the computers (most notably Intel); and makers of software—chief among them Microsoft, the most powerful new corporation to arise in American life in generations. In the 1990s, Microsoft had a virtual monopoly on the operating systems for most personal computers in the

Microsoft

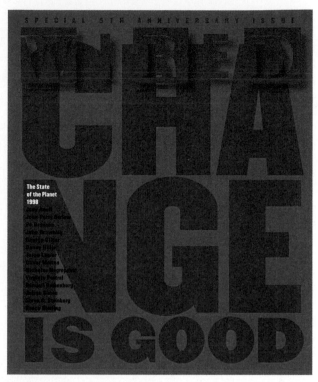

WIRED 6.01 The January 1998 issue of *Wired*, a magazine aimed at young, hip, computer-literate readers, expressed the optimistic, even visionary approach to the possibilities of new electronic technologies that was characteristic of many computer and Internet enthusiasts in the 1990s. *(Wired © Condé Nast Publications, Inc.)*

world. It had also moved into new areas: creating other kinds of software and producing software and content for the Internet.

But if Microsoft was the most conspicuous success story of the computer age, it was only one of many. Whole regions—the so-called Silicon Valley in northern California; areas around Boston, Austin, Texas, and Seattle, Washington; areas in downtown New York City—became centers of booming economic activity servicing the new computer age.

The Internet

Out of the computer revolution emerged another dramatic source of information and communication: the Internet—a vast network of computers that allows people to communicate with others all over the world. It had its beginning in 1963, in the U.S. government's Advanced Research Projects Agency (ARPA). In the early 1960s, J. C. R. Licklider, the head of ARPA's Information Processing Technique Office, launched a program to link together computers over large distances. It was known as the Arpanet. For several years, the Arpanet served mainly as a way for people to make use of what were then relatively scarce computer facilities without having to go to the site of the computer. Gradually, however, both the size and the uses of the network expanded.

Arpanet

This expansion was facilitated in part by two important new technologies. One was a system developed in the early 1960s at the RAND Corporation in the United States and the National Physical Laboratory in England. It was known as "store-and-forward packet switching," and it made possible the transmission of large quantities of data between computers without directly wiring the computers together. There could be a central communications backbone through which messages and information could be routed to individual computers. The other technological breakthrough was the development of software that would allow individual computers to handle the traffic over the network—what became known as the Interface Message Processor.

By 1971, twenty-three computers were linked together in the Arpanet, which served mostly research labs and universities. Gradually, interest in the system began to spread. By the end of 2001, there were over 650 million computers in use in the world, and over 180 million in the United States. The great majority of them had connections to the Internet. In the early 1980s, the Defense Department, an early partner in the development of the Arpanet, withdrew from the project for security reasons. The network, soon renamed the Internet, was then free to develop independently. It did so rapidly, especially after the invention of technologies that made possible electronic mail (or e-mail) and the emergence of the personal computer. In 1984, fewer than a thousand host computers connected to the Internet. A decade later, there were over 6 million. And in 2001, an estimated 400 million people around the world were using the Internet.

The Internet

As the amount of information on the Internet proliferated, new forms of software emerged to make it possible for users to navigate through the vast number of Internet sites. In 1989, a laboratory in Geneva introduced the World Wide Web, which helped establish an orderly system for both the distribution and retrieval of electronic information.

The Internet revolutionized many areas of life. E-mail replaced conventional mail, telephone calls, and even face-to-face conversation for millions of people. Newspapers, magazines, and other publications began to publish on the Internet. It became a powerful marketing tool. It is a site for vast amounts of documentary material for researchers, reporters, students and others. And it is, finally, a highly democratic medium—through which virtually anyone with access to a personal computer can establish a website and present information in a form that is available to virtually anyone in the world who chooses to look at it. New technologies that make it easier to transmit moving images over the Internet—and new forms of "broadband" access that give more users high-speed connections to the Web—promise to expand greatly the functions that the Internet can perform.

Breakthroughs in Genetics

Aided in part by computer technology, there was explosive growth in another area of scientific research: genetics. Early discoveries by Gregor Mendel, Thomas Hunt Morgan, and others laid the groundwork for more dramatic breakthroughs—the discovery of DNA by the British scientists Oswald Avery, Colin MacLeod, and Maclyn McCarty in 1944; and in 1953, the dramatic discovery by the American biochemist James Watson and the British biophysicist Francis Crick of the double-helix structure of DNA, and thus of the key to identifying genetic codes. From these discoveries emerged the new science of genetic engineering, through which new medical treatments and new techniques for hybridization of plants and animals have already become possible.

DNA

Little by little, scientists began to identify specific genes in humans and other living things that determine particular traits, and to learn how to alter or reproduce them. But the identification of genes was painfully slow; and in 1989, the federal government appropriated $3 billion to fund the National Center for the Human Genome, to accelerate the

Human Genome Project

mapping of human genes. The Human Genome Project set out to identify all of the more than 100,000 genes by 2005. But new technologies for research, and competition from other projects (some of them funded by pharmaceutical companies) drove the project forward faster than expected. In 1998, the genome project announced that it would finish its work in 2003. In the meantime, in 2000, other researchers produced a list of all the genes in the human body.

In 1997, scientists in Scotland announced that they had cloned a sheep—which they named Dolly—using a cell from an adult ewe; in other words, the genetic structure of the newborn Dolly was identical to that of the sheep from which the cell was taken. The DNA structure of an individual, scientists have discovered, is as unique and as identifiable as a fingerprint. DNA testing, therefore, makes it possible to identify individuals through their blood, semen, skin, or even hair. It played a major role first in the O. J. Simpson trial in 1995 and then in the 1998 investigation into President Clinton's relationship with Monica Lewinsky. Also in 1998, DNA testing appeared to establish with certainty that Thomas Jefferson had fathered a child with his slave Sally Hemings, by finding genetic similarities between descendants of both, thus resolving a political and scholarly dispute stretching back nearly 200 years. Genetic research has already spawned important new areas of medical treatment—and has helped the relatively new biotechnology industry to grow into one of the nation's most important economic sectors.

But genetic research was also the source of great controversy. Some critics feared genetic research on religious grounds, seeing it as an interference with God's plan. Others expressed fears that it would allow parents to choose what kinds of children they would have. And a particularly heated controversy emerged over the use in medical research of stem cells, genetic material obtained in large part from undeveloped fetuses—mostly fetuses created by couples attempting in vitro fertilization. (*In vitro fertilization* is the process by which couples unable to conceive a child have a fetus conceived outside the womb using their eggs and sperm and then implanted in the mother.) Anti-abortion advocates

Ethical Issues

denounced the research. Supporters of stem-cell research—which showed promising signs of offering cures for Parkinson's disease, Alzheimer's disease, ALS, and other previously uncurable illnesses—argued that the stem cells they used came from fetuses that would otherwise be discarded. The controversy over stem-cell research became an issue in the 2000 campaign. George W. Bush, once president, kept his promise to anti-abortion advocates and in the summer of 2001 issued a ruling barring the use of federal funds to support research using any stem cells that scientists were not already using at the time of his decision.

A CHANGING SOCIETY

The changes in the economy were only one of many factors producing major changes in the character of American society. By the end of the twentieth century, the American population was growing larger, older, and more racially and geographically diverse.

The Graying of America

One of the most important features of American life was the aging of the American

Growing Elderly Population

population. After decades of steady growth, the nation's birth rate began to decline in the 1970s and remained low through the 1980s and 1990s. In 1970, there were 18.4 births for every 1,000 people in the population. By 1996, the rate had dropped to 14.8 births. The declining birth rate and a significant rise in life expectancy produced a substantial increase in the proportion of elderly citizens. Almost 13 percent of the population was more than sixty-five years old in 2000.

The aging of the population was a cause of the increasing costliness of Social Security pensions. It meant rapidly increasing health costs. It also ensured that the elderly, who already formed one of the most powerful interest groups in America, would remain politically formidable well into the twenty-first century.

It also had important implications for the work force. In the last twenty years of the twentieth century, the number of people aged 25–54 in the native-born work force grew by over 26 million. In the first ten years of the twenty-first century, the number of workers in that age group will not grow at all. That will put increasing pressure on the economy to employ more older workers and immigrant workers.

New Patterns of Immigration and Ethnicity

The nation's immigration quotas expanded significantly in the last decades of the twentieth century, allowing more newcomers to enter the United States legally than at any point since the beginning of the twentieth century. In 2000, over 28 million Americans—over 10 percent of the total population—consisted of immigrants.

The Immigration Reform Act of 1965 had eliminated quotas based on national origin; from then on, newcomers from regions other than Latin America (who were governed by different laws) were generally admitted on a first-come, first-served basis. In 1965, 90 percent of the immigrants to the United States came from Europe. By the 1990s, only about 10 percent of the new arrivals were Europeans. The extent and character of the new immigration was causing a dramatic change in the composition of the American population. By the end of the twentieth century, people of white European background constituted under 80 percent of the population.

Latino Immigrants Particularly important to the new immigration were two groups: Latinos (people from Spanish-speaking nations, particularly Mexico) and Asians. Both experienced enormous growth after 1965. People from Latin America constituted more than a third of the total number of legal immigrants to the United States in every year after 1965. Mexico alone accounted for over one-fourth of all the immigrants living in the United States in 2000. In the 1980 census, 6 percent of the population (about 14 million) was listed as being of Hispanic origin. By 1997, census figures showed an increase to 11 percent— or 29 million people.

In the 1980s and 1990s, Asian immigrants arrived in even greater numbers than Latinos, constituting more than 40 percent of the total of legal newcomers. They swelled the already substantial Chinese and Japanese communities in California and elsewhere. And they created substantial new communities of immigrants from Vietnam, Thailand,

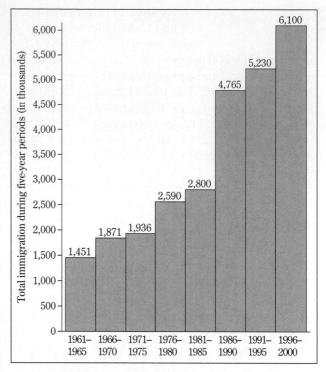

TOTAL IMMIGRATION, 1961–2000 This chart shows the tremendous increase in immigration to the United States in the decades since the Immigration Reform Act of 1965. The immigration of the 1980s and 1990s was the highest since the late nineteenth century.

Cambodia, Laos, the Philippines, Korea, and India. By 2000, there were more than 10 million Asian Americans in the United States (4 percent of the population), more than twice the number of fifteen years before.

The Black Middle Class

For the black middle class, economic progress was remarkable. Disparities between **Remarkable Black Economic Progress** black and white professionals did not vanish, but they diminished substantially. African-American families moved into more affluent communities. African Americans made up 12 percent of the college population in the 1990s. The percentage of black high-school graduates going on to college was virtually the same as that of white high-school graduates by the end of the twentieth century (although a far smaller proportion of blacks than whites managed to complete high school). And

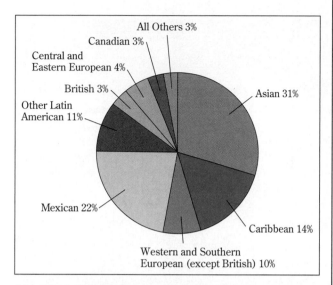

All Others 3%

Canadian 3%

Central and
Eastern European 4%

British 3%

Other Latin
American 11%

Asian 31%

Mexican 22%

Caribbean 14%

Western and Southern
European (except British) 10%

SOURCES OF IMMIGRATION, 1960–1990 The Immigration Reform Act of 1965 lifted the national quotas imposed on immigration policy in 1924 and opened immigration to large areas of the world that had previously been restricted. In 1965, 90 percent of the immigrants to the United States came from Europe. As this chart shows, by 1990 almost the reverse was true. Over 80 percent of all immigrants came from non-European sources. ▌ *What impact did this new immigration have on American politics?*

African Americans were making rapid strides in many professions from which, a generation earlier, they had been barred or within which they had been segregated.

Poor and Working-Class African Americans

But the rise of the black middle class also accentuated the plight of other African Americans, whom the economic growth and the liberal programs of the 1960s and beyond had never reached. These impoverished people—sometimes described as the "underclass"—made up as much as a third of the nation's

▌ Black "Underclass"

black population. As more successful African Americans moved out of the inner cities, the poor were left in their decaying neighborhoods. Fewer than half of young inner-city blacks finished high school; more than 60 percent were unemployed. The black family structure suffered as well. There was a radical increase in the number of single-parent, female-headed black households. In 1970, 59 percent of all black children under 18 lived with both their parents. In 2000, only 38 percent of African-American children lived in such households, while 75 percent of white children did.

Nonwhites were disadvantaged by many factors in the changing social and economic climate of the 1980s and 1990s. Among them was a growing impatience with affirmative action. They suffered as well from a steady decline in the number of unskilled jobs in the economy; the departure of businesses from their neighborhoods; the absence of adequate transportation to areas where jobs were more plentiful; and failing schools. And they suffered, in many cases, from a sense of futility born of years of entrapment in brutal urban ghettoes.

The anger and despair such conditions were creating was expressed at times artistically, as in some aspects of rap music. The frustration became visible in the summer of 1992 in Los Angeles. The previous year, a bystander had videotaped several Los Angeles police officers beating an apparently helpless black man, Rodney King, whom they had captured after an auto chase. Broadcast repeatedly around the country, the tape evoked outrage among whites and blacks alike. But an all-white jury acquitted the officers when they were tried for assault. Black residents of South Central Los Angeles erupted

▌ Los Angeles Riots

in anger—precipitating one of the largest racial disturbances of the twentieth century. There was widespread looting and arson. More than fifty people died.

Relations between white and black Americans grew increasingly sour in these difficult years. Nowhere was this mutual suspicion more evident than in the trial of the former football star O. J. Simpson, who was accused of murdering his former wife and a young man in Los Angeles in 1994. The long and costly "O. J. trial" was a media sensation for over a year. Throughout the proceedings, opinions about Simpson's guilt broke down strikingly along racial lines. A vast majority of whites believed that he was guilty, and a significant majority of blacks believed he was innocent. Simpson's acquittal in the fall of 1995, after a trial in which the defense tried to portray him as a victim of police racism, caused celebrations in many black communities and a quiet disgust among many whites.

"IGNORANCE = FEAR" The artist Keith Haring (whose work was inspired in large part by urban graffiti) created this striking poster in 1989, the year before he himself died of AIDS, to generate support for the battle against the disease. "ACT UP," the organization that distributed it, was among the most militant groups in demanding more rapid efforts to search for a cure. *(Silence = Death, Ignorance = Fear, 1989 © The Estate of Keith Haring)*

IGNORANCE = FEAR

SILENCE = DEATH ▲ FIGHT AIDS ACT UP

Modern Plagues: Drugs and AIDS

America in the 1980s and 1990s was ravaged by two new and deadly epidemics. One was a dramatic increase in drug use. The enormous demand for illegal drugs spawned a multibillion-dollar industry; and those reaping the profits fought strenuously and often savagely to protect their positions. Political figures of both parties spoke heatedly about the need for a "war on drugs"; but government efforts to stop drug imports and reduce demand had little effect. Drug use declined significantly among middle-class people beginning in the late 1980s, but the epidemic showed no signs of abating in the poor urban neighborhoods where it was doing the most severe damage.

The drug epidemic was closely related to another scourge of the 1980s and 1990s: the epidemic spread of a new and lethal disease first documented in 1981 and soon named AIDS (acquired immune deficiency syndrome). AIDS is the product of the HIV virus, which is transmitted by the exchange of bodily fluids (blood or semen). The virus gradually destroys the body's immune system and makes its victims highly vulnerable to a number of diseases (particularly to various forms of cancer and pneumonia) to which they would otherwise have a natural resistance. Those infected with the virus (i.e., HIV positive) can live for a long time without developing AIDS, but in the first years of the disease, those who

| AIDS Epidemic |

became ill were virtually certain to die. The first American victims of AIDS were homosexual men. But by the late 1980s, as the gay community began to take preventive measures, the most rapid increase in the spread of the disease occurred among heterosexuals, many of them intravenous drug users. In 2000, U.S. government agencies estimated that about 780,000 Americans were infected with the HIV virus and that another 427,000 had already died from the disease. But the United States represented only a tiny proportion of the worldwide total of people afflicted with AIDS, an estimated 36.1 million people at the end of 2000. Seventy percent (over 25 million) of those cases were concentrated in Africa. Governments and private groups, in the meantime, began promoting AIDS awareness in increasingly visible and graphic ways—urging young people, in particular, to avoid "unsafe sex" through abstinence or the use of latex condoms.

In the mid-1990s, AIDS researchers began discovering effective treatments for the disease. By taking a combination of powerful drugs on a rigorous schedule, even people with relatively advanced cases of AIDS experienced dramatic improvement. The new drugs gave promise of dramatically extending the lives of people with AIDS. The drugs were not a cure for AIDS; people who stopped taking them experienced a rapid return of the disease. And the effectiveness of the drugs varied from person to person. In addition, the drugs were very expensive and difficult to administer; poorer AIDS patients often could not obtain access to them, and they remained very scarce in less affluent parts of the world. Nevertheless, the new medications restored hundreds of thousands of desperately ill people to health and gave them realistic hopes of long and relatively normal lives.

The Decline in Crime

One of the most striking social developments of the late 1990s was a dramatic reduction in crime rates across most of the United States. The rising incidence of violent crime had been one of the most disturbing facts of American life for two generations. But beginning in the early 1990s, crime began to fall. The government's crime index—which measures the incidence of seven serious crimes—fell by 19.5 percent between 1992 and 2000, with some of the most dramatic reductions occurring in murder and other violent crimes.

Prosperity and declining unemployment were certainly factors. So were new, sophisticated police techniques that helped deter many crimes and that led to the arrest of many criminals who would previously have escaped capture. New incarceration policies— longer, tougher sentences and fewer paroles and early releases for violent criminals—led to a radical increase in the prison population and, consequently, a reduction in the number of criminals at liberty to commit crimes.

| New Police Techniques |

A CONTESTED CULTURE

Few things created more controversy and anxiety in the 1980s and 1990s than the battles over the character of American culture.

Battles over Feminism and Abortion

Among the principal goals of the New Right as it became more powerful was to challenge feminism and its achievements. Leaders of the New Right had campaigned successfully against the proposed Equal Rights Amendment to the Constitution. And they played a central role in the controversy over abortion rights.

For those who favored allowing women to choose to terminate unwanted pregnancies, the Supreme Court's decision in *Roe* v. *Wade* (1973) had seemed to settle the question. By the 1980s, abortion was the most commonly performed surgical procedure in the country. But at the same time, opposition to abortion was creating a powerful grassroots movement. The right-to-life movement, as it called itself, found its most fervent supporters among Catholics; and indeed, the Catholic Church itself lent its institutional authority to the battle against legalized abortion. Religious doctrine also motivated the anti-abortion stance of Mormons, fundamentalist Christians, and other groups. The opposition of some other anti-abortion activists had less to do with religion than with their commitment to traditional notions of gender. To them, abortion was a particularly offensive part of a much larger assault by feminists on the role of women as wives and mothers. It was also, many foes contended, a form of murder. Fetuses, they claimed, were human beings who had a "right to life" from the moment of conception.

| Right-to-Life Movement |

In the 1970s, Congress and many state legislatures began barring the use of public funds to pay for abortions, thus making them inaccessible for many poor women. The Reagan and both Bush administrations imposed further restrictions on federal funding. Extremists in the right-to-life movement began picketing, occupying, and at times bombing abortion clinics. Several anti-abortion activists murdered doctors who performed abortions.

The changing composition of the Supreme Court in the 1980s and early 1990s (when five new conservative justices were named by Presidents Reagan and Bush) renewed the right-to-life movement's hopes for a reversal of *Roe* v. *Wade*. In *Webster* v. *Reproductive Health Services* (1989), the Court upheld a Missouri law that forbade any institution receiving state funds from performing abortions. But the Court stopped short of overturning its 1973 decision.

Through much of the 1970s and 1980s, defenders of abortion had remained confident that *Roe* v. *Wade* protected their right to choose abortion. But the changing judicial climate of the late 1980s mobilized defenders of abortion as never before. They called themselves the "pro-choice" movement, because they were defending every woman's right to choose whether and when to bear a child. It quickly became clear that the pro-choice movement was at least as strong as, and in some areas much stronger than, the right-to-life movement, and it contributed substantially to the election and reelection of Bill Clinton. But abortion rights remained highly vulnerable, and Clinton's successor, George W. Bush, openly opposed abortion.

Women's Rights Expanded

Other efforts by feminists to protect and expand the rights of women continued. Women's organizations and many individual women worked strenuously in the 1980s and 1990s to improve access to child care for poor women, and to win the right to caregiver leaves for parents, which a law passed by Congress and signed by President Clinton in 1993 helped secure. They also worked to raise awareness of sexual harassment in the workplace, with considerable success. Colleges, universities, the military, government agencies, even many corporations established strict new standards of behavior for their employees in dealing with members of the opposite sex and created grievance procedures for those who believed they had been harassed.

Both the achievements and the limits of their progress on this issue were evident in the sensational controversy in 1991 over Judge Clarence Thomas, President Bush's nominee for a seat on the Supreme Court. Late in the confirmation proceed-

Anita Hill and Clarence Thomas

ings, accusations of sexual harassment from Anita Hill, a law professor and former employee of Thomas, became public. Hill's testimony before the Senate Judiciary Committee dramatically polarized both the Senate and the nation. Feminists and others tended to believe the accusations and hailed the accuser for drawing national attention to the issue of harassment; but many Americans (and most members of the virtually all-male Senate) apparently did not believe her. Thomas was ultimately confirmed by a narrow margin. Visit Chapter 34 of the book's Online Learning Center for a Where Historians Disagree essay on "Women's History."

The Changing Left and the Growth of Environmentalism

The New Left of the 1960s and early 1970s did not disappear after the end of the war in Vietnam, but it faded rapidly. Yet a left of sorts did survive. Where 1960s activists had rallied to protest racism, poverty, and war, their counterparts in the 1980s and 1990s more often worked to organize communities to fight for local concerns. A great resurgence of grassroots organizing in many parts of the country was, in part, testament to the legacy of the New Left. Most of all, activists in the 1980s and 1990s organized to stop the proliferation of nuclear weapons and power plants, to protect endangered species, to limit reckless economic development, and to otherwise protect the environment.

The environmental movement continued to expand in the last decades of the twentieth century. Several highly visible environmental catastrophes in those years greatly increased their commitment. Among them were a major oil spill off Santa Barbara, California, in 1969; the discovery of large deposits of improperly disposed toxic waste in the residential community of Love Canal in upstate New York in 1978; a frightening accident at the nuclear power plant on Three Mile Island, Pennsylvania in 1979; and the largest oil spill in American history in Alaska in 1989.

In the decades after the first Earth Day, environmental issues gained increasing attention and support. Environmentalists helped block the construc-

Global Warming

tion of roads, airports, and other projects that they claimed would be ecologically dangerous, taking advantage of new legislation protecting endangered species and environmentally fragile regions. By the end of the 1970s, many scientists were warning that the release of certain industrial pollutants (most notably chlorofluorocarbons) into the atmosphere was depleting the ozone layer of the earth's atmosphere, which protects the globe from the sun's most dangerous rays. They warned, too, of the related danger of global warming, a rise in the earth's temperature as a result of emissions from the burning of fossil fuels (coal and oil). These problems required international solutions, which were much more difficult to produce. In 1997, representatives of the major industrial nations met in Kyoto, Japan and agreed to a broad treaty banning certain emissions into the atmosphere as a step toward reversing global warming. But in March 2001, under pressure from business leaders, the second Bush administration rejected the treaty.

The concern for the environment, the opposition to nuclear power, the resistance to economic development—all were reflections of a more fundamental characteristic of the post-Vietnam left. In a sharp break from the nation's long commitment to growth and progress, many dissidents argued that only by limiting growth and curbing traditional forms of progress could society hope to survive. Such arguments evoked strong opposition from conservatives and others.

The Fragmentation of Mass Culture

One of the most powerful cultural trends throughout much of the twentieth century was the growing power and the increasing standardization of mass culture. The institutions of the media—news, entertainment, advertising, and others—grew steadily more influential. They also strove to attract the largest possible audience or market. In doing so, they attempted to standardize their products so that they would be familiar to everyone. The drive toward standardization was reinforced by the philosophy of the advertising industry to appeal to the largest possible audience.

Beginning in the 1970s, the character of mass culture changed in some important ways. There was, of course, continued standardization in many areas. McDonald's, Burger King, and other fast-food chains became the most widely known restaurants. Huge retail chains—Kmart, Bradlees, WalMart, Barnes & Noble, Blockbuster, the Gap, and others—dominated retail sales in many communities.

Growing Cultural Segmentation

The most popular Hollywood films attracted larger audiences than ever before; and the most powerful media companies—most notably, Disney—produced merchandise that made their film and television characters familiar to almost everyone in the world. But there was also a tendency in both retailing and entertainment to appeal less to mass markets and more to specific segments of the market.

This segmentation was first visible in new ideas about advertising known as "targeting." Instead of finding promotional techniques to appeal to everyone, advertisers sought to identify a product with a particular "segment" of the market (men, women, young people, old people, children) and create advertisements designed to appeal to it. As if in response, the television networks began to produce programming that focused on particular segments of the audience. Some programs were aimed at women, some at African Americans, some at affluent, urban middle-class viewers, some at more rural and provincial people. Fewer and fewer programs had a truly "mass" audience.

Even more important was the rapid proliferation of media outlets. As late as the 1970s, American television audiences overwhelmingly watched programs on the three major networks: NBC, CBS, and ABC. In the 1980s, that began to change. One reason was the proliferation of videocassette recorders (VCRs). Instead of watching network television, viewers could now rent or buy videotapes and watch movies or other programming of their own choosing. In the late 1990s, VCRs began to give way to digital video disk players (DVDs). Another reason was the increasing availability of cable and satellite television, which allowed homes to receive many more channels than ever before. The percent of television viewers watching the major networks declined steadily in the 1980s. New networks (among them Fox and Warner Brothers), along with specialized sports, movies, shopping, music, weather, and other channels, began to compete with the traditional leaders. And many people turned away from television altogether and began to explore the powerful new medium of the Internet, with its huge variety of sites tailored to almost every conceivable interest and taste.

New Consumer Technologies

As audiences fragmented among many different stations and media, the phenomenon of the national "shared experience" declined as well. Network news, once the most important source for the vast majority of information, experienced a dramatic decline in viewership. Young people found their own media world in MTV and other cable stations that focused on rock music and other elements of youth culture. Hollywood continued to turn out hugely expensive "blockbusters" in a search for a mass audience. But some filmgoers turned instead to smaller independent films, which targeted particular segments of the population.

The "Culture Wars"

Few issues attracted more attention in the 1990s than the battle over what became known as

"Multiculturalism" "multiculturalism." Multiculturalism sought to legitimize the cultural pluralism of the rapidly diversifying American population. That meant acknowledging that "American culture," which had long been defined primarily by white males of European descent, also included other traditions: female, African American, Native American, and increasingly in the late twentieth century, Hispanic, Asian, and Middle Eastern. Particular acrimony emerged out of efforts by some revisionists to portray traditional Western culture as inherently racist and imperialistic. Many critics of multiculturalism complained of a tyranny of "political correctness," by which feminists, cultural radicals, and others introduced a new form of intolerance to public discourse in the name of defending the rights of women and minorities.

The controversies surrounding multiculturalism were illustrations of a painful change in the character of American society. Traditional patterns of authority faced challenges from women, minorities, and others. The liberal belief in tolerance and assimilation was fraying in the face of the growing cultural separatism of some ethnic and racial groups. But multiculturalism was also a way of broadening the definition of American culture to include all the nation's diverse peoples. It was often an expression of confidence in society's ability to tolerate and understand its many differences.

THE PERILS OF GLOBALIZATION

The celebration of the beginning of a new millennium on January 1, 2000 was a global event—a shared and for the most part joyous experience. Television viewers around the world followed the dawn of the new century from Australia, through Asia, Africa, and Europe, and on into the Americas. Never had the world seemed more united. But if the millennium celebrations suggested the bright promise of globalization, other events at the dawn of the new century suggested its dark perils.

Opposing the "New World Order"

In the United States and other industrial nations, opposition to globalization—or to what President George H. W. Bush once called "the new world order"—took several forms. To many Americans on both the left and the right, the nation's increasingly interventionist foreign policy was deeply troubling. Critics on the left charged that the United States was using military action to advance its economic interests, most notably in the 1991 Gulf War. Critics on the right claimed that the nation was allowing itself to be swayed by the interests of other nations; they opposed such supposedly humanitarian interventions as the 1993 invasion of Somalia and the American interventions in the Balkans in the late 1990s.

But the most impassioned opposition to globalization in the West came from an array of groups that challenged the claim that the "new world order" was economically beneficial. Labor unions insisted that the rapid expansion of free-trade agreements led to the export of jobs from advanced nations to less developed ones. Other groups attacked the poor working conditions in new manufacturing countries on humanitarian grounds. Environmentalists argued that globalization exported industrial pollution and toxic waste into nations that had no effective laws to control them. And still others opposed global economic arrangements on the grounds that they enriched and empowered large multinational corporations and threatened the freedom and autonomy of individuals and communities.

The varied opponents of globalization may have had different reasons for their hostility, but they agreed on the targets of their discontent. Among them were the World Trade Organization, which monitored the enforcement of the GATT treaties of the 1990s; the International Monetary Fund, which controlled international credit and exchange rates; and the World Bank, which made money available for development projects in many countries. In November 1999, when the leaders of the seven leading industrial nations (as well as the leader of Russia) gathered for their annual meeting in Seattle, Washington, tens of thousands of protestors clashed with police, smashed store windows, and all but paralyzed the city. A few months later a smaller but still substantial demonstration disrupted meetings of the IMF and the World Bank in Washington. And in July 2001, at a meeting of the same leaders in Genoa, Italy, thousands of demonstrators clashed violently with police in a melee that left one protester dead and several hundred injured. The participants in the meeting responded to the demonstrations by pledging $1.2 billion to fight the AIDS epidemic in developing countries, and also by deciding to hold their next meeting at a remote resort in Canada.

Defending Orthodoxy

Outside the industrialized West, many people resented the way the world economy had, in their view, exploited and oppressed them. In some parts of the nonindustrialized world—the Middle East—the increasing reach of globalization created additional concerns, less rooted in economics than in religion and culture.

The Iranian Revolution of 1979, in which orthodox Muslims ousted a despotic government whose leaders had embraced many aspects of modern western culture, was one of the first manifestations of a phenomenon that would eventually reach across the Islamic world. In one Islamic nation after another, waves of fundamentalist orthodoxy (known as "Islamism") emerged to defend traditional culture against incursions from the West. The new fundamentalism met considerable resistance within much of Islam—from established governments, from affluent middle classes that had made their peace with the modern industrial world, from women who feared the antifeminist agenda of many of these movements. But it emerged nevertheless as a powerful force.

Among some particularly militant fundamentalists, the battle to preserve orthodoxy came to be defined as a battle against the West generally and the United States in particular.
Resentment of the West was rooted in the incursion of new and, in their view, threatening cultural norms into traditional societies. It was rooted as well in resentment of the support western nations gave to corrupt and tyrannical regimes in some Islamic countries, and in opposition to western (and particularly American) military incursions into the region. The continuing struggle between Palestinians and Israelis—a struggle defined in the eyes of many Muslims by American support for Israel—added further to their contempt.

One product of this combination of resentments was individuals and groups committed to using violence to fight the influence of the West. No fundamentalist movement had any advanced military capabilities. Militants resorted instead to isolated incidents of violence and mayhem, designed to disrupt societies and governments and to create fear among their peoples. Such tactics became known to the world as terrorism.

The Rise of Terrorism

The term "terrorism" was used first during the French Revolution in the 1790s to describe the actions of the radical Jacobins against the French government. The word continued to be used intermittently throughout the nineteenth and early twentieth centuries to describe the use of violence as a form of intimidation against peoples and governments. But the widespread understanding of terrorism as an important fact of modern life is largely a product of the second half of the twentieth century.

Acts of what are now known as terrorism have occurred in many parts of the world. Irish revolutionaries engaged in terrorism regularly against the English through much of the twentieth century. Jews used it in Palestine against the British before the creation of Israel, and Palestinians have used it frequently against Jews in Israel. Revolutionary groups in Italy, Germany, Japan, and France have engaged in terrorist acts intermittently over the last thirty years.

The United States, too, has experienced terrorism for many years, much of it against American targets abroad. These included bombing of the Marine barracks in Beirut in 1983, the explosion that brought down an American airliner over Lockerbie, Scotland in 1988, the bombing of American embassies in 1998, the assault on the U.S. naval vessel *Cole* in 2000, and other events around the world. Terrorist incidents were relatively rare, but not unknown, within the United States itself prior to September 11, 2001. Militants on the American left performed various acts of terror in the 1960s and early 1970s. In February, 1993, a bomb exploded in the parking garage of the World Trade Center in New York killing six people and causing serious, but not irreparable, structural damage to the towers. Several men connected with militant Islamic organizations were convicted of the crime. In April 1995, a van containing explosives blew up in front of a federal building in Oklahoma City, killing 168 people. Timothy McVeigh, a former Marine who had become part of a militant anti-government movement on the right, was convicted of the crime and eventually executed in 2001.

Most Americans, however, considered terrorism a problem that mainly plagued other nations. One of the many results of the terrible events of September 11, 2001 was to jolt the American people out of complacency and alert them to the presence of continuing danger. That awareness increased in the months and years after September 11. New security measures began to change the way in which Americans traveled. New government regulations began to alter immigration policies. Warnings of possible new terrorist attacks created widespread tension and uneasiness. A puzzling and frightening epidemic of anthrax—a potent bacterial agent that can

cause illness and death if not properly treated—began in the weeks after September 11 and spread through the mail to media outlets, members of Congress, and random others.

In the meantime, the United States government launched what President Bush called a "war against terror-ism." The attacks on the World Trade Center and the Pentagon, government intelligence indicated, had been planned and orchestrated by Middle Eastern agents of a powerful terrorist network known as Al Qaeda. Its leader, Osama Bin Laden, quickly became one of the most notorious figures in the world. Fighting a shadowy terrorist network spread out among many nations proved to be a very difficult task, and the administration made clear from the beginning that the battle would be waged in many ways, not just militarily. But the first visible act of

"War against Terrorism"

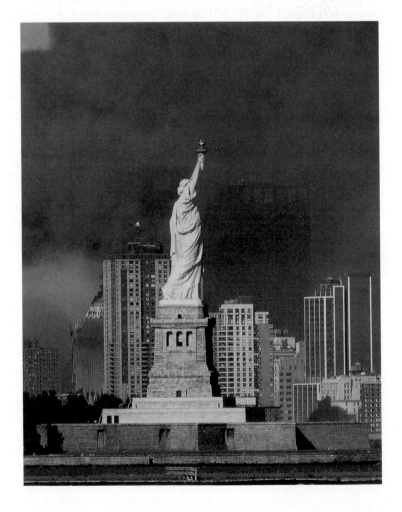

SEPTEMBER 11, 2001 One great American symbol, the Statue of Liberty, stands against a sky filled with the thick smoke from the destruction of another American symbol, New York City's World Trade Center towers, a few hours after terrorists crashed two planes into them. *(Daniel Hatshizer/AP/Wide World Photos)*

the war against terrorism was, in fact, a military one. Convinced that the militant "Taliban" government of Afghanistan had sheltered and supported Bin Laden, the United States began a sustained campaign of bombing against the regime and sent in small numbers of ground troops to help a resistance organization overthrow the Afghan government. The Taliban soon fled in disarray, and with it most of the Al Qaeda forces they had sheltered. How many survived the American onslaught remained unknown for some time, as did the fate of Osama Bin Laden himself.

In early 2002, President Bush spoke to Congress of an "axis of evil" in the world, which included

"Axis of Evil"

North Korea, Iran, and Iraq. By the end of 2002, the Bush administration was talking openly of invading Iraq and was amassing troops and weapons in the region, to topple the regime of Saddam Hussein. But it was also being drawn, reluctantly, into the turbulent politics of the Middle East, as violence between Israelis and Palestinians escalated. Palestinian "suicide bombers" terrorized the Israeli people. The hard-line Israeli prime minister, Ariel Sharon, sent troops and tanks into Palestinian areas of the West Bank. American leaders seemed torn between their desire to stop the violence and their reluctance to criticize Sharon for combating terrorism.

While the American military built up a presence in the Gulf, the Bush administration made a strenuous but unsuccessful effort to attract broad international support for the proposed war against Iraq. The United Nations voted in the fall of 2002 to demand a resumption of inspections of Iraqi weapons—mandated by the settlement of the 1991 Gulf War—and early in 2003, the new inspections began in earnest. Although the Iraqi government disclosed, and even destroyed, some forbidden weapons, the Bush administration insisted that they were not complying adequately with the UN requirements and that only a

War in Iraq

"regime change" (that is, the ouster of Hussein) would be sufficient evidence of disarmament. One by one, many of America's traditional allies in Europe and the Middle East turned against the American policy. France, Germany, Russia, and China all opposed a UN Security Council resolution in support of war in Iraq; large antiwar demonstrations

occurred across much of the world. Anti-American sentiment intensified in Europe, the Middle East, and elsewhere. In the end, only Britain among America's principal allies supported the American effort in Iraq.

By mid-March 2003, the American military build-up in the Gulf was nearing completion, and President Bush gave Hussein 48 hours to leave the country so as to avert a war. Hussein rejected that demand and on the evening of March 19, American missiles struck Baghdad. The next day American and British troops began moving into the Iraqi desert, and the second American war against Iraq in twelve years had begun.

It proved to be even briefer than the first Gulf War. Within a few weeks, the American-dominated "coalition" occupied most areas of the country, captured Baghdad, and drove Hussein and his closest aides into hiding. Over the following months, American forces hunted down and captured many of the leading figures in the deposed regime, killed Hussein's two powerful and widely feared sons in a bombing raid, and finally captured Hussein himself in the closing weeks of 2003. But Iraq remained far from stable for many months after the war, and American troops continued to face attacks from insurgent groups—some of them consisting of anti-American Iraqis, and some of them drawn from militant groups from other Middle Eastern nations. A steady stream of new American and Iraqi casualties after the war began to dilute enthusiasm for the war in the United States, and even the capture of Hussein and the creation of an interim Iraqi government did not at first seem to lead to any reduction in the violence.

A New Era?

In the immediate aftermath of September 11, 2001, many Americans came to believe that they had entered a new era in their history. The instability that had plagued so much of the rest of the world for years seemed suddenly to have arrived in the United States, opening a period of uncertainty and fear. The prospects for the future were clouded further by a significant weakening of the economy.

But fear and uncertainty were not the only results of

America United

the September 11 disasters. Americans responded to the tragedies with countless acts of courage and generosity, large and small, and with a sense of national unity and commitment that seemed, at least for a time, to resemble the unity and commitment at the beginning of World War II. The displays of courage began with the heroism of firefighters and rescue workers in New York City, who unhesitatingly plunged into the burning towers of the World Trade Center in an effort to save the people inside. Over 300 such workers died when the towers collapsed. In the weeks after the disaster, New York was flooded with volunteers who flocked to the city from around the country and the world to assist with rescue and recovery. Charitable donations to help the victims of the disasters exceeded $1 billion, the largest amount ever raised for a single purpose in such a short time in American history. Open and unembarrassed displays of patriotism and national pride—things that many Americans had once scorned—suddenly became fashionable again. Faith in government and its leaders, in decline for decades, suddenly (if not necessarily permanently) surged.

Alongside the many changes that occurred in American life and culture in the months after the attacks, many things remained constant. Most Americans continued to pursue their lives more or less as they always had. Most national institutions continued to function normally. The economy, despite its temporary weakness, remained the strongest, most diverse, and most productive in the world. "Nothing has changed. . . . Everything has changed," wrote one prominent journalist in the weeks after September 11. In fact, no one could reliably predict whether the catastrophe would prove to be a fundamental turning point in the course of American and world history, or simply another in the countless changes and adjustments, great and small, that have characterized the nation's experience for centuries.

CONCLUSION

Americans entered the twenty-first century afflicted with many anxieties, doubts, and resentments. Faith in the nation's institutions was at its lowest point in many decades. Confidence in the nation's leaders had dramatically eroded. Ugly battles over differing standards of morality and different cultural styles disturbed many communities. Vague resentments over the increasingly unequal patterns of income and wealth in the new economy increased the nation's unease.

But the United States at the end of the century was, despite its many problems, a remarkably successful society. It had made dramatic strides in improving the lives of its citizens and in dealing with many of its social problems since the end of World War II. It entered the new century with the strongest economy in the world; with violent crime in a marked decline; and with its power and stature in the world unrivaled.

The traumatic events of September 11, 2001 changed many aspects of American life, not least the nation's sense of its isolation, and insulation, from the problems of the rest of the world. But both the many long-standing problems and the many long-standing strengths of the United States survived the attacks. It seemed safe to predict that the American people would go forward into their suddenly uncertain future not simply burdened by difficult problems, but also armed with great wealth, great power, and perhaps most of all with the extraordinary energy and resilience that has allowed the nation—throughout its long and often turbulent history—to endure, to flourish, and to strive continually for a better future.

INTERACTIVE LEARNING

On the *Primary Source Investigator CD-ROM*, check out a number of valuable tools for further exploration of the content of this chapter.

Interactive Maps
- U.S. Elections (Map M7)
- Middle East Conflicts (Map M28)

Primary Sources

Documents, images, and maps related to American politics and society in the last fifteen years. Some highlights include:

- An image from Bill Clinton's first inauguration

- Text of California's controversial Proposition 187 regarding services for undocumented immigrants

*Online Learning Center
(www.mhhe.com/unfinishedinteractive)*

Explore this rich website, providing additional exploration of the material covered in this chapter, online versions of the interactive maps included on the Primary Source Investigator CD-ROM, as well as several study aids, including a multiple-choice quiz, essay questions, a glossary, and other valuable tools. In the Online Learning Center for this chapter look for an *Interactive Feature Essay* on:

- **Where Historians Disagree: Women's History**

FOR FURTHER REFERENCE

John Lewis Gaddis, *The United States and the End of the Cold War* (1992) and *We Now Know: Rethinking Cold War History* (1997) are early examinations of the transformation of the world order. E. J. Dionne, *Why Americans Hate Politics* (1991) is a perceptive discussion of the political discontents of the 1980s and early 1990s. Thomas Byrne Edsall and Mary D. Edsall, *Chain Reaction: The Impact of Race, Rights, and Taxes on American Politics* (1991) is an alternative interpretation of the changes in American politics, focusing primarily on the impact of race. David Maranniss, *First in His Class: A Biography of Bill Clinton* (1995) traces Clinton's pre-presidential career. Theda Skocpol, *Boomerang: Clinton's Health Security Effort and the Turn against Government in U.S. Politics* (1996) is an account of one of the major setbacks of Clinton's first term. Jeffrey Toobin, *A Vast Conspiracy* (1999) is an account of the scandals that rocked the Clinton presidency. Toobin is also the author of an important account of the disputed 2000 presidential election, *Too Close to Call* (2001). Haynes Johnson, *The Best of Times: America in the Clinton Years* (2001) is an account of the politics and culture of the 1990s. David Halberstam, *War in a Time of Peace: Bush, Clinton, and the Generals* (2001) examines the foreign policy and military

ventures of the Bush and Clinton years. Michael A. Bernstein and David E. Adler, *Understanding American Economic Decline* (1994) is an important collection of essays on the changes in the American economy since the 1970s. *Computer: A History of the Information Machine* by Martin Campbell-Kelly and William Aspray (1996) is an introduction to the development of one of the critical technologies of the late twentieth century, and Janet Abbate, *Inventing the Internet* (1999) examines the emergence of the powerful new vehicle of communication. Randy Shilts, *And the Band Played On: Politics, People, and the AIDS Epidemic* (1987) is a provocative discussion of the early years of AIDS in America. Andrew Hacker, *Two Nations: Black and White, Separate, Hostile, Unequal* (1992) and Michael Katz, *The Undeserving Poor: From the War on Poverty to the War on Welfare* (1989) are two contrasting arguments about the nature of African-American life and inner-city poverty. William Julius Wilson, *The Truly Disadvantaged* (1987) and *When Work Disappears* (1996) are important studies of the inner-city poor from one of America's leading sociologists. David A. Hollinger, *Postethnic America: Beyond Multiculturalism* (1995) is an intelligent and spirited comment on the debates over multiculturalism.

APPENDICES

Documents and Tables

The United States

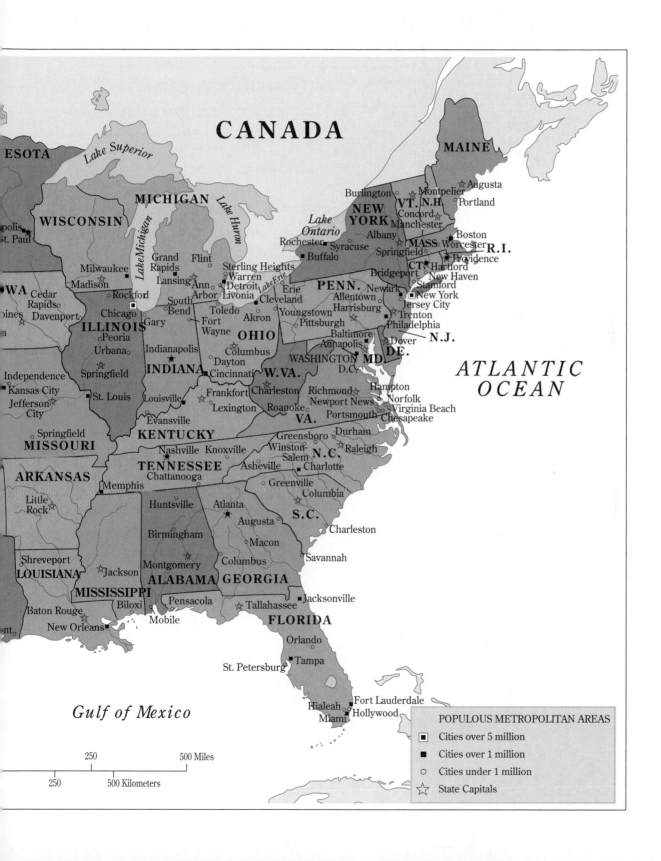

CANADA

MAINE

ESOTA

Lake Superior

MICHIGAN

Lake Huron

WISCONSIN

Lake Michigan

Burlington

Montpelier

Augusta

VT. N.H

Portland

Concord

NEW YORK

Manchester

Lake Ontario

Rochester

Albany

Springfield

MASS

Boston

Worcester

R.I.

Providence

Syracuse

Buffalo

Grand Rapids

Flint

Milwaukee

Madison

Rockford

OWA

Cedar Rapids

oines

Davenport

Sterling Heights

Lansing

Warren

Ann Arbor

Detroit

Livonia

Lake Erie

Erie

CT.

Hartford

New Haven

Bridgeport

Stamford

PENN.

Newark

New York

Jersey City

Cleveland

Youngstown

Akron

Allentown

Harrisburg

Trenton

Philadelphia

N.J.

South Bend

Toledo

Fort Wayne

Pittsburgh

Dover

Baltimore

DE.

Chicago

Gary

ILLINOIS

Peoria

OHIO

Columbus

Annapolis

MD.

Urbana

Indianapolis

Dayton

WASHINGTON D.C.

Independence

Springfield

INDIANA

Cincinnati

W.VA.

Hampton

Kansas City

Frankfort

Charleston

Richmond

Norfolk

Jefferson City

St. Louis

Louisville

Lexington

Roanoke

Newport News

Virginia Beach

Portsmouth

Chesapeake

VA.

Evansville

Springfield

KENTUCKY

Greensboro

Durham

MISSOURI

Nashville

Knoxville

Winston-Salem

N.C.

Raleigh

ARKANSAS

TENNESSEE

Asheville

Charlotte

Chattanooga

Greenville

Memphis

Columbia

Little Rock

Huntsville

Atlanta

S.C.

Augusta

Charleston

Birmingham

Macon

Shreveport

Montgomery

Columbus

Savannah

LOUISIANA

Jackson

ALABAMA

GEORGIA

MISSISSIPPI

Baton Rouge

Biloxi

Pensacola

Jacksonville

nt.

New Orleans

Mobile

Tallahassee

FLORIDA

Orlando

St. Petersburg

Tampa

Gulf of Mexico

Hialeah

Fort Lauderdale

Miami

Hollywood

ATLANTIC OCEAN

250   500 Miles

250   500 Kilometers

POPULOUS METROPOLITAN AREAS

◙ Cities over 5 million

■ Cities over 1 million

○ Cities under 1 million

☆ State Capitals

United States Territorial Expansion, 1783–1898

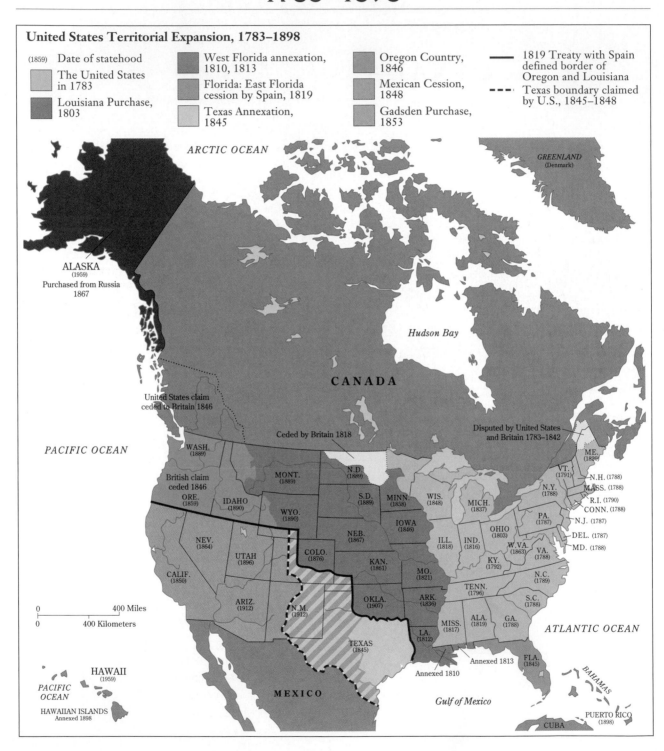

United States Territorial Expansion, 1783–1898

(1859) Date of statehood

The United States in 1783

Louisiana Purchase, 1803

West Florida annexation, 1810, 1813

Florida: East Florida cession by Spain, 1819

Texas Annexation, 1845

Oregon Country, 1846

Mexican Cession, 1848

Gadsden Purchase, 1853

1819 Treaty with Spain defined border of Oregon and Louisiana

Texas boundary claimed by U.S., 1845–1848

ARCTIC OCEAN

GREENLAND (Denmark)

ALASKA (1959)
Purchased from Russia 1867

Hudson Bay

CANADA

United States claim ceded to Britain 1846

Ceded by Britain 1818

Disputed by United States and Britain 1783–1842

PACIFIC OCEAN

WASH. (1889)

British claim ceded 1846

ORE. (1859)

IDAHO (1890)

MONT. (1889)

N.D. (1889)

S.D. (1889)

MINN. (1858)

WIS. (1848)

MICH. (1837)

ME. (1820)

VT. (1791)

N.H. (1788)

N.Y. (1788)

MASS. (1788)

R.I. (1790)

CONN. (1788)

PA. (1787)

N.J. (1787)

WYO. (1890)

NEV. (1864)

UTAH (1896)

IOWA (1846)

NEB. (1867)

ILL. (1818)

IND. (1816)

OHIO (1803)

W.VA. (1863)

VA. (1788)

DEL. (1787)

MD. (1788)

KY. (1792)

CALIF. (1850)

COLO. (1876)

KAN. (1861)

MO. (1821)

N.C. (1789)

TENN. (1796)

ARIZ. (1912)

N.M. (1912)

OKLA. (1907)

ARK. (1836)

S.C. (1788)

MISS. (1817)

ALA. (1819)

GA. (1788)

ATLANTIC OCEAN

0 400 Miles
0 400 Kilometers

TEXAS (1845)

LA. (1812)

Annexed 1810

Annexed 1813

FLA. (1845)

BAHAMAS

HAWAII (1959)
PACIFIC OCEAN
HAWAIIAN ISLANDS
Annexed 1898

MEXICO

Gulf of Mexico

Annexed 1813

PUERTO RICO (1898)

CUBA

The Declaration of Independence

In Congress, July 4, 1776,

The Unanimous Declaration of the Thirteen United States of America

When, in the course of human events, it becomes necessary for one people to dissolve the political bands which have connected them with another, and to assume, among the powers of the earth, the separate and equal station to which the laws of nature and of nature's God entitle them, a decent respect to the opinions of mankind requires that they should declare the causes which impel them to the separation.

We hold these truths to be self-evident, that all men are created equal; that they are endowed by their Creator with certain unalienable rights; that among these, are life, liberty, and the pursuit of happiness. That, to secure these rights, governments are instituted among men, deriving their just powers from the consent of the governed; that, whenever any form of government becomes destructive of these ends, it is the right of the people to alter or to abolish it, and to institute a new government, laying its foundation on such principles, and organizing its powers in such form, as to them shall seem most likely to effect their safety and happiness. Prudence, indeed, will dictate that governments long established, should not be changed for light and transient causes; and, accordingly, all experience hath shown, that mankind are more disposed to suffer, while evils are sufferable, than to right themselves by abolishing the forms to which they are accustomed. But, when a long train of abuses and usurpations, pursuing invariably the same object, evinces a design to reduce them under absolute despotism, it is their right, it is their duty, to throw off such government and to provide new guards for their future security. Such has been the patient sufferance of these colonies, and such is now the necessity which constrains them to alter their former systems of government. The history of the present King of Great Britain is a history of repeated injuries and usurpations, all having, in direct object, the establishment of an absolute tyranny over these States. To prove this, let facts be submitted to a candid world:

He has refused his assent to laws the most wholesome and necessary for the public good.

He has forbidden his governors to pass laws of immediate and pressing importance, unless suspended in their operation till his assent should be obtained; and, when so suspended, he has utterly neglected to attend to them.

He has refused to pass other laws for the accommodation of large districts of people, unless those people would relinquish the right of representation in the legislature; a right inestimable to them, and formidable to tyrants only.

He has called together legislative bodies at places unusual, uncomfortable, and distant from the depository of their public records, for the sole purpose of fatiguing them into compliance with his measures.

He has dissolved representative houses repeatedly for opposing, with manly firmness, his invasions on the rights of the people.

He has refused, for a long time after such dissolutions, to cause others to be elected; whereby the legislative powers, incapable of annihilation, have returned to the people at large for their exercise; the state remaining, in the meantime, exposed to all the danger of invasion from without, and compulsions within.

He has endeavored to prevent the population of these States; for that purpose, obstructing the laws for naturalization of foreigners, refusing to pass others to encourage their migration hither, and raising the conditions of new appropriations of lands.

He has obstructed the administration of justice, by refusing his assent to laws for establishing judiciary powers.

He has made judges dependent on his will alone, for the tenure of their offices, and the amount and payment of their salaries.

He has erected a multitude of new offices, and sent hither swarms of officers to harass our people, and eat out their substance.

He has kept among us, in time of peace, standing armies, without the consent of our legislatures.

He has affected to render the military independent of, and superior to, the civil power.

He has combined, with others, to subject us to a jurisdiction foreign to our Constitution, and unacknowledged by our laws; giving his assent to their acts of pretended legislation:

For quartering large bodies of armed troops among us:

For protecting them by a mock trial, from punishment, for any murders which they should commit on the inhabitants of these States:

For cutting off our trade with all parts of the world:

For imposing taxes on us without our consent:

For depriving us, in many cases, of the benefit of trial by jury:

For transporting us beyond seas to be tried for pretended offences:

For abolishing the free system of English laws in a neighboring province, establishing therein an arbitrary government, and enlarging its boundaries, so as to render it at once an example and fit instrument for introducing the same absolute rule into these colonies:

For taking away our charters, abolishing our most valuable laws, and altering, fundamentally, the powers of our governments:

For suspending our own legislatures, and declaring themselves invested with power to legislate for us in all cases whatsoever.

He has abdicated government here, by declaring us out of his protection, and waging war against us.

He has plundered our seas, ravaged our coasts, burnt our towns, and destroyed the lives of our people.

He is, at this time, transporting large armies of foreign mercenaries to complete the works of death, desolation, and tyranny, already begun, with circumstances of cruelty and perfidy scarcely paralleled in the most barbarous ages, and totally unworthy the head of a civilized nation.

He has constrained our fellow citizens, taken captive on the high seas, to bear arms against their country, to become the executioners of their friends, and brethren, or to fall themselves by their hands.

He has excited domestic insurrections amongst us, and has endeavored to bring on the inhabitants of our frontiers, the merciless Indian savages, whose known rule of warfare is an undistinguished destruction of all ages, sexes, and conditions.

In every stage of these oppressions, we have petitioned for redress, in the most humble terms; our repeated petitions have been answered only by repeated injury. A prince, whose character is thus marked by every act which may define a tyrant, is unfit to be the ruler of a free people.

Nor have we been wanting in attention to our British brethren. We have warned them, from time to time, of attempts made by their legislature to extend an unwarrantable jurisdiction over us. We have reminded them of the circumstances of our emigration and settlement here. We have appealed to their native justice and magnanimity, and we have conjured them, by the ties of our common kindred, to disavow these usurpations, which would inevitably interrupt our connections and correspondence. They, too, have been deaf to the voice of justice and consanguinity. We must, therefore, acquiesce in the necessity which denounces our separation, and hold them as we hold the rest of mankind, enemies in war, in peace, friends.

We, therefore, the representatives of the United States of America, in general Congress assembled, appealing to the Supreme Judge of the world for the rectitude of our intentions, do, in the name, and by the authority of the good people of these colonies, solemnly publish and declare, that these united colonies are, and of right ought to be, free and independent states: that they are absolved from all allegiance to the British Crown, and that all political connection between them and the state of Great Britain is, and ought to be, totally dissolved; and that, as free and independent states, they have full power to levy war, conclude peace, contract alliances, establish commerce, and to do all other acts and things which independent states may of right do. And, for the support of this declaration, with a firm reliance on the protection of Divine Providence, we mutually pledge to each other our lives, our fortunes, and our sacred honor.

The foregoing Declaration was, by order of Congress, engrossed, and signed by the following members:

John Hancock

NEW HAMPSHIRE

Josiah Bartlett
William Whipple
Matthew Thornton

CONNECTICUT

Roger Sherman
Samuel Huntington
William Williams
Oliver Wolcott

NEW YORK

William Floyd
Philip Livingston
Francis Lewis
Lewis Morris

NEW JERSEY

Richard Stockton
John Witherspoon
Francis Hopkinson
John Hart
Abraham Clark

PENNSYLVANIA

Robert Morris
Benjamin Rush
Benjamin Franklin
John Morton
George Clymer
James Smith
George Taylor
James Wilson
George Ross

MASSACHUSETTS BAY

Samuel Adams
John Adams
Robert Treat Paine
Elbridge Gerry

VIRGINIA

George Wythe
Richard Henry Lee
Thomas Jefferson
Benjamin Harrison
Thomas Nelson, Jr.
Francis Lightfoot Lee
Carter Braxton

DELAWARE

Caesar Rodney
George Read
Thomas M'Kean

MARYLAND

Samuel Chase
William Paca
Thomas Stone
Charles Carroll,
  of Carrollton

RHODE ISLAND

Stephen Hopkins
William Ellery

SOUTH CAROLINA

Edward Rutledge
Thomas Heyward, Jr.
Thomas Lynch, Jr.
Arthur Middleton

NORTH CAROLINA

William Hooper
Joseph Hewes
John Penn

GEORGIA

Button Gwinnett
Lyman Hall
George Walton

Resolved, That copies of the Declaration be sent to the several assemblies, conventions, and committees, or councils of safety, and to the several commanding officers of the continental troops; that it be proclaimed in each of the United States, at the head of the army.

The Constitution of the United States[1]

We the People of the United States, in Order to form a more perfect Union, establish Justice, insure domestic Tranquility, provide for the common defence, promote the general Welfare, and secure the Blessings of Liberty to ourselves and our Posterity, do ordain and establish this CONSTITUTION for the United States of America.

Article I

Section 1.

All legislative Powers herein granted shall be vested in a Congress of the United States, which shall consist of a Senate and House of Representatives.

Section 2.

The House of Representatives shall be composed of Members chosen every second Year by the People of the several States, and the Electors in each State shall have the Qualifications requisite for Electors of the most numerous Branch of the State Legislature.

No Person shall be a Representative who shall not have attained to the Age of twenty-five Years, and been seven Years a Citizen of the United States, and who shall not, when elected, be an Inhabitant of that State in which he shall be chosen.

[Representatives and direct Taxes[2] shall be apportioned among the several States which may be included within this Union, according to their respective Numbers, which shall be determined by adding to the whole Number of free Persons, including those bound to Service for a Term of Years, and excluding Indians not taxed, three fifths of all other Persons.][3] The actual Enumeration shall be made within three Years after the first Meeting of the Congress of the United States, and within every subsequent Term of ten Years, in such Manner as they shall by Law direct. The Number of Representatives shall not exceed one for every thirty Thousand, but each State shall have at Least one Representative; and until such enumeration shall be made, the State of New Hampshire shall be entitled to chuse three, Massachusetts eight, Rhode-Island and Providence Plantations one, Connecticut five, New York six, New Jersey four, Pennsylvania eight, Delaware one, Maryland six, Virginia ten, North Carolina five, South Carolina five, and Georgia three.

When vacancies happen in the Representation from any State, the Executive Authority thereof shall issue Writs of Election to fill such Vacancies.

The House of Representatives shall chuse their Speaker and other Officers; and shall have the sole Power of Impeachment.

Section 3.

The Senate of the United States shall be composed of two Senators from each State, chosen by the Legislature thereof, for six Years; and each Senator shall have one Vote.

Immediately after they shall be assembled in Consequence of the first Election, they shall be divided as equally as may be into three Classes. The Seats of the Senators of the first Class shall be vacated at the Expiration of the second Year, of the second Class at the Expiration of the fourth Year, and of the third Class at the Expiration of the sixth Year, so that one-third may be chosen every second Year; and if Vacancies happen by Resignation, or otherwise, during the Recess of the Legislature of any State, the Executive thereof may make temporary Appointments until the next Meeting of the Legislature, which shall then fill such Vacancies.

No Person shall be a Senator who shall not have attained to the Age of thirty Years, and been nine Years a Citizen of the United States, and who shall not, when elected, be an Inhabitant of that State for which he shall be chosen.

The Vice President of the United States shall be President of the Senate, but shall have no vote, unless they be equally divided.

The Senate shall chuse their other Officers, and also a President pro tempore, in the absence of the Vice President, or when he shall exercise the Office of President of the United States.

The Senate shall have the sole Power to try all Impeachments. When sitting for that purpose they shall be on Oath or Affirmation. When the President of the United States is tried, the Chief Justice shall preside: And no person shall be convicted without the Concurrence of two thirds of the Members present.

Judgment in Cases of Impeachment shall not extend further than to removal from Office, and disqualification to hold and enjoy any Office of honor, Trust, or Profit under the United States: but the Party convicted shall nevertheless be liable and subject to Indictment, Trial, Judgment, and Punishment, according to Law.

Section 4.

The Times, Places and Manner of holding Elections for Senators and Representatives, shall be prescribed in each

---

[1] This version, which follows the original Constitution in capitalization and spelling, was published by the United States Department of the Interior, Office of Education, in 1935.
[2] Altered by the Sixteenth Amendment.
[3] Negated by the Fourteenth Amendment.

State by the Legislature thereof; but the Congress may at any time by Law make or alter such Regulations, except as to the Places of Chusing Senators.

The Congress shall assemble at least once in every Year, and such Meeting shall be on the first Monday in December, unless they shall by Law appoint a different Day.

Section 5.

Each House shall be the Judge of the Elections, Returns and Qualifications of its own Members, and a Majority of each shall constitute a Quorum to do Business; but a smaller number may adjourn from day to day, and may be authorized to compel the Attendance of absent Members, in such Manner, and under such Penalties, as each House may provide.

Each House may determine the Rules of its Proceedings, punish its Members for disorderly Behaviour, and, with the Concurrence of two thirds, expel a Member.

Each House shall keep a Journal of its Proceedings, and from time to time publish the same, excepting such Parts as may in their Judgment require Secrecy; and the Yeas and Nays of the Members of either House on any question shall, at the Desire of one fifth of those Present, be entered on the Journal.

Neither House, during the Session of Congress, shall, without the Consent of the other, adjourn for more than three days, nor to any other Place than that in which the two Houses shall be sitting.

Section 6.

The Senators and Representatives shall receive a Compensation for their Services, to be ascertained by Law, and paid out of the Treasury of the United States. They shall in all Cases, except Treason, Felony, and Breach of the Peace, be privileged from Arrest during their Attendance at the Session of their respective Houses, and in going to and returning from the same; and for any Speech or Debate in either House, they shall not be questioned in any other Place.

No Senator or Representative shall, during the Time for which he was elected, be appointed to any civil Office under the Authority of the United States, which shall have been created, or the Emoluments whereof shall have been increased, during such time; and no Person holding any Office under the United States shall be a Member of either House during his continuance in Office.

Section 7.

All Bills for raising Revenue shall originate in the House of Representatives; but the Senate may propose or concur with Amendments as on other bills.

Every Bill which shall have passed the House of Representatives and the Senate, shall, before it become a Law, be presented to the President of the United States; If he approve he shall sign it, but if not he shall return it, with his Objections, to that House in which it shall have originated, who shall enter the Objections at large on their Journal, and proceed to reconsider it. If after such Reconsideration two thirds of that House shall agree to pass the bill, it shall be sent, together with the objections, to the other House, by which it shall likewise be reconsidered, and if approved by two thirds of that House, it shall become a Law. But in all such Cases the Votes of both Houses shall be determined by Yeas and Nays, and the Names of the Persons voting for and against the Bill shall be entered on the Journal of each House respectively. If any Bill shall not be returned by the President within ten Days (Sundays excepted) after it shall have been presented to him, the Same shall be a Law, in like Manner as if he had signed it, unless the Congress by their Adjournment prevent its Return, in which Case it shall not be a Law.

Every Order, Resolution, or Vote to which the Concurrence of the Senate and House of Representatives may be necessary (except on a question of Adjournment) shall be presented to the President of the United States; and before the Same shall take Effect, shall be approved by him, or being disapproved by him, shall be repassed by two thirds of the Senate and House of Representatives, according to the Rules and Limitations prescribed in the Case of a Bill.

Section 8.

The Congress shall have Power To lay and collect Taxes, Duties, Imposts and Excises, to pay the Debts and provide for the common Defence and general Welfare of the United States; but all Duties, Imposts and Excises shall be uniform throughout the United States;

To borrow money on the credit of the United States;

To regulate Commerce with foreign Nations, and among the several States, and with the Indian Tribes;

To establish an uniform rule of Naturalization, and uniform Laws on the subject of Bankruptcies throughout the United States;

To coin Money, regulate the Value thereof, and of foreign Coin, and fix the Standard of Weights and Measures;

To provide for the Punishment of counterfeiting the Securities and current Coin of the United States;

To establish Post Offices and post Roads;

To promote the Progress of Science and useful Arts, by securing for limited Times to Authors and Inventors the exclusive Right to their respective Writings and Discoveries;

To constitute Tribunals inferior to the Supreme Court;

To define and punish Piracies and Felonies committed on the high Seas, and Offenses against the Law of Nations;

To declare War, grant Letters of Marque and Reprisal, and make Rules concerning Captures on Land and Water;

To raise and support Armies, but no Appropriation of Money to that Use shall be for a longer Term than two Years;

To provide and maintain a Navy;

To make Rules for the Government and Regulation of the land and naval forces;

To provide for calling forth the Militia to execute the Laws of the Union, suppress Insurrections and repel Invasions;

To provide for organizing, arming, and disciplining the Militia, and for governing such Part of them as may be employed in the Service of the United States, reserving to the States respectively, the Appointment of the Officers, and the Authority of training the Militia according to the discipline prescribed by Congress;

To exercise exclusive Legislation in all Cases whatsoever, over such District (not exceeding ten Miles square) as may, by Cession of particular States, and the acceptance of Congress, become the Seat of the Government of the United States, and to exercise like Authority over all Places purchased by the Consent of the Legislature of the State in which the Same shall be, for the Erection of Forts, Magazines, Arsenals, Dock-yards, and other needful Buildings;—And

To make all Laws which shall be necessary and proper for carrying into Execution the foregoing Powers, and all other Powers vested by this Constitution in the Government of the United States, or in any Department or Officer thereof.

Section 9.

The Migration or Importation of such Persons as any of the States now existing shall think proper to admit, shall not be prohibited by the Congress prior to the Year one thousand eight hundred and eight, but a tax or duty may be imposed on such Importation, not exceeding ten dollars for each Person.

The privilege of the Writ of Habeas Corpus shall not be suspended, unless when in Cases of Rebellion or Invasion the public Safety may require it.

No bill of Attainder or ex post facto Law shall be passed.

No capitation, or other direct, Tax shall be laid unless in Proportion to the Census or Enumeration herein before directed to be taken.

No Tax or Duty shall be laid on Articles exported from any State.

No Preference shall be given by any Regulation of Commerce or Revenue to the Ports of one State over those of another: nor shall Vessels bound to, or from, one State, be obliged to enter, clear, or pay Duties in another.

No Money shall be drawn from the Treasury, but in Consequence of Appropriations made by Law; and a regular Statement and Account of the Receipts and Expenditures of all public Money shall be published from time to time.

No Title of Nobility shall be granted by the United States: And no Person holding any Office of Profit or Trust under them, shall, without the Consent of the Congress, accept of any present, Emolument, Office, or Title, of any kind whatever, from any King, Prince, or foreign State.

Section 10.

No State shall enter into any Treaty, Alliance, or Confederation; grant Letters of Marque and Reprisal; coin Money; emit Bills of Credit; make any Thing but gold and silver Coin a Tender in Payment of Debts; pass any Bill of Attainder, ex post facto Law, or Law impairing the Obligation of Contracts, or grant any Title of Nobility.

No State shall, without the Consent of the Congress, lay any Imposts or Duties on Imports or Exports, except what may be absolutely necessary for executing its inspection Laws; and the net Produce of all Duties and Imposts, laid by any State on Imports or Exports, shall be for the use of the Treasury of the United States; and all such Laws shall be subject to the Revision and Control of the Congress.

No state shall, without the Consent of Congress, lay any duty of Tonnage, keep Troops, or Ships of War in time of Peace, enter into any Agreement or Compact with another State, or with a foreign Power, or engage in War, unless actually invaded, or in such imminent Danger as will not admit of delay.

Article II

Section 1.

The executive Power shall be vested in a President of the United States of America. He shall hold his Office during the Term of four years, and, together with the Vice President, chosen for the same Term, be elected, as follows:

Each State shall appoint, in such Manner as the Legislature thereof may direct, a Number of Electors, equal to the whole Number of Senators and Representatives to which the State may be entitled in the Congress: but no Senator or Representative, or Person holding an Office of Trust or Profit under the United States, shall be appointed an Elector.

[The Electors shall meet in their respective States, and vote by Ballot for two persons, of whom one at least shall not be an Inhabitant of the same State with themselves. And they shall make a List of all the Persons voted for, and of the Number of Votes for each; which List they shall sign and certify, and transmit sealed to the Seat of the Government of the United States, directed to the President of the Senate. The President of the Senate shall, in the Presence of the Senate and House of Representatives, open all the Certificates, and the Votes shall then be counted. The Person having the greatest Number of Votes shall be the President, if such Number be a Majority of the whole Number of Electors appointed; and if there be more than one who have such Majority, and have an equal Number of Votes, then the House of Representatives shall immediately chuse by Ballot one of them for President; and if no Person have a Majority, then from the five highest on the List the said House shall in like Manner chuse the President. But in chusing the President, the Votes shall be taken by States, the Representation from each State having one Vote; a quorum for this Purpose shall consist of a Member or Members from two-thirds of the States, and a Majority of all the States shall be necessary to a Choice. In every Case, after the Choice of the President, the Person having the greatest Number of Votes of the Electors shall be the Vice President. But if there should remain two or more who have equal votes, the Senate shall chuse from them by Ballot the Vice President.]⁴

The Congress may determine the Time of chusing the Electors, and the Day on which they shall give their Votes; which Day shall be the same throughout the United States.

No person except a natural-born Citizen, or a Citizen of the United States, at the time of the Adoption of this Constitution, shall be eligible to the Office of President; neither shall any Person be eligible to that Office who shall not have attained to the Age of thirty-five years, and been fourteen Years a Resident within the United States.

In Case of the Removal of the President from Office, or of his Death, Resignation, or Inability to discharge the Powers and Duties of the said Office, the same shall devolve on the Vice President, and the Congress may by Law provide for the Case of Removal, Death, Resignation, or Inability, both of the President and Vice President, declaring what Officer shall then act as President, and such Officer shall act accordingly, until the disability be removed, or a President shall be elected.

The President shall, at stated Times, receive for his Services a Compensation, which shall neither be increased nor diminished during the Period for which he shall have been elected, and he shall not receive within that Period any other Emolument from the United States, or any of them.

Before he enter on the execution of his Office, he shall take the following Oath or Affirmation:—"I do solemnly swear (or affirm) that I will faithfully execute the Office of President of the United States, and will, to the best of my

---

⁴Revised by the Twelfth Amendment.

Ability, preserve, protect, and defend the Constitution of the United States."

Section 2.
The President shall be Commander in Chief of the Army and Navy of the United States, and of the Militia of the several States, when called into the actual Service of the United States; he may require the Opinion, in writing, of the principal Officer in each of the executive Departments, upon any subject relating to the Duties of their respective Offices, and he shall have Power to Grant Reprieves and Pardons for Offenses against the United States, except in Cases of Impeachment.

He shall have Power, by and with the Advice and Consent of the Senate, to make Treaties, provided two-thirds of the Senators present concur; and he shall nominate, and by and with the Advice and Consent of the Senate, shall appoint Ambassadors, other public Ministers and Consuls, Judges of the supreme Court, and all other Officers of the United States, whose Appointments are not herein otherwise provided for, and which shall be established by Law: but the Congress may by Law vest the Appointment of such inferior Officers, as they think proper, in the President alone, in the Courts of Law, or in the Heads of Departments.

The President shall have Power to fill up all Vacancies that may happen during the Recess of the Senate, by granting Commissions which shall expire at the End of their next Session.

Section 3.
He shall from time to time give to the Congress Information of the State of the Union, and recommend to their Consideration such Measures as he shall judge necessary and expedient; he may, on extraordinary occasions, convene both Houses, or either of them, and in Case of Disagreement between them, with respect to the Time of Adjournment, he may adjourn them to such Time as he shall think proper; he shall receive Ambassadors and other public Ministers; he shall take care that the Laws be faithfully executed, and shall Commission all the Officers of the United States.

Section 4.
The President, Vice President and all civil Officers of the United States, shall be removed from Office on Impeachment for, and Conviction of, Treason, Bribery, or other high Crimes and Misdemeanors.

Article III

Section 1.
The judicial Power of the United States, shall be vested in one supreme Court, and in such inferior Courts as the

Congress may from time to time ordain and establish. The Judges, both of the supreme and inferior Courts, shall hold their Offices during good Behaviour, and shall, at stated Times, receive for their Services, a Compensation, which shall not be diminished during their Continuance in Office.

Section 2.
The judicial Power shall extend to all Cases, in Law and Equity, arising under this Constitution, the Laws of the United States, and Treaties made, or which shall be made, under their Authority;—to all Cases affecting ambassadors, other public ministers and consuls;—to all cases of admiralty and maritime Jurisdiction;—to Controversies to which the United States shall be a Party;—to Controversies between two or more States;—between a State and Citizens of another State;[5]—between Citizens of different States—between Citizens of the same State claiming Lands under Grants of different States, and between a State, or the Citizens thereof, and foreign States, Citizens, or Subjects.

In all Cases affecting Ambassadors, other public Ministers and Consuls, and those in which a State shall be Party, the supreme Court shall have original Jurisdiction. In all the other Cases before mentioned, the supreme Court shall have appellate Jurisdiction, both as to Law and Fact, with such Exceptions, and under such Regulations as the Congress shall make.

The trial of all Crimes, except in Cases of Impeachment, shall be by Jury; and such Trial shall be held in the State where the said Crimes shall have been committed; but when not committed within any State, the Trial shall be at such Place or Places as the Congress may by Law have directed.

Section 3.
Treason against the United States, shall consist only in levying War against them, or in adhering to their Enemies, giving them Aid and Comfort. No Person shall be convicted of Treason unless on the Testimony of two Witnesses to the same overt Act, or on Confession in open Court.

The Congress shall have power to declare the Punishment of Treason, but no Attainder of Treason shall work Corruption of Blood, or Forfeiture except during the Life of the Person attained.

Article IV

Section 1.
Full Faith and Credit shall be given in each State to the public Acts, Records, and judicial Proceedings of every

---
[5]Qualified by the Eleventh Amendment.

other State. And the Congress may by general Laws prescribe the Manner in which such Acts, Records and Proceedings shall be proved, and the Effect thereof.

Section 2.
The Citizens of each State shall be entitled to all Privileges and Immunities of Citizens in the several States.

A Person charged in any State with Treason, Felony, or other Crime, who shall flee from Justice, and be found in another State, shall on demand of the executive Authority of the State from which he fled, be delivered up, to be removed to the State having Jurisdiction of the crime.

No Person held to Service or Labour in one State, under the Laws thereof, escaping into another, shall, in Consequence of any Law or Regulation therein, be discharged from such Service or Labour, but shall be delivered up on Claim of the Party to whom such Service or Labour may be due.

Section 3.
New States may be admitted by the Congress into this Union; but no new State shall be formed or erected within the Jurisdiction of any other State; nor any State be formed by the Junction of two or more States, or parts of States, without the Consent of the Legislatures of the States concerned as well as of the Congress.

The Congress shall have Power to dispose of and make all needful Rules and Regulations respecting the Territory or other Property belonging to the United States; and nothing in this Constitution shall be so construed as to Prejudice any Claims of the United States, or of any particular State.

Section 4.
The United States shall guarantee to every State in this Union a Republican Form of Government, and shall protect each of them against Invasion; and on Application of the Legislature, or of the Executive (when the Legislature cannot be convened) against domestic Violence.

Article V

The Congress, whenever two-thirds of both Houses shall deem it necessary, shall propose Amendments to this Constitution, or, on the Application of the Legislatures of two-thirds of the several States, shall call a Convention for proposing Amendments, which, in either Case, shall be valid to all Intents and Purposes, as part of this Constitution, when ratified by the Legislatures of three-fourths of the several States, or by Conventions in three-fourths thereof, as the one or the other Mode of Ratification may be proposed by the Congress; Provided that no Amendment which may be made prior to the Year One thousand eight hundred and eight shall in any Manner affect the first and fourth Clauses in the Ninth Section of the first Article; and that no State, without its Consent, shall be deprived of its equal Suffrage in the Senate.

Article VI

All Debts contracted and Engagements entered into, before the Adoption of this Constitution, shall be as valid against the United States under this Constitution, as under the Confederation.

   This Constitution, and the Laws of the United States which shall be made in Pursuance thereof; and all Treaties made, or which shall be made, under the Authority of the United States, shall be the supreme Law of the Land; and the Judges in every State shall be bound thereby, any Thing in the Constitution or Laws of any State to the Contrary notwithstanding.

   The Senators and Representatives before mentioned, and the Members of the several State Legislatures, and all executive and judicial Officers, both of the United States and of the several States, shall be bound by Oath or Affirmation to support this Constitution; but no religious Tests shall ever be required as a qualification to any Office or public Trust under the United States.

Article VII

The Ratification of the Conventions of nine States shall be sufficient for the Establishment of this Constitution between the States so ratifying the same.

   Done in Convention by the Unanimous Consent of the States present the Seventeenth Day of September in the Year of our Lord one thousand seven hundred and Eighty seven, and of the Independence of the United States of America the Twelfth. In Witness whereof We have hereunto subscribed our Names.[6]

---

[6] These are the full names of the signers, which in some cases are not the signatures on the document.

George Washington
President and deputy from Virginia

NEW HAMPSHIRE

John Langdon
Nicholas Gilman

MASSACHUSETTS

Nathaniel Gorham
Rufus King

CONNECTICUT

William Samuel Johnson
Roger Sherman

NEW YORK

Alexander Hamilton

NEW JERSEY

William Livingston
David Brearley
William Paterson
Jonathan Dayton

PENNSYLVANIA

Benjamin Franklin
Thomas Mifflin
Robert Morris
George Clymer
Thomas FitzSimons
Jared Ingersoll
James Wilson
Gouverneur Morris

DELAWARE

George Read
Gunning Bedford, Jr.
John Dickinson
Richard Bassett
Jacob Broom

MARYLAND

James McHenry
Daniel of
 St. Thomas Jenifer
Daniel Carroll

VIRGINIA

John Blair
James Madison, Jr.

NORTH CAROLINA

William Blount
Richard Dobbs
 Spaight
Hugh Williamson

SOUTH CAROLINA

John Rutledge
Charles Cotesworth
 Pinckney
Charles Pinckney
Pierce Butler

GEORGIA

William Few
Abraham Baldwin

Articles in Addition to, and Amendment of, the Constitution of the United States of America, Proposed by Congress, and Ratified by the Legislatures of the Several States, Pursuant to the Fifth Article of the Original Constitution.[7]

[Article I]

Congress shall make no law respecting an establishment of religion, or prohibiting the free exercise thereof; or abridging the freedom of speech, or of the press; or the right of the people peaceably to assemble, and to petition the Government for a redress of grievances.

[Article II]

A well regulated Militia, being necessary to the security of a free State, the right of the people to keep and bear Arms shall not be infringed.

[Article III]

No Soldier shall, in time of peace, be quartered in any house, without the consent of the Owner, nor in time of war, but in a manner to be prescribed by law.

[Article IV]

The right of the people to be secure in their persons, houses, papers, and effects, against unreasonable searches and seizures, shall not be violated, and no Warrants shall issue, but upon probable cause, supported by Oath or affirmation, and particularly describing the place to be searched, and the persons or things to be seized.

[Article V]

No person shall be held to answer for a capital or otherwise infamous crime, unless on a presentment or indictment of a Grand Jury, except in cases arising in the land or naval forces, or in the Militia, when in actual service in time of War or public danger; nor shall any person be subject for the same offence to be twice put in jeopardy of life or limb; nor shall be compelled in any criminal case to be a witness against himself, nor be deprived of life, liberty, or property, without due process of law; nor shall private property be taken for public use, without just compensation.

[Article VI]

In all criminal prosecutions, the accused shall enjoy the right to a speedy and public trial, by an impartial jury of the State and district wherein the crime shall have been committed, which district shall have been previously ascertained by law, and to be informed of the nature and cause of the accusation; to be confronted with the witnesses against him; to have compulsory process for obtaining witnesses in his favour, and to have the Assistance of Counsel for his defense.

[Article VII]

In suits at common law, where the value in controversy shall exceed twenty dollars, the right of trial by jury shall be preserved, and no fact tried by a jury, shall be otherwise reexamined in any Court of the United States, than according to the rules of the common law.

[Article VIII]

Excessive bail shall not be required, nor excessive fines imposed, nor cruel and unusual punishments inflicted.

[Article IX]

The enumeration of the Constitution, of certain rights, shall not be construed to deny or disparage others retained by the people.

[Article X]

The powers not delegated to the United States by the Constitution, nor prohibited by it to the States, are reserved to the States respectively, or to the people.
[Amendments I–X, in force 1791.]

[Amendment XI][8]

The Judicial power of the United States shall not be construed to extend to any suit in law or equity, commenced or prosecuted against one of the United States by Citizens of another State, or by Citizens or Subjects of any Foreign State.

[Amendment XII][9]

The Electors shall meet in their respective States and vote by ballot for President and Vice-President, one of whom, at least, shall not be an inhabitant of the same State with themselves; they shall name in their ballots the person voted for as President, and in distinct ballots the person voted for as Vice-President, and they shall make distinct lists of all persons voted for as President, and of all persons

---

[7] This heading appears only in the joint resolution submitting the first ten amendments.

[8] Adopted in 1798.
[9] Adopted in 1804.

voted for as Vice-President, and of the number of votes for each, which lists they shall sign and certify, and transmit sealed to the seat of the government of the United States, directed to the President of the Senate;—The President of the Senate shall, in the presence of the Senate and House of Representatives, open all the certificates and the votes shall then be counted;—The person having the greatest number of votes for President, shall be the President, if such number be a majority of the whole number of Electors appointed; and if no person have such majority, then from the persons having the highest numbers not exceeding three on the list of those voted for as President, the House of Representatives shall choose immediately, by ballot, the President. But in choosing the President, the votes shall be taken by states, the representation from each state having one vote; a quorum for this purpose shall consist of a member or members from two-thirds of the states, and a majority of all the states shall be necessary to a choice. And if the House of Representatives shall not choose a President whenever the right of choice shall devolve upon them, before the fourth day of March next following, then the Vice-President shall act as President, as in the case of the death or other constitutional disability of the President.—The person having the greatest number of votes as Vice-President, shall be the Vice-President, if such number be a majority of the whole number of Electors appointed, and if no person have a majority, then from the two highest numbers on the list, the Senate shall choose the Vice-President; a quorum for the purpose shall consist of two-thirds of the whole number of Senators, and a majority of the whole number shall be necessary to a choice. But no person constitutionally ineligible to the office of President shall be eligible to that of Vice-President of the United States.

[Amendment XIII][10]

Section 1.
Neither slavery nor involuntary servitude, except as a punishment for crime whereof the party shall have been duly convicted, shall exist within the United States, or any place subject to their jurisdiction.

Section 2.
Congress shall have power to enforce this article by appropriate legislation.

[Amendment XIV][11]

Section 1.
All persons born or naturalized in the United States, and subject to the jurisdiction thereof, are citizens of the United States and of the State wherein they reside. No State shall make or enforce any law which shall abridge the privileges or immunities of citizens of the United States; nor shall any State deprive any person of life, liberty, or property, without due process of law; nor deny to any person within its jurisdiction the equal protection of the laws.

Section 2.
Representatives shall be apportioned among the several States according to their respective numbers, counting the whole number of persons in each State, excluding Indians not taxed. But when the right to vote at any election for the choice of electors for President and Vice-President of the United States, Representatives in Congress, the Executive and Judicial officers of a State, or the members of the Legislature thereof, is denied to any of the male inhabitants of such State, being twenty-one years of age, and citizens of the United States, or in any way abridged, except for participation in rebellion, or other crime, the basis of representation therein shall be reduced in the proportion which the number of such male citizens shall bear to the whole number of male citizens twenty-one years of age in such State.

Section 3.
No person shall be a Senator or Representative in Congress, or elector of President and Vice-President, or hold any office, civil or military, under the United States, or under any State, who, having previously taken an oath, as a member of Congress, or as an officer of the United States, or as a member of any State legislature, or as an executive or judicial officer of any State, to support the Constitution of the United States, shall have engaged in insurrection or rebellion against the same, or given aid or comfort to the enemies thereof. But Congress may by a vote of two-thirds of each House, remove such disability.

Section 4.
The validity of the public debt of the United States, authorized by law, including debts incurred for payment of pensions and bounties for services in suppressing insurrection or rebellion, shall not be questioned. But neither the United States nor any State shall assume or pay any debts or obligation incurred in aid of insurrection or rebellion against the United States, or any claim for the loss or emancipation of any slave; but all such debts, obligations, and claims shall be held illegal and void.

Section 5.
The Congress shall have the power to enforce, by appropriate legislation, the provisions of this article.

[10] Adopted in 1865.
[11] Adopted in 1868.

[Amendment XV][12]

Section 1.
The right of citizens of the United States to vote shall not be denied or abridged by the United States or by any State on account of race, color, or previous condition of servitude—

Section 2.
The Congress shall have power to enforce this article by appropriate legislation.

[Amendment XVI][13]

The Congress shall have power to lay and collect taxes on incomes, from whatever source derived, without apportionment among the several States, and without regard to any census or enumeration.

[Amendment XVII][14]

The Senate of the United States shall be composed of two Senators from each State, elected by the people thereof, for six years; and each Senator shall have one vote. The electors in each State shall have the qualifications requisite for electors of the most numerous branch of the State legislatures.

When vacancies happen in the representation of any State in the Senate, the executive authority of such State shall issue writs of election to fill such vacancies: *Provided,* That the legislature of any State may empower the executive thereof to make temporary appointments until the people fill the vacancies by election as the legislature may direct.

This amendment shall not be so construed as to affect the election or term of any Senator chosen before it becomes valid as part of the Constitution.

[Amendment XVIII][15]

Section 1.
After one year from the ratification of this article the manufacture, sale, or transportation of intoxicating liquors within, the importation thereof into, or the exportation thereof from the United States and all territory subject to the jurisdiction thereof for beverage purposes is hereby prohibited.

Section 2.
The Congress and the several States shall have concurrent power to enforce this article by appropriate legislation.

Section 3.
This article shall be inoperative unless it shall have been ratified as an amendment to the Constitution by the legislatures of the several States, as provided in the Constitution, within seven years from the date of the submission hereof to the States by the Congress.

[Amendment XIX][16]

The right of citizens of the United States to vote shall not be denied or abridged by the United States or by any State on account of sex.

Congress shall have power to enforce this article by appropriate legislation.

[Amendment XX][17]

Section 1.
The terms of the President and Vice-President shall end at noon on the 20th day of January, and the terms of Senators and Representatives at noon on the 3d day of January, of the years in which such terms would have ended if this article had not been ratified; and the terms of their successors shall then begin.

Section 2.
The Congress shall assemble at least once in every year, and such meeting shall begin at noon on the 3d day of January, unless they shall by law appoint a different day.

Section 3.
If, at the time fixed for the beginning of the term of the President, the President elect shall have died, the Vice-President elect shall become President. If a President shall not have been chosen before the time fixed for the beginning of his term or if the President elect shall have failed to qualify, then the Vice-President elect shall act as President until a President shall have qualified; and the Congress may by law provide for the case wherein neither a President elect nor a Vice-President elect shall have qualified, declaring who shall then act as President, or the manner in which one who is to act shall be selected, and such person shall act accordingly until a President or Vice-President shall have qualified.

---

[12] Adopted in 1870.
[13] Adopted in 1913.
[14] Adopted in 1913.
[15] Adopted in 1918.

[16] Adopted in 1920.
[17] Adopted in 1933.

Section 4.

The Congress may by law provide for the case of the death of any of the persons from whom the House of Representatives may choose a President whenever the right of choice shall have devolved upon them, and for the case of the death of any of the persons from whom the Senate may choose a Vice-President whenever the right of choice shall have devolved upon them.

Section 5.

Sections 1 and 2 shall take effect on the 15th day of October following the ratification of this article.

Section 6.

This article shall be inoperative unless it shall have been ratified as an amendment to the Constitution by the legislatures of three-fourths of the several States within seven years from the date of its submission.

[Amendment XXI][18]

Section 1.

The eighteenth article of amendment to the Constitution of the United States is hereby repealed.

Section 2.

The transportation or importation into any State, Territory, or possession of the United States for delivery or use therein of intoxicating liquors, in violation of the laws thereof, is hereby prohibited.

Section 3.

This article shall be inoperative unless it shall have been ratified as an amendment to the Constitution by conventions in the several States, as provided in the Constitution, within seven years from the date of the submission hereof to the States by the Congress.

[Amendment XXII][19]

No person shall be elected to the office of the President more than twice, and no person who has held the office of President, or acted as President, for more than two years of a term to which some other person was elected President shall be elected to the office of the President more than once.

But this Article shall not apply to any person holding the office of President when this Article was proposed by the Congress, and shall not prevent any person who may be holding the office of President, or acting as President, during the term within which this Article becomes operative from holding the office of President or acting as President during the remainder of such term.

This article shall be inoperative unless it shall have been ratified as an amendment to the Constitution by the legislatures of three-fourths of the several states within seven years from the date of its submission to the states by the Congress.

[Amendment XXIII][20]

Section 1.

The District constituting the seat of Government of the United States shall appoint in such manner as the Congress may direct:

A number of electors of President and Vice-President equal to the whole number of Senators and Representatives in Congress to which the District would be entitled if it were a State, but in no event more than the least populous State; they shall be in addition to those appointed by the States, but they shall be considered, for the purposes of the election of President and Vice-President, to be electors appointed by a State; and they shall meet in the District and perform such duties as provided by the twelfth article of amendment.

Section 2.

The Congress shall have power to enforce this article by appropriate legislation.

[Amendment XXIV][21]

Section 1.

The right of citizens of the United States to vote in any primary or other election for President or Vice President, for electors for President or Vice President, or for Senator or Representative in Congress, shall not be denied or abridged by the United States or any state by reason of failure to pay any poll tax or other tax.

Section 2.

The Congress shall have the power to enforce this article by appropriate legislation.

[Amendment XXV][22]

Section 1.

In case of the removal of the President from office or of his death or resignation, the Vice President shall become President.

---

[18] Adopted in 1933.
[19] Adopted in 1961.

[20] Adopted in 1961.
[21] Adopted in 1964.
[22] Adopted in 1967.

Section 2.

Whenever there is a vacancy in the office of the Vice President, the President shall nominate a Vice President who shall take office upon confirmation by a majority vote of both Houses of Congress.

Section 3.

Whenever the President transmits to the President Pro Tempore of the Senate and the Speaker of the House of Representatives his written declaration that he is unable to discharge the powers and duties of his office, and until he transmits to them a written declaration to the contrary, such powers and duties shall be discharged by the Vice President as Acting President.

Section 4.

Whenever the Vice President and a majority of either the principal officers of the executive departments or of such other body as Congress may by law provide, transmit to the President Pro Tempore of the Senate and the Speaker of the House of Representatives their written declaration that the President is unable to discharge the powers and duties of his office, the Vice President shall immediately assume the powers and duties of the office as Acting President.

Thereafter, when the President transmits to the President Pro Tempore of the Senate and the Speaker of the House of Representatives his written declaration that no inability exists, he shall resume the powers and duties of his office unless the Vice President and a majority of either the principal officers of the executive departments or of such other body as Congress may by law provide, transmit within four days to the President Pro Tempore of the Senate and the Speaker of the House of Representatives

their written declaration that the President is unable to discharge the powers and duties of his office. Thereupon Congress shall decide the issue, assembling within forty-eight hours for that purpose if not in session. If the Congress, within twenty-one days after receipt of the latter written declaration, or, if Congress is not in session, within twenty-one days after Congress is required to assemble, determines by two-thirds vote of both Houses that the President is unable to discharge the powers and duties of his office, the Vice President shall continue to discharge the same as Acting President; otherwise, the President shall resume the powers and duties of his office.

[Amendment XXVI][23]

Section 1.

The right of citizens of the United States, who are eighteen years of age or older, to vote shall not be denied or abridged by the United States or by any State on account of age.

Section 2.

The Congress shall have power to enforce this article by appropriate legislation.

[Amendment XXVII][24]

No law varying the compensation for the services of the Senators and Representatives shall take effect until an election of Representatives shall have intervened.

---

[23] Adopted in 1971.
[24] Adopted in 1992.

Presidential Elections

Year	Candidates	Parties	Popular Vote	Percentage of Popular Vote	Electoral Vote	Percentage of Voter Participation
1789	GEORGE WASHINGTON (VA.)*				69	
	John Adams				34	
	Others				35	
1792	GEORGE WASHINGTON (VA.)				132	
	John Adams				77	
	George Clinton				50	
	Others				5	
1796	JOHN ADAMS (MASS.)	Federalist			71	
	Thomas Jefferson	Democratic Republican			68	
	Thomas Pinckney	Federalist			59	
	Aaron Burr	Dem.-Rep.			30	
	Others				48	
1800	THOMAS JEFFERSON (VA.)	Dem.-Rep.			73	
	Aaron Burr	Dem.-Rep.			73	
	John Adams	Federalist			65	
	C. C. Pinckney	Federalist			64	
	John Jay	Federalist			1	
1804	THOMAS JEFFERSON (VA.)	Dem.-Rep.			162	
	C. C. Pinckney	Federalist			14	
1808	JAMES MADISON (VA.)	Dem.-Rep.			122	
	C. C. Pinckney	Federalist			47	
	George Clinton	Dem.-Rep.			6	
1812	JAMES MADISON (VA.)	Dem.-Rep.			128	
	De Witt Clinton	Federalist			89	
1816	JAMES MONROE (VA.)	Dem.-Rep.			183	
	Rufus King	Federalist			34	
1820	JAMES MONROE (VA.)	Dem.-Rep.			231	
	John Quincy Adams	Dem.-Rep.			1	

NOTE: *State of residence at time of election.

(continued)

Year	Candidates	Parties	Popular Vote	Percentage of Popular Vote	Electoral Vote	Percentage of Voter Participation
1824	JOHN Q. ADAMS (MASS.)	Dem.-Rep.	108,740	30.5	84	26.9
	Andrew Jackson	Dem.-Rep.	153,544	43.1	99	
	William H. Crawford	Dem.-Rep.	46,618	13.1	41	
	Henry Clay	Dem.-Rep.	47,136	13.2	37	
1828	ANDREW JACKSON (TENN.)	Democratic	647,286	56.0	178	57.6
	John Quincy Adams	National Republican	508,064	44.0	83	
1832	ANDREW JACKSON (TENN.)	Democratic	687,502	55.0	219	55.4
	Henry Clay	National Republican	530,189	42.4	49	
	John Floyd	Independent			11	
	William Wirt	Anti-Mason	33,108	2.6	7	
1836	MARTIN VAN BUREN (N.Y.)	Democratic	765,483	50.9	170	57.8
	W. H. Harrison	Whig			73	
	Hugh L. White	Whig	739,795	49.1	26	
	Daniel Webster	Whig			14	
	W. P. Magnum	Independent			11	
1840	WILLIAM H. HARRISON (OHIO)	Whig	1,274,624	53.1	234	80.2
	Martin Van Buren	Democratic	1,127,781	46.9	60	
	J. G. Birney	Liberty	7,069		—	
1844	JAMES K. POLK (TENN.)	Democratic	1,338,464	49.6	170	78.9
	Henry Clay	Whig	1,300,097	48.1	105	
	J. G. Birney	Liberty	62,300	2.3	—	
1848	ZACHARY TAYLOR (LA.)	Whig	1,360,967	47.4	163	72.7
	Lewis Cass	Democratic	1,222,342	42.5	127	
	Martin Van Buren	Free-Soil	291,263	10.1	—	
1852	FRANKLIN PIERCE (N.H.)	Democratic	1,601,117	50.9	254	69.6
	Winfield Scott	Whig	1,385,453	44.1	42	
	John P. Hale	Free-Soil	155,825	5.0	—	
1856	JAMES BUCHANAN (PA.)	Democratic	1,832,955	45.3	174	78.9
	John C. Frémont	Republican	1,339,932	33.1	114	
	Millard Fillmore	American	871,731	21.6	8	
1860	ABRAHAM LINCOLN (ILL.)	Republican	1,865,593	39.8	180	81.2
	Stephen A. Douglas	Democratic	1,382,713	29.5	12	

Year	Candidates	Parties	Popular Vote	Percentage of Popular Vote	Electoral Vote	Percentage of Voter Participation
	John C. Breckinridge	Democratic	848,356	18.1	72	
	John Bell	Union	592,906	12.6	39	
1864	**ABRAHAM LINCOLN (ILL.)**	Republican	2,213,655	55.0	212	73.8
	George B. McClellan	Democratic	1,805,237	45.0	21	
1868	**ULYSSES S. GRANT (ILL.)**	Republican	3,012,833	52.7	214	78.1
	Horatio Seymour	Democratic	2,703,249	47.3	80	
1872	**ULYSSES S. GRANT (ILL.)**	Republican	3,597,132	55.6	286	71.3
	Horace Greeley	Democratic; Liberal Republican	2,834,125	43.9	66	
1876	**RUTHERFORD B. HAYES (OHIO)**	Republican	4,036,298	48.0	185	81.8
	Samuel J. Tilden	Democratic	4,300,590	51.0	184	
1880	**JAMES A. GARFIELD (OHIO)**	Republican	4,454,416	48.5	214	79.4
	Winfield S. Hancock	Democratic	4,444,952	48.1	155	
1884	**GROVER CLEVELAND (N.Y.)**	Democratic	4,874,986	48.5	219	77.5
	James G. Blaine	Republican	4,851,981	48.2	182	
1888	**BENJAMIN HARRISON (IND.)**	Republican	5,439,853	47.9	233	79.3
	Grover Cleveland	Democratic	5,540,309	48.6	168	
1892	**GROVER CLEVELAND (N.Y.)**	Democratic	5,556,918	46.1	277	74.7
	Benjamin Harrison	Republican	5,176,108	43.0	145	
	James B. Weaver	People's	1,041,028	8.5	22	
1896	**WILLIAM McKINLEY (OHIO)**	Republican	7,104,779	51.1	271	79.3
	William J. Bryan	Democratic People's	6,502,925	47.7	176	
1900	**WILLIAM McKINLEY (OHIO)**	Republican	7,207,923	51.7	292	73.2
	William J. Bryan	Dem.-Populist	6,358,133	45.5	155	
1904	**THEODORE ROOSEVELT (N.Y.)**	Republican	7,623,486	57.9	336	65.2
	Alton B. Parker	Democratic	5,077,911	37.6	140	
	Eugene V. Debs	Socialist	402,283	3.0	—	
1908	**WILLIAM H. TAFT (OHIO)**	Republican	7,678,908	51.6	321	65.4
	William J. Bryan	Democratic	6,409,104	43.1	162	
	Eugene V. Debs	Socialist	420,793	2.8	—	
1912	**WOODROW WILSON (N.J.)**	Democratic	6,293,454	41.9	435	58.8
	Theodore Roosevelt	Progressive	4,119,538	27.4	88	

(continued)

A–21

Year	Candidates	Parties	Popular Vote	Percentage of Popular Vote	Electoral Vote	Percentage of Voter Participation
	William H. Taft	Republican	3,484,980	23.2	8	
	Eugene V. Debs	Socialist	900,672	6.0	—	
1916	**WOODROW WILSON (N.J.)**	Democratic	9,129,606	49.4	277	61.6
	Charles E. Hughes	Republican	8,538,221	46.2	254	
	A. L. Benson	Socialist	585,113	3.2	—	
1920	**WARREN G. HARDING (OHIO)**	Republican	16,152,200	60.4	404	49.2
	James M. Cox	Democratic	9,147,353	34.2	127	
	Eugene V. Debs	Socialist	919,799	3.4	—	
1924	**CALVIN COOLIDGE (MASS.)**	Republican	15,725,016	54.0	382	48.9
	John W. Davis	Democratic	8,386,503	28.8	136	
	Robert M. LaFollette	Progressive	4,822,856	16.6	13	
1928	**HERBERT HOOVER (CALIF.)**	Republican	21,391,381	58.2	444	56.9
	Alfred E. Smith	Democratic	15,016,443	40.9	87	
	Norman Thomas	Socialist	267,835	0.7	—	
1932	**FRANKLIN D. ROOSEVELT (N.Y.)**	Democratic	22,821,857	57.4	472	56.9
	Herbert Hoover	Republican	15,761,841	39.7	59	
	Norman Thomas	Socialist	881,951	2.2	—	
1936	**FRANKLIN D. ROOSEVELT (N.Y.)**	Democratic	27,751,597	60.8	523	61.0
	Alfred M. Landon	Republican	16,679,583	36.5	8	
	William Lemke	Union	882,479	1.9	—	
1940	**FRANKLIN D. ROOSEVELT (N.Y.)**	Democratic	27,244,160	54.8	449	62.5
	Wendell L. Willkie	Republican	22,305,198	44.8	82	
1944	**FRANKLIN D. ROOSEVELT (N.Y.)**	Democratic	25,602,504	53.5	432	55.9
	Thomas E. Dewey	Republican	22,006,285	46.0	99	
1948	**HARRY S. TRUMAN (MO.)**	Democratic	24,105,695	49.5	304	53.0
	Thomas E. Dewey	Republican	21,969,170	45.1	189	
	J. Strom Thurmond	State-Rights Democratic	1,169,021	2.4	38	
	Henry A. Wallace	Progressive	1,156,103	2.4	—	
1952	**DWIGHT D. EISENHOWER (N.Y.)**	Republican	33,936,252	55.1	442	63.3
	Adlai E. Stevenson	Democratic	27,314,992	44.4	89	
1956	**DWIGHT D. EISENHOWER (N.Y.)**	Republican	35,575,420	57.6	457	60.6

Year	Candidates	Party	Popular Vote	Percentage of Popular Vote	Electoral Vote	Percentage of Voter Participation
	Adlai E. Stevenson	Democratic	26,003,066	42.1	73	
	Other	—	—		1	
1960	JOHN F. KENNEDY (MASS.)	Democratic	34,227,096	49.9	303	62.8
	Richard M. Nixon	Republican	34,108,546	49.6	219	
	Other	—	—		15	
1964	LYNDON B. JOHNSON (TEX.)	Democratic	43,126,506	61.1	486	61.7
	Barry M. Goldwater	Republican	27,176,799	38.5	52	
1968	RICHARD M. NIXON (N.Y.)	Republican	31,770,237	43.4	301	60.6
	Hubert H. Humphrey	Democratic	31,270,533	42.7	191	
	George Wallace	American Independent	9,906,141	13.5	46	
1972	RICHARD M. NIXON (N.Y.)	Republican	47,169,911	60.7	520	55.2
	George S. McGovern	Democratic	29,170,383	37.5	17	
	Other	—	—		1	
1976	JIMMY CARTER (GA.)	Democratic	40,828,587	50.0	297	53.5
	Gerald R. Ford	Republican	39,147,613	47.9	241	
	Other	—	1,575,459	2.1	—	
1980	RONALD REAGAN (CALIF.)	Republican	43,901,812	50.7	489	52.6
	Jimmy Carter	Democratic	35,483,820	41.0	49	
	John B. Anderson	Independent	5,719,722	6.6	—	
	Ed Clark	Libertarian	921,188	1.1	—	
1984	RONALD REAGAN (CALIF.)	Republican	54,455,075	59.0	525	53.3
	Walter Mondale	Democratic	37,577,185	41.0	13	
1988	GEORGE BUSH (TEX.)	Republican	47,946,422	54.0	426	50.2
	Michael S. Dukakis	Democratic	41,016,429	46.0	112	
1992	WILLIAM J. CLINTON (ARK.)	Democratic	43,728,375	43.0	370	55.0
	George Bush	Republican	38,167,416	38.0	168	
	Ross Perot	Independent	19,237,247	19.0	0	
1996	WILLIAM J. CLINTON (ARK.)	Democratic	47,401,185	49.3	379	49.0
	Robert Dole	Republican	39,197,469	40.7	159	
	Ross Perot	Reform	8,085,294	8.4	—	
2000	GEORGE W. BUSH (TEXAS)	Republican	50,459,211	47.89	271	51.0
	Albert Gore, Jr.	Democratic	51,003,894	48.41	266	
	Ralph Nader	Green	2,834,410	2.69	—	

Population of the United States, 1790–2000

Year	Population	Percent Increase	Population per Square Mile	Percent Urban/ Rural	Percent White/ Nonwhite	Median Age
1790	3,929,214		4.5	5.1/94.9	80.7/19.3	NA
1800	5,308,483	35.1	6.1	6.1/93.9	81.1/18.9	NA
1810	7,239,881	36.4	4.3	7.3/92.7	81.0/19.0	NA
1820	9,638,453	33.1	5.5	7.2/92.8	81.6/18.4	16.7
1830	12,866,020	33.5	7.4	8.8/91.2	81.9/18.1	17.2
1840	17,069,453	32.7	9.8	10.8/89.2	83.2/16.8	17.8
1850	23,191,876	35.9	7.9	15.3/84.7	84.3/15.7	18.9
1860	31,443,321	35.6	10.6	19.8/80.2	85.6/14.4	19.4
1870	39,818,449	26.6	13.4	25.7/74.3	86.2/13.8	20.2
1880	50,155,783	26.0	16.9	28.2/71.8	86.5/13.5	20.9
1890	62,947,714	25.5	21.2	35.1/64.9	87.5/12.5	22.0
1900	75,994,575	20.7	25.6	39.6/60.4	87.9/12.1	22.9
1910	91,972,266	21.0	31.0	45.6/54.4	88.9/11.1	24.1
1920	105,710,620	14.9	35.6	51.2/48.8	89.7/10.3	25.3
1930	122,775,046	16.1	41.2	56.1/43.9	89.8/10.2	26.4
1940	131,669,275	7.2	44.2	56.5/43.5	89.8/10.2	29.0
1950	150,697,361	14.5	50.7	64.0/36.0	89.5/10.5	30.2
1960	179,323,175	18.5	50.6	69.9/30.1	88.6/11.4	29.5
1970	203,302,031	13.4	57.4	73.5/26.5	87.6/12.4	28.0
1980	226,545,805	11.4	64.0	73.7/26.3	86.0/14.0	30.0
1990	248,709,873	9.9	70.3	77.5/22.5	80.3/19.7	32.9
2000	281,421,906	13.0	79.6	NA/NA	83.0/17.0	35.3

NA = Not available.

Employment, 1870–2000

Year	Number of Workers (in millions)	Male/Female Employment Ratio	Percentage of Workers in Unions
1870	12.5	85/15	—
1880	17.4	85/15	—
1890	23.3	83/17	—
1900	29.1	82/18	3
1910	38.2	79/21	6
1920	41.6	79/21	12
1930	48.8	78/22	7
1940	53.0	76/24	27
1950	59.6	72/28	25
1960	69.9	68/32	26
1970	82.1	63/37	25
1980	108.5	58/42	23
1985	108.9	57/43	19
1990	118.8	55/45	16
2000	134.3	53/47	13.5

Production, Trade, and Federal Spending/Debt, 1790–2000

Year	Gross National Product (GNP) (in billions $)	Balance of Trade (in millions $)	Federal Budget (in billions $)	Federal Surplus/Deficit (in billions $)	Federal Debt (in billions $)
1790	—	−3	.004	+0.00015	.076
1800	—	−20	.011	+0.0006	.083
1810	—	−18	.008	+0.0012	.053
1820	—	−4	.018	−0.0004	.091
1830	—	+3	.015	+0.100	.049
1840	—	+25	.024	−0.005	.004
1850	—	−26	.040	+0.004	.064
1860	—	−38	.063	−0.01	.065
1870	7.4	−11	.310	+0.10	2.4
1880	11.2	+92	.268	+0.07	2.1
1890	13.1	+87	.318	+0.09	1.2
1900	18.7	+569	.521	+0.05	1.2
1910	35.3	+273	.694	−0.02	1.1
1920	91.5	+2,880	6.357	+0.3	24.3
1930	90.7	+513	3.320	+0.7	16.3
1940	100.0	−3,403	9.6	−2.7	43.0
1950	286.5	+1,691	43.1	−2.2	257.4
1960	506.5	+4,556	92.2	+0.3	286.3
1970	992.7	+2,511	196.6	+2.8	371.0
1980	2,631.7	+24,088	579.6	−59.5	914.3
1985	4,087.7	−148,480	946.3	−212.3	1,827.5
1990	5,764.9	−101,012	1,251.8	−220.5	4,064.6
2000	9,860.8	−369.7	1,789.6	+237.0	5,674.2

Index

Note: Page numbers followed by *i* or *m* refer to illustrations and maps, respectively. Appendices are indicated as follows: *A25*